READINGS IN THE ECONOMICS OF LAW
AND REGULATION

READINGS IN THE ECONOMICS OF LAW AND REGULATION

EDITED BY
A. I. OGUS
Professor of Law, University of Newcastle upon Tyne
AND
C. G. VELJANOVSKI
Lecturer in English Law, University College London

CLARENDON PRESS · OXFORD
1984

Oxford University Press, Walton Street, Oxford OX2 6DP

London New York Toronto
Delhi Bombay Calcutta Madras Karachi
Kuala Lumpur Singapore Hong Kong Tokyo
Nairobi Dar es Salaam Cape Town
Melbourne Auckland

and associated companies in
Beirut Berlin Ibadan Mexico City Nicosia

Oxford is a trade mark of Oxford University Press

Published in the United States
by Oxford University Press, New York

British Library Cataloguing in Publication Data
Readings in the economics of law and regulation.
1. Law – England – Economic aspects
I. Ogus, A. I.   II. Veljanovski , Cento G.
340'.115'0942   KD660
ISBN 0-19-876142-2
ISBN 0-19-876143-0 Pbk

Library of Congress Cataloging in Publication Data
Main entry under title:
Readings in the economics of law and regulation.
Includes index.
1. Law – Great Britain. 2. Economics. I. Ogus, A. I.
II. Veljanovski, C. G.
KD658.R4 1984   338.5'142   83-25189
ISBN 0-19-876142-2
ISBN 0-19-876143-0 (pbk.)

Typeset by Oxford Verbatim Limited
Printed in Great Britain
at the University Press, Oxford

PREFACE

The application of economic theory to law and legal institutions has developed rapidly over the last two decades or so. While the main impetus and most of the literature are American, the importance of the subject has gradually become more widely recognized. An appreciation of the way in which the law, in part at least, determines how society deals with problems of scarce resources has enabled lawyers to gain a more profound understanding of their subject, and economists to sharpen their awareness of the impact of different institutional arrangements. In America these developments have taken place in a context in which most lawyers have some background in economics. This is not generally true elsewhere, and the lawyer who wishes to inform himself is faced with a literature which, quite apart from the obvious handicap that it might not be easily available to him, is awesome in terms of both its volume and its technical content. This book is aimed at such a person.

Our primary concern has been to select readings which may readily be assimilated by those without formal training in economics and which, at the same time, reflect the major achievements of scholarship in this field. The first chapter includes materials designed to introduce economic theory and while these may usefully be supplemented by the standard economic textbooks they should enable the reader to understand and benefit from all that follows. In the notes which accompany the extracts we incorporate references which the more ambitious and those with greater technical ability may wish to pursue.

If economics fundamentally deals with problems arising from choice, this is well illustrated by our difficulties in selecting appropriate areas of analysis. In the end, we considered (perhaps paternalistically) that the utility of the work to our readers was likely to be maximized by our concentrating on those subjects with which lawyers will be most familiar – the so-called 'core subjects': property, tort, contract and crime – and which have received significant economic analysis, together with aspects of regulation, an area of law shamefully neglected in traditional legal education. That the source of most of our material is American publications does not seem to us to constitute a serious problem. For the purposes of the analysis, American law is typically sufficiently similar to English law, and, where it is not, we indicate the fact in our notes. On the other hand, we have not been generous in the supply of legal references. We have assumed that the majority of our readers will understand the basic legal ideas considered in the analysis without further assistance, or will know where to turn for some succinct explanation. In any event, very few of the readings discuss legal doctrine of a substantially technical character.

Some may find surprising our relatively brief treatment of monopoly and other aspects of competition law. The fact that the law is here dealing directly and overtly with economic concepts has given rise to a long history of interdisciplinary work and consequently to a literature that is both voluminous and highly specific in its orientation. There are, indeed, several excellent texts which do justice to the many facets of the subject in a way which would not have been possible in our book. On the other hand, some account of the general notions of monopoly and a competitive market was essential since they have an impact on other legal topics.

We have benefited from the guidance and critical scrutiny of a number of our colleagues, notably Ed Belobba, Dennis Carlton, Tim Frazer, Roger Halson, Dick Helmholz, Gareth Jones, Dick Markovits, Iain Ramsay and Brian Simpson. We are grateful, too, for the tireless secretarial efforts of Yolanda Fowler, Christine Markham and Beverly Rogers and the remarkable skills of the OUP editorial staff. We also are grateful to the Centre for Socio-Legal Studies, Oxford, for secretarial support and the encouragement that its Directors and staff have given law-and-economics generally and this book in particular. A substantial part of the book was prepared while one of us was Visiting Law and Economics Fellow at the University of Chicago Law School. This institution has, more than any other, been responsible for the rapid growth of scholarship on our subject, so that we can truly say, in more than one sense, that without it this book would not exist.

Newcastle upon Tyne AIO
Oxford CGV

April 1983

CONTENTS

PART I

*

Introduction

1

THE ECONOMIC FRAMEWORK

A. Nature and Scope of Economic Reasoning

R. H. COASE

*

Economics and Contiguous Disciplines[1]

If we look at the work that economists are doing at the present time, there can be little doubt that economics is expanding its boundaries or, at any rate, that economists are moving more and more into other disciplines . . . One striking example, with which I am familiar, is the use of economics in the study of law. The general movement is clear. Economists are extending the range of their studies to include all of the social sciences, which I take to be what we mean when we speak of economics' contiguous disciplines.

What is the reason why this is happening? One completely satisfying explanation (in more than one sense) would be that economists have by now solved all of the major problems posed by the economic system, and, therefore, rather than become unemployed or be forced to deal with the trivial problems which remain to be solved, have decided to employ their obviously considerable talents in achieving a similar success in the other social sciences. However, it is not possible to examine any area of economics with which I have familiarity without finding major puzzles for which we have no agreed solution or, indeed, questions to which we have not answers at all . . . [I]t would perhaps be more plausible to argue that economists are looking for fields in which they can have some success.

Another explanation for this interest in neighbouring fields might be that modern economists have had a more broadly based education than those who preceded them and that, in consequence, their interests are wider, with the result that they are naturally dissatisfied with being restricted to so narrow a range of problems as that presented by the

[1] (1978) 7 J. Legal Stud. 201, 202–17. First published in Mark Perlman (ed.), *The Organisation and Retrieval of Economic Knowledge* (Macmillan, London: Westview Press, Colorado, 1977). Reprinted by permission of Macmillan, London and Basingstoke.

economic system. Such an explanation seems to me largely without merit. If we think of Adam Smith or John Stuart Mill or Alfred Marshall, the range of questions with which they deal is greater than is commonly found in a modern work on economics. This impression is reinforced if we have regard to the articles which appear in most of the economics journals, which, to an increasingly great extent, tend to deal with highly formal technical questions of economic analysis, usually treated mathematically. The general impression one derives, particularly from the journals, is of a subject narrowing, rather than extending, the range of its interest. This seems inconsistent with the concurrent movement of economists into the other social sciences, but I believe that there is a connection between these two apparently contradictory developments.

If we are to attempt to forecast what the scope of economists' work is likely to be in the future . . . we have to understand the reason why economists have been moving into the other social sciences and what the situation is likely to be in future. To do this, we have to consider what it is that binds together a group of scholars so that they form a separate profession and enables us to say that someone is an economist, someone else a sociologist, another a political scientist, and so on. It seems to me that what binds such a group together is one or more of the following: common techniques of analysis, a common theory or approach to the subject, or a common subject matter. I need not conceal from you at this stage my belief that in the long run it is the subject matter, the kind of question which the practitioners are trying to answer, which tends to be the dominant factor producing the cohesive force that makes a group of scholars a recognizable profession with its own university departments, journals, and libraries. I say this, in part, because the techniques of analysis and the theory or approach used are themselves, to a considerable extent, determined by what it is that the group of scholars is studying, although scholars in a particular discipline may use different techniques or approaches in answering the same questions. . . . If my description of the binding forces of a scholarly discipline is correct . . . then we will have to decide whether the current movement by economists into the other social sciences is the triumph of a technique or of an approach, or whether such an extension of their work illuminates, and is interrelated with, the solution of the central questions which economists attempt to answer, that is, is necessitated by the nature of the subject matter which they study. To the extent that this movement is based on technique or approach, we can expect a gradual displacement of economists from their newly-won ground. To the extent that it is necessitated by their subject matter, we may expect the range of studies undertaken by economists to be permanently enlarged.

What do economists study? What do they do? They study the economic system. Marshall, in the first edition of the *Principles of Economics*, defined economics thus: 'Political Economy, or Economics, is a study of man's actions in the ordinary business of life; it inquires how he gets his income and how he uses it.' A modern economist, Stigler, has phrased it differently: 'Economics is the study of the operation of economic organizations, and economic organizations are social (and rarely individual) arrangements to deal with the production and distribution of economic goods and services.'[2] Both of these definitions of economics emphasize that economists study certain kinds of activity. And this accords well with the actual topics dealt with in a book on economics. What economists study is the working of the social institutions which bind together the economic system: firms, markets for goods and services, labour markets, capital markets, the banking system, international trade, and so on. It is the common interest in these social institutions which distinguishes the economics profession.

A very different kind of definition is that of Robbins: 'Economics is the science which studies human behaviour as a relationship between ends and scarce means which have alternative uses.'[3] Such a definition makes economics a study of human choice. It is clearly too wide if regarded as a description of what economists do. Economists do not study all human choices, or, at any rate, they had not done so as yet. However, the view that economics is a study of all human choice, although it does not tell us the nature of the economic theory or approach which is to be employed in all of the social science, certainly calls for the development of such a theory . . .

The nature of this general approach has been described by Posner in his *Economic Analysis of Law*:

Economics, the science of human choice in a world in which resources are limited in relation to human wants, explores and tests the implications of the assumption that man is a rational maximizer of his ends in life, his satisfactions – what we shall call his 'self-interest'.[4]

By defining economics as the 'science of human choice', economics becomes the study of all purposeful human behaviour and its scope is, therefore, coterminous with all of the social sciences. It is one thing to make such a claim, it is quite another to translate it into reality. At a time when the King of England claimed to be also King of France, he was not always welcome in Paris. The claim that economics is the science of human choice will not be enough to cause sociologists, political scientists, and lawyers to abandon their field or, painfully, to

[2] G. J. Stigler, *The Theory of Price* (1952), p. 1.
[3] L. C. Robbins, *An Essay on the Nature and Significance of Economic Science* (1932), p. 15.
[4] (2nd edn, 1977), p. 3.

become economists. The dominance of the other social sciences by economists, if it happens, will not come about simply by redefining economics, but because of something which economists possess and which enables them to handle sociological, political, legal, and similar problems better than the practitioners in these other social sciences. I take it to be the view of Becker and Posner that the decisive advantage which economists possess in handling social problems is their theory of, or approach to, human behaviour, the treatment of man as a rational, utility-maximizer.

Since the people who operate in the economic system are the same people who are found in the legal or political system, it is to be expected that their behaviour will be, in a broad sense, similar. But it by no means follows that an approach developed to explain behaviour in the economic system will be equally successful in the other social sciences. In these different fields, the purposes which men seek to achieve will not be the same, the degree of consistency in behaviour need not be the same and, in particular, the institutional frameworks within which the choices are made are quite different. It seems to me probable that an ability to discern and understand these purposes and the character of the institutional framework (how, for example, the political and legal systems actually operate) will require specialized knowledge not likely to be acquired by those who work in some other discipline. Furthermore, a theory appropriate for the analysis of these other social systems will presumably need to embody features which deal with the important specific interrelationships of that system.

I am strengthened in this view by a consideration of the part played by utility theory in economic analysis. Up to the present it has been largely sterile. To say that people maximize utility tells us nothing about the purposes for which they engage in economic activity and leaves us without any insight into why people do what they do . . .

Economics, it must be admitted, does appear to be more developed than the other social sciences. But the great advantage which economics has possessed is that economists are able to use the 'measuring rod of money'. This has given a precision to the analysis, and since what is measured by money are important determinants of human behaviour in the economic system, the analysis has considerable explanatory power. Furthermore, the data (on prices and incomes) is generally available, so that hypotheses can be examined and checked . . . [This] suggests that the problems faced by practitioners in these other fields are not likely to be dissipated simply by an infusion of economists, since in moving into these fields, they will commonly have to leave their strength behind them. The analysis developed in economics is not likely to be successfully applied in other subjects without major modifications.

If I am right about the relative unimportance of technique as a basis for the choice of professional groupings, if subject matter is really the dominant factor, with the theory or approach in large part determined by the subject matter, what is the outlook for the work of economists in other social sciences? I would not expect them to continue indefinitely their triumphal advance and it may be that they will be forced to withdraw from some of the fields which they are now so busily cultivating. But such a forecast depends on the practitioners in the other disciplines making a competitive response. The success of economists in moving into the other social sciences is a sign that they possess certain advantages in handling the problems of those disciplines. One is, I believe, that they study the economic system as a unified interdependent system and, therefore, are more likely to uncover the basic interrelationships within a social system than is someone less accustomed to looking at the working of a system as a whole. Another is that a study of economics makes it difficult to ignore factors which are clearly important and which play a part in all social systems. The economist's analysis may fail to touch some of the problems found in the other social systems, but often the analysis can be brought to bear. And the economist will take full advantage of those opportunities which occur when the 'measuring rod of money' can be used.

Economists may, however, study other social systems, such as the legal and political ones, not with the aim of contributing to law or political science, but because it is necessary if they are to understand the working of the economic system itself. It has come to be realized by many economists in recent times that parts of these other social systems are so intermeshed with the economic system as to be as much a part of that system as they are of a sociological, political, or legal system. Thus, it is hardly possible to discuss the functioning of a market without considering the nature of the property right system, which determines what can be bought and sold and which, by influencing the cost of carrying out various kinds of market transactions, determines what is, in fact, bought and sold, and by whom. Similarly, the family or household and the educational system are of concern to the sociologist, but their operations affect the supply of labour to different occupations and the patterns of consumption and production and are, therefore, also of concern to the economist. In the same way, the administration of the regulatory agencies and antitrust policy, while part of the legal system and, as such, studied by lawyers, also provides the framework within which firms and individuals decide on their actions in the economic sphere.

The need to take into account the influence of other social systems, above all the legal system, in analysing the working of the economic system, is now widely accepted by economists. It has resulted in numerous studies of the effect of the legal system on the performance of the economic system. Such work, because of its focus on the economic system, is likely, in general, to be best done by economists. Unlike the movement by economists into the other social sciences which has as its aim the improvement of these other social sciences, a movement which, for reasons I have already given, seems to me likely to be temporary, the study by economists of the effects of the other social systems on the economic system will, I believe, become a permanent part of the work of economists. It cannot be done effectively by social scientists unfamiliar with the economic system. Such work may be carried out in collaboration with other social scientists, but it is unlikely to be well done without economists. For this reason, I think we may expect the scope of economics to be permanently enlarged to include studies in other social sciences. But the purpose will be to enable us to understand better the working of the economic system.

G. S. BECKER

*

The Economic Approach to Human Behavior[5]

Although few persons would dispute the distinctiveness of an economic approach, it is not easy to state exactly what distinguishes the economic approach from the sociological, psychological, anthropological, political, or even genetical approaches. In this essay I attempt to spell out the principal attributes of the economic approach. . . .

The combined assumptions of maximizing behaviour, market equilibrium, and stable preferences, used relentlessly and unflinchingly, form the heart of the economic approach as I see it. . . .

Everyone recognizes that the economic approach assumes maximizing behaviour more explicitly and extensively than other approaches do, be it the utility or wealth function of the household, firm, union, or government bureau that is maximized. Moreover, the economic approach assumes the existence of markets that with varying degrees of efficiency coordinate the actions of different participants – individuals, firms, even nations – so that their behaviour becomes mutually consistent. Since economists generally have had little to contribute, especially in recent times, to the understanding of how preferences are formed, preferences are assumed not to change substantially over time, nor to be very different between wealthy and poor persons, or even between persons in different societies and cultures ...

The assumption of stable preferences provides a stable foundation for generating predictions about responses to various changes, and prevents the analyst from succumbing to the temptation of simply postulating the required shift in preferences to 'explain' all apparent contradictions to his predictions.

The economic approach is clearly not restricted to material goods and wants, nor even to the market sector ... Consider, for example, a person whose only scarce resource is his limited amount of time. This time is used to produce various commodities that enter his preference function, the aim being to maximize utility. Even without a market sector, either directly or indirectly, each commodity has a relevant marginal 'shadow' price, namely, the time required to produce a unit change in that commodity ... Most importantly, an increase in the relative price of any commodity – i.e., an increase in the time required to produce a unit of that commodity – would tend to reduce the consumption of that commodity.

The economic approach does not assume that all participants in any market necessarily have complete information or engage in costless transactions. Incomplete information or costly transactions should not, however, be confused with irrational or volatile behaviour. The economic approach has developed a theory of the optimal or rational accumulation of costly information that implies, for example, greater investment in information when undertaking major than minor decisions – the purchase of a house or entrance into marriage versus the purchase of a sofa or bread. The assumption that information is often seriously incomplete because it is costly to acquire is used in the economic approach to explain the same kind of behaviour that is explained by irrational and volatile behaviour, or traditional behaviour, or 'nonrational' behaviour in other discussions.

When an apparently profitable opportunity to a firm, worker, or household is not exploited, the economic approach does not take refuge in assertions about irrationality, contentment with wealth already acquired, or convenient ad hoc shifts in values (i.e., preferences). Rather it postulates the existence of costs, monetary or psychic, of taking advantage of these opportunities that eliminate their profitability – costs that may not be easily 'seen' by outside observers. Of course, postulating the existence of costs closes or 'completes' the economic approach in the same, almost tautological, way that postulating the existence of (sometimes unobserved) uses of energy completes the energy system, and preserves the law of the conservation of energy ... The critical question is whether a system is completed in a useful way; the important theorems derived from the economic approach indicate that it has been completed in a way that yields much more than a bundle of empty tautologies in good part because, as I indicated earlier, the assumption of stable preferences provides a foundation for predicting the responses to various changes.

Moreover, the economic approach does not assume that decision units are necessarily conscious of their efforts to maximize or can verbalize or otherwise describe in an informative way reasons for the systematic patterns in their behaviour. . . . In addition, the economic approach does not draw conceptual distinctions between major and minor decisions, such as those involving life and death in contrast to the choice of a brand of coffee; or between decisions said to involve strong emotions and those with little emotional involvement, such as in choosing a mate or the number of children in contrast to buying paint; or between decisions by persons with different incomes, education, or family backgrounds.

Indeed, I have come to the position that the economic approach is a comprehensive one that is applicable to all human behaviour . . .

The heart of my argument is that human behaviour is not compartmentalized, sometimes based on maximizing, sometimes not, sometimes motivated by stable preferences, sometimes by volatile ones, sometimes resulting in an optimal accumulation of information, sometimes not. Rather, all human behaviour can be viewed as involving participants who maximize their utility from a stable set of preferences and accumulate an optimal amount of information and other inputs in a variety of markets.

Notes

1. During the last decade, economics has been applied to law, sociology and political science at the same time as it has become increasingly narrow, abstract, mathematical and, some would argue, irrelevant to practical affairs. 'It is as if our subject', state two economists, 'were progressing rapidly at the frontier, while disintegrating at the centre' (P. Bauer and A. Walters, 'The State of Economics' (1975) 18 J. Law and Econ. 1, 7). This trend has frequently been blamed on the economists' increasing use of, if not preoccupation with, mathematical theory and unwillingness to emphasize empirical research (W. Leontief, 'Theoretical Assumptions and Nonobserved Facts' (1971) 61 Am. Econ. Rev. 1). The application of economics to law and politics is in part an attempt by some economists to give the subject more policy relevance – a return to the political economy of the classical economists. It is noteworthy, however, that while other disciplines have drawn on economics for some time in the study of government regulation (see infra, Chapter 6) it only became a serious preoccupation among economists after it had been modelled mathematically (H. Averch and L. Johnson, 'Behavior of

the Firm Under Regulatory Constraint' (1962) 52 Am. Econ. Rev. 1052; P. A. Samuelson, 'The Pure Theory of Public Expenditure' (1954) 36 Rev. Econ. and Statistics 27).

2. Coase and Becker view the widening applications of economics differently. For Coase, the 'permanent' contribution will be to increase the economists' understanding of the operation of the economic system, while Becker portrays economics as the 'science' of all purposeful individual and collective behaviour, capable of making substantial contributions to other disciplines. His work represents the most ambitious attempt yet to give economics an unrestricted scope and has been responsible for a large literature on the economics of crime, nonmarket activities (such as altruism), the family and politics (*The Economics of Discrimination* (1st edn, 1957); *The Economic Approach to Human Behavior* (1976); *A Treatise on the Family* (1982)). The methodological issues raised by this all-embracing definition of economics have only recently received critical attention: W. Nutter, 'On Economism' (1979) 22 J. Law and Econ. 263; R. B. McKenzie, *The Limits of Economic Science* (1982); N. Komesar, 'In Search of a General Approach to Legal Analysis: A Comparative Institutional Alternative (1981) 79 Mich. L. R. 1350.

3. L. Robbins in *An Essay on the Nature and Significance of Economic Science* (1932), p. 15, defines economics as the 'science which studies human behaviour as a relationship between ends and scarce means which have alternative uses'; continuing, 'when time and the means for achieveing ends are limited and capable of being distinguished in order of importance, then behaviour necessarily assumes the form of choice . . . it has an economic aspect'. Thus the defining characteristics of economics are choice and scarcity, rather than material welfare or market activity. This definition is also wider than Becker's, which restricts the economic approach to maximizing behaviour (cf. L. Robbins, 'Economics and Political Economy' (1981) 71 Am. Econ. Rev. 1, 2). Economists have, however, frequently employed models based on bounded rationality – the limited human capacity to formulate and solve complex problems – and game theory – strategies engaged in by individuals with imperfect information – which do not necessarily generate utility maximizing solutions (H. Simon, 'From Substantive to Procedural Rationality' in F. Hahn and M. Hollis (eds.), *Philosophy and Economic Theory* (1979), ch. 5; O. E. Williamson, *Markets and Hierarchies* (1975); M. Peston and A. Coddington, 'The Elementary Ideas of Game Theory' in H. Townsend (ed.), *Price Theory* (2nd edn, 1980), ch. 18.

4. Becker succinctly states the theoretical basis of the so-called Chicago School of Law and Economics as exemplified by the work of Stigler and Posner (G. J. Stigler, *The Citizen and the State* (1975); R. A. Posner, *Economic Analysis of Law* (2nd edn, 1977)). This approach is almost exclusively concerned with developing testable predictions using the utility maximizing model (i.e. it is positive economics; see Veljanovski infra, Section B.). The 'Chicago Credo' is that 'individuals act efficiently in their own interests' (G. J. Stigler, 'Economists and Public Policy' [1982] Regulation 13,

16) and that 'tastes neither change capriciously not differ importantly between people' (G. S. Becker and G. J. Stigler, '*De Gustibus Non Est Disputandum*' (1977) 67 Am. Econ. Rev. 76). Hence, all differences between, and changes in, the behaviour of individuals are assumed to be determined by objective constraints, such as prices, costs and income (M. W. Reder, 'Chicago Economics: Performance and Change' (1982) 20 J. Econ. Litt. 1. See also the critical views of E. J. Mishan, 'The Folklore of the Market – An Inquiry into the Economic Doctrines of the Chicago School' (1975) 9 J. Econ. Issues 681; and R. S. Markovits, 'A Basic Structure for Microeconomic Policy Analysis in Our Worse-than-Second-Best World: A Proposal and Related Critique of the Chicago Approach to the Study of Law and Economics' [1975] Wisc. L.R. 750). Stigler (op. cit., p. 17) has claimed that these assumptions build a 'powerful and versatile theory' that eliminates the 'ad hocery of special explanations and recourse to exceptions that prove no rule'. This, however, is not frequently the case since the maximization calculus, although rigorous and logical, does not always yield unambiguous predictions without resorting to arbitrary assumptions about preferences and the relative magnitudes of key variables (M. Blaug, *The Methodology of Economics* (1980), ch. 14). There is, thus, a real danger that economics especially when applied to phenomena that are not quantifiable, will verge on the 'scientistic' – the uncritical application of the methods of the natural sciences to problems for which they are not apt (F. von Hayek, 'The Pretence of Knowledge' (1977) 4 Swedish J. Econ. 433). If so, the new vocabulary and approach of economics will merely lend the appearance of scientific precision to speculative theories about law which are impossible to 'test'.

B. Assumptions and Concepts

C. G. VELJANOVSKI

*

The New Law-and-Economics: A Research Review[6]

Economic analysis of law is foremost a theoretical approach. Great emphasis is placed on developing a coherent and consistent theoretical model that will provide the basis for interpreting economic and legal phenomena . . .

NATURE OF MODELS

Models simplify in order to enable a better understanding of the real world. Because legal and economic processes are complex, a thorough understanding of the underlying forces and interrelationships is generally impossible. Models break up phenomena into more manageable portions by abstracting those variables that are believed to be a significant influence on choice and subjecting them to deductive reasoning based on a set of accepted axioms. Logical conclusions are then derived which must be translated into propositions about the real world. These propositions or predictions must then be compared to actual behaviour and experience, either by observation or statistical methods.

Types of Theory

In economics there are two modes of discourse: positive (what is) and normative (what ought to be). To this I would add a third: descriptive economic analysis. The success of positive, normative and descriptive theory are to be judged by different criteria and hence they are *not* susceptible to the same criticisms. Critics of the economic approach often confuse these three modes of analysis resulting in much ill-conceived criticism. Here a very simplified account of economic methodology is given.

Positive Economics

Positive economics is the empirical branch of economics. It seeks to generate a set of testable, that is potentially refutable, predictions that can be verified by the empirical evidence. A positive economic model is a meaningful model if it is both correct and useful. It is correct if it is internally consistent; it is useful if it focuses on a significant influence on choice. A meaningful model is thus one that generates predictions to which behaviour conforms more frequently that those generated by some alternative competing theory. If the model is successful in predicting, then the *negative judgment* can be made that the model has not been falsified. Positive economic analysis is used to make qualitative predictions and to organize data for the testing of these predictions. It is predictive and empirical economics.

The predictions of positive economic models must be interpreted with some care. First, such models only establish partial relationships. For example, one of the most common predictions in economics is the inverse relationship between the price of a good and the quantity demanded. However, this statement must be read with an important caveat – the caveat of *ceteris paribus*. The prediction states that in practice the quantity demanded will decrease as price increase *only if all other factors affecting demand such as income, tastes, and the relative prices of other goods remain constant.* Thus the predictions of positive economic models are in the nature of conditional statements 'if A – then B, given C', but B may never be observed to occur because other influences on A (C) have also changed.

Secondly, since positive economic models only deal with partial relationships they do not imply that other factors, economic and non-economic, are of no, or less, importance in explaining behaviour. An economist may argue, for example, that people will respond to cost-pressures (such as liability for damages) in the care they take in an activity which places the safety of others at risk, and he may empirically establish this proposition. But this finding does not naturally lead to the conclusion that pecuniary incentives are the only, or even the best, means of achieving an increase in the level of safety.

Positive economic analysis is most relevant to *impact studies* of the law. Legal impact studies seek to identify and quantify the effects of law on measurable variables, e.g. the extent to which safety legislation reduces the accident rate.

Normative Economics

Normative or welfare economics is the study of criteria that can be used to rank alternative economic situations on a scale of better or worse or in terms of their ability to raise or lower 'social welfare'. In one sense, normative economics is the ethical branch of economics concerned with allocative efficiency, distributive and social justice and prescribing corrective measures to improve social welfare. For the most part welfare economics has been based on the market failures or efficiency framework and a concern for distributive justice, i.e. the optimal level of wealth inequality.

There is an apparent inconsistency between the views that economics is a science and that welfare economics is normative. Normative propositions cannot, as a matter of fact, be verified, nor are they in principle verifiable. Value judgments cannot be tested to see whether they are true or false; they are either acceptable or unacceptable.

Some economists have argued that welfare economics should be treated as a branch of positive economics confined to the study of the economic factors affecting some index of social welfare derived from elsewhere, without arguing that the index is itself desirable. Welfare economics would then simply analyse the economic means of attaining a desired result. The conclusions of these analyses would then be falsifiable in the same way as the predictions of positive economics.

Descriptive Economics

Much economic analysis does not fall neatly into either positive or normative categories. Indeed the bulk of economic theory is not designed to generate testable predictions nor to determine the social desirability of a set of policies. It is abstract theory of economic problems whose sole function is to generate logical deductions and to *describe* economic phenomena.

It is useful to distinguish a third (though not exhaustive) category of economic analysis – descriptive economic analysis. Descriptive economics attempts to model/analyse actual processes and to describe the economic influences that affect them. It is thus based on assumptions that are more or less realistic and therefore subject to empirical verification.

Much of the literature by lawyers using economics falls into this category. It seeks to provide a comprehensive model of law based on economics that is alleged to explain the content of the law. *Descriptive law-and-economics* can be defined as an approach concerned with the principle of allocative efficiency as a concept to rationalize existing legal rules.

Descriptive economics must be judged by different criteria to positive economics for two reasons. First, since its purpose is to *describe* the existing system of law, rather than to predict the impact of changes in the law, the assumptions upon which the theory is built must be descriptively accurate, and these assumptions need to be subject to empirical verification. Thus the statement that 'common law is efficient' is a hypothesis that can be tested by showing that its benefits exceed its costs. Second, descriptive economic theories of law have not been subject to the type of rigorous empirical testing which is deemed appropriate to predictive economics, and there are serious doubts as to whether the descriptive theories are even potentially refutable in this way. The difficulty of testing the theories strengthens the need for descriptive accuracy, otherwise neither assumptions nor conclusions will be subject to verification.

BASIC PREMISES

Although there are a number of schools of economic thought the dominant approach used in the economic analysis of law is neo-classical economics. Here the main ingredients of this approach are outlined.

Methodological Individualism

Neoclassical economics builds on the postulate of methodological individualism – the view that social theories must be based on the attitudes and behaviour of individuals. The basic unit of analysis is thus the rational individual and the behaviour of groups is assumed to be the outcome of the decisions taken by the individuals who compose them. Neoclassical economics is, in other words, *individualistic economics* based on the behavioural model of rational choice.

Maximization Principle

Economic man is assumed to be a self-interested egotist who maximizes his utility. The assumptions of utility (and profit) maximization, or economic rationality as it is sometimes referred to, have given rise to much criticism and confusion. When an economist says that an individual is acting rationally or maximizing his utility he is saying no more than that the individual is making *consistent* choices, and that he chooses the preferred alternative(s) from those available to him. That is, it is assumed the individual is the best judge of his own welfare – the notion of consumer sovereignty.

The economic approach does *not* contend that all individuals are rational nor that these assumptions are necessarily realistic. Rather economic man is some weighted average of the individuals under study in which the non-uniformities and extremes in behaviour are evened out. The theory allows for irrationality but argues that *groups* of individuals behave *as if* their members are rational. Also the utility maximizing postulate does not assert that individuals consciously calculate the cost and benefits of all actions, only that their behaviour can be 'explained' as if they did so.

Stable Preferences

The tastes and preferences of individuals are assumed to be given and stable. This assumption is related to and implied by rational behaviour because if tastes change over time or with past choices preferences may not be consistent. For positive economics the assumption of given tastes thus prevents the economist from rationalizing inconsistencies between theory and the evidence by *ad hoc* claims that tastes have changed. For normative economics changing tastes would render measures of economic welfare unreliable indicators of changes in an individual's well-being. For example, if tastes are constant one can say that a fall in the price of a good improves the (economic) welfare of consumers of that good. However, if at the same time the consumers' tastes alter and they come to regard the good as less desirable, it would not be possible to make such a statement.

Economic Value

The final ingredient of the economic approach concerns the valuation of alternatives. The economic value of a good, service or activity is measured by the individual's willingness to pay, either in money or in kind, to acquire it. Value in economics is exchange or scarcity value – that is, preferences backed by willingness to pay by giving up alternative choices. The economic cost of a resource used for any purpose is equal to its value in the next best alternative use; its *opportunity cost*. The notion of opportunity cost captures elegantly both the concepts of scarcity and the need to choose among competing alternatives, and emphasizes that the economic value of resources is not necessarily the same as their financial costs. For example, the financial cost of a motor car may be less than its social opportunity costs if the car industry is a major polluter and imposes losses on neighbouring residents for which it does not pay compensation.

MARKET AND PRICES

The concepts of a market and price play key rôles in economics. Even in areas where there is not an explicit market, the economic approach will often analyse the subject by analogy with the market concepts of supply, demand and price. A market is simply a decentralized mechanism for allocating resources. Since Adam Smith's *Wealth of Nations*, economists have assumed that individuals trade in markets because exchange is mutually advantageous. The interaction between buyers and sellers in the market has been formalized by economists in the so-called Laws of Supply and Demand. They are 'Laws' in the sense that they have been repeatedly verified by empirical analysis.

The Law of Demand posits an inverse relationship between the price of a commodity and the quantity demanded, holding all other things constant. The Law of Demand states that as the price of a good rises, less is consumed as the consumer reduces his purchases or turns to substitute goods.

The willingness of individuals to produce goods is also assumed to depend on the price. The Law of Supply states that there is a positive relationship between the price received by a producer and the quantity he is willing to produce and supply to the market.

Economists usually portray the market in terms of a supply-and-demand diagram (Figure 1). The demand for a commodity is drawn as a negatively inclined line. It describes the relationship between price

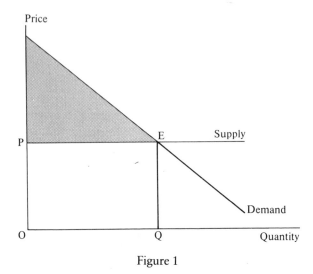

Figure 1

per unit of a good and the quantity consumers are willing to buy at each price. It is negatively sloped because of the assumption of diminishing satisfaction from increased consumption (diminishing marginal utility). To take an extreme example, a person's willingness to pay for a loaf of bread is greater when he is hungry than after he has consumed his second loaf. The *market* demand curve is also negatively sloped because as the price decreases individuals with lower valuations of the commodity enter the market. Each point on the demand curve or schedule therefore shows the maximum price consumers are willing to pay for an addition unit of the good.

The supply line shows the *marginal* cost of producing an additional unit of the good. For convenience, it has been assumed that the marginal costs of production are the same regardless of the level of production. Usually the supply schedule is drawn with a positive slope thus indicating increasing marginal opportunity costs. The assumption of rising marginal costs reflects the increasing scarcity, and hence opportunity costs, of resources drawn into the industry as output expands.

The first economic proposition illustrated in Figure 1 is the allocative function of price. Price *rations* the supply of goods and provides *incentives* for production. It does both of these simultaneously by itself adjusting until the plans of consumers and producers are mutually consistent. If supply exceeds demand, the price will fall to encourage more purchases and discourages production; if demand exceeds supply the price will rise to choke off the excess demand. The price that achieves this is given by the intersection of the two schedules at E in Figure 1. The market is said to be cleared at this price, or in *equilibrium* in the sense that at E the quantity demanded is equal to the quantity supplied and neither consumers nor producers have any desire or incentive to alter their actions.

The market price, P, also provides information to individuals in the economy. In a competitive market the price of a good or service equals the marginal opportunity costs of the resources used to produce it. Thus, a competitive price equal to marginal costs conveys to consumers the sacrifice in the alternative uses of resources that their consumption of an additional unit of the good entails. Price equal to marginal cost informs both consumers and producers of the full (or social) economic cost of expanding or contracting production and consumption, and hence ensures that resources are allocated efficiently.

Figure 1 also enables the economist's measure of value, consumers' surplus or willingness-to-pay, to be distinguished from market price. The market value of the goods produced and consumed in Figure 1 is equal to the price multiplied by the quantity (given by the area OQEP). This sum does not however equal the value that consumers place on the good, which is equal to the market value plus the shaded area in Figure 1. This additional value is known as the consumers' surplus – the excess of what a person is willing to pay for a good or service over the amount that he actually pays. The concept of consumers' surplus provides a quantitative measure of the economic value of changes in prices and quantities of goods and services.

CONCEPTS OF EFFICIENCY

Economists usually separate allocative efficiency from distributional matters. The former refers to the composition of output that satisfies consumer demand as measured by willingness to pay at the lowest costs of production; the latter to the division of wealth in society.

Allocative efficiency is the organizing principle of much of the economic analysis of law. This concept can be defined more formally in two ways which must be clearly distinguished.

Pareto Efficiency

A Pareto efficient situation is one in which the welfare of one individual cannot be improved without reducing the welfare of any other member of society. This criterion is based on several ethical premises:

1. that the individual is the best judge of his own welfare;
2. that the welfare of society depends on the welfare of individuals that comprise it;

3. that any change that increases the welfare of at least one individual without diminishing the welfare of any other improves social welfare.
(This is often termed *the Pareto Criterion*).

The concept of Pareto efficiency is usually linked to the model of perfect competition. Perfect competition is a textbook model of a market that assumes that, *inter alia*, individuals maximize utility, firms are profit maximizers, no individual seller or buyer has the ability to influence a commodity's price by his/her actions (this is the assumption of 'price-taking behaviour'), products are homogeneous, all resources (including firms and individuals) are costlessly mobile and individuals have perfect information about market opportunities. *Given these stringent assumptions*, a perfectly competitive market produces a Pareto efficient allocation of resources in the sense that resources gravitate to those uses where their economic value is greatest. The criterion of maximum value is Pareto efficient because there exist no further trading opportunities between any two (or more) individuals in the market that would be mutually beneficial.

Kaldor–Hicks Efficiency

The Pareto Criterion is an immensely restrictive tool for policy analysis. It precludes the economist from making any interpersonal comparisons of utility; the welfare of one individual cannot be offset or compared to that of another. Since even the most trivial policy change is likely to harm at least one person's interests, the economist will be left with little to say even on matters involving clear net gains.

To circumvent this difficulty the concept of Kaldor–Hicks efficiency (also referred to as potential Pareto improvement, hypothetical compensation test, cost–benefit analysis, wealth maximization, allocative efficiency or simply efficiency) is used. A policy is Kaldor–Hicks efficient if those that gain can in principle compensate those that have been 'harmed' and still be better off. Or simply, the cost–benefit test that the gains exceed the losses to whomsoever they accrue. The major difference between Kaldos–Hicks efficiency and Pareto-efficiency is that in the former the compensation is only hypothetical and the improvement in everyone's welfare is only potential. Kaldor–Hicks efficiency thus *appears* to separate efficiency from the question of wealth distribution and provides the theoretical underpinning for social cost–benefit analysis.

DIFFICULTIES WITH THE EFFICIENCY CRITERION

First-Best Problems

There are several limitations to the Kaldor–Hicks approach. First, unlike Pareto efficiency, there is no sense of voluntarism in Kaldor–Hicks efficiency; the efficient solution is coercively imposed after some third-party determination of costs and benefits. Secondly, because losers of 'efficient' legal reforms go uncompensated for their losses, the criterion is capable of generating quite drastic, capricious and inequitable redistributions of wealth. Thirdly, it is not self-evident why an increase in potential welfare is the relevant maximand particularly when there are individuals suffering losses and others reaping windfall gains more than sufficient to compensate losses. Improvements in actual welfare would appear to be the more appropriate benchmark. Fourthly, it is frequently, but wrongly, claimed that Kaldor–Hicks efficiency obviates the need to make inter-personal comparisons of utility. It assumes that a £1 is a £1 to whomsoever it accrues. But this is as much an interpersonal comparison as one that weighs the gains and losses on the basis of some normative and/or ethical value judgment regarding the relative 'worthiness' of individuals. The Kaldor–Hicks approach in practice assumes that the worth of a £1 (in technical terms its marginal utility) is the same to everyone, and this is a demonstrably false assumption. Moreover, judging from public policy and political rhetoric it is not a widely held one. In fact most governments have legislated against this assumption of economists by introducing progressive personal income taxation. Finally, Kaldor–Hicks efficiency does not rest on the same value premises underlying Pareto efficiency and since it violates the third premise (the no-loss requirement), it has a much narrower ethical appeal.

Second-Best Problems

In an imperfect world where some sectors of the economy persistently and irremediably deviate from efficiency it will no longer be true that fostering efficiency in other sectors will maximize economic efficiency. The constraint imposed by deviant sectors of the economy must be taken into consideration and this will require immensely complex, if not impossible, calculations to determine the optimal policy. This is know as the problem of the 'second-best'.

Although the theory underlying the second-best is difficult, its logic is not and can be easily illustrated by an example. Suppose there is an inefficient industry which prices its goods below marginal social costs because it inflicts uncompensated damage on local residents. Further assume that for some reason the government cannot impose a corrective policy on the industry. From an economic efficiency point of view this industry's production is overexpanded. Given that this cannot be rectified it may no longer be efficient for the government to encourage all other sectors to price at marginal cost. For example, for products that are highly complementary to those of the inefficient sector, it may be efficient to price above marginal cost so as to discourage their production and indirectly the overexpansion of the inefficient sector. The implication of the problem of second-best is that piecemeal applications of the Kaldor–Hicks criterion may not bring about a more efficient allocation of resources in the economy.

DISTRIBUTIVE JUSTICE

Each allocative change not only alters total wealth but distributes it in different proportions among individuals. The latter is also an economic problem, one that economists have had little success in modelling. Even if one is not principally concerned with the distribution of wealth, it is necessary to recognize that efficiency and the economic value of goods and services cannot be separated from distributional questions.

The distribution of wealth (or entitlements which confer legal rights to wealth) determine in part both the economic value and optimal allocation of resources in an economy. To say that a situation is allocatively efficient is to say only that all the (potential or actual) gains from trade have been exhausted, given the initial distribution of wealth among individuals. If the wealth in society were redistributed then there would be a different efficient allocation of resources. To take a rather extreme example, if wealth is concentrated in the hands of a few rich landowners who buy Rolls Royces and caviar, then allocative efficiency will be consistent with the poor starving and the economy's productive activity channelled into the manufacture of these luxury items. If wealth were to be distributed more equitably, less Rolls Royces and caviar and more of the necessities of life would be produced.

Thus each different distribution of wealth generates a different pattern of demand, a different set of prices and different production decisions. Economic value and the efficient allocation of resources are both intractably related and vary according to the distribution of wealth in society. There thus exists literally an infinite number of allocatively efficient outcomes that differ only with respect to the distribution of welfare among individuals in society. Efficiency is therefore little more than a *technocratic principle of unimprovability*; there is no rearrangement of society's productive activity or allocation of goods and services that will improve the economic welfare of society *given the distribution of wealth* upon which market transactions are based.

Allocative efficiency is a necessary but not sufficient condition for the maximization of a social welfare function that incorporates a value judgement regarding the ethical deserts of various members of society. The orthodox view is that the desirability of a given income distribution is not a question of efficiency. The attainment of an optimum that maximizes social welfare is seen as involving state intervention to rectify the initial distribution of resources so as to make each consumer £1 voting in the market of equal social deserts.

The recognition of the inseparable relationship between the distribution of wealth and efficiency gives rise to certain propositions that have not been sufficiently emphasized in the literature:

1. the only Pareto efficient outcome that is socially desirable is that based on a just distribution of income and property rights and;
2. inefficiency may be acceptable in practice if it leads to a more desirable or ethically attractive distribution of wealth.

Thus it is apparent that normative economics needs a theory of distributive justice that will enable the analyst to rank efficient outcomes in terms of their ethical attractiveness. Economists have shied away from this task largely because of a widely held professional view that distributive justice is a nebulous concept that defies scientific evaluation and the obvious difficulties of defining and enforcing a social welfare function which would at the same time be consistent with the Paretian assumptions.

Notes

1. Market analysis is extensively used in economics (Scherer, infra, Chapter 5, Section B.; R. B. McKenzie and G. Tullock, *Modern Political Economy* (1978) chs. 2–4). This has led to a widespread belief that economic analysis of law is based on a market philosophy which can be rejected by those who hold different ideological beliefs. While it is true that economists start with assumptions that the market is the natural state of affairs, the substance of their analysis would not change if central planning were taken as the norm, provided that in each case departures from the chosen norm were permitted on efficiency grounds. The critics of economics, unfortunately, have been misled by the terminology of the subject. Many articles begin by using a market analogy – the economist will conceptualize, say crime, in terms of a supply of and demand for offences and characterize the penalty as a 'price' to engage in crime (Ehrlich, infra, Chapter 8, Section A). This conveys the impression that he believes that provided criminals are willing to pay an

appropriate price they can rape, rob and pillage at will. This is a misconception caused by a confusing if not unnecessary vocabulary used to rigorously analyse the supply of criminal offences and the demand of prospective victims to prevent crime, both of which use scarce resources, involve choices and are therefore economic problems.

2. Positive economic theory is used to model the law and predict its effects. Multiple regression analysis is the statistical technique most frequently employed to test these predictions. It is a device for making precise and quantitative estimates of the (separate) effects of different factors on some variable of interest (F. M. Fisher, 'Multiple Regression in Legal Proceedings' (1980) 80 Col. L.R. 702; C. H. Lee, *The Quantitative Approach to Economic History* (1977)). Its procedures form a highly specialized branch of study called econometrics. Regression analysis has been widely used to estimate the impact of regulation (infra, Chapter 7) and as evidence in some American civil cases (M. O. Finkelstein, 'The Judicial Reception of Multiple Regression Studies in Race and Sex Discrimination Cases' (1980) 80 Col. L.R. 737; and *Quantitative Methods in Law* (1978)).

3. Welfare economics, of which the concept of allocative efficiency is a component, is a well developed branch of economic analysis (J. de Graaf, *Theoretical Welfare Economics* (1957); P. Bohm, *Social Efficiency* (1974); C. M. Price, *Welfare Economics in Theory and Practice* (1977); J. L. Coleman, 'Efficiency, Exchange and Auction: Philosophic Aspects of the Economic Approach to Law' (1980) 68 Calif. L.R. 221). The efficiency analysis of law, in the guise of social loss minimization, wealth maximization or cost–benefit analysis, is based on the Kaldor–Hicks criterion. Since this criterion compares only aggregate costs and benefits without regard to their incidence, or whether some individuals are harmed, its ethical propriety differs substantially from Pareto efficiency. A stronger and substantially more controversial value judgement must be made, namely, that maximizing net monetary gains is a normatively attractive criterion or else instrumental in promoting some other desired goal (see Dworkin, infra, Section C).

G. J. STIGLER

*

The Theory of Price[7]

THE NATURE OF COSTS

Occasionally one walks into the shop of a lazy man and observes identical goods with two prices, and is told that the lower priced items were in an earlier shipment that cost less. This is foolish merchandising unless the cost of remarking the price is more than the rise in price. It is

---

[7] From *The Theory of Price* (3rd edn., 1966), pp. 104–14, with omissions. Copyright © 1942, 1946, 1952 by Macmillan Publishing Company; copyright © 1966 by George J. Stigler. Reprinted by permission of the Macmillan Company (New York).

also symptomatic of the layman's tendency to identify 'cost' with outlays actually incurred or historical costs.

Historical costs have powerful sway over untutored minds. The Internal Revenue Service insists that corporation assets be so valued. The public utility commissions consider historical costs a relevant or even decisive item in setting rates. Men incur additional losses trying to 'get their money' out of a venture. They all fly in the face of a basic principle of rational behaviour, 'By-gones are forever by-gones'.

It is easy to manufacture cases in which historical costs are seen to be irrelevant to price. Smith produces a commodity for $3, Jones for $4 – will they receive different prices? Johnson builds a house for $20,000 which termites mostly devour – will it sell for $20,000? I buy a rock for $10, and it proved to be a diamond of remarkable purity – will I sell it for $10? . . .

In every case, of course, there was a miscalculation of some sort: Jones should have been more efficient; Johnson should have beaten off the termites; the seller should have known it was a diamond (and possibly nature should have hidden it deeper in the ground); . . . But even with perfect foresight historical costs can be irrelevant: they exclude interest (as accountants reckon costs) whereas a wine should sell for C per cent more after a year, if C is the carrying cost (as a per cent of last year's value).

The basic concept of cost is therefore something different: the cost of any productive service to use A is the maximum amount it could produce elsewhere. The foregone alternative is the cost. Note that the alternative cost sets the *value* of the resource to use A; it does not by itself set the cost of producing A's product. To determine the cost of production of A's product, we must know also the amounts of resources used to produce a given amount of A. . . .

The alternative uses of a resource depend upon the use for which the cost is being reckoned:

1. The cost of an acre of land to agricultural uses is the amount the land could yield in nonagricultural uses (residences, parks, and so on).

2. The cost of an acre of land to the wheat-growing industry is the amount it would yield in other agricultural crops (oats, corn, and so on), as well as in nonagricultural uses.

3. The cost of an acre of land to wheat farmer X is the amount the land could yield to other wheat farmers, as well as all non-wheat uses.

If all land were homogeneous in all relevant respects (including location, fertility, and the like), obviously all three of these alternative costs would be the same. For if land yielded more in nonagricultural uses than in agricultural uses, some of it would be transferred to the nonagricultural uses, and the transfer would go on until the yields in all uses were equal (under competition). Equality of yields of a resource in every feasible use is necessary to maximum return for the individual owners of the resource; any discrepancy in yields is (with competition) an opportunity to someone to increase his income.

But if the land is not homogeneous, it is not necessary that these alternative costs be equal. Suppose that due to locational and other factors, an acre of one type of land will yield $50 in wheat, $30 in other farm crops, and $5 in nonagricultural uses. Then the cost of the land to the wheat industry is $30 an acre – the best foregone alternative. This cost is decisive to the land's use: even if a declining demand forces the yield in wheat down to $31, the land will not be transferred to other uses. But from the viewpoint of any tenant wheat farmer, a rent of $50 is the cost because at $49.99 it will be rented to another farmer.

This definition of cost clearly avoids the paradoxes encountered by historical costs. All productive services which are identical necessarily have the same alternative cost, no matter what the differences in their historical costs. It is also a powerful weapon in analyzing fallacies, of which a few samples may be appropriate.

With conscription an army pays its soldiers whatever it wishes, and it is sometimes said that the relatively high wage rates of American soldiers make national defense more expensive for the United States than for other countries. The cost of a soldier to an economy, however, is his foregone product as a civilian, and this is not directly affected by his rate of pay. The dollars which are given to the soldier involve a real cost to the community only to the extent that higher wage rates lead to the employment of more tax collectors . . .

The alternative uses of a resource will often be different, and in fact fewer, in the short run from what they are in the long run. This is obviously true of specialized machinery: during its life it can be used only for the purpose for which it was designed, or as scrap. But over time it earns depreciation reserves which can be reinvested in other forms of capital. The same situation holds with respect to labor: a carpenter has as alternative occupations only those fields which requires his skills or are less skilled (he can become an unskilled laborer, for example). But given sufficient time to be retrained, he can work in a sash and door plant or become an electrician. Given still more time, every young man who otherwise would have entered this occupation will enter one of a hundred others with demands for a comparable quality of labor. . . .

There is a widespread tendency to look at only the short run alternatives in judging the cost of a commodity (when alternatives are considered at all). When France froze rents during a substantial inflation, there seemed to be no serious costs in the alternative sense.

Dwellings are durable and specialized, so the supply can be assumed to remain the same with low rents as with high. For a week this is true. Over time, however, a landlord can and will (and did!) reduce maintenance, as a device for withdrawing capital from this unprofitable field of investment. Over a still longer period the supply of houses will shrink – none will be built (privately) and the elements will erode those in existence. In the long run houses can be built and maintained only with resources that have many other uses, and no scheme of financing can avoid the alternative costs of these resources. The alternative cost theory is sometimes rephrased as the theorem that there is no such thing as a free lunch even in France.

Nonmonetary Alternatives. The alternatives to a given use of a resource often include also nonmonetary elements. In the employment of labor, they include riskiness, the conditions of work (cleanliness, 3 vs. 9 coffee breaks, and so forth), prestige, and similar factors, but *not* the prospective increase in earnings with time, which is a monetary element. In the employment of capital, riskiness is the main factor, although in some areas the ability to withdraw funds rapidly (liquidity) is also important. These nonmonetary elements obviously must be reckoned with monetary returns in analysing the allocation of resources among uses.

It would be an immense boon if one could always translate nonmonetary elements into 'monetary equivalents'. We would obviously prefer to say that the alternative cost of a man to the legal professions is $14,000 or its equivalent, rather than $12,000 plus the amenities of being a professor.

Within limits it is possible to make direct estimates of the monetary value of these elements. For example, the longer vacation of an occupation can be appraised at the time rate of the basic salary, and income in kind (as food grown and consumed on farms) can be appraised at appropriate market costs.

This method is not available for elements such as prestige or risk of death. Here we may *deduce* the monetary equivalent by comparing returns to the factors in equilibrium if there is free competition. If in equilibrium a professor earns $3,000 less than a dentist, after adjustment for differences in training, income in kind, and so on, we may assert that this is the money value of the nonmonetary returns of the one occupation relative to the other. There are difficult, but not insoluble, problems in determining whether an equilibrium has existed during a given period. A more important limitation in principle is that the occupations may not be equally open to men of equal and appropriate ability: this is obviously the difficulty with comparing Supreme Court Justices and lawyers or comparing airline pilots (who have a strong union) and other pilots.

The equilibrium difference in money returns will measure the difference in nonmonetary elements only at the margin. If the equilibrium money labor income of a farmer is 20 per cent less than that of a comparable urban worker, there will be many farmers for whom nonmonetary returns are larger, and some who would not leave farming if incomes fell to 50 per cent of the urban level. In our terminology, the earnings of these ardent farmers contain rents.

The nonmonetary returns are seldom an invariable part of the use of a resource. If men love a rural setting, industrial plants will move to the country to supply this desire (or, what is simply another way of viewing it, to pay lower wages). If workers wish the opportunity to acquire additional training, the employers will institute programs or allow time off to take courses. If lenders are fearful of losing their capital, they are supplied with senior obligations by the borrower.

Private Costs and Social Costs

A chemical plant, let us assume, collects waste products and discharges them into a stream which flows by the plant. The cost to this plant of disposing of waste is then the cost of pumping the waste to the stream (or, in more precise language, the cost is the foregone alternatives of the resources necessary to do the pumping). If pollution of the stream reduces the income of other people (destroying recreational uses, making the water unpotable, and so on), there are additional costs borne by others. The costs to the individual firm are termed *private* costs, while the sum of costs to everyone is called the *social cost* of waste disposal.

There can be no doubt of the existence of these external effects of an individual's behaviour. In fact, in strictest logic there are very few actions whose entire consequences accrue to the actor. If I educate my children well, the community (it is hoped) will benefit by reduced crime, more enlightened citizenship, and so forth. If I grow an attractive lawn, my neighbours are pleased . . .

One of the most tendentious questions in economics has been: when social and private costs diverge appreciably, will competition lead to correct amounts (and prices) of goods? Will not the chemical plant, under competition, sell at a price which does not cover the costs of pollution, so its costs will be too low and its output too large (with given demands for chemicals)?

To answer the queston, let us shift to another example, which happens to have a long legal history, that of wandering cattle. In a region hitherto devoted to unfenced farms growing grain, a cattle raiser comes. His cattle will, unless fenced in, occasionally wander into the neighboring grain fields and damage the crops.

Taking account of this damage, from the social viewpoint the use of the farm for cattle is desirable only if the additional net income of the land is larger that that in growing grain by the lesser of the two amounts: (1) the annual cost of fencing the cattle farm, or (2) the damage to the neighboring crops. Let us assume that cattle raising just meets this test.

If the cattle raiser has no responsibility, or only partial responsibility, for the costs imposed upon others by his wandering cattle, it appears that he will earn a larger rent in cattle than in grain. As a result, more farms will be converted to cattle, and there will be too much meat and not enough grain in the community.

We mean a specific thing by too much meat and not enough grain. Suppose the social costs of 100 bushels of wheat and 400 pounds of meat are the same – the same resources can produce either. Then if their prices (for these quantities) are not equal, consumers will buy relatively more of the cheaper product. Perhaps the equilibrium is reached when 500 pounds of meat sells for the same price as 100 bushels of wheat. The consumer is then indifferent if one bushel of wheat is added and 5 pounds of meat taken away from him. But given the social costs, it would be impossible by reducing meat output 5 pounds to obtain 1.25 bushels of wheat, and the consumer would consider this 0.25 bushels a clear gain.

This is in fact an instance of a general theorem: consumers will be best off . . . when the relative prices of goods are equal to their relative (marginal) social costs. Where private costs differ from social costs, obviously this optimum position will not be reached, because producers will gear output to their private costs.

The differences between private and social costs or returns have provided a fertile field for public control of economic activity. In fact on can attribute most limitations on private ownership or control of property to this source. These controls are of every degree of perspicacity, ranging from traffic controls (where private contracts between rapidly converging drivers would be difficult to arrange) to petroleum import restrictions (designed to conserve the supply of domestic petroleum!).

Notes

1. The economist's definition of cost differs from that normally used by accountants. Opportunity costs relate not to items of expenditure but *courses of action* (R. Sugden and A. Williams, *The Principles of Practical Cost–Benefit Analysis* (1978), ch. 3; D. W. Pearce, *The Valuation of Social Cost* (1978)). Some economists have disputed that the 'costs' that influence individual

decisions can be objectively measured by an external observer. This minority view holds that costs are subjective phenomena (J. M. Buchanan, *Cost and Choice* (1969); J. M. Buchanan and G. F. Thirlby (eds.) *L.S.E. Essays on Cost* (1973)).

2. The concepts of social costs and benefits play key roles in normative economic analysis. The difference between social and private costs (or benefits) is frequently referred to as an externality (also spillover, third-party effect or external cost/benefit). To quote A. C. Pigou (*The Economics of Welfare* (4th edn, 1932), p. 183) an externality where 'one person . . . in the course of rendering some service, for which payment is made, to a second person, . . . incidentally also renders services or disservices to other persons, of such a sort that payment cannot be extracted from the benefited party or compensation enforced on behalf of the injured parties'. Externalities thus have two essential characteristics: (1) they are incidental by-products of some other market or productive activity; and (2) the effects are unpriced (J. G. Head, *Public Goods and Public Welfare* (1969), ch. 9; E. J. Mishan, '–The Postwar Literature on Externalities; An Interpretative Essay' (1971) 9 J. Econ. Litt. 1). All forms of market failure (e.g. monopoly, public goods, imperfect information) imply a divergence between social and private costs/benefits (see Breyer, infra, Chapter 6, Section B). Much of the normative economic analysis of law rationalizes the law in terms of rules that redistribute losses in an attempt to remedy the inefficiency resulting from externalities (see Coase, infra, Chapter 2, Section C).

3. Not all uncompensated third-party effects cause market failure. Economists distinguish the above technological externalities from 'pecuniary' externalities. A technological externality is a *direct* interdependence that affects production or utility. A pecuniary externality on the other hand is the natural consequence of the interdependence of market relations. For example, if an individual enters the market for apples and places a large order, his additional demand will raise the price of apples to all other consumers thus adversely affecting their welfare. Such third-party effects do not cause a problem for market efficiency because the loss to existing consumers of apples, due to the higher price, is exactly counter-balanced by the gain to the producers of apples (for an application of this distinction see Bishop, infra, Chapter 3, Section E).

C. Applications of Economics to Law

A. K. KLEVORICK

*

Law and Economic Theory: An Economist's View[8]

The first kind of contribution an economic theorist can make in law arises when economic concepts become important in understanding some aspect of a particular legal case. Although the overall question raised by the case may not be economic in nature, at some point an understanding of how markets work, how markets value commodities, services, and assets, and how individuals interact in their economic roles may become critical in deciding the ultimate disposition of the case. One can take an example as basic as the valuation of a capital asset. Suppose, for example, that through some set of circumstances (which we will not inquire into now), A has destroyed B's widget-making machine. The latter has no sentimental attachment to his machine, but values it only for the widgets it enables him to produce and sell. Without inquiring how the court reaches this position, suppose the court decides to award B an amount in damages equal to the value of the machine A has destroyed. An economist armed with his understanding of how markets value capital assets should be able to help the court in deciding the appropriate amount for B to receive in damages, given the court's decision that B should be compensated for the loss he has incurred because of A's destruction of the machines. An economist should also be able to help the court if B returns, as some real-world plaintiffs have, and asks for compensation, *in addition to* the amount the court has already awarded him, for the loss of profits he will incur until he can replace his widget-making machine with the new one he had just ordered.

In such a situation, the economist essentially plays the role of technician. He takes the problem facing the legal decision maker framed the way the legal decision maker has posed it, and he bring his expertise to bear in dealing with a specific part of the case. The economist draws upon his understanding of the way in which particular functions of society are performed, and he uses that understanding to shed light on specific issues in a given case. It is not a

[8] (1975) 65 Am. Econ. Rev. 237, 237–43, with omissions. Reprinted by permission of the American Economic Association.

terribly imaginative role, but it is undoubtedly a terribly important one.

The second type of contribution an economist can make to law might be described as the economist in the role of 'supertechnician'. Once again, the economist takes the problem as set by the lawyer or by the legal decision maker, but in this instance the entire structure of the problem area has economic roots. The objectives and design of the institutions and doctrine are explicitly stated in economic terms, and the economist is called upon to evaluate and give advice about the best ways to achieve the specified objective(s). Most of the traditional areas of interaction between law and economics would fall, I think, into this category. They include, for example, the areas of antitrust law, public utility regulation, and labour law. When the issues at hand concern the most efficient way, or at least more efficient ways, of structuring an industry or a sector of the economy or the relationship between economic agents, the question comes ready-made for the economist to make an important contribution.

One particularly important function the economist can play in his role as supertechnician is to question whether the legal decision maker's general approach in a particular area actually helps to achieve the end the legal decision maker has in mind. For example, putting aside for the moment the multiplicity of reasons and rationales that might lie behind the institution of public utility regulation, suppose the legal decision maker asserts and believes that the primary objective of a system of public utility regulation is efficiency in the economist's strictly defined sense. The economist should be able to point out the kinds of characteristics commonly associated with natural monopoly and the kinds of characteristics which might suggest the need for special concern about the efficient functioning of an industry. He can help to focus the discussion to see whether the industry for which regulation has been proposed is indeed a natural monopoly. If the answer is yes, the economist can – and should – then suggest to the decision maker the variety of possible responses to the natural monopoly situation, responses ranging from having the natural monopoly privately owned and unregulated, to the general type of public utility regulation we have today, to an alternative type of regulation, or, finally, to public enterprise.

One thing the economist should do is provide the decision maker with an evaluation of the advantages and disadvantages of each of these alternative approaches. He should frame the discussion so that it encompasses not only the direct impacts each of these systems will have on the efficiency of the sector or industry whose regulation is being contemplated, but also the side effects or indirect effects that such regulation might have on this industry and its consumers and on other industries and other consumers in the economy. It would also seem to be incumbent upon the economist to try, to whatever extent possible, to indicate the income- (or wealth-) distributional impacts of such a regulatory policy. For although we have assumed (for the sake of this discussion) that the averred and true goal of the decision maker's use of regulation is to achieve efficiency, there are undoubtedly some tradeoffs between efficiency and distribution in the choice of a response to the natural monopoly problem, and the economist is particularly well suited to the task of pointing out what kinds of tradeoffs exist. Of course, while most of my discussion is concerned with the role of the economic theorist, the kinds of judgments that would be important, indeed critical, in such a balancing act are empirical judgments (and empirical guesses if hard data do not exist concerning these alternative costs and benefits). But even the theorist can help, and should help, to focus the discussion at the level of a comparative institutional analysis – a comparison of the alternative systems available for trying to achieve the given objectives.

In the context of this role as supertechnician, the economic theorist can also have a considerable input in designing the particular legal structure that is eventually chosen to cope with the given legal problem. For example, in the public utility area the economic theorist may be able to indicate which kinds of regulatory structures are most likely to achieve the goal of efficiency. He would be able to delineate, from an efficiency point of view, which kinds of issues are best handled using automatic adjustment clauses and which types of issues are best thrashed out in an alternative procedural setting.

In sum, when the economic theorist acts as a supertechnician for the lawyer, he draws on his expertise in analyzing a problem posed by the lawyer, just as he did in the role I described as economist as technician. But now the problem he is addressing is in its own terms economic in nature.

The third role I see for the economic theorist in the joint enterprise of law and economics is one that has come to flourish quite recently. Put briefly, it envisions the economist or economic theorist as the propounder of a new vocabulary, a new analytical structure for viewing a traditional legal problem. In contrast to the economist's approach in the first two categories of interaction I discussed, in this third role he no longer takes the problem as framed by the lawyer. Rather he takes the general problem area with which the lawyer is concerned – say, torts, or property, or procedure – and poses in his own terms – that is, in economic terms – the problem he sees the legal structure or legal doctrine confronting. He provides, thereby, a different way of looking at the legal issue which yields alternative explanations of how current law came to be what it is and new proposals for new law.

In the area of torts, for example, some economic theorists have posed the problem facing society as minimization of the expected social costs of accidents, taking account of: the costs incurred when accidents occur and the probabilities that such accidents will occur; the relationship between those accident costs and probabilities and the steps people take to avoid accidents; the costs of the resources devoted to avoiding accidents and the costs any administrative structure used to make decisions about the optimal level and allocation of these several kinds of costs among members of society. Economic theorists have used this type of framework to discuss and evaluate the traditional negligence rules, to provide a critique of the fault system of accident law, and to evaluate new proposals for automobile accident law, for example, no-fault plans . . .

This third role is probably the most exciting one the economic theorist can currently play. This form of interaction with the lawyer appears to be the most creative and the most challenging. Hence, it is interesting to ask whether particular kinds of problems confront the economist when he presents a new vocabulary or a new structure for analyzing a legal problem. I think two such problems are particularly important – one arises from a constraint imposed by the economist's tools while the other is a limitation imposed by the lawyer's formulation of the problem area.

The constraint imposed by the economist's tools is perhaps seen best in the context of a concrete example. Consider the problem of designing a set of liability rules for accident law in the world in which we live today. It should be clear that any attempt to analyze reality, to make meaningful statements about it, requires some abstraction from the richness of the phenomena being studied. The lawyer's world view is an abstraction just as the economist's is. The economic theorist's approach is to begin with the simplest possible model which captures important structural elements of the problem and to analyze that model as carefully as possible. As a theorist, I think this is a wise strategy. Having analyzed the simplest model, one might then proceed by relaxing some of the unrealistic assumptions which made one's first construction so tractable. For example, one might assume at the first step that all accident costs are, in fact, known to all parties making decisions about what levels of care to exercise. The second level of analysis might involve a relaxation of that assumption and a recognition that some parties will not be fully aware of these costs. The single (certain) values individuals attached to accident costs in the first model might now be replaced by subjective probability distributions people have about the accident costs that will be incurred.

Now suppose that in the simplest model several different liability rules would each yield the full-information social optimum by leading individual decision makers to attain the social-cost-minimizing combination of care levels. As one relaxes the assumptions of the model, the set of liability rules that will achieve the social optimum will undoubtedly become smaller. Further relaxations of the original assumptions – further gropings toward a more realistic representation of the world and people's decision-making processes – will undoubtedly reduce even further the number of liability rules that yield the social-cost-minimizing solution. Indeed, it is most likely that before long the set of socially optimal liability rule structures will become empty. In short, there is no first-best solution in the real world or, for that matter, in the most complicated, yet tractable model we may construct.

The question then is: If the economic theorist is going to use his theoretical analysis to make policy recommendations, how should he proceed? It would be tempting simply to consider those policies that were socially optimal in, say, the next-to-the-most complicated model he had. The problem with this, of course, is that the order in which the theorist relaxes his original assumptions to arrive at the most complicated model he analyses – that is, the path that leads to the continually shrinking set of socially optimal policies – has no particular normative justification. He could follow an alternative complicating path which might well generate an alternative second-best policy.

The realization that we are making decisions in second-best (indeed, an nth-best) setting does not imply that the theorist's models and analyses should be dispensed with or ignored. Nor should the second-best nature of the decision problem be used by the economist as an excuse for avoiding statements of a policy nature. To evaluate alternative policies, however, the theoretical model must be used in conjunction with careful, empirically rooted judgments (guesses?) about which of the theorist's original simplifying assumptions are most likely to affect the applicability of his model's results. And the order in which the theorist relaxes these assumptions in building successively more realistic models need not reflect the empirical importance of the various assumptions. Hence, there is no reason to evaluate second-best policies by simply removing, in reverse order, the complications introduced to obtain the most realistic model.

The theorist can contribute in two ways to the comparative institutional analysis the law and economics enterprise should produce in such situations. First, by providing a new and different way of looking at the traditional legal issue, he will, hopefully, provide clarification and new insights into that issue. Second, he will provide an indication of the kinds of empirical guesses that are needed in order to use his theoretical investigation for policy formulation in the world in which lawyers actually operate.

A different, but equally important, difficulty arises when the economic theorist provides a new vocabulary for a problem which the lawyer poses in a form not really amenable to economic analysis. While the theorist might be tempted to show how his analytical structures can be applied to particular issues in such areas, it is simply the case that his tools are inappropriate to the overall task. I have particularly in mind those areas in which lawyers or legal scholars have framed the legal question in process-oriented rather than outcome-oriented terms, that is, as a question about how a decision will be made rather than about what the decision will be. Questions of institutional competence, questions of whether a particular issue is one that should be taken up by legislatures or by courts, are questions which are not easily comprehended within the economist's framework.

To be sure, questions of relative institutional competence can be stated in economic terms. One can talk about which institution has a comparative advantage in performing which function. We can ask whether courts or legislatures are 'better' at developing liability rules, whether courts or administrative agencies are 'better' at determining the value of a fair rate of return to a public utility, whether legislatures or courts are 'better situated' to decide which interests are fundamental and which interests are not (alternatively, which wants are merit wants), or whether the judiciary or the legislature or the executive is the appropriate institution to decide if and when prior restraint over publication should be exercised. One can use the terminology of economics and talk about the costs and benefits of using one institution rather than the other. But when the legal scholar has posed the problem in process terms, the analytical structure the economist offers for the given legal issue may not prove very helpful to the lawyer. . . .

We come now to the question of what happens after the economist has proposed a new vocabulary for viewing a traditional area of legal concern. One possibility, of course, is that the new vocabulary will simply be rejected, and I have tried to indicate at least one reason why that may occur. A second possibility is that the new vocabulary, the new way of viewing the problem, will come to displace the old. While I regard this outcome as highly unlikely, it nevertheless suggests the major danger that I see, and that I hope will be averted, in the application of economic theory to legal problems: namely, a type of intellectual imperialism on the part of the economic theorist or the lawyer-economist. It is the danger that, having created or at least suggested a new vocabulary for viewing the legal issue, the economic theorist or the lawyer-economist will develop – or even worse, try to generate in others – a form of tunnel vision in which he sees the new vocabulary as the only 'reasonable' one for viewing the area. While I firmly believe that economics can make a contribution to law and that economic theory in particular can make such a contribution, I do not believe that the analytical grid the economic theorist imposes on the legal problem is the only one worth examining. . . .

Economic theory's contribution to law is likely to be greatest if, in proposing new analytical structures for traditional legal issues, the economist or lawyer-economist takes a constructive eclectic view and welcomes the contributions other social scientists may be able to make to our understanding of these areas. For psychologists, historians, sociologists, and others can also suggest new and potentially useful approaches to legal issues, approaches which will undoubtedly complement the economist's with its relative inattention to a variety of questions − like historical development, the formation of individual and social tastes, and so on. The economic theorist's new formulation essentially provides a new metaphor for viewing the particular area of legal concern. But the economist's suggested metaphor is only one among many, and in attempting to understand, to analyze, and to aid in the development of the law, an approach which draws upon the variety of ways the several social sciences analyze human behaviour is likely to be the most helpful and the most successful.

A. E. LEFF

*

Economic Analysis of Law: Some Realism about Nominalism[9]

With the publication of Richard A. Posner's *Economic Analysis of Law*,[10] that field of learning known as 'Law and Economics' has reached a stage of extended explicitness that requires and permits extended and explicit comment.

THE WAY WE LIVE TODAY

Let us start with a couple of vicious intellectual parodies. Once upon a time there was Formalism. The Law itself was a deductive system, with unquestionable premises leading to ineluctable conclusions. . . . The job of legal commentators, and a fortiori of treatise writers, was to find the consistent thread in the inconsistent statements of others and pull it

[9] (1974) 60 Virginia L. R. 451, 451−61, with omissions. Reprinted by permission of Fred B. Rothman & Co.
[10] (1st edn, 1972).

all together along the seam of what was implicit in 'the logic of the system'. . . .

Then, out of the hills, came the Realists. What their messianic message was has never been totally clear. But it is generally accepted that, at least in comparison to the picture of their predecessors which they drew for themselves, they were much more interested in the way law actually functioned in society. There were *men* in law, and the law created by men had an effect on other men in society. The critical questions were henceforward no longer to be those of systematic consistency, but of existential reality. You could no longer criticize law in terms of logical operations, but only in terms of operational logic.

Now such a move, while liberating, was also ultimately terrifying. For if you were interested in a society, and with law as an operative variable within that society, you would have to find out something about that subject matter and those operations. You would, it seems, have to become an empiricist. . . .

Let us say you found yourself facing a universe normatively empty and empirically overflowing. What I suppose you would want most to do, if you wanted to talk at all, would be to find some grid you could place over this buzzing data to generate a language which would at the same time provide a critical terminology ('*X* is bad because . . .') and something in terms of which the criticism could be made (that is, something to follow the 'because . . .'). . . . [Posner] does indeed solve the normative 'oughtness' problems by the neo-Panglossian move: good is defined as that which is in fact desired. But then he makes a very pretty move, one that renders his work, and work like it, so initially attractive . . . in place of what one might have expected (and feared) – a complex regimen for an empirical investigation of human wants and values – he puts a single-element touchstone, so narrow a view of the critical empirical question as to be, essentially, a definition. 'What people want' is presented in such a way that while it is in form empirical, it is almost wholly non-falsifiable by anything so crude as fact.

To follow this initially attractive development in legal criticism (for purposes both of admiration and scorn), one will have to master the critical early moves. The first and most basic is 'the assumption that man is a rational maximizer of his ends in life. . . .' In connection with this assumption, several 'fundamental economic concepts' emerge. 'The first is that of the inverse relation between price charged and quantity demanded.' The second is the economist's definition of cost, 'the price that the resources consumed in making (and selling) the seller's product would command in their next best use – the alternative price.'

The third basic concept, which is also derived from reflection on how self-interested people react to a change in their surroundings, is the tendency of resources to gravitate toward their highest valued uses if exchange is permitted. . . . By a process of voluntary exchange, resources are shifted to those uses in which the value to the consumer, as measured by the consumer's willingness to pay, is highest. When resources are being used where their value is greatest, we may say that they are being employed efficiently.[11]

Now it must immediately be noted, and never forgotten, that these basic propositions are really not empirical propositions at all. They are all generated by 'reflection' on an 'assumption' about choice under scarcity and rational maximization. While Posner states that 'there is abundant evidence that theories derived from those assumptions have considerable power in predicting how people in fact behave', he cites none. And it is in fact unnecessary to cite any, for the propositions are not empirically falsifiable at all.

Efficiency is a technical term: it means exploiting economic resources in such a way that human satisfaction *as measured by aggregate consumer willingness to pay* for goods and services is maximized. Value too is defined by willingness to pay.[12]

In other words, since people are rationally self-interested, what they *do* shows what they value, and their willingness to pay for what they value is proof of their rational self-interest. Nothing merely empirical could get in the way of such a structure because it is definitional. That is why the assumptions can predict how people behave: in *these* terms there is no other way they can behave. . . .

Thus what people do is good, and its goodness can be determined by looking at what it is they do. In place of the more arbitrary normative 'goods' of Formalism, *and* in place of the more complicated empirical 'goods' of Realism, stands the simple definitionally circular 'value' of Posner's book. If human desire itself becomes normative (in the sense that it cannot be criticized), and if human desire is made definitionally identical with certain human acts, then those human acts are also beyond criticism in normative or efficiency terms; everyone is doing as best he can exactly what he set out to do which, by definition, is 'good' for him. In those terms, it is not at all surprising that economic analyses have 'considerable power in predicting how people in fact behave'.

I shall argue that lovely as all of this is, it is still unsatisfactory as anything approaching an adequate picture of human activity, even as expressed in that subcategory of living loosely called 'law'. . . . All of us are unable to tell (or at least to tell about) the difference between right and wrong. All of us want to go on talking. If we could find a way to slip in our normatives in the form of descriptives, within a discipline offering narrow and apparently usable epistemological categories, we would

---

[11] Ibid., p. 4.
[12] Ibid.

all be pathetically grateful for such a new and more respectable formalism in legal analysis. We would leap to embrace it. Since that is the promise of economic analysis of law, to an increasing (and not wholly delusive or pernicious) extent, many of us are leaping.

To summarize, the move to economic analysis in law schools seems an attempt to get over, or at least get by, the complexity thrust upon us by the Realists. . . . Now we have a book in which it is apparently plausible to declare, 'it may be possible to deduce the basic formal characteristics of law itself from economic theory . . .' *and then do it in a two-page chapter.* What bliss.

We are, I think, beginning to see in the speedy spread of economic analysis of law the development of a new basic academic theory of law. [I]ts basic intellectual technique is the substitution of definitions for both normative and empirical propositions, . . .

THE POWER OF POSITIVE ECONOMICS

. . . I would rather not leave any impression of thorough negativism, if for no reason other than that such a response would be stupid. The economic analysis of law (including *The Economic Analysis of Law*) continually manages to provide rich and varied insights into legal problems. Its growing popularity among legal scholars is, as I have noted, no accident. But in addition to its value as a way to continue to ignore our otherwise desperate intellectual straits, it frequently serves intelligently to inform actual legal choices. For the central tenet and most important operative principle of economic analysis is to ask, of every move (1) how much it will cost; (2) who pays; and (3) who ought to decide both questions.

That might seem obvious. In fact, it is not. It is a most common experience in law schools to have someone say, of some action or state of events, 'how awful', with the clear implication that reversing it will de-awfulize the world to the full extent of the initial awfulness. But the true situation, of course, is that eliminating the 'bad' state of affairs will not lead to the opposite of that bad state, but to a third state, neither the bad one nor its opposite. That is, before agreeing with any 'how awful' critic, one must always ask him the really nasty question, 'compared to what?' Moreover, it should be, but often is not, apparent to everyone that the process of moving the world from one state to another is itself costly. If one were not doing *that* with those resources (money, energy, attention), one could be doing something else, perhaps righting a few different wrongs, a separate pile of 'how ghastly's'.

One can illustrate this basic kind of economic analysis by working with quite simple fact situations. There is this old widow, see, with six children. It is December and the weather is rotten. She defaults on the mortgage on her (and her babies') family home. The mortgagee, twirling his black moustache, takes the requisite legal steps to foreclose the mortgate and throw them all out into the cold. She pleads her total poverty to the judge. Rising behind the bench, the judge points her and her brood out into the swirling blizzard. 'Go', he says. 'Your plight moves me not.' 'How awful', you say?

'Nonsense', says the economic analyst. 'If the old lady and kids slip out into the storm, they most likely won't die. There are people a large part of whose satisfactions come from relieving the distress of others, who have, that is, high utilities for beneficence and gratitude. So the costs to the widow are unlikely to be infinite. Moreover, look at the other side of the (you should pardon the expression) coin. What would happen if the judge let the old lady stay on just because she was out of money? First of all, lenders would in the future be loathe to lend to old widows with children. I don't say that they wouldn't lend at all; they'd just be more careful about marginal cases, and raise the price of credit for the less marginal cases. The aggregate cost to the class of old ladies with homesteads would most likely rise much more than the cost imposed on this particular widow. That is, the aggregate value of all their homes (also known as their wealth) would fall, and they'd all be worse off.'

'More than that, look at what such a decision would do to the motivation of old widows. Knowing that their failure to pay their debts would not be visited with swift retribution, they would have less incentive to prevent defaults. They might start giving an occasional piece of chicken to the kids, or even work up to a fragment of beef from time to time. Profligacy like that would lead to even less creditworthiness as their default rates climbed. More and more of them would be priced out of the money market until no widow could ever *decide for herself* to mortgage her house to get the capital necessary to start a seamstress business to pull herself (and her infants) out of poverty. What do you mean, "awful"? What have you got against widows and orphans?'

Now, I have with malice aforethought tendentiously chosen and written this particular example sharply to highlight an otherwise unexpected possibility: the economic analyst may well be right. He is not necessarily 'right' in the sense that one ought to throw out this particular old lady (for the analysis is too sketchy and data-free to decide that). But he is certainly 'right' in this sense: the effect of not throwing her out is not a net gain, to society in general, or even to others in her 'class', equal to what she personally is saved by staying in possession. Choosing to favor her is not cost free, *even to others like her.*

Notes

1. The economics of law can be separated into two somewhat arbitrary categories – the old and new. The old law-and-economics restricts its subject matter to legal arrangements affecting explicit 'economic relationships' and economic variables such as prices, profits, investment and output. Competition law and public utility regulation fall into this category (see infra, Chapters 5 and 7). The new law-and-economics takes as its subject matter the legal system itself and principles of both private and public law (such as tort, property, crime and civil procedure) whether they ostensibly affect economic variables or not. For surveys see: R. A. Posner, 'The Economic Approach to Law' (1975) 53 Texas L.R. 757; R. A. Posner, 'Some Uses and Abuses of Economics in Law' (1979) 46 U. Chi. L.R. 281; C. G. Veljanovski, 'The Economic Approach to Law: A Critical Introduction' (1980) 7 Brit. J. Law and Soc. 158; C. G. Veljanovski, *The New Law-and-Economics – A Research Review* (1983); 'Symposium: The Place of Economics in Legal Education' (1983) 33 J. Legal Educ. 183–368. The subject is also covered by a growing number of texts and anthologies: G. Tullock, *The Logic of Law* (1970); R. A. Posner, *Economic Analysis of Law* (2nd edn, 1977); W. Z. Hirsch, *Law and Economics: An Introductory Analysis* (1979); H. G. Manne (ed.), *The Economics of Legal Relationships* (1975); A. T. Kronman and R. A. Posner (eds.), *The Economics of Contract Law* (1979); P. Burrows and C. G. Veljanovski (eds.), *The Economic Approach to Law* (1981); R. A. Bowles, *Law and the Economy* (1982); A. M. Polinsky, *An Introduction to Law and Economics* (1983).

2. The typical training of British lawyers does not equip them to deal adequately with the policy questions surrounding legal change and reform. 'Law', states L. Fuller (*The Anatomy of Law* (1968), p. 4), 'is the only human study having no distinctive end of its own. Where its ends can be regarded as grounded in reason . . . they must be derived not from law itself but from ethics, sociology and economics.' A major contribution of economics is the framework (or theory) that it gives the lawyer systematically to evaluate legal policy, reveal important tradeoffs and interrelationships between legal goals, and trace through the probable effects, costs and benefits of different laws. While the application of economics does not yield precise answers, it can draw attention to some important questions that would otherwise be ignored and its insights can complement those of the other social sciences. It is interesting to note that in several countries cost–benefit analysis has been used by law reform bodies and governments to assist in the development of more cost-effective laws and to guide or control administrative discretion (Australian Law Reform Comm., *Insurance Agents and Brokers* (ALRC 16, 1980); Health and Safety Comm., *Cost/benefit assessment of health, safety and pollution controls* (1982)).

3. As Leff emphasizes, the economic analysis of law, treats legal rules as a system of incentives and disincentives which influence the actions of *potential* litigants. The law is seen as guiding the behaviour of groups or individuals

and, on the assumption of economic reationality, the economic model is able to predict the direction (though not the size) of the response. Thus, economists tend to focus on the general effects of law such as, for example, the deterrent effect of tort liability rules and the impact on trading behaviour of different contract remedies. This emphasis differs significantly from the way most lawyers are accustomed to analyse law – primarily as a means of redressing grievances and of resolving individual disputes peacefully, fairly and consistently with legal doctrine.

4. Another approach to the analysis of law and collective behaviour which flourished in the United States during the early part of this century is Institutional Economics. It is most associated with the name of John R. Commons (*Legal Foundations of Capitalism* (1924); *Institutional Economics* (1934), best summarized in W. C. Mitchell, 'Commons on Institutional Economics' (1935) 25 Am. Econ. Rev. 635). According to M. Blaug (*Economic Theory in Retrospect* (2nd edn, 1968, p. 678)) institutionalism has at least two main features: a dissatisfaction with the high level of abstraction and static nature of neoclassical economics (i.e. price or microeconomic theory); and an interdisciplinary approach, combining economics with law and other social sciences. The Institutionalist movement did not succeed as a serious challenge to neoclassical economics although it survives today as a minor school of economic thought. (W. J. Samuels and A. Schmid, *Law and Economics – An Institutional Perspective* (1980); and articles published in J. Econ. Issues). A related approach, but which draws much more extensively on the externalities literature, is Williamson's transaction cost analysis (O. E. Williamson, *Markets and Hierarchies* (1975); 'Transaction Cost Economics: The Governance of Contractual Relations; (1979) 22 J. Law and Econ. 233). Williamson, like Commons, regards the transaction, rather than the individual, as the basic unit of analysis. His approach focusses on the costs that attend alternative institutional arrangements (contract, market, the firm, regulation) and postulates that the form they take can be explained in terms of minimizing these costs.

R. A. POSNER

*

The Economic Approach to Law[13]

The economic approach to law has aroused a good deal of antagonism among academic lawyers. . . . It seems worthwhile, therefore, to attempt to answer the criticisms . . .

One criticism that is silly but too frequently made to ignore is that since economists cannot explain this or that (*e.g.*, our current recession *cum* inflation), they have nothing to say to lawyers about the legal

---

[13] Published originally in slightly different form in (1975) 53 Texas L. Rev. Copyright © 1975 by the Texas Law Review. Reprinted by permission.

system. Because economics is an incomplete and imperfect science, it is easy to poke fun at, just as it is easy to poke fun at medicine for the same reason. But it is as foolish to write off economics as it would be to write off medicine.

A closely related criticism of the economic approach to law is that since economics has its limitations – for example, there is no widely accepted economic theory of the optimum distribution of income and wealth – the lawyer can ignore or even reject the approach until these limitations are overcome. This is tantamount, however, to the absurd proposition that unless a method of analysis is at once universal and unquestioned it is unimportant. A variant of this criticism is made by some legal philosophers who argue that since the philosophical basis of economics is utilitarianism, which they consider discredited, economics has no foundation and must collapse, carrying the economic approach to law with it. Admittedly, economics does not provide a basis for unconditional normative statements of the form, 'because the most efficient method of controlling crime would be to cut off the ears and nose of a convicted felon and brand him on the forehead, society should adopt these penalties'. What the economist might be able to say, by way of normative analysis, is that a policy such as mutilation of felons increases efficiency and should therefore be adopted, unless its adoption would impair some more important social value. The economist's ability to make conditional suggestions of this sort is not endangered by the debate over the merits of utilitarianism, unless the challenge to utilitarianism is a challenge to ascribing *any* value to promoting economic efficiency. Even more clearly, the economist's ability to enlarge our understanding of how the legal system actually operates is not undermined by the attacks on utilitarianism. If the participants in the legal process act as rational maximizers of their satisfactions, or if the legal process itself has been shaped by a concern with maximizing economic efficiency, the economist has a rich field of study whether or not a society in which people behave in such a way or institutions are shaped by such concerns can be described as 'good'.

Another common criticism of the economic approach to law is that the attempt to explain the behaviour of legal institutions, and of the people operating or affected by them, on economic grounds must fail because, surely, much more than rational maximizing is involved in such behaviour. The motivations of the violent criminal cannot be reduced to income maximization nor the goals of the criminal justice system to minimizing the costs of crime and its control. This criticism reflects a fundamental misunderstanding of the nature of scientific inquiry. A scientific theory necessarily abstracts from the welter of experience that it is trying to explain, and is therefore necessarily 'unrealistic' when compared directly to actual conditions. Newton's law of falling bodies is 'unrealistic' in assuming that bodies fall in a vacuum, but it is still a useful theory because it correctly predicts the behaviour of a wide variety of falling bodies in the real world. Similarly, an economic theory of law is certain not to capture the full complexity, richness, and confusion of the phenomena – criminal activity or whatever – that it seeks to illuminate. That lack of realism does not invalidate the theory; it is, indeed, the essential precondition of a theory. . . .

Still another common criticism of the 'new' law and economics is that it manifests a strongly conservative political bias. Its practitioners have found, for example, that capital punishment has a deterrent effect and that legislation designed to protect the consumer frequently ends up hurting him. Findings such as these provide ammunition to the supporters of capital punishment and the opponents of consumerist legislation. The oddest thing about this criticism is that economic research that provides support for liberal positions is rarely acknowledged, at least by liberals, as manifesting political bias. The theory of public goods, for example, could be viewed as one of the ideological underpinnings of the welfare state, but it is not so viewed. . . .

Another criticism leveled against the economic approach is that it ignores 'justice', which in these critics' view is and should be the central concern of the legal system and of the people who study it. In evaluating this criticism, it is necessary to distinguish different senses in which the word justice is used in reference to the legal system. It is sometimes used to mean 'distributive justice', which can be defined very crudely as the 'proper' degree of economic inequality. Although economists cannot tell you what that degree is, they have much to say that is extremely relevant to the debate over inequality – about the actual amounts of inequality in different societies and in different periods, the difference between real economic inequality and inequalities in pecuniary income that merely compensate for cost differences or reflect different positions in the life cycle, and the costs of achieving greater real or nominal equality . . .

A second meaning of 'justice', and the most common I would argue, is simply 'efficiency'. When we describe as 'unjust' convicting a person without a trial, taking property without just compensation, or failing to require a negligent automobile driver to answer in damages to the victim of his carelessness, we can be interpreted as meaning simply that the conduct or practice in question wastes resources. It is no surprise that in a world of scarce resources, waste is regarded as immoral. There may be, however, more to notions of justice than a concern with efficiency, for many types of conduct widely condemned as unjust may well be efficient. . . . I doubt, however, that . . . [our] views are completely impervious to what an economic study might show. For example, would the objection to medical experimentation on convicts remain unshaken if it were shown persuasively that the social benefits of such experiments greatly exceeded the costs? Would the objections to capital punishment survive a convincing demonstration that capital punishment had a significantly greater deterrent effect than life imprisonment? All of these are studiable issues, and since no rational society can ignore the costs of its public policies, they are issues to which economics has great relevance. The demand for justice is not independent of its price.

R. M. DWORKIN

*

Is Wealth a Value?[14]

In this essay I consider and reject a political theory about law often called the economic analysis of law. . . .

Wealth maximization, as defined, is achieved when goods and other resources are in the hands of those who value them most, and someone values a good more only if he is both willing and able to pay more in money (or in the equivalent of money) to have it. An individual maximizes his own wealth when he increases the value of the resources he owns; whenever he is able, for example, to purchase something he values for any sum less than the most he would be willing to pay for it. Its value to him is measured by the money he would pay if necessary . . .

. . . Economic analysis holds, on its normative side, that social wealth maximization is a worthy goal so that judicial decisions should try to maximize social wealth, for example, by assigning rights to those who would purchase them but for transaction costs. But it is unclear *why* social wealth is a worthy goal. Who would think that a society that has more wealth, as defined, is either better or better off than a society that has less? . . .

There are several possible answers to this question . . . (I) Social wealth may be thought to be itself a component of social value – that is, something worth having for its own sake. . . .

(II) Social wealth may be thought to be, not a component, but an instrument of value. Improvements in social wealth are not valuable in themselves, but valuable because they may or will produce other improvements that are valuable in themselves . . . I shall begin by considering whether the claim that social wealth is a component of value . . . is a defensible idea.

[14] (1980) 9 J. Legal Stud. 191, 191–208, with omissions. Copyright © 1980 by the University of Chicago. All rights reserved. Reprinted by permission of the University of Chicago Press.

I think it is plain it is not. . . . If economic analysis argues that law suits should be decided to increase social wealth, defined in the particular way described, then it must show why a society with more wealth is, for that reason alone, better or better off than a society with less. I have distinguished, and now propose to consider, one form of answer: social wealth is in itself a component of value. That answer states a theory of value. It holds that if society changes so that there is more wealth then that change is in itself, at least *pro tanto*, an improvement in value even if there is no other change that is also an improvement in value, and even if the change is in other ways a fall in value. The present question is not whether a society that follows the economic analysis of law will produce changes that are improvements in wealth with nothing else to recommend them. The question is whether such a change would be an improvement in value. That is a question of moral philosophy, in its broadest sense, not of how economic analysis works in practice. If the answer to my question is no – a bare improvement in social wealth is not an improvement in value – the claim that social wealth is a component of value fails, and the normative claim of economic analysis needs other support. . . .

Once social wealth is divorced from utility, at least, it loses all plausibility as a component of value . . . It is false that even an individual is necessarily better off if he has more wealth, once having more wealth is taken to be independent of utility information. . . . [I]mprovements in wealth do not necessarily lead to improvements in happiness . . . [and] they sometimes lead to a loss in happiness because people want things other than wealth, and these further preferences may be jeopardized by more wealth. . . . Suppose, therefore, that an individual faces a choice between a life that will make him happier (or more fulfilled, or more successful in his own lights, or whatever) and a life that will make him wealthier in money or the equivalent of money. It would be irrational of him to choose the latter. Nor – and this is the crux – does he lose or sacrifice anything of value in choosing the former. It is not that he should, on balance, prefer the former, recognizing that in the choice he sacrifices something of value in the latter. Money or its equivalent is useful so far as it enables someone to lead more valuable, successful, happier, or more moral life. . . .

I now turn to the claim that a society with more wealth is better because wealth bears some important instrumental connection – whether as cause, as ingredient, or as false-target – to some independent component of value. . . . Supporters of economic analysis might have any number of independent values in mind, or some structured or intuitionistic mix of different independent values. We cannot test the instrumental claim for wealth maximization until the independent value or mix of these is at least roughly specified. . . . [I]n a

recent article, . . . Posner suggests . . . that wealth maximization is a
value because a society that takes wealth maximization to be its central
standard for political decisions will develop other attractive features.[15]
In particular, it will honor individual rights. . . .

The argument has the form of a strong instrumentalist claim of the
causal variety. It has very wide scope. It specifies a set of features of
society – individual rights, agreeable virtues, and humane instincts –
that can plausibly be taken to be components of value. It then suggests
that the 'right' mix of these will be best obtained by a single-minded
attention to wealth maximization as a standard for political decisions,
including judicial decisions. The trouble begins, however, when we ask
what arguments he might offer to support this strong and wide
instrumentalist claim.

We may begin with the claim that wealth maximization will encourage respect for individual rights. A society that sets out to
maximize social wealth will require, of course, some assignment of
rights to property, labor, and so forth. That is a conceptual requirement, because wealth is measured by what people are willing to pay, in
money or its equivalent, but no one can pay what he does not own, or
borrow if he has nothing to pledge or if others have nothing to lend.
Society bent on maximizing wealth must specify what rights people
have to money, labor, or other property so that it can be determined
what is theirs to spend and, in this way, where wealth is improved. A
society is, however, not a better society just because it specifies that
certain people are entitled to certain things. Witness South Africa.
Everything depends on which rights society recognizes, and on whether
those rights should be recognized according to some independent test.
It cannot, that is, provide an instrumental claim for wealth maximization that it leads to the recognition of certain individual rights, if all
that can be said, in favor of the moral value of these rights, is that
these are the rights that a system of wealth maximization would
recognize.

There is, however, a danger that Posner's argument will become
circular in that way. According to the economic analysis of law, rights
should be assigned instrumentally, in such a way that the assignment
of rights will advance wealth maximization. That is, indeed, the
principal use of the standard of wealth maximization in the judicial
context . . . Economic analysis does not suppose that there is some
independent moral argument in favor of giving or withholding that
right. So it *cannot* be claimed, in favor of economic analysis, that it
points to what is independently, on moral grounds, the right answer.
On the contrary, it claims that the right answer is right only because
the answer increases social wealth.

[15] 'Utilitarianism, Economics, and Legal Theory' (1979) 8 J. Legal Stud. 103.

Nor does Posner limit the scope of that argument – that assignments of rights must be made instrumentally – to what might be called less important rights, like the right to an injunction in nuisance or to damages in negligence. On the contrary, he is explicit that the same test must be used in determining the most fundamental human rights of citizens, including their right to life and to control their own labor rather than be slaves to others. He counts it an important virtue of wealth maximization that it explains why people have those rights. But if wealth maximization is only to be an instrumental value . . . then there must be some independent moral claim for the rights that wealth maximization recommends. These rights cannot have a moral claim on us simply because recognizing those rights advances wealth.

Let us, therefore, suppose that Posner believes people have a right to their own bodies, and to direct their own labor as they wish, for some independent moral reason. Suppose he also argues that wealth maximization is of instrumental value because a society that maximizes wealth will recognize just those rights. There remains a serious conceptual difficulty. The argument supposes that a social order bent only on wealth maximization, which makes no independent judgments about the fairness of distributions of resources, will recognize the rights of the 'natural' owner to his own body and labor. That is true only if the assumption of those rights can be justified by the wealth maximization test, which requires that if rights to the 'natural owner's' body or labor are in fact assigned to someone else, he will nevertheless be willing and able to purchase these rights, at least, if we assume no transaction costs.

We cannot, however, speculate intelligibly about whether someone would purchase the right to his own labor unless we make some assumptions about the distribution of wealth. Posner acknowledges this. Indeed, he uses this example – someone's ability to purchase the right to his own labor if he is made a slave – to make the point that whether someone can purchase that right depends on his and others' wealth, and in particular how large a share of that wealth is that right. He says that in such a case 'economic analysis does not predict a unique allocation of resources unless the initial assignment of rights is specified'. If A is B's slave he may not be able to buy back the right to his labor, although if he were not B would not be able to buy that right from him. If economic analysis makes someone's initial right to his own labor depend upon whether he would purchase the right if assigned to another, that right cannot be 'derived' from economic analysis unless we already know who initially has the right. This appears to be a serious circle. We cannot specify an initial assignment of rights unless we answer questions that cannot be answered unless an initial assignment of rights is specified.

Notes

1. The third category of law-and-economics distinguished by Klevorick has attracted considerable criticism and controversy, to which Posner, a principal exponent, responds. Much of such criticism focusses on the claim that allocative efficiency (i.e. the Kaldor–Hicks criterion) can produce positive and normative theories that explain and provide moral support for the common law (R. A. Posner, *Economic Analysis of Law* (2nd edn, 1977) ch. 6; R. A. Posner, *The Economics of Justice* (1981)).

The critics, while accepting that economics can make a contribution to legal studies, have disputed both these claims, i.e. that the common law is allocatively efficient (M. J. Rizzo, 'Uncertainty, Subjectivity and the Economic Analysis of Law' in M. J. Rizzo (ed.), *Time, Uncertainty and Disequilibrium* (1979); F. I. Michelman, 'A Comment on Some Uses and Abuses of Economics in Law' (1979) 46 U. Chi. L.R. 307) and that it yields a philosophically coherent theory of rights, duties, morality or justice (E. J. Weinrib, 'Utilitarianism, Economics and Legal Theory' (1980) 30 U. Toronto L.J. 307; 'Symposium: Efficiency as a Legal Concern' (1980) 8 Hofstra L.R. 485; 'Symposium: Change in the Common Law: Legal and Economic Perspectives' (1980) 9 J. Legal Stud. 189, 199–252; C. G. Veljanovski, 'Wealth Maximisation Law and Ethics – on the Limits of Economic Efficiency' (1981) 1 Int. Rev. Law and Econ. 5; J. R. Pennock and J. W. Chapman (eds.), *Ethics, Economcs and the Law* (1982)). It should also be noted, parenthetically, that in large part this debate rehearses at great length that which took place among economists in the 1930s and 1940s over the Kaldor–Hicks approach (J. S. Chipman and J. C. Moore, 'The New Welfare Economics, 1937–1974' (1974) 19 Int. Econ. Rev. 547).

2. Economic analysis of rights is another area that has excited much controversy. Economists treat rights as a 'factor of production', i.e. they are valued only to the extent they increase production, allocative efficiency or promote a more desirable distribution of wealth. The cost–benefit assignment of legal rights suffers, as Dworkin points out, from an inherent circularity. Expressed in economic language, willingness-to-pay is determined in part by an individual's bundle of rights (i.e. wealth) and therefore cannot be used to determine fundamental rights. See: W. J. Samuels, 'Welfare Economics, Power and Property' in Samuels and Schmid, op. cit., ch. 1; C. Fried, 'Difficulties in the Economic Analysis of Rights' in G. Dworkin *et al.* (eds.), *Markets and Morals* (1977), pp. 175–94; D. Kennedy, 'Cost/Benefit Analysis of Entitlement Problems – A Critique' (1981) 22 Stan. L.R. 387.

PART II

*

Private Law

2

PROPERTY

A. The Economic Basis of Property

S. PEJOVICH

*

Towards an Economic Theory of the Creation and Specification of Property Rights[1]

The alleged failure of the standard theory of production and exchange to explain a wide class of empirical observations has led to proliferation of *ad hoc* theorizing. Without questioning the validity of some of those *ad hoc* theories, it is important to recognize that they are valid only for a small class of events. A generalization of the standard theory of production and exchange to obtain an expanded scope of its validity should, therefore, be regarded as a preferred alternative. The *property rights approach* represents such an attempt.

The line of reasoning that underlies the property rights approach to the explanation of economic events can be summarized as follows: the purpose of trade is to exchange bundles of property rights *to do things* with goods and services that are exchanged. The value of the goods that are traded and, consequently, the terms of trade depend on the content of property rights in those goods. For example, I will pay more for a house if the bundle of property rights I acquire permits me to exclude gasoline stations, chemical plants, etc. from the surrounding area. The possession of various property rights affects the allocation of resources, composition of output, income distribution, etc. . . .

That a relationship exists between property rights assignments and the allocation of resources might be intuitively obvious and readily observable. Yet, to convert this relationship into an analytically useful and testable theory it is necessary to demonstrate that:

[1] (1972) 30 Rev. Soc. Econ. 309, 310–25, with omissions. Reprinted by permission of the Association for Social Economics.

(i) Property rights assignments affect the allocation of resources in a *specific* and *predictable* way. This is an essential requirement that should help us to deduce some analytically important and empirically refutable propositions *re* the effects of changes in property rights assignments over scarce resources on formal equilibrium solutions. The on-going research on externalities, large corporations and regulated firms, and the economics of socialism has already provided strong evidence that the allocation and use of resources *is* constrained in a specific and predictable way by the prevailing property rights assignments.

(ii) The creation and specification of property rights over scarce resources is endogenously determined; that is, it takes place in response to the desire of the interacting persons for more utility....

A student of economics discovers early that the entire body of the standard theory of production and exchange is built upon the assumption of private property rights over resources with zero detection, police and enforcement costs, and the appreciation of the negatively sloped demand curve (which is independent of property rights assignments). He also learns that private property rights are a powerful and possibly necessary condition for the most efficient allocation of resources. The compulsive desire for more utility and the law of negatively sloped demand schedule combine with the right of private ownership to induce the utility maximizing individuals to increase the extent of exchange to the point where privately perceived marginal costs and benefits equal social costs and benefits.

An intelligent student will reject the idea that it is a mere accident when and where the importance of property rights assignments over resources is discovered. He will instead address himself to a fundamental economic question: is the standard theory of production and exchange capable of explaining the emergence of the institution of property rights over scarce resources. That is, can we deduce the development of property rights theoretically?...

Let us begin our discussion with the case where property rights in a resource are absent. A non-owned resource is a free good for individuals. However, it is a scarce good for society. The relevant questions are: what type of competition is used to allocate a non-owned good among the competing claimants, what is the cost of 'purchasing' it, and what are the implications of the absence of property rights in a resource for its rate of exploitation and reproduction?

A person can derive utility (non-pecuniary as well as pecuniary) from a non-owned good only by taking it into his physical possession and for only as long as it remains in his possession. That is, the individual who postpones using that good *now* will find it taken by someone else. The rationing criterion is clearly: first come, first served. This type of competition suggests that the individual could hardly concern himself with either the cost of 'planting' a non-owned good or its future value consequences (e.g., the value of lumber in the tree associated with aging). It follows that each person's 'purchase' costs of a non-owned good equals his outlaid expenses (e.g., hunting rifle) and the highest-valued alternative. The latter can be taken to be of primary importance here.

The logic of economics then suggests that the rate of exploitation of a non-owned resource should be expected to exceed the rate that would prevail if some kind of transferable property rights in that good is established. Cheung[2] and Gordon[3] deduced the equilibrium solution of the industry as it occurs in the state of uncontrolled exploitation of a non-owned resource and demonstrated that the rent is completely eliminated and the *average* product of labor equals the *average* opportunity income. That is, the marginal product of labor is below the social cost as represented by opportunity income. From the social point of view this situation implies economic waste. From the individual's point of view it implies a zero rent. Quite importantly this wasteful use of a resource should be attributed to the absence of property rights assignments in that good rather than the individual's greed or lack of social responsibility.

The rate of investment in a non-owned resource is also affected by the absence of property rights assignments. First, the investor must feel insufficiently confident that he will be able to capture the expected future value consequences of his investment decision. This would shorten his time horizon, raise the discount rate and, consequently, investment activity will stop short of what it would otherwise be. And this conclusion remains valid even if we assume that the investor is willing to incur the costs of policing his investment inputs. In that case the result will be a longer time horizon, lower discount rate, but also much higher costs associated with investment in a non-owned resource.

Second, the absence of property rights in a resource is also likely to affect the form of investment activity. For example, non-owned land in Tripolitania is used as a pasture by cattle owners rather than for planting more profitable almond trees. The reason for this wasteful behaviour is that the costs of policing one's use of land for raising cattle that can be driven home at night is lower relative to the costs of policing investment in almond trees.

The logic of economics is then capable of explaining that (i) from the social point of view the creation of property rights assignments is a

[2] 'The Structure of a Contract and the Theory of a Non-Exclusive Resource' (1970) 13 J. Law and Econ. 49.
[3] 'The Economic Theory of a Common-Property Resource: The Fishery' (1954) 62 J. Pol. Econ. 124.

powerful and possibly necessary condition for more efficient allocation and use of resources, and (ii) from the individual's point of view
the specification of property rights is associated with his search for
more utility. I conjecture that this latter point relates the standard
theory of production and exchange to the creation of property rights
over scarce resources.

The analysis of a non-owned resource indicates that the person
would capture some rent for himself if he could exclude others from
the free access to that good. The logic of economics then suggests that
the individual or a group of individuals will try to exclude others from
using a good whenever the expected benefits (rent) exceed the cost of
policing and enforcing the 'claim' to that resource. We note that to
exclude others from the free access to a resource *means* to specify
property rights over that good. For property rights are defined not as
relations between men and things but, rather, as *the behavioural
relations among men that arise from the existence of things and
pertain to their use.* The prevailing system of property rights assignments in the community is, in effect, the set of economic and social
relations defining the position of interacting individuals with respect to
the utilization of scarce resources.

Probably the first step towards the creation of individual property
rights was for a tribe to establish or to try to establish its exclusive right
over a piece of land, fishing, or hunting grounds in order to consume
some rent. Yet, privately perceived costs and benefits from the exploitation of a commonly held resource are different from total costs
and benefits for at least two reasons: (i) not all costs of a person's
activity are borne by himself (e.g., over-hunting, over-intensive use of
land), and (ii) non-transferability of a commonly owned resource
prevents a person from capturing for himself the full value of that
good. It follows that each member of the community could increase his
benefits by either reducing the size of the group or capturing *more*
property rights for himself. In other words, whenever contractual
relationships result in the dissipation of a part of the rent to third
parties there will be an incentive to alter the contractual relationship
as long as the gains from so doing exceed the costs of specifying new
property rights assignments. The marginal equivalences between the
costs and benefits then become a major factor that governs the size of
the group as well as changes in the content of property rights over a
resource. As the size of the group is reduced and/or individuals acquire
more property rights in a resource the difference between private and
social costs as well as private and social benefits narrows down to be
finally eliminated in a world of private property rights with zero
transaction costs. This situation might easily amount to no more than
a pious wish, but it is important to note that the man's compulsive

desire for more utility combined with the cost–benefit calculus provides a rational explanation for both the creation as well as endogenously determined changes in the content of property rights assignments over scarce resources. Moreover, this explanation of the creation and specification of property rights is free from historical determinism. It does not proclaim a definite and pre-ordained sequence of changes in the specification of property rights. It merely suggests that the prevailing property rights assignments in the community reflect the costs and benefits of specifying property rights over scarce resources, and that changes in the property rights assignments are endogenously determined by changes in the cost–benefit ratio. Finally, the analysis does not preclude the possible influence of exogenous factors which could and indeed have affected the content of property rights over scarce resoures (Communist revolution in Russia, governmental regulation of radio frequencies in the USA, etc.)

To incorporate our discussion into an expanded framework of the classical marginalism we have to specify all the important variables and parameters that affect, or might affect at various stages of the community's economic development, the determination of the costs and benefits of specifying property rights assignments over scarce resources. More importantly, we must also specify those factors that could bring about changes in the cost–benefit ratio and, thus, changes in the content of property rights. The result would be a formal and fully testable theory capable of explaining and possibly predicting the development of property rights assignments in response to changing economic conditions. Moreover, a generalization of the standard theory of production and exchange *via* the effects of property rights assignments on the penalty-reward system would substitute an integrated economic theory for *ad hoc* theorizing and hopefully improve our understanding of the economic processes, income distributions and resource allocations in various regions and at different times.

This is yet to be done. However, recent contributions have shown that the logic of economics and empirical evidence combine to suggest that the following three factors have frequently been responsible for changes in the cost–benefit ratio and, consequently, for changes in the content of property rights over resources.

(i) Technological Changes and Opening of New Markets. For example, the substitution of arabic numbers for Roman numerals and the invention of watches changed the extent of trade, the content of contractual stipulations, and provided incentives for the alteration of property rights; also, when people learned how to survey land, the cost of defining property rights in land fell relative to the gains from doing so. . . .

(ii) A Change in Relative Factor Scarcities and factor prices results in a change in the cost–benefit ratio and provides incentives for the modification of the existing or the creation of new property rights. North wrote:

The revival of population growth as a result of the relative improvement in order led to local crowding and diminishing returns [in feudal Europe] . . . General diminishing returns appear to have set in the 12th century leading to changing relative factor scarcities. The rising value of land led to increasing efforts to provide for exclusive ownership and transferability. 13th century England witnessed the development of an extensive body of land law, the beginning of enclosure and finally the ability to alienate land.[4]

(iii) An Economic Theory of the State. Our comprehension of the development of property rights is obviously incomplete without an economic theory of the state. This is so because a political organization (tribe, princedom, kingdom, modern state, etc.) can be regarded as the firm that produces and sells protection and justice in exchange for revenue (taxes). The authority define property rights over resources (including human resources, of course) *via* customs and/or laws and enforces those rights against both 'insiders' (police, courts) and 'outsiders' (military). The subjects pay for this service. The source of this payment is the rent which better specification of property rights makes possible. For example, Kings and Princes granted (and en-forced) various property rights to merchants. This led to an expansion of trade, higher revenues, and the sharing of these gains by the authority and tradesmen. Similar events frequently occur in modern times. The states are known to close markets to all potential com-petitors by granting licenses to a selected few (a very valuable property right). This, in turn, is expected to raise the average return in the industry, a part of which then goes to the state treasury as license fees. . . .

Let us now summarize our discussion. The creation and specification of property rights over scarce resources is deduced from the standard theory of production and exchange. They both occur in response to the man's desire for more utility and, in turn, lead towards a more efficient allocation of resources. The term efficiency is defined here as the narrowing of the gap between privately perceived costs and benefits and social costs and benefits. As long as those are different, not all costs and benefits of a contract are borne by contractual parties and the inducements for better specification of property rights exist. Some important factors which govern changes in the content of property

---

[4] *The Creation of Property Rights in Western Europe 900–1700 A.D.* (1972), unpublished.

rights are asserted to be: technological innovations and opening of new markets, changes in relative factor scarcities, and the behaviour of the state.

W. S. BOWMAN

*

Patent and Antitrust Law: A Legal and Economic Appraisal[5]

PATENT LAW

Patent law, thought by some to be an exception to a general rule in favor of competition, shares with antitrust law its central purpose – efficiently providing those things consumers value. But the means are different. Patent law pursues this goal by encouraging the invention of new and better products. Invention, like other forms of productive activity, is not costless. Those who undertake it, therefore, must be rewarded. And so elusive a commodity as an idea which qualifies as invention is peculiarly susceptible to being freely appropriated by others. A patent is a legal device to insure that there can be a property right in certain ideas. Thus the temporary right of a patentee to exclude others is a means of preventing 'free riding' so that the employment of useful private resources may be remunerated. Without a patent system, prevention of 'free riding' would be severely limited. Ability to keep secrets and to enforce private 'know-how' contracts would, without patent law, provide inventors very limited protection from rapid and widespread copying by others. Central to the economic justification of a patent system is the presumption that without the patent right, too few resources would be devoted to invention.

The 'exclusive right to make, use and vend the invention or discovery', which Congress has long granted patentees, is thus a legal monopoly exempt from the more general proscription of trade restraints and monopolization under early common law and more recent antitrust statutes.

GOAL EVALUATION

The goal of both antitrust law and patent law is to maximize allocative efficiency (making what consumers want) and productive efficiency (making these goods with the fewest scarce resources). In achieving this goal under either antitrust or patent law the detriment to be avoided is output restriction. This may arise from monopolization which diverts production from more urgent to less urgent use or from legal rules requiring inefficient methods of production. The evil, then, may be viewed as net output restriction after efficiency increases are accounted for. Both antitrust and patent law seek output expansion, not output restriction. Competition deserves support insofar as it brings about this result. And so it is with patents. The temporary monopoly afforded by a patent, once a particular invention has come into being, will have all the output-restrictive disabilities of any monopoly. The argument for patents is that without this temporary monopoly there would be insufficient profit incentives to produce the invention, and that because an invention is profitable only if consumers are willing to pay what the patentee charges, the consumers are therefore better off than they would be without the invention, even if they are charged 'monopoly' prices. If this is so, a trade-off (some monopoly restraint for greater output in the long run) is in the interest of socially desirable resource allocation. . . .

An economic appraisal of a patent system must resolve three basic problems. The first is the incentive question itself. Some have argued that invention is simply not profit motivated or is motivated by profit in so small a degree that a special reward is not needed. If invention is generated by such motives as instinct for contrivance or creative curiosity rather than by a search for profit, any patent monopoly will be hard to justify. Second, the amount of innovation is not solely a function of either pecuniary incentive or instinctive curiosity. It also depends upon the availability of previously accumulated knowledge. Whether a patent reward system deters this accumulation or facilitates it will also determine whether it deserves support as an efficient resource allocator. Third, appraisal of a patent system must also take into account the standards applied to determine which inventions qualify for the monopoly and make a judgment whether these inventions are, as a result, overrewarded or underrewarded. The ultimate purpose of pursuing these three lines of inquiry is to determine whether a patent system aids consumers in achieving more of what they want at the lowest cost. Obviously this cannot easily be appraised with precision, and 'on balance' judgments will be necessary. . . .

LIMITS OF REWARD FROM PATENT MONOPOLY

The revenue obtainable from the right granted an inventor depends ultimately upon how users evaluate the benefits of the invention. Informed users can be expected to pay no more than the added value the invention makes possible. The limitation of the user's willingness to pay is, of course, applicable to all monopolies, whether condemned by the antitrust laws or permissible under the patent system. The benefits of a patent system, if they exist, must be assessed in terms of what alternatives consumers have with or without the disadvantage of the temporary monopoly a patent system imposes upon them. The most obvious case of net social advantage of a patent system arises when except for the patent protection the product of the invention would not be available. In such a case anything users would be willing to pay would be an improvement (wealth increasing) over not having the product. If, however, to take an opposite extreme case, a patent monopoly were granted for a product which would have been forthcoming anyway, then the restricted output caused by the patent monopoly leads to a net social loss to the community.

There is considerable divergence of opinon about whether on balance a patent system makes for better or worse resource allocation. The product of a patent is information. Information lacks one aspect of scarceness which other economic goods share. Most goods are exhaustible; they can be used up. When one person gets a unit of physical product another gives up a unit. Not so with information. Requisition of information by a second person leaves the first with the same information he had. This is not to say that keeping information to oneself would not make it more valuable to that one person, but it raises marketability problems. In terms of either private interest or community interest, there is optimal utilization when a commodity with such properties is distributed to everybody who has use for it, so long as the value of that use is greater than the cost of its distribution. Because a rational patent monopolist can be expected in his own interest to exploit a wide use pattern, this minimizes the output-restrictive effects of the legalized monopoly. Insofar as secrecy is a practicable alternative to a patent system, it also results in output restriction by deliberately not taking advantage of the widespread uses to which information can be put. The problem should thus be recognized as involving a trade-off between the short-run disadvantages of monopoly on already granted patents and the possibly greater advantages of having new or better products not otherwise available.

INVESTMENT IN INNOVATION AND THE MISALLOCATION PROBLEM: OVERREWARDING INNOVATION

All investments are uncertain, all involve risks, and all would be increased if they were made more remunerative. A rational patent system should be able to identify the unique attributes of investment in

ideas which qualify them for special treatment as opposed to investment in alternatives.

For Plant[6] the temporary patent monopoly entails a subsidy for
invention, causing overinvestment in this form of economic activity.
Since economic resources are scarce, overinvestment in invention leads
to underinvestment in other forms of activity. As Plant says, 'It enables
those who have monopoly of the right to use a patented invention to
raise the price of using it for the whole term of the patent within the
limits fixed by the elasticity of demand, and in that way derive a larger
profit from invention than they could otehwise obtain. The effect must
surely be to induce a considerable volume of activity to be diverted
from other spheres to the attempt to make inventions of a patentable
type.' Without the patent laws, according to Plant, people who spend
their time inventing would serve the community better by doing
something else. . . .

The second basis for Plant's criticism of patents relates to the system of
reward itself. Here the argument is closely related to, and in some
respects is a part of, the incentive problem just discussed. For example,
the problem of almost simultaneous discovery is set forth as an
example of how the patent system rewards the 'first inventor' with a
monopoly and renders almost nugatory the labors of all the rest. And
the existence of the first monopoly diverts the efforts of the losers (and
nonparticipants) in this race away from what might well be the most
fruitful field for further invention. Except for the winner of the first
patent, Plant suggests, efforts are diverted from the most socially
useful activity – improving the best – to finding possibly inferior
alternatives to circumvent the original patent monopoly.

INVESTMENT IN INNOVATION AND THE MISALLOCATION PROBLEM:
UNDERREWARDING INNOVATION

. . . Professor Arrow, writing a quarter of a century later, focused
directly upon the special nature of information in a provocative
theoretical probe of market allocation of this unique commodity.[7] His
conclusion, in contrast to Plant's, is that innovation is underrewarded
rather than overrewarded.

A unique aspect of information as a commodity, Arrow noted, is the
nature of its marketability: 'In the absence of special legal protection,
the owner cannot . . . sell information in the open market. Any one

---

[6] 'The Economic Theory of Patents for Invention' (1934) 1 Economica 30.

[7] 'Economic Welfare and the Allocation of Resources' in National Bureau Committee for
Economic Research, *The Rate and Direction of Inventive Activity: Economic and Social Factors*
(1962).

purchaser can destroy the monopoly, since he can reproduce the information at little or no cost. Arrow stressed the high cost of secrecy. Not only is there high and increasing mobility of personnel among firms, as Arrow indicated, but in addition and perhaps more important, one might add, embodying information in a product will often provide information freely without its direct sale. Because of the 'enormous difficulties in defining in any sharp way an item of information and differentiating it from other similar sounding items', he concluded that only legal property rights in information can provide a partial barrier to appropriation by others. . . .

PATENT REWARD FOR THE INCONSEQUENTIAL

According to Knight the patent reward system is undesirable not because it overrewards innovation but because it underrewards true innovators and gives an undeserved monopoly to the last-step routinizers. To him, investing in some form of innovation is what the profit system is all about. In his classic work *Risk, Uncertainty and Profit*,[8] Knight emphasizes that incurring uninsurable risks – specializing in uncertainty – is the economic service provided by entrepreneurship, the reward for which is the chance of acquiring what economists define as profit. . . .

Knight viewed the patent system as a means of misdirecting rewards for innovation. Patent reward, he contended, went to the one who puts on the 'finishing touch'. The routinizer thus gets the reward while the *real* pioneering and exploration are done by others. He thus concluded: 'It would seem to be a matter of political intelligence and administrative capacity to replace artificial monopoly with some direct method of stimulating and rewarding research'. What he had in mind as that *direct* method which would improve upon 'artificial monopoly' as a means of stimulating and rewarding research was not revealed. The 'direct' method suggests the need for a direction of rewards. If this is so it has the inherent difficulty of choosing a rewarder who would predictably be better than the consumers, even those too few who participate in a monopolized market.

Notes

1. It will be apparent from the first paper that economists have a far broader notion of property than lawyers. See, also, A. A. Schmid, *Property, Power and Public Choice* (1978), p. 5: 'the term "property right" includes both real and personal property. It includes both tort and contract law, common and

---

[8] (8th impression, 1957.)

statutory law, civil and criminal law, vested and nonvested rights, and civil rights. It includes informal practices and traditions embedded in the culture as well as formal legal institutions.' For lawyers, property involves a relationship between people and 'things', but if the latter is allowed to include all forms of wealth (cf. C. Reich, 'The New Property' (1964) 73 Yale L.J. 733) then the limits of the concept are very uncertain: see, generally, K. J. Gray and P. D. Symes, *Real Property and Real People* (1981), pp. 7–20.

2. What Pejovich describes as the 'property rights' approach emerged as economists began to appreciate that the institutional arrangements which constrain the behaviour of firms and individuals, but which had been ignored in traditional analysis, might have a crucial effect on the allocation of resources. See, especially: A. A. Alchian, *Some Economics of Property* (1961); H. Demsetz, 'Towards a Theory of Property Rights' (1967) 57 Am. Econ. Rev. (Proc) 347; and, for surveys of the literature, E. Furuboth and S. Pejovich, 'Property Rights and Economic Theory: A Survey of Recent Literature' (1972) 10 J. Econ. Lit. 1137; L. De Alessi, 'The Economics of Property Rights: A Review of the Evidence' (1980) 2 Research in Law and Econ. 1.

3. The primary economic explanation for the introduction of property rights is derived from the concept of an externality (cf. supra, Chapter 1, Section B). In his classic paper, op. cit., Demsetz demonstrates how the absence of private property rights may lead to an overutilization of natural resources. Those exploiting the resource (in Demsetz's example, fur hunters), in determining the extent of this activity, take account of their individual costs (capital and labour) but not the social costs arising from the depletion of the resource, which will be suffered by all potential future exploiters. The creation of a private property right in the resource enables its owner to take into account the costs and benefits of the resource's present and future uses. As will be seen, infra, Chapter 4, Section A, the existence of *corporate* property rights in companies may be understood in the light of the additional economic goal of reducing the costs of transacting in the market.

4. The creation of private property rights involves enforcement costs which must be balanced against the benefits of internalization. Improvement in technology and communications will reduce these costs, leading to an increase in the number of resources which are governed by private property rights (see, e. g., T. Anderson and P. Hill, 'The Evolution of Property Rights: A Study of the American West' (1975) 18 J. Law and Econ. 162, 175, where it is suggested that the introduction of barbed wire influenced the development of property rights in the territories of the pioneers; also L. E. Davis and D. C. North, *Institutional Change and American Economic Growth* (1973)). Conversely, there are some resources which, by their nature, are not susceptible to *private* enforcement of property rights, and for which, therefore, some form of state regulation becomes justified. Sea fisheries provide the classic example: H. S. Gordon, 'The Economic Theory of a Common Property Resource: the Fishery' (1954) 62 J. Pol. Econ. 124.

5. An external benefit arises where some consumers do not pay for a product

(they are 'free-riders'); in consequence, the producer has insufficient incentive to respond to what is society's true demand for the product. As the second extract reveals, private property rights can attempt to solve this problem of misallocation (see also F. Machlup, 'An Economic Review of the Patent System', Study No. 15 of the Subcommittee on Patents, Trademarks and Copyrights of the Committee on the Judiciary – U.S. Senate (1958)). However, the very nature of 'intangible' property gives rise to problems both of enforcement (cf. the difficulties currently being experienced by 'piracy' of videos and cassettes: *Report of the Committee to consider the Law on Copyright and Designs* (1977, Cmnd. 6732)) and of monopoly. The right to exclude others may be uncontroversial when the object is tangible property but not where it is information or an idea, since that can be acquired simultaneously and independently by a number of individuals. As Bowman shows, the trade-off between the benefit of a property right and the cost arising from a monopoly (on which see generally infra, Chapter 5) is often difficult to evaluate.

B. Different Property Interests

D. R. DENMAN

*

The Place of Property[9]

THE FIRST LAW OF PROPRIETARY MAGNITUDES

[T]he first law of proprietary magnitudes . . . states that the degree of competence with which the power of decision-making inherent in the property power is used moves in inverse ratio to the number of joint owners. Aristotle's dictum 'that which is common to the greatest number has the least care bestowed upon it', is substantiated not only in the indifference of commoners towards what they hold in common but in the inability of the many to reach decisions in time to ensure expeditious action in care and management. . . .

THE SECOND LAW OF PROPRIETARY MAGNITUDES

[The] relationship between the competence of human actions, the intensity of human activity and the measure of land space leads to the second law of proprietary magnitudes. The law is this: the physical

---

[9] From *The Place of Property* (Geographical Publications Ltd., 1978), pp. 39–44, with omissions. Reprinted by permission of the author.

extent of land most conducive to competent effective decision-making and action is a function of the intensity of human activity over the land implicit in the rights of property over that land and vested in he who takes the decisions. The relationship can be expressed symbolically as:

$$O_s = f(i)$$

where O_s is the optimum size of the unit of proprietorship, the proprietary land unit, and (i) an index of the intensity of human activity to the degree which the property rights over the land permit. Put another way: the optimum physical size of a proprietary land unit changes inversely with the intensity of human activity on the land of the unit within the sanction of its right of property. . . .

While universally valid optima are difficult to establish, the optimum size of the decision-making unit is usually known, however vaguely, to the decision-maker. In the nature of things he will be restless with second best and ever wanting to reach the optimum. In the expression $O_s = f(i)$, if the human activity is too great, ways will be sought to reduce the size of the actual unit so as to conform with O_s. . . .

Proprietary land units are protean and can change in numerous ways, not only in physical size but in the range, nature and potency of the property rights which constitute them. Thus it is possible for the (i) factor in the equation to be manipulated by reducing or increasing the content of the property rights. If for example the owner of a fee simple estate on the fringe of a developing township were to go in for building shops where previously he had been farming, it would be impossible and absurd for him to occupy all the shops he built as the owner of the fee simple estate in them. The range of rights pertaining to a fee simple in possession could not be exercised by an individual person in more than two of the shops. In the notation of our equation, (i) would be too intense to make $O_s > (n)$ shops where $n = 2$. But the fee simple owner of the farmland could cut out of his fee simple derivative interests as leases and convey each shop to a lessee. So doing, the builder would retain the fee simple estate but it would be in reversion, the reversion [falling in after the expiry of] the leases of the shops. Now the human activity (i) would be reduced to rent collecting, the maintenance of roads and buildings and other acts of estate management, an intensity sufficient for $O_s = 200$ shops. . . .

J. S. MILL

*

Principles of Political Economy[10]

The imperfections of the law, both in its substance and in its procedure, fall heaviest upon the interests connected with what is technically called *real* property; in the general language of European
jurisprudence, immoveable property. With respect to all this portion
of the wealth of the community, the law fails egregiously in the
protection which it undertakes to provide. It fails, first, by the uncertainty, and the maze of technicalities, which make it impossible for
any one, at however great an expense, to possess a title to land which
he can positively know to be unassailable. It fails, secondly, in omitting
to provide due evidence of transactions, by a proper registration of
legal documents. It fails, thirdly, by creating a necessity for operose
and expensive instruments and formalities (independently of fiscal
burthens) on occasion of the purchase and sale, or even the lease or
mortgage, of immoveable property. And, fourthly, it fails by the
intolerable expense and delay of law proceedings, in almost all cases in
which real property is concerned. There is no doubt that the greatest
sufferers by the defects of the higher courts of civil law are the
landowners. Legal expenses, either those of actual litigation, or of the
preparation of legal instruments, form, I apprehend, no inconsiderable
item in the annual expenditure of most persons of large landed
property, and the saleable value of their land is greatly impaired, by the
difficulty of giving to the buyer complete confidence in the title;
independently of the legal expenses which accompany the transfer. . . .

In so far as the defects of legal arrangements are a mere burthen on
the landowner, they do not much affect the sources of production; but
the uncertainty of the title under which land is held, must often act as a
great discouragement to the expenditure of capital in its improvement;
and the expense of making transfers, operates to prevent land from
coming into the hands of those who would use it to most advantage;
often amounting, in the case of small purchases, to more than the price
of the land, and tantamount, therefore, to a prohibition of the purchase
and sale of land in small portions, unless in exceptional circumstances.
Such purchases, however, are almost everywhere extremely desirable,
there being hardly any country in which landed property is not either
too much or too little subdivided, requiring either that great estates

[10] From *Principles of Political Economy*, pp. 884–94, with omissions (Collected Works of
John Stuart Mill, ed. J. M. Robson, 1965). Copyright © University of Toronto Press 1965.
Reprinted by permission of Routledge & Kegan Paul Ltd., and the University of Toronto Press.

should be broken down, or that small ones should be bought up and consolidated. To make land as easily transferable as stock, would be one of the greatest economical improvements which could be bestowed on a country; and has been shown, again and again, to have no insuperable difficulty attending it. . . .

[*Law and Custom of Primogeniture*] There are two arguments of an economical character, which are urged in favour of primogeniture. One is, the stimulus applied to the industry and ambition of younger children, by leaving them to be the architects of their own fortunes. . . .

The other economical argument in favour of primogeniture, has special reference to landed property. It is contended that the habit of dividing inheritances equally, or with an approach to equality, among children, promotes the subdivision of land into portions too small to admit of being cultivated in an advantageous manner. This argument, eternally reproduced, has again and again been refuted by English and Continental writers. It proceeds on a supposition entirely at variance with that on which all the theorems of political economy are grounded. It assumes that mankind in general will habitually act in a manner opposed to their immediate and obvious pecuniary interest. For the division of the inheritance does not necessarily imply division of the land; which may be held in common, as is not unfrequently the case in France and Belgium; or may become the property of one of the coheirs, being charged with the shares of the others by way of mortgage; or they may sell it outright, and divide the proceeds. When the division of the land would diminish its productive power, it is the direct interest of the heirs to adopt some one of these arrangements. Supposing, however, what the argument assumes, that either from legal difficulties or from their own stupidity and barbarism, they would not, if left to themselves, obey the dictates of this obvious interest, but would insist upon cutting up the land bodily into equal parcels, with the effect of impoverishing themselves; this would be an objection to a law such as exists in France, of compulsory division, but can be no reason why testators should be discouraged from exercising the right of bequest in general conformity to the rule of equality, since it would always be in their power to provide that the division of the inheritance should take place without dividing the land itself. . . .

Unless a strong case of social utility can be made out for primogeniture, it stands sufficiently condemned by the general principles of justice; being a broad distinction in the treatment of one person and of another, grounded solely on an accident. There is no need, therefore, to make out any case of economical evil *against* primogeniture. Such a case, however, and a very strong one, may be made. It is a natural effect of primogeniture to make the landlords a needy class. The object of the institution, or custom, is to keep the land together in large masses, and this it commonly accomplishes; but the legal proprietor of a large domain is not necessarily the *bonâ fide* owner of the whole income which it yields. It is usually charged, in each generation, with provisions for the other children. . . . The same desire to keep up the 'splendour' of the family, which gives rise to the custom of primogeniture, indisposes the 'owner' to sell a part in order to set free the remainder; their apparent are therefore habitually greater than their real means, and they are under a perpetual temptation to proportion their expenditure to the former rather than to the latter. From such causes as these, in almost all countries of great landowners, the majority of landed estates are deeply mortgaged; and instead of having capital to spare for improvements, it requires all the increased value of land, caused by the rapid increase of the wealth and population of the country, to preserve the class from being impoverished.

[*Entails*] To avert this impoverishment, recourse was had to the contrivance of entails, whereby the order of succession was irrevocably fixed, and each holder, having only a life interest, was unable to burthen his successor. The land thus passing, free from debt, into the possession of the heir, the family could not be ruined by the improvidence of its existing representative. The economical evils arising from this disposition of property were partly of the same kind, partly different, but on the whole greater, than those arising from primogeniture. The possessor could not now ruin his successors, but he could still ruin himself: he was not at all more likely than in the former case to have the means necessary for improving the property: while, even if he had, he was still less likely to employ them for that purpose, when the benefit was to accrue to a person whom the entail made independent of him, while he had probably younger children to provide for, in whose favour he could not now charge the estate. While thus disabled from being himself an improver, neither could he sell the estate to somebody who would; since entail precludes alienation. In general he has even been unable to grant leases beyond the term of his own life; 'for,' says Blackstone, 'if such leases had been valid, then, under cover of long leases, the issue might have been virtually disinherited;'[11] and it has been necessary in Great Britain to relax, by statute, the rigour of entails, in order to allow either of long leases, or of the execution of improvements at the expense of the estate. It may be added that the heir of entail, being assured of succeeding to the family property, however undeserving of it, and being aware of this from his earliest years, has much more than the ordinary chances of growing up idle, dissipated, and profligate.

---

[11] *Commentaries on the Laws of England* (ed. J. Chitty, 1826), vol. 2, p. 116.

In England, the power of entail is more limited by law, than in Scotland and in most other countries where it exists. A landowner can settle his property upon any number of persons successively who are living at the time, and upon one unborn person, on whose attaining the age of twenty-one, the entail expires, and the land becomes his absolute property. An estate may in this manner be transmitted through a son, or a son and grandson, living when the deed is executed, to an unborn child of that grandson. It has been maintained that this power of entail is not sufficiently extensive to do any mischief: in truth, however, it is much larger than it seems. Entails very rarely expire; the first heir of entail, when of age, joins with the existing possessor in resettling the estate, so as to prolong the entail for a further term. Large properties, therefore, are rarely free for any considerable period, from the restraints of a strict settlement; though the mischief is in one respect mitigated, since in the renewal of the settlement for one more generation, the estate is usually charged with a provision for younger children.

In an economical point of view, the best system of landed property is that in which land is most completely an object of commerce; passing readily from hand to hand when a buyer can be found to whom it is worth while to offer a greater sum for the land, than the value of the income drawn from it by its existing possessor. This of course is not meant of ornamental property, which is a source of expense, not profit; but only of land employed for industrial uses, and held for the sake of the income which it affords. Whatever facilitates the sale of land, tends to make it a more productive instrument of the community at large; whatever prevents or restricts its sale, subtracts from its usefulness. Now, not only has entail this effect, but primogeniture also. The desire to keep land together in large masses, from other motives than that of promoting its productiveness, often prevents changes and alienations which would increase its efficiency as an instrument.

Notes

1. The fundamental aspect of property law with which most law students are familiar, the division of interests in land, has, so far, been poorly served by the law-and-economics literature. The two extracts chosen and the commentary which follows should give an indication of some of the economic issues involved.

2. The simple idea of division of labour (cf. A. Smith, *The Wealth of Nations*, Bk I, chs. 1–2) helps to explain the benefits to an owner of carving out lesser interests in his land. Denman is concerned to locate the optimal size of such

interests (for analogous discussion of different forms of *contractual* arrangements, see S. Cheung, 'Transaction Costs, Risk Aversion and the Choice of Contractual Arrangements' (1969) 12 J. Law and Econ. 23). Where possessory rights are divorced from ownership, a potential conflict arises between the tenant in possession's desire to maximize the income from the land during the period of his interest and the owner's concern to preserve the capital value of the land, which may be diminished by overutilization. In economic terms, the tenant can impose an external cost on the owner (cf. supra, Chapter 1, Section B). Two legal methods were evolved to deal with the problem (cf. R. Posner, *Economic Analysis of Law* (2nd edn, 1977), pp. 52–4: the doctrine of waste which rendered the tenant liable for adverse changes in the nature of the property; and the trust which conferred on the trustee general powers of supervision, so that he could maintain a balance between the various beneficial interests in the property.

3. According to traditional welfare economics, there is a gain in allocative efficiency whenever resources shift to a more highly valued use. Mill's criticisms of the then existing state of English land law focus on two causes of inefficiency in this sense, and provide an economic basis for the important legislative reforms which ensued (though it should be noted that his notion of social utility, which is identified almost exclusively with land productivity, is narrower than that currently adopted in economic theory). First, the desire of landowners to keep property within the family by means of entails and settlements thwarted alienability. Although the matter is not free from controversy (cf. L. M. Simes, *Public Policy and the Dead Hand* (1955) and A. B. W. Simpson, 'Entails and Perpetuities' [1979] Jurid. Rev. 1), the rule against perpetuities can be regarded as an attempt to balance the utility derived from this form of patriarchal expression and the social costs which it generated. Much more significant were the reforms of the nineteenth and twentieth century which converted future interests from legal rights in the property *in specie* to equitable rights in the proceeds of sale and enabled entails to be enlarged into freely alienable interests. F. H. Lawson, *The Rational Strength of English Law* (1951), p. 95, comments: 'the rigour with which the legal estates were regulated in 1925 is very noteworthy, for all family interests have, as it were, been taken off the land itself and have become interests in a notional entity, a capital fund . . . We have . . . been far more ruthless than even the Romans in making land freely marketable, and we have been able to be so because we have detached the management, including the alienation of land, from the beneficial interest in it.'

4. The second weakness of traditional land law, uncertainty of title, was linked to the first, for it hindered alienation and reduced the value of property; clearly, the greater the risk of being ousted, the less a purchaser is willing to pay (see, generally, O. E. G. Johnson, 'Economic Analysis, the Legal Framework and Land Tenure Systems' (1972) 15 J. Law and Econ. 259). The situation is not much ameliorated if title can be made secure but only by highly expensive investigation of previous property dealings. Legal complexity generates high transaction costs. The 1925 legislation promoted efficiency by reducing the number of legal estates, enabling equitable interests

to be overreached and extending registration both of title and of land charges: see, generally on the latter, J. T. Janczyk, 'An Economic Analysis of the Land Title Systems for Transferring Real Property' (1977) 6 J. Legal Stud. 213.

C. Conflicts in Land Use and Externalities

R. H. COASE

The Problem of Social Cost[12]

I. THE PROBLEM TO BE EXAMINED

This paper is concerned with those actions of business firms which have harmful effects on others. The standard example is that of a factory the smoke from which has harmful effects on those occupying neighbouring properties. The economic analysis of such a situation has usually proceeded in terms of a divergence between the private and social product of the factory, in which economists have largely followed the treatment of Pigou in *The Economics of Welfare*. The conclusions to which this kind of analysis seems to have led most economists is that it would be desirable to make the owner of the factory liable for the damage caused to those injured by the smoke, or alternatively, to place a tax on the factory owner varying with the amount of smoke produced and equivalent in money terms to the damage it would cause, or finally, to exclude the factory from residential districts (and presumably from other areas in which the emission of smoke would have harmful effects on others). It is my contention that the suggested courses of action are inappropriate, in that they lead to results which are not necessarily, or even usually, desirable.

II. THE RECIPROCAL NATURE OF THE PROBLEM

The traditional approach has tended to obscure the nature of the choice that has to be made. The question is commonly thought of as one in which A inflicts harm on B and what has to be decided is: how should we restrain A? But this is wrong. We are dealing with a problem of a reciprocal nature. To avoid the harm to B would inflict harm on A.

The real question that has to be decided is: should A be allowed to harm B or should B be allowed to harm A? The problem is to avoid the more serious harm. I instanced in my previous article[13] the case of a confectioner the noise and vibrations from whose machinery disturbed a doctor in his work. To avoid harming the doctor would inflict harm on the confectioner. The problem posed by this case was essentially whether it was worth while, as a result of restricting the methods of production which could be used by the confectioner, to secure more doctoring at the cost of a reduced supply of confectionery products. Another example is afforded by the problem of straying cattle which destroy crops on neighbouring land. If it is inevitable that some cattle will stray, an increase in the supply of meat can only be obtained at the expense of a decrease in the supply of crops. The nature of the choice is clear: meat or crops. What answer should be given is, of course, not clear unless we know the value of what is obtained as well as the value of what is sacrificed to obtain it. . . . It goes almost without saying that this problem has to be looked at in total *and* at the margin.

III. THE PRICING SYSTEM WITH LIABILITY FOR DAMAGE

I propose to start my analysis by examining a case in which most economists would presumably agree that the problem would be solved in a completely satisfactory manner: when the damaging business has to pay for all damage caused *and* the pricing system works smoothly (strictly this means that the operation of a pricing system is without cost).

A good example of the problem under discussion is afforded by the case of straying cattle which destroy crops growing on neighbouring land. Let us suppose that a farmer and a cattle-raiser are operating on neighbouring properties. Let us further suppose that, without any fencing between the properties, an increase in the size of the cattle-raiser's herd increases the total damage to the farmer's crops. What happens to the marginal damage as the size of the herd increases is another matter. This depends on whether the cattle tend to follow one another or to roam side by side, on whether they tend to be more or less restless as the size of the herd increases and on other similar factors. For my immediate purpose, it is immaterial what assumption is made about marginal damage as the size of the herd increases.

To simplify the argument, I propose to use an arithmetical example. I shall assume that the annual cost of fencing the farmer's property is $9 and that the price of the crop is $1 per ton. Also, I assume that the relation between the number of cattle in the herd and the annual crop loss is as follows:

[13] 'The Federal Communications Commission' (1959) 2 J. Law and Econ. 26.

Number in Herd (Steers)	Annual Crop Loss (Tons)	Crop Loss per Additional Steer (Tons)
1	1	1
2	3	2
3	6	3
4	10	4

Given that the cattle-raiser is liable for the damage caused, the additional annual cost imposed on the cattle-raiser if he increased his herd from, say 2 to 3 steers is $3 and in deciding on the size of the herd, he will take this into account along with his other costs. That is, he will not increase the size of the herd unless the value of the additional meat produced (assuming that the cattle-raiser slaughters the cattle), is greater than the additional costs that this will entail, including the value of the additional crops destroyed. Of course, if, by the employment of dogs, herdsmen, aeroplanes, mobile radio and other means, the amount of damage can be reduced, these means will be adopted when their cost is less than the value of the crop which they prevent being lost. Given that the annual cost of fencing is $9, the cattle-raiser who wished to have a herd with 4 steers or more would pay for fencing to be erected and maintained, assuming that other means of attaining the same end would not do so more cheaply. When the fence is erected, the marginal cost due to the liability for damage becomes zero, except to the extent that an increase in the size of the herd necessitates a stronger and therefore more expensive fence because more steers are liable to lean against it at the same time. But, of course, it may be cheaper for the cattle-raiser not to fence and to pay for the damaged crops, as in my arithmetical example, with 3 or fewer steers.

It might be thought that the fact that the cattle-raiser would pay for all crops damaged would lead the farmer to increase his planting if a cattle-raiser came to occupy the neighbouring property. But this is not so. If the crop was previously sold in conditions of perfect competition, marginal cost was equal to price for the amount of planting undertaken and any expansion would have reduced the profits of the farmer. In the new situation, the existence of crop damage would mean that the farmer would sell less on the open market but his receipts for a given production would remain the same, since the cattle-raiser would pay the market price for any crop damaged. Of course, if cattle-raising commonly involved the destruction of crops, the coming into existence of a cattle-raising industry might raise the price of the crops involved and farmers would then extend their planting. But I wish to confine my attention to the individual farmer.

I have said that the occupation of a neighbouring property by a cattle-raiser would not cause the amount of production, or perhaps more exactly the amount of planting, by the farmer to increase. In fact, if the cattle-raising has any effect, it will be to decrease the amount of planting. The reason for this is that, for any given tract of land, if the value of the crop damaged is so great that the receipts from the sale of the undamaged crop are less than the total costs of cultivating that tract of land, it will be profitable for the farmer and the cattle-raiser to make a bargain whereby that tract of land is left uncultivated. This can be made clear by means of an arithmetical example. Assume initially that the value of the crop obtained from cultivating a given tract of land is $12 and that the cost incurred in cultivating this tract of land is $10, the net gain from cultivating the land being $2. I assume for purposes of simplicity that the farmer owns the land. Now assume that the cattle-raiser starts operations on the neighbouring property and that the value of the crops damaged is $1. In this case $11 is obtained by the farmer from sale on the market and $1 is obtained from the cattle-raiser for damage suffered and the net gain remains $2. Now suppose that the cattle-raiser finds it profitable to increase the size of his herd, even though the amount of damage rises to $3; which means that the value of the additional meat production is greater than the additional costs, including the additional $2 payment for damage. But the total payment for damage is now $3. The net gain to the farmer from cultivating the land is still $2. The cattle-raiser would be better off if the farmer would agree not to cultivate his land for any payment less than $3. The farmer would be agreeable to not cultivating the land for any payment greater than $2. There is clearly room for a mutually satisfactory bargain which would lead to the abandonment of cultivation. But the same argument applies not only to the whole tract cultivated by the farmer but also to any subdivision of it. Suppose, for example, that the cattle have a well-defined route, say, to a brook or to a shady area. In these circumstances, the amount of damage to the crop along the route may well be great and if so, it could be that the farmer and the cattle-raiser would find it profitable to make a bargain whereby the farmer would agree not to cultivate this strip of land.

But this raises a further possibility. Suppose that there is such a well-defined route. Suppose further that the value of the crop that would be obtained by cultivating this strip of land is $10 but that the cost of cultivation is $11. In the absence of the cattle-raiser, the land would not be cultivated. However, given the presence of the cattle-raiser, it could well be that if the strip was cultivated, the whole crop would be destroyed by the cattle. In which case, the cattle-raiser would be forced to pay $10 to the farmer. It is true that the farmer would lose $1. But the cattle-raiser would lose $10. Clearly this is a situation which is not likely to last indefinitely since neither party would want this to happen. The aim of the farmer would be to induce the cattle-raiser to make a payment in return for an agreement to leave this land uncultivated. The farmer would not be able to obtain a payment greater than the cost of fencing off this piece of land nor so high as to lead the cattle-raiser to abandon the use of the neighbouring property. What payment would in fact be made would depend on the shrewdness of the farmer and the cattle-raiser as bargainers. But as the payment would not be so high as to cause the cattle-raiser to abandon this location and as it would not vary with the size of the herd, such an agreement would not affect the allocation of resources but would merely alter the distribution of income and wealth as between the cattle-raiser and the farmer.

I think it is clear that if the cattle-raiser is liable for damage caused and the pricing system works smoothly, the reduction in the value of production elsewhere will be taken into account in computing the additional cost involved in increasing the size of the herd. This cost will be weighed against the value of the additional meat production and, given perfect competition in the cattle industry, the allocation of resources in cattle-raising will be optimal. What needs to be emphasized is that the fall in the value of production elsewhere which would be taken into account in the costs of the cattle-raiser may well be less than the damage which the cattle would cause to the crops in the ordinary course of events. This is because it is possible, as a result of market transactions, to discontinue cultivation of the land. This is desirable in all cases in which the damage that the cattle would cause, and for which the cattle-raiser would be willing to pay, exceeds the amount which the farmer would pay for use of the land. In conditions of perfect competition, the amount which the farmer would pay for the use of the land is equal to the difference between the value of the total production when the factors are employed on this land and the value of the additional product yielded in their next best use (which would be what the farmer would have to pay for the factors). If damage exceeds the amount the farmer would pay for the use of the land, the value of the additional product of the factors employed elsewhere would exceed the value of the total product in this use after damage is taken into account. It follows that it would be desirable to abandon cultivation of the land and to release the factors employed for production elsewhere. A procedure which merely provided for payment for damage to the crop caused by the cattle but which did not allow for the possibility of cultivation being discontinued would result in too small an employment of factors of production in cattle-raising and too large an employment of factors in cultivation of the crop. But given the possibility of market transactions, a situation in which damage to crops exceeded the rent of the land would not endure. Whether the cattle-raiser pays the farmer to leave the land uncultivated or himself rents the land by paying the land-owner an amount slightly greater than the farmer would pay (if the farmer was himself renting the land), the final result would be the same and would maximize the value of production. Even when the farmer is induced to plant crops which it would not be profitable to cultivate for sale on the market, this will be a purely short-term phenomenon and may be expected to lead to an agreement under which the planting will cease. The cattle-raiser will remain in that location and the marginal cost of meat production will be the same as before, thus having no long-run effect on the allocation of resources.

IV. THE PRICING SYSTEM WITH NO LIABILITY FOR DAMAGE

I now turn to the case in which, although the pricing system is assumed to work smoothly (that is, costlessly), the damaging business is not liable for any of the damage which it causes. This business does not have to make a payment to those damaged by its actions. I propose to show that the allocation of resources will be the same in this case as it was when the damaging business was liable for damage caused. As I showed in the previous case that the allocation of resources was optimal, it will not be necessary to repeat this part of the argument.

I return to the case of the farmer and the cattle-raiser. The farmer would suffer increased damage to his crop as the size of the herd increased. Suppose that the size of the cattle-raiser's herd is 3 steers (and that this is the size of the herd that would be maintained if crop damage was not taken into account). Then the farmer would be willing to pay up to $3 if the cattle-raiser would reduce his herd to 2 steers, up to $5 if the herd were reduced to 1 steer and would pay up to $6 if cattle-raising was abandoned. The cattle-raiser would therefore receive $3 from the farmer if he kept 2 steers instead of 3. This $3 foregone is therefore part of the cost incurred in keeping the third steer. Whether the $3 is a payment which the cattle-raiser has to make if he adds the third steer to his herd (which it would be if the cattle-raiser was liable to the farmer for damage caused to the crop) or whether it is a sum of money which he would have received if he did not keep a third steer (which it would be if the cattle-raiser was not liable to the farmer for damage caused to the crop) does not affect the final result. In both cases $3 is part of the cost of adding a third steer, to be included along with the other costs. If the increase in the value of production in cattle-raising through increasing the size of the herd from 2 to 3 is greater than the additional costs that have to be incurred (including the $3 damage to crops), the size of the herd will be increased. Otherwise, it will not. The size of the herd will be the same whether the cattle-raiser is liable for damage caused to the crop or not.

It may be argued that the assumed starting point – a herd of 3 steers – was arbitrary. And this is true. But the farmer would not wish to pay to avoid crop damage which the cattle-raiser would not be able to cause. For example, the maximum annual payment which the farmer could be induced to pay could not exceed $9, the annual cost of fencing. And the farmer would only be willing to pay this sum if it did not reduce his earnings to a level that would cause him to abandon cultivation of this particular tract of land. Furthermore, the farmer would only be willing to pay this amount if he believed that, in the absence of any payment by him, the size of the herd maintained by the cattle-raiser would be 4 or more steers. Let us assume that this is the case. Then the farmer would be willing to pay up to $3 if the cattle-raiser would reduce his herd to 3 steers, up to $6 if the herd were reduced to 2 steers, up to $8 if one steer only were kept and up to $9 if cattle-raising were abandoned. It will be noticed that the change in the starting point has not altered the amount which would accrue to the cattle-raiser if he reduced the size of his herd by any given amount. It is still true that the cattle-raiser could receive an additional $3 from the farmer if he agreed to reduce his herd from 3 steers to 2 and that the $3 represents the value of the crop that would be destroyed by adding the third steer to the herd. Although a different belief on the part of the farmer (whether justified or not) about the size of the herd that the cattle-raiser would maintain in the absence of payments from him may affect the total payment he can be induced to pay, it is not true that this different belief would have any effect on the size of the herd that the cattle-raiser will actually keep. This will be the same as it would be if the cattle-raiser had to pay for damage caused by his cattle, since a receipt foregone of a given amount is the equivalent of a payment of the same amount.

It might be thought that it would pay the cattle-raiser to increase his herd above the size that he would wish to maintain once a bargain had been made, in order to induce the farmer to make a larger total payment. And this may be true. It is similar in nature to the action of the farmer (when the cattle-raiser was liable for damage) in cultivating land on which, as a result of an agreement with the cattle-raiser, planting would subsequently be abandoned (including land which would not be cultivated at all in the absence of cattle-raising). But such manoeuvres are preliminaries to an agreement and do not affect the long-run equilibrium position, which is the same whether or not the cattle-raiser is held responsible for the crop damage brought about by his cattle.

It is necessary to know whether the damaging business is liable or not for damage caused since without the establishment of this initial delimitation of rights there can be no market transactions to transfer and recombine them. But the ultimate result (which maximizes the value of production) is independent of the legal position if the pricing system is assumed to work without cost.

V. THE PROBLEM ILLUSTRATED ANEW...

[In] *Sturges v. Bridgman*[14] . . . a confectioner (in Wigmore Street) used two mortars and pestles in connection with his business (one had been in operation in the same position for more than 60 years and the other for more than 26 years). A doctor then came to occupy neighbouring premises (in Wimpole Street). The confectioner's machinery caused the doctor no harm until, eight years after he had first occupied the premises, he built a consulting room at the end of his garden right against the confectioner's kitchen. It was then found that the noise and vibration caused by the confectioner's machinery made it difficult for the doctor to use his new consulting room. 'In particular . . . the noise prevented him from examining his patients by auscultation for diseases of the chest. He also found it impossible to engage with effect in any occupation which required thought and attention.' The doctor therefore brought a legal action to force the confectioner to stop using his machinery. The courts had little difficulty in granting the doctor the injunction he sought. 'Individual cases of hardship may occur in the strict carrying out of the principle upon which we found our judgment, but the negation of the principle would lead even more to individual hardship, and would at the same time produce a prejudicial effect upon the development of land for residential purposes.'

The court's decision established that the doctor had the right to prevent the confectioner from using his machinery. But, of course, it would have been possible to modify the arrangements envisaged in the legal ruling by means of a bargain between the parties. The doctor would have been willing to waive his right and allow the machinery to continue in operation if the confectioner would have paid him a sum of money which was greater than the loss of income which he would suffer from having to move to a more costly or less convenient location or from having to curtail his activities at this location or, as was suggested as a possibility, from having to build a separate wall which would deaden the noise and vibration. The confectioner would have been willing to do this if the amount he would have to pay the doctor was less than the fall in income he would suffer if he had to change his mode of operation at this location, abandon his operation or move his confectionery business to some other location. The solution of the

[14] (1879) 11 Ch. D. 852.

problem depends essentially on whether the continued use of the machinery adds more to the confectioner's income than it subtracts from the doctor's. But now consider the situation if the confectioner had won the case. The confectioner would then have had the right to continue operating his noise and vibration-generating machinery without having to pay anything to the doctor. The boot would have been on the other foot: the doctor would have had to pay the confectioner to induce him to stop using the machinery. If the doctor's income would have fallen more through continuance of the use of this machinery than it added to the income of the confectioner, there would clearly be room for a bargain whereby the doctor paid the confectioner to stop using the machinery. That is to say, the circumstances in which it would not pay the confectioner to continue to use the machinery and to compensate the doctor for the losses that this would bring (if the doctor had the right to prevent the confectioner's using his machinery) would be those in which it would be in the interest of the doctor to make a payment to the confectioner which would induce him to discontinue the use of the machinery (if the confectioner had the right to operate the machinery). The basic conditions are exactly the same in this case as they were in the example of the cattle which destroyed crops. With costless market transactions, the decision of the courts concerning liability for damage would be without effect on the allocation of resources. It was of course the view of the judges that they were affecting the working of the economic system – and in a desirable direction. Any other decision would have hd 'a prejudicial effect upon the development of land for residential purposes', an argument which was elaborated by examining the example of a forge operating on a barren moor, which was later developed for residential purposes. The judges' view that they were settling how the land was to be used would be true only in the case in which the costs of carrying out the necessary market transactions exceeded the gain which might be achieved by any rearrangement of rights. And it would be desirable to preserve the areas (Wimpole Street or the moor) for residential or professional use (by giving non-industrial users the right to stop the noise, vibration, smoke, etc., by injunction) only if the value of the additional residential facilities obtained was greater than the value of cakes or iron lost. But of this the judges seem to have been unaware. . . .

Bryant v. Lefever[15] raised the problem of the smoke nuisance in a novel form. The plaintiff and the defendants were occupiers of adjoining houses, which were of about the same height.

Before 1876 the plaintiff was able to light a fire in any room of his house without the chimneys smoking; the two houses had remained in the same

[15] (1879) 4 C.P.D. 172.

condition some thirty or forty years. In 1876 the defendants took down their house, and began to rebuild it. They carried up a wall by the side of the plaintiff's chimneys much beyond its original height, and stacked timber on the roof of their house, and thereby caused the plaintiff's chimneys to smoke whenever he lighted fires.

The reason, of course, why the chimneys smoked was that the erection of the wall and the stacking of the timber prevented the free circulation of air. In a trial before a jury, the plaintiff was awarded damages of £40. The case then went to the Court of Appeal where the judgment was reversed. Bramwell, L. J., argued:

. . . it is said, and the jury have found, that the defendants have done that which caused a nuisance to the plaintiff's house. We think there is no evidence of this. No doubt there is a nuisance, but it is not of the defendants' causing. They have done nothing in causing the nuisance. Their house and their timber are harmless enough. It is the plaintiff who causes the nuisance by lighting a coal fire in a place the chimney of which is placed so near the defendants' wall, that the smoke does not escape, but comes into the house. Let the plaintiff cease to light his fire, let him move his chimney, let him carry it higher, and there would be no nuisance. Who then, causes it? It would be very clear that the plaintiff did, if he had built his house or chimney after the defendants had put up the timber on theirs, and it is really the same though he did so before the timber was there. But (what is in truth the same answer), if the defendants cause the nuisance, they have a right to do so. If the plaintiff has not the right to the passage of air, except subject to the defendants' right to build or put timber on their house, then his right is subject to their right, and though a nuisance follows from the exercise of their right, they are not liable. . . .

I do not propose to show that any subsequent modification of the situation, as a result of bargains between the parties (conditioned by the cost of stacking the timber elsewhere, the cost of extending the chimney higher, etc.), would have exactly the same result whatever decision the courts had come to since this point has already been adequately dealt with in the discussion of the cattle example and the two previous cases. What I shall discuss is the argument of the judges in the Court of Appeal that the smoke nuisance was not caused by the man who erected the wall but by the man who lit the fires. The novelty of the situation is that the smoke nuisance was suffered by the man who lit the fires and not by some third person. The question is not a trivial one since it lies at the heart of the problem under discussion. Who caused the smoke nuisance? The answer seems fairly clear. The smoke nuisance was caused both by the man who built the wall *and* by the man who lit the fires. Given the fires, there would have been no smoke nuisance without the wall; given the wall, there would have been no smoke nuisance without the fires. Eliminate the wall *or* the fires and the smoke nuisance would disappear. On the marginal principle it is clear that *both* were responsible and *both* should be forced to include the loss of amenity due to the smoke as a cost in deciding whether to continue the activity which gives rise to the smoke. And given the possibility of market transactions, this is what would in fact happen. Although the wall-builder was not liable legally for the nuisance, as the man with the smoking chimneys would presumably be willing to pay a sum equal to the monetary worth to him of eliminating the smoke, this sum would therefore become for the wall-builder, a cost of continuing to have the high wall with the timber stacked on the roof.

The judges' contention that it was the man who lit the fires who alone caused the smoke nuisance is true only if we assume that the wall is the given factor. This is what the judges did by deciding that the man who erected the higher wall had a legal right to do so. The case would have been even more interesting if the smoke from the chimneys had injured the timber. Then it would have been the wall-builder who suffered the damage. The case would then have closely paralleled *Sturges v. Bridgman* and there can be little doubt that the man who lit the fires would have been liable for the ensuing damage to the timber, in spite of the fact that no damage had occurred until the high wall was built by the man who owned the timber.

Judges have to decide on legal liability but this should not confuse economists about the nature of the economic problem involved. In the case of the cattle and the crops, it is true that there would be no crop damage without the cattle. It is equally true that there would be no crop damage without the crops. The doctor's work would not have been disturbed if the confectioner had not worked his machinery; but the machinery would have disturbed no one if the doctor had not set up his consulting room in that particular place. . . . If we are to discuss the problem in terms of causation, both parties cause the damage. If we are to attain an optimum allocation of resources, it is therefore desirable that both parties should take the harmful effect (the nuisance) into account in deciding on their course of action. It is one of the beauties of a smoothly operating pricing system that, as has already been explained, the fall in the value of production due to the harmful effect would be a cost for both parties.

Notes

1. This classic paper is the basis of much economics of law analysis and its importance in the development of our subject cannot be overestimated. Coase's policy prescription differs from the hitherto traditional economic approach derived from Pigou (*The Economics of Welfare* (4th edn, 1932)), which assumed that externalities could be corrected by imposing a tax on the externality-creating activity equal to its marginal external cost. A first proposition to be derived from the Coase paper is that, on the assumption that transactions between the affected parties are costless, allocative efficiency will be reached without government intervention and, indeed, whether or not the imposition of the externality is permitted under *private* law.

2. A second proposition, and one perhaps equally startling to economists and lawyers, is concerned with the reciprocal nature of externalities; a potential misallocation of resources occurs not simply where one activity imposes harm on another but as the result of an interaction of two (or more) conflicting uses of the resources. The presence of the farmer is as much a 'cause' of the conflict as the straying cattle. Hence the social losses caused by 'harm' are the 'joint costs' of both activities. It should be noted that this is not consistent with the way in which courts and lawyers (also laymen?) use causation language – see, especially, R. Epstein, 'A Theory of Strict Liability' (1973) 2 J. Legal Stud. 151, 164–6. This may suggest that the law has regard to ethical or other non-economic considerations in formulating principles of liability.

3. The effects on the distribution of wealth of different principles of liability are not explored by Coase. Clearly a householder granted a property right to stop a neighbouring industrialist polluting is wealthier than if he had no such right; although in the latter case allocative efficiency will be achieved if an appropriate bargain is struck, the payment made will reduce the householder's wealth. The redistribution of wealth arising from alternative legal assignments will also affect the allocation of resources, since it may be the case that an individual benefiting from a property right (and therefore wealthier) will demand a price to sell it which is higher than what he would have paid to acquire it: see E. J. Mishan, 'The Economics of Disamenity' (1974) 14 Nat. Res. J. 55, 62–4; P. Burrows, 'On External Costs and the Visible Arm of the Law' (1970) 22 Oxford Economic Papers 39. If such 'wealth effects' exist then the law will affect the allocation of resources but not the efficiency of the bargained-for solution. Note also that in situations where the parties have a pre-existing or concurrent contractual relationship, the ex ante redistributive effects of liability rules will disappear (e.g. an employer liable for all accident costs will reduce the wage rate): see, infra, Chapter 3, Section D.

4. In the real world, as Coase of course recognizes, transactions are not costless. It therefore follows that the achievement of allocative efficiency might, in a given situation, depend crucially how legal principles are formu-

lated because of the magnitude and nature of transaction costs. Much of the subsequent literature is concerned, as we shall see, with how the differing impact of transaction costs can justify variations in legal principles. Transaction costs are usually defined to include those incurred in communicating with other parties, negotiations leading to a bargain, and initiating or compromising a legal claim (Mishan, op. cit., pp. 66–75) but, on a broader view, may include the acquiring of information relevant to decision-making (see Beale *et al.*, infra, Chapter 7, Section D). For an empirical study of the significance of transaction costs, see T. Crocker, 'Externalities, Property Rights, and Transaction Costs: An Empirical Study' (1971) 14 J. Law and Econ. 451.

5. It has been argued that, quite apart from transaction costs, there are fundamental problems arising from Coase's 'bargaining' solution. Game theory suggests that where two parties have no alternatives to dealing with each other – what is called 'bilateral monopoly' – disputes and strategies may occur over the division of the potential gains from trade which may preclude the efficient solution from being attained: R. Cooter, 'The Cost of Coase' (1982) 11 J. Legal Stud. 1; C. G. Veljanovski 'The Coase Theorems, and the Economic Theory of Markets and Law' (1972) 24 Kyklos 66.

D. Property Rules and Liability Rules

G. CALABRESI and A. D. MELAMED

*

Property Rules, Liability Rules and Inalienability: One View of the Cathedral[16]

The first issue which must be faced by any legal system is one we call the problem of 'entitlement'. Whenever a state is presented with the conflicting interests of two or more people, or two or more groups of people, it must decide which side to favor. Absent such a decision, access to goods, services, and life itself will be decided on the basis of 'might makes right' – whoever is stronger or shrewder will win. Hence the fundamental thing that law does is to decide which of the conflicting parties will be entitled to prevail. The entitlement to make noise versus the entitlement to have silence, the entitlement to pollute versus

[16] (1972) 85 Harv. L.R. 1089, 1093–1124, with omissions. Copyright © 1972 by the Harvard Law Review Association. Reprinted by permission of the authors and Harvard Law Review.

the entitlement to breathe clean air, the entitlement to have children versus the entitlement to forbid them – these are the first order of legal decisions. . . .

The state not only has to decide whom to entitle, but it must also simultaneously make a series of equally difficult second order decisions. These decisions go to the manner in which entitlements are protected and to whether an individual is allowed to sell or trade the entitlement. In any given dispute, for example, the state must decide not only which side wins but also the kind of protection to grant. It is with the latter decisions, decisions which shape the subsequent relationship between the winner and the loser, that this article is primarily concerned. We shall consider three types of entitlements – entitlements protected by property rules, entitlements protected by liability rules, and inalienable entitlements. . . .

An entitlement is protected by a property rule to the extent that someone who wishes to remove the entitlement from its holder must buy it from him in a voluntary transaction in which the value of the entitlement is agreed upon by the seller. It is the form of entitlement which gives rise to the least amount of state intervention: once the original entitlement is decided upon, the state does not try to decide its value. It lets each of the parties say how much the entitlement is worth to him, and gives the seller a veto if the buyer does not offer enough. Property rules involve a collective decision as to who is to be given an initial entitlement but not as to the value of the entitlement.

Whenever someone may destroy the initial entitlement if he is willing to pay an objectively determined value for it, an entitlement is protected by a liability rule. This value may be what it is thought the original holder of the entitlement would have sold it for. But the holder's complaint that he would have demanded more will not avail him once the objectively determined value is set. Obviously, liability rules involve an additional stage of state intervention: not only are entitlements protected, but their transfer or destruction is allowed on the basis of a value determined by some organ of the state rather than by the parties themselves.

An entitlement is inalienable to the extent that its transfer is not permitted between a willing buyer and a willing seller. The state intervenes not only to determine who is initially entitled and to determine the compensation that must be paid if the entitlement is taken or destroyed, but also to forbid its sale under some or all circumstances. Inalienability rules are thus quite different from property and liability rules. Unlike those rules, rules of inalienability not only 'protect' the entitlement; they may also be viewed as limiting or regulating the grant of the entitlement itself. . . .

II. THE SETTING OF ENTITLEMENTS

A. Economic Efficiency

Perhaps the simplest reason for a particular entitlement is to minimize the administrative costs of enforcement. . . . By itself this reason will never justify any result except that of letting the stronger win, for obviously that result minimizes enforcement costs. Nevertheless, administrative efficiency may be relevant to choosing entitlements when other reasons are taken into account. This may occur when the reasons accepted are indifferent between conflicting entitlements and one entitlement is cheaper to enforce than the others. It may also occur when the reasons are not indifferent but lead us only slightly to prefer one over another and the first is considerably more expensive to enforce than the second.

But administrative efficiency is just one aspect of the broader concept of economic efficiency. Economic efficiency asks that we choose the set of entitlements which would lead to that allocation of resources which could not be improved in the sense that a further change would not so improve the condition of those who gained by it that they could compensate those who lost from it and still be better off than before. . . .

Recently it has been argued that on certain assumptions, usually termed the absence of transaction costs, Pareto optimality or economic efficiency will occur regardless of the initial entitlement.[17] . . . But no one makes an assumption of no transaction costs in practice. Like the physicist's assumption of no friction or Say's law in macro-economics, the assumption of no transaction costs may be a useful starting point, a device which helps us see how, as different elements which may be termed transaction costs become important, the goal of economic efficiency starts to prefer one allocation of entitlements over another.

Since one of us has written at length on how in the presence of various types of transaction costs a society would go about deciding on a set of entitlements in the field of accident law,[18] it is enough to say here: (1) that economic efficiency standing alone would dictate that set of entitlements which favors knowledgeable choices between social benefits and the social costs of obtaining them, and between social costs and the social costs of avoiding them; (2) that this implies, in the absence of certainty as to whether a benefit is worth its costs to society, that the cost should be put on the party or activity best located to make such a cost-benefit analysis; (3) that in particular contexts like accidents

---

[17] Coase, supra, Section C.
[18] G. Calabresi, *The Costs of Accidents* (1970), pp. 135–97.

or pollution this suggests putting costs on the party or activity which can most cheaply avoid them; (4) that in the absence of certainty as to who that party or activity is, the costs should be put on the party or activity which can with the lowest transaction costs act in the market to correct an error in entitlements by inducing the party who can avoid social costs most cheaply to do so; and (5) that since we are in an area where by hypothesis markets do not work perfectly – there are transaction costs – a decision will often have to be made on whether market transactions or collective fiat is most likely to bring us closer to the Pareto optimal result the 'perfect' market would reach.

Complex though this summary may suggest the entitlement choice to be, in practice the criteria it represents will frequently indicate which allocations of entitlements are most likely to lead to optimal market judgments between having an extra car or taking a train, getting an extra cabbage and spending less time working in the hot sun, and having more widgets and breathing the pollution that widget production implies. Economic efficiency is not, however, the sole reason which induces a society to select a set of entitlements. Wealth distribution preferences are another, and thus it is to distributional grounds for different entitlements to which we must now turn.

B. Distributional Goals ...

Difficult as wealth distribution preferences are to analyze, it should be obvious that they play a crucial role in the setting of entitlements. For the placement of entitlements has a fundamental effect on a society's distribution of wealth. It is not enough, if a society wishes absolute equality, to start everyone off with the same amount of money. A financially egalitarian society which gives individuals the right to make noise immediately makes the would-be noisemaker richer than the silence loving hermit.

The consequence of this is that it is very difficult to imagine a society in which there is complete equality of wealth. Such a society either would have to consist of people who were all precisely the same, or it would have to compensate for differences in wealth caused by a given set of entitlements. The former is, of course, ridiculous, even granting cloning. And the latter would be very difficult; it would involve knowing what everyone's tastes were and taxing every holder of an entitlement at a rate sufficient to make up for the benefits the entitlement gave him. For example, it would involve taxing everyone with an entitlement to private use of his beauty or brains sufficiently to compensate those less favourably endowed but who nonetheless desired what beauty or brains could get.

If perfect equality is impossible, a society must choose what entitlements it wishes to have on the basis of criteria other than perfect equality. In doing this, a society often has a choice of methods, and the method chosen will have important distributional implications. Society can, for instance, give an entitlement away free and then, by paying the holders of the entitlement to limit their use of it, protect those who are injured by the free entitlement. Conversely, it can allow people to do a given thing only if they buy the right from the government. Thus a society can decide whether to entitle people to have children and then induce them to exercise control in procreating, or to require people to buy the right to have children in the first place. A society can also decide whether to entitle people to be free of military service and then induce them to join up, or to require all to serve but enable each to buy his way out. Which entitlement a society decides to sell, and which it decides to give away, will likely depend in part on which determination promotes the wealth distribution that society favors.

III. RULES FOR PROTECTING AND REGULATING ENTITLEMENTS

A. *Property and Liability Rules*

Why cannot a society simply decide on the basis of the already mentioned criteria who should receive any given entitlement, and then let its transfer occur only through a voluntary negotiation? Why, in other words, cannot society limit itself to the property rule? To do this it would need only to protect and enforce the initial entitlements from all attacks, perhaps through criminal sanctions, and to enforce voluntary contracts for their transfer. Why do we need liability rules at all?

In terms of economic efficiency the reason is easy enough to see. Often the cost of establishing the value of an initial entitlement by negotiation is so great that even though a transfer of the entitlement would benefit all concerned, such a transfer will not occur. If a collective determination of the value were available instead, the beneficial transfer would quickly come about.

Eminent domain[19] is a good example. A park where Guidacres, a tract of land owned by 1,000 owners in 1,000 parcels, now sits would, let us assume, benefit a neighboring town enough so that the 100,000 citizens of the town would each be willing to pay the average of $100 to have it. The park is Pareto desirable if the owners of the tracts of land in Guidacres actually value their entitlements at less than $10,000,000 or an average of $10,000 a tract. Let us assume that in fact the parcels are all the same and all the owners value them at $8,000. On this assumption, the park is, in economic efficiency terms, desirable – in values foregone it costs $8,000,000 and is worth

---

[19] [*Editors' Note*: the power to take private property for public use.]

$10,000,000 to the buyers. And yet it may well not be established. If enough of the owners hold out for more than $10,000 in order to get a share of the $2,000,000 that they guess the buyers are willing to pay over the value which the sellers in actuality attach, the price demanded will be more than $10,000,000 and no park will result. The sellers have an incentive to hide their true valuation and the market will not succeed in establishing it. . . .

Whenever this is the case an argument can readily be made for moving from a property rule to a liability rule. If society can remove from the market the valuation of each tract of land, decide the value collectively, and impose it, then the holdout problem is gone. Similarly, if society can value collectively each individual citizen's desire to have a park and charge him a 'benefits' tax based upon it, the freeloader problem is gone. If the sum of the taxes is greater than the sum of the compensation awards, the park will result. . . .

We should also recognize that efficiency is not the sole ground for employing liability rules rather than property rules. Just as the initial entitlement is often decided upon for distributional reasons, so too the choice of a liability rule is often made because it facilitates a combination of efficiency and distributive results which would be difficult to achieve under a property rule. As we shall see in the pollution context, use of a liability rule may allow us to accomplish a measure of redistribution that could only be attained at a prohibitive sacrifice of efficiency if we employed a corresponding property rule.

More often, once a liability rule is decided upon, perhaps for efficiency reasons, it is then employed to favor distributive goals as well. Again accidents and eminent domain are good examples. In both these areas the compensation given has clearly varied with society's distributive goals, and cannot be readily explained in terms of giving the victim, as nearly as possible, an objectively determined equivalent of the price at which he would have sold what was taken from him. . . .

IV. THE FRAMEWORK AND POLLUTION CONTROL RULES

Nuisance or pollution is one of the most interesting areas where the question of who will be given an entitlement, and how it will be protected, is in frequent issue. Traditionally, and very ably in the recent article by Professor Michelman, the nuisance-pollution problem is viewed in terms of three rules.[20] First, Taney may not pollute unless his neighbor (his only neighbor let us assume), Marshall, allows it (Marshall may enjoin Taney's nuisance). Second, Taney may pollute but must compensate Marshall for damages caused (nuisance is found

[20] 'Pollution as a Tort: a Non-Accidental Perspective on Calabresi's Costs' (1971) 80 Yale L.J. 647.

but the remedy is limited to damages). Third, Taney may pollute at will and can only be stopped by Marshall if Marshall pays him off (Taney's pollution is not held to be a nuisance to Marshall). In our terminology rules one and two (nuisance with injunction, and with damages only) are entitlements to Marshall. The first is an entitlement to be free from pollution and is protected by a property rule; the second is also an entitlement to be free from pollution but is protected only by a liability rule. Rule three (no nuisance) is instead an entitlement to Taney protected by a property rule, for only by buying Taney out at Taney's price can Marshall end the pollution.

The very statement of these rules in the context of our framework suggests that something is missing. Missing is a fourth rule representing an entitlement in Taney to pollute, but an entitlement which is protected only by a liability rule. The fourth rule, really a kind of partial eminent domain coupled with a benefits tax, can be stated as follows: Marshall may stop Taney from polluting, but if he does he must compensate Taney.

As a practical matter it will be easy to see why even legal writers as astute as Professor Michelman have ignored this rule. Unlike the first three it does not often lend itself to judicial imposition for a number of good legal process reasons. For example, even if Taney's injuries could practicably be measured, apportionment of the duty of compensation among many Marshalls would present problems for which courts are not well suited. If only those Marshalls who voluntarily asserted the right to enjoin Taney's pollution were required to pay the compensation, there would be insuperable freeloader problems. If, on the other hand, the liability rule entitled one of the Marshalls alone to enjoin the pollution and required all the benefited Marshalls to pay their share of the compensation, the courts would be faced with the immensely difficult task of determining who was benefited how much and imposing a benefits tax accordingly, all the while observing procedural limits within which courts are expected to function.

The fourth rule is thus not part of the cases legal scholars read when they study nuisance law, and is therefore easily ignored by them. But it is available, and may sometimes make more sense than any of the three competing approaches. Indeed, in one form or another, it may well be the most frequent device employed. To appreciate the utility of the fourth rule and to compare it with the other three rules, we will examine why we might choose any of the given rules.

We would employ rule one (entitlement to be free form pollution protected by a property rule) from an economic efficiency point of view if we believed that the polluter, Taney, could avoid or reduce the costs of pollution more cheaply than the pollutee, Marshall. Or to put it another way, Taney would be enjoinable if he were in a better position to balance the costs of polluting against the costs of not polluting. We would employ rule three (entitlement to pollute protected by a property rule) again solely from an economic efficiency standpoint, if we made the converse judgment on who could best balance the harm of pollution against its avoidance costs. If we were wrong in our judgments and if transactions between Marshall and Taney were costless or even very cheap, the entitlement under rules one or three would be traded and an economically efficient result would occur in either case. If we entitled Taney to pollute and Marshall valued clean air more than Taney valued the pollution, Marshall would pay Taney to stop polluting even though no nuisance was found. If we entitled Marshall to enjoin the pollution and the right to pollute was worth more to Taney than freedom from pollution was to Marshall, Taney would pay Marshall not to seek an injunction or would buy Marshall's land and sell it to someone who would agree not to seek an injunction. As we have assumed no one else was hurt by the pollution, Taney could now pollute even though the initial entitlement, based on a wrong guess of who was the cheapest avoider of the costs involved, allowed the pollution to be enjoined. Wherever transactions between Taney and Marshall are easy, and wherever economic efficiency is our goal, we could employ entitlements protected by property rules even though we would not be sure that the entitlement chosen was the right one. Transactions as described above would cure the error. While the entitlement might have important distributional effects, it would not substantially undercut economic efficiency.

The moment we assume, however, that transactions are not cheap, the situation changes dramatically. Assume we enjoin Taney and there are 10,000 injured Marshalls. Now *even if* the right to pollute is worth more to Taney than the right to be free from pollution is to the sum of the Marshalls, the injunction will probably stand. The cost of buying out all the Marshalls, given holdout problems, is likely to be too great, and an equivalent of eminent domain in Taney would be needed to alter the initial injunction. Conversely, if we denied a nuisance remedy, the 10,000 Marshalls could only with enormous difficulty, given freeloader problems, get together to buy out even one Taney and prevent the pollution. This would be so even if the pollution harm was greater than the value to Taney of the right to pollute.

If, however, transaction costs are not symmetrical, we may still be able to use the property rule. Assume that Taney can buy the Marshalls' entitlements easily because holdouts are for some reason absent, but that the Marshalls have great freeloader problems in buying out Taney. In this situation the entitlement should be granted to the Marshalls unless we are sure the Marshalls are the cheapest avoiders of pollution costs. Where we do not know the identity of the cheapest cost avoider it is better to entitle the Marshalls to be free of pollution because, even if we are wrong in our initial placement of the entitlement, that is, even if the Marshalls are the cheapest cost avoiders, Taney will buy out the Marshalls and economic efficiency will be achieved. Had we chosen the converse entitlement and been wrong, the Marshalls could not have bought out Taney. Unfortunately, transaction costs are often high on both sides and an initial entitlement, though incorrect in terms of economic efficiency, will not be altered in the market place.

Under these circumstances – and they are normal ones in the pollution area – we are likely to turn to liability rules whenever we are uncertain whether the polluter or the pollutees can most cheaply avoid the cost of pollution. We are only likely to use liability rules where we are uncertain because, if we are certain, the costs of liability rules – essentially the costs of collectively valuing the damages to all concerned plus the cost in coercion to those who would not sell at the collectively determined figure – are unnecessary. They are unnecessary because transaction costs and bargaining barriers become irrelevant when we are certain who is the cheapest cost avoider; economic efficiency will be attained without transactions by making the correct initial entitlement.

As a practical matter we often are uncertain who the cheapest cost avoider is. In such cases, traditional legal doctrine tends to find a nuisance but imposes only damages on Taney payable to the Marshalls. This way, if the amount of damages Taney is made to pay is close to the injury caused, economic efficiency will have had its due; if he cannot make a go of it, the nuisance was not worth its costs. The entitlement to the Marshalls to be free from pollution unless compensated, however, will have been given *not* because it was thought that polluting was probably worth less to Taney than freedom from pollution was worth to the Marshalls, nor even because on some distributional basis we preferred to charge the cost to Taney rather than to the Marshalls. It was so placed *simply because we did not know* whether Taney desired to pollute more than the Marshalls desired to be free from pollution, and the only way we thought we could test out the value of the pollution was by the only liability rule we thought we had. This was rule two, the imposition of nuisance damages on Taney. At least this would be the position of a court concerned with economic efficiency which believed itself limited to rules one, two, and three.

Rule four gives at least the possibility that the opposite entitlement may also lead to economic efficiency in a situation of uncertainty. Suppose for the moment that a mechanism exists for collectively assessing the damage resulting to Taney from being stopped from polluting by the Marshalls, and a mechanism also exists for collectively assessing the benefit to each of the Marshalls from such cessation. Then – assuming the same degree of accuracy in collective valuation as exists in rule two (the nuisance damage rule) – the Marshalls would stop the pollution if it harmed them more than it benefited Taney. If this is possible, then even if we thought it necessary to use a liability rule, we would still be free to give the entitlement to Taney or Marshall for whatever reasons, efficiency or distributional, we desired.

Actually, the issue is still somewhat more complicated. For just as transaction costs are not necessarily symmetrical under the two converse property rule entitlements, so also the liability rule equivalents of transaction costs – the cost of valuing collectively and of coercing compliance with that valuation – may not be symmetrical under the two converse liability rules. Nuisance damages may be very hard to value, and the costs of informing all the injured of their rights and getting them into court may be prohibitive. Instead, the assessment of the objective damage to Taney from foregoing his pollution may be cheap and so might the assessment of the relative benefits to all Marshalls of such freedom from pollution. But the opposite may also be the case. As a result, just as the choice of which property entitlement may be based on the asymmetry of transaction costs and hence on the greater amenability of one property entitlement to market corrections, so might the choice between liability entitlements be based on the asymmetry of the costs of collective determination.

The introduction of distributional considerations makes the existence of the fourth possibility even more significant. One does not need to go into all the permutations of the possible tradeoffs between efficiency and distributional goals under the four rules to show this. A simple example should suffice. Assume a factory which, by using cheap coal, pollutes a very wealthy section of town and employs many low income workers to produce a product purchased primarily by the poor; assume also a distributional goal that favors equality of wealth. Rule one – enjoin the nuisance – would possibly have desirable economic efficiency results (if the pollution hurt the homeowners more than it saved the factory in coal costs), but it would have disastrous distribution effects. It would also have undesirable efficiency effects if the initial judgment on costs of avoidance had been wrong and transaction costs were high. Rule two – nuisance damages – would allow a testing of the economic efficiency of eliminating the pollution, even in the presence of high transaction costs, but would quite possibly put the factory out of business or diminish output and thus have the same income distribution effects as rule one. Rule three – no nuisance – would have favorable distributional effects since it might protect the income of the workers. But if the pollution harm was greater to the homeowners than the cost of avoiding it by using a better coal, and if transaction costs – holdout problems – were such that homeowners could not unite to pay the factory to use better coal, rule three would have unsatisfactory efficiency effects. Rule four – payment of damages to the factory after allowing the homeowners to compel it to use better coal, and assessment of the cost of these damages to the homeowners – would be the only one which would accomplish both the distributional and efficiency goals.

An equally good hypothetical for any of the rules can be constructed. Moreover, the problems of coercion may as a practical matter be extremely severe under rule four. How do the homeowners decide to stop the factory's use of low grade coal? How do we assess the damages and their proportional allocation in terms of benefits to the homeowners? But equivalent problems may often be as great for rule two. How do we value the damages to each of the many homeowners? How do we inform the homeowners of their rights to damages? How do we evaluate and limit the administrative expenses of the court actions this solution implies?

The seriousness of the problem depends under each of the liability rules on the number of people whose 'benefits' or 'damages' one is assessing and the expense and likelihood of error in such assessment. A judgment on these questions is necessary to an evaluation of the possible economic efficiency benefits of employing one rule rather than another. The relative ease of making such assessments through different institutions may explain why we often employ the courts for rule two and get to rule four – when we do get there – only through political bodies which may, for example, prohibit pollution, or 'take' the entitlement to build a supersonic plane by a kind of eminent domain, paying compensation to those injured by these decisions. But all this does not, in any sense, diminish the importance of the fact that an awareness of the possibility of an entitlement to pollute, but one protected only by a liability rule, may in some instances allow us best to combine our distributional and efficiency goals.

A. I. OGUS and G. M. RICHARDSON

*

Economics and the Environment: A Study of Private Nuisance[21]

To meet the efficiency criteria . . . tort law may choose between three solutions.

[21] (1977) 36 Camb. L.J. 284, 293–314, with omissions. Reprinted by permission of Cambridge University Press and the authors.

(i) Liability on discharger – specific enforcement. The pollution resulting from the discharge may be abated by an injunction.
(ii) Liability on discharger – monetary payment. Discharger liable in damages but on payment he may continue discharging. He effectively compulsorily purchases the right to pollute.
(iii) No liability on discharger – the discharger has a right to pollute. He is subject to no legal remedy and must be 'bought off' at an agreed price.

But, as Calabresi and Melamed have revealed, there exists a theoretical fourth solution to complete the symmetry.

(iv) The discharger's right to pollute may be bought at a judicially determined price. . . .

A. ACTIONABILITY

If the English courts decide that a nuisance is actionable they are in effect preferring the solution in rules i, ii, or iv to that in rule iii. To satisfy economic efficiency criteria they should, in broad terms, only refuse the plaintiff a remedy when they are certain that he is either the cheaper cost-abater or the better briber. It remains to be seen whether the law of nuisance is consistent with these precepts. Broadly defined, the tort embraces any condition or activity which unduly interferes with the use or enjoyment of land. To succeed the plaintiff must overcome [a number of] hurdles.   ₁

(i) He must have a legal interest in the occupation or enjoyment of land. . . . The requirement of an interest in land may thus be crucial. Yet it is difficult to rationalise the limitation in efficiency terms, except perhaps in so far as it increases the certainty of legal decision-making. . . .

(ii) The interest must be of a kind which the law of nuisance will protect. It is true that the nuisance action has extended its protection beyond tangible physical harm to cover such loss of amenities as that resulting from noise and smell. But, in contrast to other legal systems, English law has persistently refused to condemn aesthetic nuisances. . . . For the purposes of economic efficiency these distinctions seem to be of dubious validity – the deprivation of such facilities, as much as other forms of interference, result in the diminution of land value and there are certainly no grounds for assuming that the plaintiff here will be the cheaper cost-abater. . . .

(iii) The plaintiff must prove interference with the enjoyment of his interest and the extent of the interference required will depend on the nature of that interest. Some rights are drawn in almost absolute terms and damage will be presumed (*e.g.*, a riparian owner need only show a 'sensible' alteration in water quality or quantity). Others require proof of actual damage, *e.g.*, fumes, smell or noise. There appears to be no historical justification behind the attribution of absolute status to certain interests, and equally in economic efficiency terms the elevated status of certain interests appears to be somewhat arbitrary. No doubt in a fair proportion of water pollution cases it may be proper to assume that the discharger will be the cheapest cost-abater or, failing this, the best briber, but the same may be equally the case for other less favoured land users. It is, of course, true that an absolute standard may reduce dispute costs.

(iv) In cases of interference with amenity rather than physical damage the plaintiff must show that the defendant's activities constituted an unreasonable use of his land. . . . In theory, to achieve an efficient allocation of land use, the court might indulge in balancing between the costs of pollution, individual and social, and those of abatement, individual and social. These will include the nature of the area in terms of amenities, employment and general welfare, balance of payments, relative social utility of the parties and community morale. In cases of physical damage, following the decision in *St. Helens Smelting Co.* v. *Tipping*,[22] such balancing is excluded: liability follows automatically on proof of injury. As regards amenity damage, in practice the courts have limited themselves to the so-called 'neighbourhood test': analogously to a zoning process, they attribute land use characteristics to specific areas. The plaintiff may expect only standards considered appropriate for his particular neighbourhood. . . .

But the neighbourhood test can at best provide a crude guide to cost-abatement. Were the court to have regard to *all* factors relevant to determine the actual costs of abatement in some cases it might reach a different conclusion. For example in *Rushmer* v. *Polsue and Alfieri*[23] a milkman who had lived and managed his dairy for eighteen years in a neighbourhood devoted to printing and allied trades brought an action against a neighbouring printing firm which had installed a new machine. When normally operated at night it interfered with his sleep. The court upheld an injunction imposed on the night activities on the basis that the inconvenience was unreasonable even within such an area. Here the court can be seen to be focusing solely on its conception of the neighbourhood, to the exclusion of such relevant factors as the unique nature of the plaintiff's land use (he was the only resident in the area), the changing techniques and needs of the printing trade and the importance to the trade of night work. . . .

Quite apart from the limited nature of the neighbourhood test, the distinction between physical and amenity damage derived from the *St. Helens* case is itself extremely suspect. Why should zoning techniques

[22] (1865) 11 H.L.C. 642.   [23] [1906] 1 Ch. 234.

be relevant to the latter but not the former? One possible justification which is evident on the face of the opinions in the *St. Helens* case is that property damage rather than amenity damage leads to a diminution in land value – a fallacious argument since land values clearly reflect environmental amenities. A second possible rationalisation may be based on cost-abatement considerations. It might be argued that an inflicter of physical harm is invariably the cheapest cost-abater. Such an assumption is demonstrably false: if cost abatement may be considered when smoke gets in your eyes, it is equally relevant when smoke gets at your cabbages. . . .

(v) The plaintiff must establish that the interference resulted from the defendant's activity. This may give rise to serious problems in cases involving multiple-polluters. Once able to establish the causal link with one polluter, a plaintiff who suffers indivisible harm, as is likely with most forms of industrial discharge, may recover from that polluter damages for the whole. The principle of contribution enables the defendant to recover a proportionate indemnity from the other tortfeasors. The combination of these two rules constitutes an efficient method of achieving the allocation of resources chosen on grounds of, for example, cost-abatement or justice. . . .

(vi) The defendant must not have acquired the right to pollute by prescription. It is necessary that for a period of at least twenty years the nuisance has existed, it has been exercised as of right, the owner of the servient tenement knew of its existence and the nature of the nuisance has been certain and uniform throughout that period. . . . Where the discharger has acquired a prescriptive right the assumption is that the victim has consciously been prepared to bear the cost. The discharger has presumably relied on this fact and has organised his business accordingly. If the victim were suddenly to prevent the polluter from discharging it might involve the latter in considerable expenditure or could result in the closure of his plant. The law will not contemplate such a result and will uphold the prescriptive right to discharge in the absence of statutory regulation. Where a change of mind on the part of the plaintiff is involved this will probably be the efficient solution: it should be cheaper for him to adapt than for the polluter to abate. On the other hand, where a change of use is involved the situation may be different. No doubt in many cases it will still be cheaper for the new use to be located elsewhere and the prescriptive rule should apply. But account should be taken of the social costs resulting from the freezing of land use. If these exceed the cost of abating the first use, the rule will be inappropriate. . . . Where the social costs issue does not intrude, the defence of prescription achieves efficiency. There is, however, no magic in the twenty years and a general defence of 'coming to the nuisance' would not tie the court to any such arbitrary period.

(vii) The discharger may plead in defence that the plaintiff's activity was unduly sensitive. The law will not allow an individual by virtue of his special land use to make unusual demands on his neighbours. It lays down environmental standards which, though to some extent relate to general neighbourhood conditions, do not cater for individual needs. If individuals require greater protection they must procure it through private transactions governed by the law of contract. Although for these reasons a legal solution imposing liability on the discharger can only be regarded as hypothetical, nevertheless the question remains whether the present legal solution is efficient. In cases where the sensitive user is outnumbered by many dischargers, it is reasonable to assume, as in the neighbourhood test, that the former is the cheapest cost-abater. So also where the sensitive use is subsequent in time to the more normal use. On the arguments developed in the last section it is contended that the present solution will usually be efficient. . . .

B. REMEDIES

Availability of Injunctions. On satisfying the criteria of actionability, the plaintiff is entitled to common law damages as of right. Both the equitable remedies, damages and injunction, are at the discretion of the court and the question now to be considered is how it is exercised, in particular whether regard is had to efficiency objectives. There are two fundamental principles. The first, expressing the primacy of injunctive relief, was enunciated by Sir Raymond Evershed M.R. in the leading pollution nuisance case of *Pride of Derby* v. *British Celanese*[24] 'if A proves that his proprietary rights are being wrongfully interfered with by B, and that B intends to continue his wrong, then A is prima facie entitled to an injunction, and he will be deprived of that remedy only if special circumstances exist'. The second, complementary, principle specifies the situations in which the damages alternative is to be preferred:

'(1) If the injury to the plaintiff's legal right is small,
 (2) and is one which is capable of being estimated in money,
 (3) and is one which can be adequately compensated by a small money payment,
 (4) and the case is one in which it would be oppressive to the defendant to grant an injunction –
   then damages in substitution for an injunction may be given'.[25]

The principles reveal the clear English judicial preference for rule i over rule ii. Only where it is certain that the defendant is either the cheapest

---

[24] [1953] Ch. 149, 181.
[25] *Shelfer* v. *City of London Electric Lighting Co.* [1895] 1 Ch. 287, 322, *per* A. L. Smith L.J.

cost-abater or the best briber should the injunction be preferred if the result is to accord with the economic analysis. But the case law manifestly demonstrates that in their initial preference for the injunction, the judiciary have little regard for economic considerations. They have not in general been prepared to 'balance the equities', to weigh up the detrimental consequences to the defendant of granting an injunction against those to the plaintiff of refusing one. . . .

Suspension of injunction. While economic factors are generally regarded as irrelevant in the choice of remedy, they re-emerge as significant factors in deciding how the remedy is to be implemented. In particular, great flexibility is achieved through the ability to suspend the injunction. This device has been used by the court to achieve the efficient result in three different situations.

(i) In the first, efficiency demands the eventual abatement of the nuisance but also that time is necessary to achieve that goal. The costs, both individual and collective, resulting from the immediate disruption of the defendant's activities would be much greater than those incurred by the plaintiff, pending more gradual abatement. . . .

(ii) The second category involves situations where there is real uncertainty as to the identity of both the cheapest cost-abater, and the best briber and for which a rule ii damages award would provide the efficient solution. . . . [H]owever, the judges feel compelled by their distrust of 'compulsory purchase' to avoid this solution. They choose instead to suspend the injunction, thus mitigating the defendant's burden. . . .

(iii) In some circumstances there is no uncertainty: it is clear on the evidence available that the plaintiff is the least cost-abater. Here efficiency would dictate the adoption of rule iii and confer no remedy on the plaintiff, but as has been seen there are several areas where the law will hold a nuisance actionable despite efficiency criteria. This is particularly evident in cases where physical damage is inflicted or in which the property right is absolute. Of course, in the eyes of the proponents of the economic model, this selection of the rule is not fatal to an efficient outcome: it is assumed that market transactions will achieve the appropriate relocation. The court, having imposed liability, is faced with a choice between rules i, ii and iv. If forced to consider this problem the model would favour that rule which would encourage a satisfactory bargain at least cost. Rule i would be appropriate where transaction costs are low and the parties might easily reach a bargain. Otherwise rule ii, judicial evaluation of abatement cost, should apply. The typical response of the English court does not proceed along such lines. Unlike economists, judges seldom contemplate that parties to an action will immediately resort to the market place and reverse the effect of their ruling. Accordingly, in their eyes, there can be no justification for rule i. For reasons already given rule ii is generally not favoured, and they have no conception of rule iv as such. They are left then with their dependable compromise solution, the suspended injunction. . . .

Suspension with or without damages. The suspension of an injunction leaves open the question of who is to bear the cost before the order takes effect. If the defendant is to bear the cost the court will award damages for the interim period, thereby selecting rule ii for the short term and rule i for the long term. In the language of property law this is tantamount to a compulsory leasehold of the plaintiff's right to quiet enjoyment. It also conforms with the standard practice of the courts. If the plaintiff so requests it seems that damages will usually be granted, but generally in the form of an undertaking by the defendant to pay either at the time the injunction takes effect or from 'time to time' throughout the suspension, for damage actually inflicted. The decision to impose the interim costs on the plaintiff by not awarding damages is a short-term rule iii, forcing the plaintiff to pay the market price if he wants to secure abatement for the earlier period. The combination of this solution with an eventual injunction (rule i) could be the closest analogy in English law to rule iv: the plaintiff gets his injunction but the price he pays for it is the period of delay. . . .

Notes

1. The paper by Calabresi and Melamed constitutes an important development of the Coasian analysis in several respects. First, it distinguishes between different forms of rights (or entitlements). The most significant for present purposes are property rules, when the law enforces entitlement *in specie*, and liability rules, when it restricts the right to a monetary equivalent. The distinction was formulated in F. Michelman, 'Pollution as a Tort: A Non-Accidental Perspective on Calabresi's Costs' (1971) 80 Yale L.J. 647, 670–2. Calabresi and Melamed recognize that the distinction can be applied not only where entitlement is drawn in favour of the plaintiff – injunction (rule one); damages (rule two) – but also where entitlement lies with the defendant: no liability (rule three) and an injunction at a judicially determined price (rule four – for a rare example of this, see *Spur Industries* v. *Del E. Webb Development* 494 P.2d 700 (1972)). Note that liability rules (rules two and four) involve a compulsory sale of property rights and thus raise constitutional issues concerning the proper function of the state and the method of quantifying compensation: cf. F. Michelman, 'Property, Utility and Fairness: Limits on the Ethical Foundations of "Just Compensation" Law' (1967) 80 Harv. L.R. 1165; E. Rabin, 'Nuisance Law: Rethinking Fundamental Assumptions' (1977) 63 Virginia L.R. 1229, 1302–9. The

third form of entitlement is an 'inalienable right', one which the parties may not vary or exclude by contract. We have omitted the discussion of Calabresi and Melamed on this, because it it more germane to regulatory law which we consider in Chapter 7.

2. Secondly, Calabresi and Melamed introduce distributional considerations into the analysis. Normatively, we cannot be sure that the efficient solution is also the socially desirable solution unless we can be satisfied that it is also consistent with society's distributional objectives. No doubt, it is difficult to determine what these objectives are, and some writers argue that it is better to pursue distributional goals *directly* through a combination of taxation and social welfare benefits rather than *indirectly* through property rights (e.g. M. Friedman, *Capitalism and Freedom* (1962), pp. 190–2; and for a more comprehensive analysis, see E. K. Browning, *Redistribution and the Welfare System* (1975)). But in efficiency terms this method of redistribution might be more costly, where for example higher tax rates reduce work incentives. See A. M. Polinsky, 'Resolving Nuisance Disputes: The Simple Economics of Injunctive and Damage Remedies' (1980) 32 Stan. L.R. 1075, 1084–5, which ambitiously attempts to integrate distributional objectives into the economic analysis of nuisance.

3. Thirdly, Calabresi and Melamed relax Coase's key assumption of zero transaction costs. In the absence of bargaining, it is clearly important in terms of efficiency that the legal principle should approximate to the optimal solution. For the nuisance/pollution problem, Calabresi and Melamed suggest that entitlement should be granted *against* the party who is the 'least-cost-avoider' (generally in the form of a liability rule), and if there is insufficient information as to who that might be, then against the party who is the 'best-briber'. For criticism, see P. Burrows, 'Nuisance, legal rules and de-centralized decisions: a different view of the cathedral crypt' in P. Burrows and C. Veljanovski (eds.), *The Economic Approach to Law* (1981), ch. 6. He argues (1) that it is illogical to have regard to the best-briber when *ex hypothesi* there are obstacles to bargaining and (2) in the absence of informa-tion on the efficient level of pollution, identification of the cheapest cost-avoider is an insufficient criterion. Conversely, Demsetz claims that for the purposes of transactions the liability rule does not matter, for the party who can initiate the bargaining process more cheaply will in any event do so: 'Theoretical Efficiency in Pollution Control: Comment on Comments' (1971) 9 W. Econ. J. 444.

4. Ogus and Richardson conclude that some of the principles of the English law of nuisance are hard to reconcile with the goal of allocative efficiency (that is, on the assumption that the parties do not engage in Coasian bargaining). For an alternative view based on American Law, see R. C. Ellickson, 'Alternatives to Zoning: Covenants, Nuisance Rules and Fines as Land Use Control' (1972) 40 U. Chi. L.R. 681. In passages omitted from this book – (1977) 36 Camb. L.J. 284, 317–23 – other policy objectives are considered which may account for the rules. The most important appears to be that of corrective justice, according to which the judges see their role

primarily in terms of preserving the status quo ante and protecting the parties only against unanticipated changes, those which they feel able to characterize as giving rise to 'damage'. Somewhat analogous is the analysis of R. Epstein, 'Nuisance Law: Corrective Justice and Its Utilitarian Constraints' (1979) 8 J. Legal Stud. 49. He finds the basis of nuisance law in the idea of corrective justice (A being prevented from, or liable to pay compensation for, the causing of harm to B) which must nevertheless be overriden by utilitarian (i.e. allocative efficiency) considerations in certain situations, notably 'as the following four factors become dominant: 1. high administrative costs for claim resolution 2. high transaction costs for voluntary reassignment of rights 3. low value to the interested parties of the ownership rights whose rearrangement is mandated by public rule 4. presence of implicit in-kind compensation from all to all that precludes any systematic redistribution of wealth among the interested parties' (op. cit., p. 79).

3

TORT

A. Objectives

G. WILLIAMS

*

The Aims of the Law of Tort[1]

An intelligent approach to the study of law must take account of its purpose, and must be prepared to test the law critically in the light of its purpose. The question that I shall propound is the end or social function or *raison d'être* of the law of tort, and particularly of the action in tort for damages.

It is commonly said that the civil action for damages aims at compensation, as opposed to the criminal prosecution which aims at punishment. This, however, does not look below the surface of things. Granted that the immediate object of the tort action is to compensate the plaintiff at the expense of the tortfeasor, why do we wish to do this? Is it to restore the *status quo ante?* – but if so, why do we want to restore the *status quo ante?* And could not we restore this *status* in some other and better way, for instance by a system of national insurance? Or is it really that we want to deter people from committing torts? Or, again, is it that the payment of compensation is regarded as educational, or as a kind of expiation for a wrong? . . .

There are four possible bases of the action for damages in tort: appeasement, justice, deterrence and compensation.

Appeasement. Crime and tort have common historical roots. The object of early law is to prevent the disruption of society by disputes arising from the infliction of injury. Primitive law looks not so much to preventing crime in general as to preventing the continuance of this squabble in particular. The victim's vengeance is bought off by compensation, which gives him satisfaction in two ways: he is comforted to

[1] (1951) 4 Current Legal Problems 137, 137–52, with omissions. Reprinted by permission of Sweet & Maxwell Ltd.

receive the money himself, and he is pleased that the aggressor is discomfited by being made to pay. By this means the victim is induced to 'let off steam' within the law rather than outside it. . . .

Justice. With the growth of moral ideas it came to be thought that the law of tort was the expression of a moral principle. One who by his fault has caused damage to another ought as a matter of justice to make compensation. Two variants of this theory may be perceived: (1) The first places emphasis upon the fact that the payment of compensation is an evil for the offender, and declares that justice requires that he should suffer this evil. This is the principle of ethical retribution. . . . (2) The second variant looks at the same situation from the point of view of the victim; it emphasises the fact that the payment of compensation is a benefit to the victim of the wrong, and declares that justice requires that he should receive this compensation. We may call this ethical compensation.

It may be thought that these two variants are simply two different ways of stating the same thing, but that is not entirely true. (1) Many people who would not subscribe generally to the principle of ethical retribution would nevertheless assert the principle of ethical compensation. The principle of ethical retribution goes much beyond anything needed to justify the law of tort, because it requires the wrongdoer to be punished generally. Making him pay compensation is only one form of punishment. It is quite possible to take the view that the wrongdoer ought to make amends without thinking that he ought to suffer in any other way. Again, (2) one who asserts the principle of ethical compensation does not necessarily say that the wrongdoer must himself be afflicted. If no one else will pay the compensation, the wrongdoer must; but if someone (such as the State or an insurance company) steps in and pays for him, the requirement of recuperation is satisfied even though there is no ethical retribution against the offender. . . .

Deterrence. Ranged against the theory of tort as part of the moral order are those who believe that it is merely a regime of prevention. The action in tort is a 'judicial parable', designed to control the future conduct of the community in general. In England this view seems to have been first expounded by Bentham. . . . Austin followed Bentham in this. The proximate end of the civil sanction, said Austin, is redress to the injured party; but its remote and paramount end is the same as that of the criminal sanction: the prevention of offences generally.[2] . . .

Compensation. Finally there is the compensatory or reparative theory, according to which one who has caused injury to another must make good the damage whether he was at fault or not. This . . . does not require culpability on the part of the defendant. If valid, it justifies strict liability. . . . The difficulty is, however, to state it in such a form as

---

[2] *Jurisprudence* (5th edn, ed. R. Campbell, 1911), vol. I, p. 504.

to make it acceptable. If it is said that a person who has been damaged by another ought to be compensated, we readily assent, moved as we are by sympathy for the victim's loss. But what has to be shown is not merely that the sufferer ought to be compensated, but that he ought to be compensated by the defendant. In the absence of any moral blame of the defendant, how is this demonstration possible?

It is fashionable to say that the question is simply one of who ought to bear the risk. This, however, is a restatement of the problem rather than a solution of it. A more satisfactory version is that known as . . . the enterprise theory. This regards liability for torts connected with an enterprise as a normal business expense. Nothing can be undertaken without some risk of damage to others, and if the risk eventuates it must be shouldered by the undertaker in the same way as the cost of his raw materials. That this attitude has come into prominence in the present century, though not unknown in the last, is symptomatic of the general search for security at the cost, if need be, of freedom of enterprise. . . . From this it looks as though the cry 'no liability without fault' comes from those who wish to maximise the national income, while the present apotheosis of strict liability is the result of a majority preference for security and broad equality, even if this means some stifling of progress. However, the actual rules of strict liability are so haphazard that they can hardly be fitted into any rational pattern. If the enterprise theory were consistently applied it would result in strict liability in respect of all acts done in the course of manufacture or business; but, in fact, the law does not go so far as this.

Whichever theory we think ought to be adopted as the basis of the law of tort, it is profitable to ask which one best fits the existing rules. It may be that the law of tort has grown without conscious purpose, or with a jumble of purposes; yet the law as it stands may be found to express one philosophy better than another.

Notes

1. Many have attempted to rationalize tort law in terms of a single objective. This reflects a 'belief' among a growing number of legal scholars 'in the rational foundations of law and in the feasibility of a systematic theory or model': I. Englard, 'The System Builders: A Critical Appraisal of North American Tort Theory' (1980) 9 J. Legal Stud. 27, 30. Economics and philosophy have frequently provided the basis for these theoretical approaches (surveyed in E. G. White, *Tort Law in America: An Intellectual History* (1980); P. Cane, 'Justice and Justifications for Tort Liability' (1982) 2 Oxford J. Legal Stud. 30).

2. Tort law may have several conflicting objectives. In order simultaneously

to achieve two objectives in full it is generally necessary to use at least two policy instruments. If only a single instrument is available some trade-off between objectives will be necessary. Tort law's requirement that damages equal the plaintiff's loss and be paid to the plaintiff, implies that it can achieve only one objective fully or more than one imperfectly (R. L. Birmingham, 'The Theory of Economic Policy and the Law of Torts' (1970) 55 Minn. L.R. 1). The damage measure necessary fully to compensate the wronged plaintiff may not be appropriate for efficient deterrence (Shavell, infra, Section E); or a rule, like fault liability, may encourage individuals to take adequate *care* but encourage excessive levels of dangerous *activity* (too many motorists all exercising the efficient level of care) because injurers do not pay the full social costs of accidents (see Posner, infra, Section B). In particular there will usually be a conflict between risk-spreading and deterrence objectives.

G. CALABRESI

*

The Costs of Accidents[3]

Apart from the requirements of justice, I take it as axiomatic that the principal function of accident law is to reduce the sum of the costs of accidents and the costs of avoiding accidents. . . . This cost, or loss, reduction goal can be divided into three subgoals.

The first is reduction of the number and severity of accidents. This 'primary' reduction of accident costs can be attempted in two basic ways. We can seek to forbid specific acts or activities thought to cause accidents, or we can make activities more expensive and thereby less attractive to the extent of the accident costs they cause. These two methods of primary reduction of accident costs are not clearly separable; a number of difficulties of definition will become apparent as we consider them in detail. . . .

The second cost reduction subgoal is concerned with reducing neither the number of accidents nor their degree of severity. It concentrates instead on reducing the societal costs resulting from accidents. I shall attempt to show that the notion that one of the principal functions of accident law is the compensation of victims is really a rather misleading, though occasionally useful, way of stating this 'secondary' accident cost reduction goal. The fact that I have termed this compensation notion secondary should in no way be taken as belittling its importance. There is no doubt that the way we provide for accident victims *after* the accident is crucially important and that the

---

[3] From *The Costs of Accidents* (1970), pp. 26–136, with omissions. Copyright © 1970 by Yale University Press. By permission.

real societal costs of accidents can be reduced as significantly here as by taking measures to avoid accidents in the first place. This cost reduction subgoal is secondary only in the sense that it does not come into play until after earlier primary measures to reduce accident costs have failed.

The secondary cost reduction goal can be accomplished through . . . two methods . . . both of which usually involve a shifting of accident losses: the risk (or loss) spreading method and the deep pocket method.

The third subgoal of accident cost reduction . . . involves reducing the costs of administering our treatment of accidents. It may be termed 'tertiary' because its aim is to reduce the costs of achieving primary and secondary cost reduction. But in a very real sense this 'efficiency' goal comes first. It tells us to question constantly whether an attempt to reduce accident costs, either by reducing accidents themselves or by reducing their secondary effects, costs more than it saves. By forcing us to ask this, it serves as a kind of general balance wheel to the cost reduction goal.

These, then, are the principal subgoals into which the goal of accident cost reduction can be divided – primary accident cost reduction . . . secondary accident cost reduction, which includes the risk spreading and the deep pocket methods; and the tertiary or efficiency cost reduction.

. . . It should be noted in advance that these subgoals are not fully consistent with each other. For instance, a perfect system of secondary cost reduction is, . . . inconsistent with the goals of reducing primary accident costs. We cannot have more than a certain amount of reduction in one category without forgoing some of the reduction in the other, just as we cannot reduce all accident costs beyond a certain point without incurring costs in *achieving* the reduction that are greater than the reduction is worth. Our aim must be to find the best combination of primary, secondary, and tertiary cost reduction taking into account what must be given up in order to achieve that reduction.

. . .

. . . [T]he primary way in which a society may seek to reduce accident costs is to discourage activities that are 'accident prone' and substitute safer activities as well as safer ways of engaging in the same activities. But such a statement suggests neither the degree to which we wish to discourage such activities nor the means for doing so. . . . [W]e certainly do not wish to avoid accident costs at all costs by forbidding all accident-prone activities. Most activities can be carried out safely enough or be sufficiently reduced in frequency so that there is a point at which their worth outweighs the costs of the accidents they cause. Specific prohibition or deterrence of most activities would cost society more than it would save in accident costs prevented. We want the fact that activities cause accidents to influence our choices among activities and among ways of doing them. But we want to limit this influence to a degree that is justified by the cost of these accidents. The obvious question is, how do we do this?

There are two basic approaches to making these difficult 'decisions for accidents', and our society has always used both, though not always to the same degree. The first, which I . . . term . . . the specific deterrence or collective approach, . . . involves deciding collectively the degree to which we want any given activity, who should participate in it, and how we want it done. These decisions may or may not be made solely on the basis of the accident costs the activity causes. The collective decisions are enforced by penalties on those who violate them.

The other approach . . . involves attempting instead to decide what the accident costs of activities are and letting the *market* determine the degree to which, and the ways in which, activities are desired given such costs. Similarly, it involves giving people freedom to choose whether they would rather engage in the activity and pay the costs of doing so, including accident costs, or, given the accident costs, engage in safer activities that might otherwise have seemed less desirable. I call this approach general, or market, deterrence.

The crucial thing about the general deterrence approach to accidents is that it does not involve an a priori collective decision as to the correct number of accidents. General deterrence implies that accident costs would be treated as one of the many costs we face whenever we do anything. Since we cannot have everything we want, individually or as a society, whenever we choose one thing we give up others. General deterrence attempts to force individuals to consider accident costs in choosing among activities. The problem is getting the best combination of choices available. The general deterrence approach would let the free market or price system tally the choices. . . .

The general deterrence approach operates in two ways to reduce accident costs. The first and more obvious one is that it creates incentives to engage in safer activities. Some people who would engage in a relatively dangerous activity at prices that did not reflect its accident costs will shift to a safer activity if accident costs *are* reflected in prices. The degree of the shift will depend on the relative difference in accident costs and on how good a substitute the safer activity is. Whatever the shift, however, it will reduce accident costs, since a safer activity will to some degree have been substituted for a dangerous one.

The second and perhaps more important way general deterrence reduces accident costs is that it encourages us to make activities safer. This is no different from the first if every variation in the way an activity is carried out is considered to be a separate activity, but since that is not how the term activity is used in common language, it may be useful to show how general deterrence operates to cause a given activity to become safer. Taney drives a car. His car causes, on the average, $200 per year in accident costs. If a different kind of brake were used in the car, this would be reduced to $100. The new kind of brake costs the equivalent of $50 per year. If the accident costs Taney causes are paid either by the state out of general taxes or by those who are injured, he has no financial incentive to put in the new brake. But if Taney has to pay, he will certainly put the new brake in. He will thus bear a new cost of $50 per year, but it will be less than the $100 per year in accident costs he will avoid. As a result, the cost of accidents to society will have been reduced by $50.

This example of how general deterrence operates to reduce costs is, of course, highly simplified. It assumes, for instance, that we know that Taney 'causes' the $200 in accident costs. It also assumes that the government or the victims, if they bear the losses, cannot cause the brakes to be installed as readily as Taney. Indeed, the assumptions are so simple that they lead one to ask, why we do not simply make all Taneys install the new brakes. Why, in short, do we not specifically deter the 'dangerous conduct' instead of bothering with so cumbersome a method as general deterrence?

Mentioning a few more of the many complications inherent in the situation may make clearer why general deterrence is worthwhile. Suppose that Marshall, who uses old-style brakes, has only $25 worth of accidents per year. It is not worth our while to force him to install the new brakes. Indeed, if he were made to install new brakes and if we can assume our measurements of costs to be accurate . . . forcing Marshall to install new brakes would add an unnecessary $25 to our cost burden. Yet we would still wish to have Taney install the brakes in order to get his $50 saving. It will be expensive, if not impossible, to make collective decisions distinguishing the Taneys from the Marshalls. It will, in fact, be much easier if we let the distinction be made by Taney and Marshall themselves by letting them choose between paying for the accidents and paying for the new brakes.

Another complication may be even more significant. Suppose we do not yet have the safe brakes, and requiring such brakes is therefore impossible. Placing the cost on cars may still bring about general deterrence in the form of a continuous pressure to develop something – such as new brakes – that would avoid the accident costs and would be cheaper to make and sell than paying the accident costs. General deterrence creates a market for this cost-saving substitute and, there-fore, an incentive for someone to develop it and bring about a cost reduction. . . .

A pure market approach to primary accident cost avoidance would require allocation of accident costs to those acts or activities (or combinations of them) which could avoid the accident costs most cheaply. This is the same as saying that the system would allocate the costs to those acts or activities that an arbitrary initial bearer of accident costs would (in the absence of transaction and information costs) find it most worthwhile to 'bribe' in order to obtain that modification of behavior which would lessen accident costs most.

This formulation implies several things. If there were no transaction or information costs associated with paying people to alter their behavior, it would not matter (in terms of market control of accidents) who bore the accident costs initially. Regardless of who was initially liable, there would be bribes or transactions bringing about any change in the behavior of any individual that would cause a greater reduction in accident costs than in pleasure. Since in reality transactions are often terribly expensive, it is often not worthwhile spending both the cost of the transaction and the amount needed to bribe someone else to diminish the accident-causing behavior. As a result, the accident cost is not avoided by society, while another allocation that could eliminate or lessen the transaction cost is available and would result in the avoidance of the accident cost. The aim of . . . a pure market approach is, then, how we should determine who, in practice, is the cheapest cost avoider.

Notes

1. The 'newer' economics of tort, exemplified by the work of Calabresi and Posner (W. M. Landes and R. A. Posner, 'The Positive Economic Theory of Tort Law' (1981) 15 Georgia L.R. 851) proceeds on a radically different assumption from that adopted by critics of tort law in the 1950s and 1960s. The latter emphasized the compensatory aspects of tort; as 'public law in disguise', having a regulatory and distributional character which aimed at shifting and spreading the costs of injuries (R. E. Keeton and J. O'Connell, *Basic Protection for Accident Victims* (1965); T. Ison, *The Forensic Lottery* (1967)). In Calabresi's approach, risk spreading and administrative economy are only components of the more general objective of accident cost reduction. The new tort scholarship using economics focuses almost exclusively on deterrence issues (e.g. J. P. Brown, 'Toward an Economic Theory of Liability' (1973) 2 J. Legal Stud. 323). So long as those who can avoid accidents most cheaply have appropriate incentives, the compensation of accident victims is generally regarded as being irrelevant.

2. Another school of thought examines tort liability in terms of justice. The extent to which cost-reduction and justice are compatible and, if not, how they are to be balanced is an area of lively controversy between tort theorists (G. P. Fletcher, 'Fairness and Utility in Tort Theory' (1972) 85 Harv. L.R.

537; R. A. Epstein, 'Nuisance Law: Corrective Justice and Its Utilitarianism Constraints' (1979) 8 J. Legal Stud. 49; cf. R. A. Posner, 'The Concept of Corrective Justice in Recent Theories of Tort' (1981) 10 J. Legal Stud. 187). Calabresi, for example, would accord 'justice' veto power over morally unacceptable cost-reduction liability rules (G. Calabresi and R. M. Dworkin, 'An Exchange' (1980) 8 Hofstra L.R. 553).

3. Calabresi's approach is normative and prescriptive. The objective of accident law is to allocate losses to classes of individuals who can best reduce accident costs when transaction costs are high (cf. Coase supra, Chapter 2, Section C). In practice, the identity of the 'cheapest-cost avoider' is not always obvious, although a number of guidelines can be used to identify the party who should bear the loss (G. Calabresi, 'Fault, Accidents and the Wonderful World of Blum and Kalven' (1965) 75 Yale L.J. 216, 230). According to Calabresi's criterion, he will be the party who can: (1) better evaluate the risk involved; (2) better evaluate the accident-proneness of potential parties on the other side; (3) cause prices to reflect this knowledge; (4) insure most cheaply against liability; or/and (5) is less likely to have the loss shifted in a way that reduces the incentives to avoid the loss. For critical evaluation Calabresi's approach, see England op. cit.; P. S. Atiyah, *Accidents, Compensation and the Law* (3rd edn, 1980), ch. 24.

4. 'To say that the goal of the law of tort is deterrence' states Williams (op. cit., p. 149), 'is not the same as saying that it actually does deter'. Critics of economic analysis have questioned the assumptions that individuals are deterred from accident-causing behaviour by financial penalties and that tort does deter, given the widespread availability and nature of liability insurance. Unfortunately the evidence either way is very meagre, although several studies do indicate that changes in tort law and financial penalties do have an impact on accident rates: R. W. Grayson, 'Deterrence in Automobile Liability Insurance – The Empirical Evidence' (1973) 40 Ins. Counsel J. 117; S. Rottenberg (ed.) *The Economics of Medical Malpractice* (1978); E. Landes, 'Insurance, Liability and Accidents: A Theoretical and Empirical Investigation of the Effect of No-Fault on Accidents' (1982) 25 J. Law and Econ. 49; C. J. Bruce, 'The Deterrent Effects of Automobile Insurance and Tort Law: A Survey of the Empirical Literature' (1984) 6 Law and Policy Q (forthcoming).

B. Negligence and Strict Liability

R. A. POSNER

*

Tort Law – Cases and Economic Analysis[4]

In United States v. Carroll Towing Co., 159 F. 2d 169 (2d Cir. 1947), the question was presented whether it was negligent for the Conners Company, the owner of a barge, to leave it unattended for several hours in a busy harbor. While unattended, the barge broke away from its moorings and collided with another ship. Judge Learned Hand stated for the court (at p. 173):

there is no general rule to determine when the absence of a bargee or other attendant will make the owner of the barge liable for injuries to other vessels if she breaks away from her moorings. . . . It becomes apparent why there can be no such general rule, when we consider the grounds for such a liability. Since there are occasions when every vessel will break from her moorings, and since, if she does, she becomes a menace to those about her, the owner's duty, as in other similar situations, to provide against resulting injuries is a function of three variables: (1) The probability that she will break away; (2) the gravity of the resulting injury, if she does; (3) the burden of adequate precautions. Possibly it serves to bring this notion into relief to state it in algebraic terms: if the probability be called P; the injury, L; and the burden, B; liability depends upon whether B is less that L multiplied by P: i.e., whether $B < PL$. . . . In the case at bar the bargee left at five o'clock in the afternoon of January 3rd, and the flotilla broke away at about two o'clock in the afternoon of the following day, twenty-one hours afterwards. The bargee had been away all the time, and we hold that his fabricated story was affirmative evidence that he had no excuse for his absence. At the locus in quo – especially during the short January days and in the full tide of war activity – barges were being constantly 'drilled' in and out. Certainly it was not beyond reasonable expectation that, with the inevitable haste and bustle, the work might not be done with adequate care. In such circumstances we hold – and it is all that we do hold – that it was a fair requirement that the Conners Company should have a bargee aboard (unless he had some excuse for his absence), during the working hours of daylight.

By redefinition of two terms in the Hand formula it is easy to bring out its economic character. B, the burden of precautions, is the cost of avoiding the accident, while L, the loss if the accident occurs, is the cost of the accident itself. P times L ($P \times L$) – the cost of the accident if it occurs, multiplied (or as is sometimes said, 'discounted') by the

[4] From *Tort Law – Cases and Economic Analysis* (1982), pp. 1–8, with omissions. Reprinted by permission of Little, Brown and Company.

probability that the accident will occur, is what an economist would call the 'expected cost' of the accident. Expected cost is most easily understood as the average cost that will be incurred over a period of time long enough for the predicted number of accidents to be the actual number. For example, if the probability that a certain type of accident will occur is .001 (one in a thousand) and the accident cost if it does occur is $10,000, the expected accident cost is $10 ($10,000 × .001); and this is equivalent to saying that if we observe the activity that gives rise to this type of accident for a long enough period of time we will observe an average accident cost of $10. Suppose the activity in question is automobile trips from point A to point B. If there are 100,000 trips, there will be 100 accidents, assuming that our probability of .001 was correct. The total cost of the 100 accidents will be $1 million ($10,000 × 100). The average cost, which is simply the total cost ($1 million) divided by the total number of trips (100,000), will be $10. This is the same as the expected cost.

Another name for expected accident costs – for P × L, the right-hand side of the Hand formula – is the benefits from accident avoidance. If one incurs B, the burden of precautions or cost of accident avoidance, one produces a benefit – namely, avoidance of the expected accident costs. The Hand formula is simply an application to accidents of the principle of cost–benefit analysis. Negligence means failing to avoid an accident where the benefits of accident avoidance exceed the costs.

The Hand formula shows that it is possible to think about tort law in economic terms. . . .

Many questions about the Hand formula will *not* be answered in this chapter. The unanswered questions include: Does the Hand formula provide a good description of what judges and juries do in tort cases in general or negligence cases in particular? Do courts have enough information to apply the formula intelligently? *Should* the courts use either an explicit or implicit economic approach to questions of tort liability, or should noneconomic factors weigh as or more heavily on their decisions? . . . [Here] the further explication of the formula will be limited to two rather technical but important qualifications:

1. The relevant cost of accident avoidance is not total cost, but marginal cost. For our purposes, the marginal cost of accident avoidance can be defined as the additional cost that has to be incurred to prevent *this* accident (i.e., the accident that imposes a cost of L with a probability of P). Suppose that a person slips on a staircase and is hurt. The probability that he would slip and fall is .001, the cost of the accident is $25,000, and the cost of preventing the accident (say by installing rubber mats on each stair and by providing a guard rail)

would be $50. Since $50 is more than $25, the expected accident cost, it might seem that the failure to prevent the accident was not negligent. But this conclusion is not necessarily correct. Suppose that if $10 were spent on just installing rubber mats, the probability of an accident would drop by one half. The expected accident cost would then be $12.50 rather than $25. Thus it is clear that the benefits of the rubber mats in accident avoidance ($12.50) exceed their cost ($10). But once the mats are installed, a guard rail costing $40 would not be worth having since it would avoid only a $12.50 expected accident cost. Thus, to be a correct economic test, the Hand formula must be applied at the margin: the court must examine the incremental benefit in accident avoidance of an incremental expenditure on safety.

2. An *expected* value (whether cost or benefit) – that is, a value the receipt or expenditure of which is uncertain – may confer less or more utility or disutility than its certain equivalent. Compare a 1 percent chance of winning $100 with a certainty of receiving $1. Are these 'worth' the same? They are in the sense that $1 is the expected benefit of a 1 percent chance of obtaining $100. Some people, at least some of the time, are indifferent between the certain amount and its uncertain or expected equivalent. These people are said to be 'risk neutral'. Many people, however, are 'risk averse', meaning that they prefer the certain equivalent; and some are 'risk preferring', meaning that they prefer the expected to the certain amount. Gamblers are risk preferring; people who buy insurance are risk averse. . . .

The Hand formula implicity assumes risk neutrality. That is, it compares a (more or less) certain sum, the cost of accident avoidance, with an uncertain sum, the expected cost of the accident, without adjusting for the fact that one cost is certain and the other uncertain. The formula yields the same result – no negligence – whether B is $2, P 100 percent, and L $1, or B is $2, P is 1 percent and L is $100. However, a strongly risk-averse person might think that a 1 percent change of incurring a $100 loss was more costly – imposed greater disutility on him – than a certain cost of $2. He might be willing to pay $2 to insure himself against such a loss, and if so this would show that he considered a 1 percent chance of losing $100 to be the equivalent of a 100 percent chance of losing $2. . . .

Assuming, though only provisionally, that despite the above qualifications the Hand formula provides a generally sound guide to determining the economically correct investment in care and safety, let us now see how the formula might be used to induce potential injurers (and potential victims) to make that invesment: how, in other words, it might be used to shape conduct towards efficient ends.

Let us imagine the world divided strictly into injurers and victims – those who inflict injury (though they are themselves unharmed) and those who are injured. The fact that an individual is sometimes one and sometimes the other – and sometimes both at the same time – will be ignored for now. Let us begin with injurers, and assume for the moment (but just for the moment) that victims are helpless to avoid being injured. Two basic approaches could be taken to the liability of injurers. First, they could be made strictly liable, meaning that if an injury occurs, for whatever reason, and however unavoidable it may have been, the injurer must compensate the victim for the latter's loss. Under strict liability, and assuming that the court assesses damages equal to the loss suffered by the victim, the right-hand side of the Hand formula becomes an expected-damages figure. L is replaced by D (standing for damages) because every time a loss is suffered by an accident victim the injurer must pay for it. $P \times D$ is then the expected damages of the injurer if he does not avoid the accident.

In a system of strict liability the injurer must pay the injured victim regardless of the left-hand side of the Hand formula – regardless of whether B is greater than or less that $P \times L$. That is what strict liability means. It does not follow, however, that the Hand formula becomes irrelevant to the level of safety. Although the court will not apply the Hand formula – it will inquire simply whether the accident occurred and not whether the accident could have been prevented at a lower cost than the expected accident cost – rational potential injurers will apply the formula (i.e., use cost-benefit analysis) in order to determine whether to take steps to avoid the accident. And if the cost of avoidance turns out to be greater than the expected accident cost, the rational profit-maximizing (or utility-maximizing) potential injurer will not incur the cost of avoidance. He will prefer a lower expected damages cost to a higher accident-avoidance cost.

A negligence standard differs from strict liability in that under negligence the injurer is liable only for those accidents that he could have avoided at a lower cost than the expected accident cost. This is what Judge Hand suggests in the quotation at the beginning of this chapter. Notice that, at least as a first approximation, the number of accidents is the same under strict liability and negligence. This is because, as just mentioned, a potential injurer in a system of strict liability will not invest in safety beyond the point at which the costs of safety are equal to the benefits in accident avoidance. The difference between strict and negligence liability is that under the former system injurers must pay the losses of victims of accidents that are not worth preventing, whereas under the latter system injurers have no duty to pay victims of such accidents.

The comparison of strict liability and negligence can be clarified by thinking of accidents as falling into two classes: those that can be avoided at a cost lower than the expected accident cost, and those that cannot be avoided at such a cost. The latter are 'unavoidable' (in an economic, not necessarily a literal, sense) accidents. Someone who is strictly liable for all accidents he causes will not thereby be induced to avoid those accidents that are unavoidable. By definition, it doesn't pay to avoid them; it is cheaper to compensate the victim. Neither will someone who is liable only if negligent seek to prevent them; he is not liable for his unavoidable accidents and so has no incentive to avoid them.

The fact that negligence and strict liability lead, at least as a rough first approximation, to the same level of accidents may seem to provide an economic argument in favor of negligence. The argument is this: A system of strict liability provides no more (or less) safety than a negligence system. Thus the allocation of resources to safety is unchanged. But strict liability involves more claims than negligence, since under strict liability victims of unavoidable as well as avoidable accidents have claims against their injurers. The additional claims are costly to process, and the added costs confer no benefit in preventing additional accidents: no additional accidents are prevented.

In fact, the economic comparison of negligence and strict liability is more complicated than this. . . . [One complication] is as follows. There are two ways of avoiding an accident. One is to conduct the activity giving rise to the accident more carefully; the other is to reduce the amount, or change the nature, of the activity. Suppose that damage to crops from locomotive sparks can be reduced either by installing better spark-arresting equipment (or perhaps maintaining it better) or by running fewer trains. The first alternative relates to the care with which the activity of railroading is conducted, the second to the amount of activity. Under strict liability, the railroad will consider the costs of both alternatives, since both are methods of accident avoidance. What is the situation under negligence? . . . [N]egligence usually (though not always) connotes failure to use the right amount of care rather than failure to reduce the amount of activity to the correct level or change the activity (e.g., from railroading to trucking, or from growing wheat to burning trash). If so, negligence and strict liability may result in a different number of accidents after all. Strict liability will deter certain accidents where the cost of avoiding the accident by reducing the amount of activity is less than the expected accident cost; negligence will not deter such accidents.

However, before concluding that strict liability yields a more efficient allocation of resources to accident avoidance than negligence does, we must consider accident avoidance by victims. We assumed that victims were helpless, but this is not true in general. Suppose that a particular accident, having an expected cost of $100, could be avoided either by the injurer at a cost of $50 or by the victim at a cost of

$10. Clearly, it would be more efficient for the victim to avoid than for the injurer to do so. This is a case where we want the victim to bear the full costs of the accident so that he will be induced to avoid it. We want a principle of contributory negligence whereby if the victim could have avoided the accident at a cost lower than the expected accident cost and also lower than the injurer's cost of avoidance, the injurer is not liable for the victim's loss.

It might appear that the easiest way to implement this principle would be simply to apply the Hand formula to victims as well as injurers – to say that if the cost of avoidance to the victim is less than the expected accident cost, he is guilty of contributory negligence (because B is smaller than $P \times L$) and therefore 'liable' (i.e., not entitled to recover his damage from the injurer). This approach will yield the economically correct result in many cases, but not in all. The victim might be negligent under the Hand formula because his accident-avoidance cost was lower than the expected accident cost, but at the same time the injurer's accident-avoidance cost might be lower still. In that event we would want the injurer to be liable after all, even though the victim was contributorily negligent. . . .

Once the possibility of accident avoidance by victims is admitted, the earlier point (that strict liability results in fewer accidents than negligence liability because it induces adjustments in the level of, as well as care taken in, the activity giving rise to the accidents) becomes uncertain. Suppose there is a class of accidents that cannot be avoided by either injurers' or victims' taking more care, but can be avoided – and at lower cost than the expected accident cost – by a reduction in the amount of activity. Under a rule of strict liability potential injurers will reduce their activity because they will be liable for the cost of these accidents; under negligence they will not reduce their activity because they will not be liable for the accident costs. But precisely the reverse is true of potential victims. If injurers are liable only for their negligent accidents, and not for accidents avoidable only by reducing the level of activity, victims will have an incentive to reduce *their* level of activity because they will bear the costs of nonnegligent accidents. If injurers are strictly liable, however, victims will not curtail their activity, because they will be compensated for accidents arising from it.

To be concrete, under strict liability the railroad in our earlier example will run fewer trains but farmers will plant more crops; under negligence liability, the railroad will run more trains and the farmers plant fewer crops. Because it is impossible to say a priori which is the more efficient adjustment, we cannot conclude that strict liability will generally result in fewer accidents than negligence liability. Of course, if we know that in some particular class of accidents victims or injurers are helpless (in the economic sense that it would cost them more to avoid an accident, whether through more care or less activity, than the expected cost of the accident), that is a reason for preferring strict liability, or negligence liability, or even no liability . . . for that class, depending on which is the helpless group. . . .

In comparing strict liability and negligence, we have emphasized possible differences in the allocation of resouces to safety. This is one important dimension of efficiency, but another, which should always be kept in mind as well, is administrative cost. Strict liability increases the number of claims but reduces the cost of processing each one by eliminating the issue of negligence; whether the total costs of administering a strict liability system are lower or higher than those of administering a negligence system are unclear. In any event, the optimum liability rule is the one that minimizes the sum of allocative (expected-accident plus accident-avoidance) and administrative costs.

The Hand formula was announced in a negligence case but, it should be clear by now, can be applied to other issues in tort law besides the determination of negligence. It can be used . . . to answer the question whether a victim is contributorily negligent, or to justify a rule of strict liability in a class of accidents where it is clear that the cost of accident avoidance to injurers is lower than the accident-avoidance cost to victims. The Hand formula can also be used where, unlike the typical accident case, the probability of harm is one. Many pollution cases are of this type. . . .

The Hand formula can be applied even to cases of deliberate injury. Because the injurer in such a case is *trying* to hurt the victim, rather than just hurting him as a by-product of other activity, P tends to be very high in such cases. At the same time, B will often be very low, and even negative, especially if it is interpreted, as it should be, to refer to *social* as distinct from purely *private* costs. What is the social cost of refraining from spitting in someone's face? It is very low – zero or even negative (because it takes an effort to spit, not to avoid spitting). Although the injury cost is also small, it is higher than the social cost of avoidance and is inflicted with a probability close to one. Thus, application of the Hand formula to cases of deliberate harm will typically result in a decision to condemn the defendant's conduct. Nor would a different result be reached by considering the victim's conduct; in most cases of a deliberate or malicious infliction of harm, the injurer is clearly the cheaper harm-avoider than the victim.

Notes

1. Posner's approach differs from that of Calabresi. It is positive (or descriptive) law-and-economics designed to 'explain' the law rather than evaluate and prescribe reform. His central hypothesis is that 'the common

law is best explained as if judges who create the law through decisions operating as precedents in subsequent cases were trying to promote efficient resource allocation' (W. M. Landes and R. A. Posner, 'The Positive Theory of Tory Law' (1981) 15 Georgia L.R. 851, 851; also *Economic Analysis of Law* (2nd edn, 1977) pt. II). This theory has been criticized on legal, theoretical and factual grounds ('Symposium on Efficiency as a Legal Concern' (1980) 8 Hofstra L.R. 485; 'Symposium on Change in the Common Law: Legal and Economic Perspectives' (1980) 9 J. Legal Stud. 189). Perhaps the gravest criticism is that the hypothesis has at best a meagre empirical foundation and that its attempt to rationalize doctrines without an independent factual inquiry into actual costs and the law's impact on accident rates is a questionable test of the theory (C. G. Veljanovski, 'The Economic Approach to Law: A Critical Introduction' (1980) 7 Brit. J. Law and Soc. 158, 180–7; cf. Landes and Posner, op. cit., pp. 852–64; R. A. Posner, 'Some Uses and Abuses of Economics in Law' (1979) 46 U. Chi. L.R. 281).

2. Negligence and strict liability (with defences of contributory negligence) are two of several liability rules capable of inducing optimal care in the idealized economists' model, i.e. perfectly informed rational individuals and costless legal system (J. P. Brown, 'Toward and Economic Theory of Liability' (1973) 2 J. Legal Stud. 323; G. Calabresi and J. T. Hirschoff, 'Toward a Test for Strict Liability in Torts' (1972) 81 Yale L.J. 1055). But, in the long run, when both the victim's and injurer's level of care *and* decision to engage in the hazardous activity can be varied none of the rules can guarantee allocative efficiency. This is because they can satisfy only one of the two requirements necessary for efficiency: namely, (1) *care (or marginal) condition*, that for each party the marginal cost of care be equal to the marginal expected damage cost and; (2) *activity (or total) condition*, that the total social costs of participation in the risky activity do not exceed the total social benefits. Liability rules typically satisfy the former but not the latter (S. Shavell, 'Strict Liability versus Negligence' (1980) 9 J. Legal Stud. 1; A. M. Polinsky, 'Strict Liability vs. Negligence in a Market Setting' (1980) 70 Am. Econ. Rev. 363).

3. When the assumptions of the economic model are relaxed, it is no longer possible to indicate which liability rule is more efficient. It requires balancing a number of conflicting factors that can only be resolved empirically. As Posner points out, the change from negligence to strict liability has an ambiguous effect on the total administration costs of processing claims. These two rules will also have different effects on investment in safety research and development (R & D). Negligence, relative to strict liability, reduces the injurer's return on investment in R & D, but increases the victim's. In many cases, it may be reasonable to assume that those creating the risk (i.e. potential defendants) are better placed to undertake safety R & D. In any case, research costs are not taken into account in the Hand or negligence calculus. It is very hard, for example, to establish negligence in, say, the design of a motor car (P. S. Atiyah, *Accidents, Compensation and the Law* (3rd edn, 1980), pp. 59–64) even though redesign may be the most cost-effective method of reducing road accidents.

4. Negligence and strict liability have markedly different effects on the wealth of accident victims. Under a negligence regime, victims unable to satisfy the Hand formula for liability are without a remedy, whereas, under a strict liability regime, they are fully compensated. Some have inferred that the prevalence of the negligence standard in tort law reflects not so much a concern for efficiency but a preference on the part of judges to subsidize industry and risk-taking (M. J. Horwitz, *The Transformation of American Law 1790–1860* (1977); R. L. Abel, 'A Critique of American Tort Law' (1981) 8 Brit. J. Law and Soc. 199. Cf. G. T. Schwartz, 'Tort Law and the Economy in Nineteenth Century America: A Reinterpretation' (1981) 90 Yale L.J. 1717; R. A. Epstein, 'The Social Consequences of Common Law Rules' (1982) 95 Harv. L.R. 1717). Regardless of the validity of this inter-pretation, liability rules can be used to achieve distributional goals (A. M. Polinsky, 'Resolving Nuisance Disputes: The Simple Economics of Injunctive and Damage Remedies' (1980) 32 Stan. L.R. 1075; S. Shavell, 'A Note on Efficiency vs. Equity in Legal Rulemaking' (1981) 71 Am. Econ. Rev. 414.

C. Contributory Negligence

G. T. SCHWARTZ
*

Contributory and Comparative Negligence: A Reappraisal[5]

The justification that the new law-and-economics literature offers for a contributory negligence defense is not at all esoteric or highly tech-nical; it is easy enough to understand and indeed had been anticipated by traditional tort writings. By denying recovery, in whole or in part, to the victim who has been contributorily negligent, the law can dis-courage people from engaging in conduct that involves an unreasonable risk to their own safety. . . .

The economic justification for a contributory negligence defense runs as follows. Assume a $100 risk that the defendant could prevent for $60, but that the plaintiff could himself prevent for $25. Although the defendant may be negligent, the plaintiff is the more efficient accident preventer. To give the plaintiff the incentive to spend this $25, the plaintiff should be the party who is 'liable' – that is, a doctrine of contributory negligence should require him to bear the $100 loss.

---

[5] (1978) 87 Yale L.J. 697, 703–10, with omissions. Reprinted by permission of the author and the Yale Law Journal Co., and Fred B. Rothman & Company.

Although hypotheticals of this sort seem to support some version of a contributory negligence rule, they clearly do not support the rule in its traditional form. Assume a reversal of the $60/$25 figures: the plaintiff can prevent the risk for $60, the defendant for only $25. Although the plaintiff is contributorily negligent, the defendant should be held liable, since the defendant is in the better position to eliminate the risk. These converse results can be reconciled into a single contributory negligence rule: the plaintiff's contributory negligence should bar his recovery if, but only if, the plaintiff's prevention costs were lower than the defendant's. Although this rule contemplates a comparison of the negligence of the plaintiff and defendant, it does not amount to customary comparative negligence, since it is an either/or liability rule that does not involve the division of damages between the two parties. It somewhat resembles the *Galena* rule, which flourished for a few years in nineteenth century Illinois,[6] and for the sake of convenience, it will be referred to as the *Galena* rule hereafter.

Although the *Galena* rule avoids the problem of barring recovery by a plaintiff whose prevention costs were higher than the defendant's, it is beset by other problems, several of which it shares with the liability-dividing rule of comparative negligence. Consider, for example, the situation in which the defendant could prevent the risk for $60, and the plaintiff for $65 – but in which the risk could also be prevented if the plaintiff and defendant took complementary measures that would cost the defendant $9 and the plaintiff $10. This combined cost of $19 is the least expensive way to prevent the risk. Yet the *Galena* rule would give the plaintiff no incentive to take the $10 measure, since pursuant to *Galena* the fact that the defendant's prevention costs are lower than the plaintiff's (under either prevention alternative) means that the defendant will bear the entire liability. A liability-dividing rule of comparative negligence would encourage the complementary measures: the plaintiff and the defendant, each facing a liability in the vicinity of $50, would be willing to spend $10 and $9 to avoid that liability.

When the cheapest means of prevention are independent rather than complementary, however, comparative negligence can sometimes be successful, but only on a fortuitous basis. When, for example, one party's prevention costs are $25 and the other's $60, the party with the lower costs will face an expected liability of either $65 or $70, depending on the method of calculation, and will rationally spend $25 to prevent the risk. Meanwhile, the party with the $60 costs, facing an expected liability of only $30 or $35, will not spend $60 to prevent the risk. In such a case, comparative negligence produces the right result. But now assume that the risk can be prevented either by the plaintiff

---

[6] *Galena and Chicago Union R. R. v. Jacobs* 20 Ill. 478 (1858).

for $70 or by the defendant for $68. This is a risk that it would be efficient to eliminate. Yet under comparative negligence the do-nothing plaintiff and the do-nothing defendant each face a liability in the vicinity of $50; each will therefore abstain from preventive measures and allow the risk to materialize.

Finally, assume that the risk could be prevented by one party for $10 or by the other party for $20. Since under comparative negligence both parties will face liabilities in excess of their prevention costs, either party would be impelled to engage in risk prevention, which would lead to duplication and hence to wasted expenditure. Of course, if the $20 party correctly predicts that comparative negligence will motivate the $10 party to pay for prevention, the former party will neglect his own $20 option, and the desired result will be obtained. But by the same token, if the $10 party correctly predicts that comparative negligence will lead the $20 party to incur the safety expenditure, the $10 party will abstain. In this latter circumstance, duplication is avoided, but the more costly of the two 'independent' solutions results. Worse yet, each party may predict that comparative negligence will induce the other party to prevent; if so, neither will himself prevent, and the uneconomical risk will occur. . . .

Thus comparative negligence, although appropriate in situations in which complementary accident prevention is desirable, offers no assurance of the right result in those situations in which independent prevention is required. Of course, the law could adopt a two-level rule that applies *Galena* to independent-action cases while retaining comparative negligence for complementary-action cases. But it would be extremely difficult to make these characterizations after the accident and more vexing still to make them before the event, which is of course the relevant time if the rule is to achieve its purposes in influencing the actors' conduct.

In any event, several other problems afflict both *Galena* and comparative negligence and would remain even if the two rules could somehow be accommodated. In the $60/$25 hypothetical used to illustrate the *Galena* rule, assume that the opportunities to take preventive measures are sequential in time and that the $25 opportunity occurs first. If the plaintiff is the $25 preventer, the *Galena* rule would recognize his contributory negligence as a complete defense. But people often make mistakes, and the plaintiff may fail to incur the $25 expense. Once the plaintiff has so erred, the goal of efficiency suggests that liability be returned to the defendant; with the plaintiff's $25 opportunity squandered, the defendant's $60 measure is the best way to prevent the risk. This suggests a rule akin to the rule of last clear chance – one that would eliminate all effects of the plaintiff's contributory negligence. Now reverse the parties, so that the defendant's

$25 opportunity precedes the plaintiff's $60 opportunity; the idea can here be developed of last clear chance running against the plaintiff, thus reinstating his contributory negligence as a complete defense. With either of these last clear chance rules, however, the party with the earlier opportunity, knowing of the rule, might deliberately err so as to shift the safety expense to the party with the subsequent opportunity. Since the party acting first was assumed to have the lower safety costs, the possibility of such strategems perplexes the efficiency of the two-fold last clear chance rule. Moreover, in those situations in which complementary safety measures are most efficient and in which comparative negligence therefore has immediate appeal, there are related last clear chance issues that are equally complicated.

Additionally, if a two-fold last clear chance rule were adopted, there would be major difficulties in working out its elements. What fact would 'trigger' the rule: simply that the first party has squandered his opportunity, or instead that the second party knows (or has reason to know) of this squandering? What if the first party's error, although commencing early, is of a continuing nature – that is, it consists of inattentiveness that remains capable of being corrected at any moment before the accident? . . .

A further problem afflicting both *Galena* and comparative negligence concerns their implicit assumptions about each party's awareness of the other's prevention possibilities. Assuming a party who could purchase safety for $60, *Galena* would advise him to do so if, but only if, the other party's safety costs are greater than $60. This is advice on which the party can take action only if he has knowledge of what the other party's safety costs actually are. Under comparative negligence, what each party is intended to do similarly depends on his knowledge of the other party's prevention costs. Now in some situations, one party has or can easily obtain adequate knowledge of the other party's safety circumstances; but in other situations, this knowledge will be difficult or impossible to acquire. Lacking this knowledge, neither rule can give the parties the guidance they need if they are to make the balanced, efficient decisions that the rules expect. In the economists' terms, the safety arguments on behalf of both *Galena* and comparative negligence presupposes that the cost of obtaining a certain kind of information is very low. In fact, however, this information often will be quite costly to obtain and frequently will simply be unavailable in any practical sense.

What the previous analysis adds up to is this: in thinking about contributory negligence, the starting assumption is the negligence of the defendant – that is, that the defendant could efficiently have eliminated the risk. The point behind contributory negligence is that the plaintiff may have been an efficient risk preventer as well. This point is a relevant one, in the sense that insofar as the analysis has been accurate in its understanding of plaintiff conduct, negligence law without any contributory negligence defense would fail to achieve full efficiency. However, the effort to develop a defense that will take the plaintiff's conduct into account runs up against a wide range of serious theoretical and practical obstacles. Although the absence of any contributory negligence rule may be inefficient, the traditional rule of contributory negligence as a complete defense seems equally inefficient. And when their numerous complications are duly considered, intermediate rules like *Galena* and comparative negligence cannot necessarily be counted on to produce any net reduction in this inefficiency.

To be sure, none of these assessments establishes that a contributory negligence defense decreases efficiency; rather, they weaken the claim that such a defense produces positive results. When recognition is given to relevant complexities of the accident situation, an economic analysis of the contributory negligence issue is unable to yield any determinate formula.

Notes

1. The economic justification for the contributory negligence defence is that it provides an incentive to the plaintiff to take care where it is efficient for him or both parties to avoid the loss. Economists refer to the reduced incentives of those at risk to take self-protective and loss avoidance measures, because of the possibility of compensation, as 'moral hazard' (K. Arrow, 'Uncertainty and the Welfare Economics of Medical Care' (1963) 53 Am. Econ. Rev. 941; Shavell, infra, Section E). The absolute defence of contributory negligence controls moral hazard, although as Schwartz points out it sometimes does this imperfectly.

2. It is sometimes argued that comparative negligence, i.e. the English defence of contributory negligence which reduces damages according to the degree to which the plaintiff is at 'fault' (Law Reform (Contributory Negligence) Act 1945), is inefficient (Brown, op. cit., pp. 346–7; R. A. Posner, *Economic Analysis of Law* (2nd edn, 1977), pp. 123–4). But as Schwartz shows there are situations where the defence produces optimal results. (Also see W. M. Landes and R. A. Posner, 'Joint and Multiple Tortfeasors: An Economic Analysis' (1980) 9 J. Legal Stud. 517, 537–9).

D. Liability in Market Settings

BARON BRAMWELL

*

Letter to Sir Henry Jackson, Q.C.[7]

Those who propose to make a law, in truth propose to alter what exists, and should give a good reason for the change in all cases. But most certainly should they do so when the new law is proposed on account of some alleged hardship or anomaly in the old law.

This is the case in the proposed alteration of the law as to the liability of employers for negligence of a servant causing damage to a fellow-servant. It is said that the existing law is anomalous, and that it is an exception to the general rule that makes employers liable for the negligence of their servants, a grievance to workmen, and a grievance without justification. It is somehow supposed that, as a matter of natural right, something that exists in the nature of things, employers are liable for injuries occasioned by their servants' negligence, and that to except fellow-servants from this rule is unjust and unreasonable. . . .

There is, then, no general rule which makes one man liable for the negligence of another. The general rule is the other way. There are exceptions. The case of one servant injuring another is not within those exceptions nor the reason of them, but the contrary. It has been said that the servant contracts himself out of the right of compensation. It would be better to say he does not contract himself into it. He can if he and his master agree. Nay, he can stipulate for compensation where there is no negligence. He does not contract that his case shall be an exception to the general rule that a man is not liable for the acts of another. There is no injustice in this. There is in the proposition the other way. For no one can doubt that the dangers of an employment are taken into account in its wages. No one can doubt that the unpleasantness and risk of a miner's work add to his wages. Put sixpence out of his daily wage of five shillings as being on account of that risk – a sum which he may save or use as a premium of insurance. What is the proposal of those who would make the employer liable but this, that the servant shall keep the premium in his own pocket, and yet treat his master as the insurer? I do not believe that this is understood, or it would not be asked for; but it is the truth.

So much for the existing law, and so much for the reason of it. Now for the proposed change and the reason of it.

---

[7] (1880), reprinted in T. Beven, *The Law of Employers' Liability* (1881).

The largest proposed change is, that the master should be liable to his servant for the negligence of a fellow servant. . . . Why? Why if I have two servants, A. and B., and A. injures B. and B. injures A. by negligence, should I be liable to both when, if each had injured himself, I should not be to either? There can be but one reason for it – viz., that on the whole, looking at the interest of the public, the master, and the servants, it would be a better state of things than exists at present. Is that so? Now, we must start with this, that it is under the present law competent for a servant to stipulate with his master that the master shall be liable for the negligence of a fellow-servant, or in respect of any hurt or injury the servant may receive in the service. So that the difference in the law, if changed as proposed, would be this. At present the master is not liable, unless he agrees to be; on the change he would be, unless he and the servant agreed he should not be. For I suppose it is not intended to forbid the master and servant contracting themselves out of the law. That is to say, if a man prefers to take 5s. a day and no liability for accidents, rather than 4s. 6d., and the master prefers the former terms, it is not, as I understand, proposed to prevent their entering into a binding agreement to that effect. That would be a most mischievous interference with the freedom of contract, and would give rise to gross injustice and fraud on the master. I cannot suppose anything so outrageous, and proceed to consider what will follow if the liability is optional, but to exist where the parties have not agreed to the contrary. Every prudent employer of labour will immediately draw up a form to be signed by his workmen that the master shall not by liable for a fellow-servant's negligence. Or he will hire men somewhat on these terms: – '5s. a day, and no liability; 4s. 6d., and liability; and I will either compensate you myself, or apply the 6d. to an insurance for you.' I have put 6d., but I believe the difference of a farthing would make the men choose no liability. The present claim for liability, I repeat, arises from the workman not appreciating that he receives the premium now, yet would make the master the insurer.

The great employers of labour will understand the change in the law and guard against it. The mischief and wrong will be in the case of men who, not knowing of the change, will go on paying the wages which include the compensation for risk, the premium of insurance, and yet find they have to pay compensation when the risk happens, and that they are insurers though they have not received the premium.

What good, then, will the change do? The only thing I have ever heard suggested is, that it will make the master more careful in the choice of his servants. I suppose it would. For it would not have an opposite tendency. But is it just or reasonable that for this small good masters should be made liable to the extent intended? That, to prevent one accident through careless hiring of an incompetent fellow-workman, the master should pay a thousand compensations where he has done his best to get careful men? Is he not under sufficient inducements to be careful already? How rarely does an accident happen to the workman without mischief to the master, and without an appeal to his charity? Further, I ask, would the workman like that system which has prevailed in some employments, and to which the masters would be obliged to have recourse – viz., not employing a workman unless he produced a certificate of competency and fitness from his former employer? Still further, if some good would be done in this way, would there not be more mischief in another? Every one knows the recklessness bred by familiarity with danger. The man who would not open his lamp in a mine at first, will do so after a time. Another thing. It is a respectable feeling, though mistaken, which prevents servants doing what they call 'split' on each other, the consequence being that negligence, leading to danger, by one workman, is concealed from the master by the others. Now, I do not say that workmen will injure themselves for the sake of compensation; but I do say that whatever tends to lessen their reason for care and good conduct, as compensation would, tends to make them less careful in themselves and more disposed to conceal want of care in others.

I say, then, that the proposal to make the master liable to a servant for the negligence of a fellow-servant is contrary to principle, unjust, unreasonable, and calculated to produce, if not no good, at least more harm than good. . . .

R. N. McKEAN

*

Products Liability: Implications of some Changing Property Rights[8]

I shall attempt not to identify optimal policies, but simply to discuss some of the consequences of alternative products-liability arrangements. . . . These consequences will be mainly certain costs generated by the alternative arrangements – costs in terms of the price tags that are implicit in a predominantly voluntary exchange system and that would help direct one toward Pareto-optimal policies. . . .

[8] (1970) 84 Quart. J. Econ. 611, 616–24, with omissions. Reprinted by permission of the author and John Wiley & Sons, Inc.

CAVEAT EMPTOR

As a starter, what would be the consequences of complete caveat emptor – of having customers watch out for themselves and bear the losses that occur during the use of a product? As Coase has shown, that arrangement would lead to economic efficiency – to the production of safety features, caution in using products, and so on, by those parties having a comparative advantage in accident prevention – *if* there were zero transaction costs, and *if* people agreed to accept the results of voluntary exchanges. Purchasers of products would hire producers to include safety features and hire themselves to be careful as long as these actions paid. What about third parties who were injured? If owners of products were liable, they would modify their choices of products and hire bystanders to be careful as long as the gains out-weighed the costs. Bargaining would lead to economic efficiency in producing safety features, warnings, instructions to users, instructions to bystanders, caution in using products, caution in standing or walking nearby, and so on. . . .

Transaction costs, it might be noted, include the costs of negotiation, contracting, and enforcement, which therefore include the costs of acquiring information about the features of products and about contract violations. . . .

In actuality, of course, there are heavy transaction costs. Sometimes one may judge that alternative assignments of rights would bring roughly equivalent results, but often transaction costs vary markedly with different right assignments. With customer liability, however, note that *certain* transaction costs are in fact *comparatively* low. The costs of hiring producers to make safer products and issue warnings and instructions are relatively low, for the market is a mechanism through which customers are able to bid for safer products, instructions, and so on. If one is injured, financially or physically, by defective merchandise, he feels after the event that he has been at the mercy of producers and completely without influence on the design of products. . . . Nonetheless, as disappointments occur to thousands of customers, they turn to rival products or producers – unless upon reflection they prefer the lower price plus that risk to higher prices with reduced risks; and producers find it profitable to make a larger percentage of their products relatively safe, to issue instructions and warnings, to carry liability insurance, and to have broader warranties or more generous returned-goods policies. Hence, while disappointments and injuries never cease, users are able in the aggregate to register their preferences by turning to competitors and bidding more for the goods that they prefer. . . .

Customer liability would hold another kind of transaction cost in check: the cost of information about what degree of product safety in particular uses is economical. The buyer is in a better position than anyone else to know the exact use to which he plans to put a product and what alternative qualities, or degrees of safety, in the product would mean to his costs and gains. The customer, if he is liable, has an extra incentive to acquire and make appropriate use of information. To get the information, he must deal not with thousands of individuals, but with the seller and a few other identifiable persons. . . .

On the other hand, caveat emptor may keep other types of information cost comparatively high. The manufacturers do know more than anyone else about the nature of their products, and unless they probe and offer consumers numerous alternative amounts of information, customers may never know how much information they would be willing to pay for. This could be especially serious with enterprises that do not count heavily on repeat business and customer goodwill. With any arrangement, many resources will go into acquiring and providing information about products. At present, buyers utilize consumer reports, producer brochures, telephone enquiries, conversations with friends and salesmen, advertisements that convey information, engineers' and other experts' services, and directories and the Yellow Pages to help them find out where to make enquiries. But useful information about products is very costly. How difficult it is to inspect many modern products; how little one discovers about color TV sets or psychiatric treatment or new plumbing fixtures even after investigation. With high costs, potential buyers settle for relatively little information and either forego exchanges that might be mutually advantageous or accept risks that would be rejected – *if* information costs were lower. One may judge that overall costs – information, transaction, foregone-exchange, and accident costs – could be reduced by directing government, or inducing producers, to provide additional information.

The amount of information that it is economical to generate and the costs of generating information will be different for different products. For example, producers surely provide all the information that customers are willing to pay for in the case of simple familiar products like ordinary tools and supplies. When one considers new, changing, or complex products like new drugs or power tools, however, it may take years of transactions before customers can determine what kind of extra information can be offered and how much various amounts will cost. For complex secondhand items, great effort to gather information will still leave enormous uncertainty. Information about items that one does not buy frequently – e.g., swimming pools, gas furnaces, specialized medical-care equipment, food at unknown restaurants, a house in an unfamiliar city – is also comparatively expensive per unit of the product purchased. . . . Thus different treatment, e.g., liability assignments, for different product categories (such as 'ultrahazardous' or 'highly complex' products) may make sense even though it might be foolish in some ideal world with zero transaction costs.

Caveat emptor would also keep another transaction cost relatively low — that of hiring the users to be careful in employing the product. For the user is most frequently the buyer of the product or an acquaintance or a member of his family. Thus if he is liable for losses, he has to obtain the cooperation not of thousands of strangers, but of himself and a few individuals with whom he has direct personal contact, in seeing that an appropriate degree of care is exercised. This does not mean that he will be as careful as it is humanly possible to be; it merely means that he will choose by weighing the costs of extra care, such as loss of time, against the gains, such as the reduced risk of suffering uncompensated losses or injuries. . . .

PRODUCER LIABILITY WITH DEFECT

What are the consequences of moving further toward producer liability? . . . In my judgment the effects would not have great quantitative significance but would be along the following lines. I would expect more court cases and court costs, since under complete customer liability, the product owner is not compensated, and there is no court determination of the extent of injury. The presence of defects, or the existence of negligence. There would now be higher costs of hiring purchasers to exercise care, for this would now require myriad special contracts with prohibitive enforcement costs, and those higher transaction costs would result in the existence of more externalities, i.e., accident rates would rise. Producers would turn increasingly to liability insurance, and since it would not be economical to adjust the premiums continuously or precisely, producers might, up to certain thresholds, find it efficient to neglect safety features . . . diluting the shift toward safer products that is noted below.

With the customer facing a lower probability of being liable, relatively hazardous designs would be less unattractive to him, and the demand . . . for such products would rise relative to the demand . . . for comparatively safe products. With the producer facing a higher probability of being liable and with his either carrying liability insurance or paying damages, relatively hazardous designs would be more costly. . . . On the basis of this shift in liability assignment by itself, there is no presumption that the quantity of hazardous products sold would change, and while the consumer would pay a higher price to the producer, he would simply be forced to buy insurance from the producer instead of having the option of insuring himself. The only thing that would happen to the consumer's position is that he would be denied the opportunity of taking the risk. Since that option would be preferred by some consumers, especially by the poor, this would mean in effect a rise in the price of hazardous products relative to the price of 'safe' products, resulting in the end in some shift toward safer products and working to the detriment of the poor.

The shift in liability assignment would decrease efficiency, however, if there were a net increase in transaction costs . . ., resulting in higher prices for hazardous relative to safer products and in a net shift from hazardous to safer products.

PRODUCER LIABILITY WITHOUT DEFECT

Let us turn now to a rather extreme arrangement that has been mentioned in recent years – producer liability *without fault or defect*. The manufacturer would simply be held liable for all injuries occurring with the use of his product, regardless of circumstances. As in the other cases, if there were zero transaction costs . . . resource use would end up at an efficient point. With transaction costs, however, manufacturer liability without fault or defect would alter resource allocation, and, unless the transactions costs could be measured, it would be uncertain which liability assignment would lead to an efficient point.

I conjecture that costs would be affected in the following ways and that the changes would be important quantitatively. The cost of hiring thousands of purchasers or third parties to exercise care would be enormous, and therefore these persons would now find it relatively inexpensive to be careless. Accident rates would rise. Insurance premiums would become high except on relatively safe products, increasing the net price of hazardous products relative to the price of safe products. As in the preceding case, there would be a shift away from the comparatively hazardous product lines toward the safer products. The net impact on accident costs is not clear, but total costs would rise, because accident prevention would not be produced by those having a comparative advantage in doing so. Court costs per case would decline in comparison with the fault system, but the number of claims would rise; and, unlike the case of caveat emptor, disputes and court costs would not be nil, because even if fault did not have to be established, the fact and extent of injury would have to be determined. . . . Consumers would face a narrower range of choice – a significant sacrifice, but one that is impossible to quantify in any generally valid fashion. As far as this particular sacrifice is concerned, poor people would be hardest hit, because their options would now be to buy relatively expensive safe products, or hazardous products plus high producer-insurance costs, or nothing at all.

The higher accident prevention costs would be borne largely by the customers and potential customers in each industry in the form of higher prices and restricted choice. . . . Some of the burden might be passed on to customers in other industries, as people shifted their purchases, and input rents might be reshuffled somewhat.

Notes

1. In perfect labour and product markets liability rule changes do not affect the accident rate (or costs) or the distribution of wealth. When there is no liability the market price/wage will adjust to reflect the risks faced by potential victims. If the law imposes the loss on the firm the market price will adjust, so that price plus damages equals price without liability. Bargaining between workers or consumers and the firm will ensure the optimal level of safety and compensation of each group is unaffected. Of course changes in liability rules will affect the post-injury wealth of individuals vis-à-vis those who are not injured. For formal analyses, see H. Demsetz, 'Wealth Distribution and the Ownership of Rights' (1972) 1 J. Legal Stud. 223; K. Hamada, 'Liability Rules and Income Distribution in Product Liability' (1976) 66 Am. Econ. Rev. 228.

2. Bramwell's assertion that wage rates reflect accident and health risks has been much disputed. J. S. Mill (*Principles of Political Economy* (ed. Ashley, 1848), p. 388) attacked the proposition as 'an altogether false view of the facts'. It is only recently that empirical research has been undertaken to test the proposition. These studies provide some support for the theory. See R. S. Smith, 'Compensating Wage Differentials and Public Policy' (1979) 32 Indus. and Lab. Relations Rev. 339; L. Needleman, 'The Valuation of Changes in the Risk of Death by Those at Risk' (1980) 44 Manchester School 229; A. Marin and G. Psacharopolous, 'The Reward for Risk in the Labour Market: Evidence from the United Kingdom and a Reconciliation with Other Studies' (1982) 80 J. Pol. Econ. 827.

3. In practice, liability rules do affect safety levels and the distribution of wealth because of transaction costs. The major friction is information costs, resulting from the ignorance of workers, consumers and firms regarding risks and prospective losses. (G. Akerlof, 'The Market for Lemons: Qualitative Uncertainty and the Market Mechanisms' (1970) 84 Quart. J. Econ. 488; Beales *et al.* infra, Chapter 7, Section D; C. G. Veljanovski, 'The Employment and Safety Effects of Employers' Liability' (1982) 29 Scot. J. Pol. Econ. 256.) As McKean emphasizes, liability rules can economize on different transaction cost factors. See, generally, 'Symposium on Products Liability: Economic Analysis and the Law' (1970) 38 U. Chi. L.R. 1.

4. McKean's conclusion that caveat venditor increases the price of risky products and denies consumers the opportunity to buy unsafe, but cheaper, goods has been challenged. It has been shown (W. Y. Oi, 'The Economics of

Product Safety' (1973) 4 Bell J. Econ. 3; and 'A Rejoinder' (1974) 5 Bell J. Econ. 689) that there is no necessary reason why caveat venditor should raise the *full* price (actual price plus imputed expected losses) of a risky product to individual consumers or reduce the output of risky products. The eventual outcome depends on the relationship between average compensation payments which determine price and production decisions under caveat venditor and the expected losses to the marginal consumer under caveat emptor. If average expected compensation is less than the expected losses to the marginal consumer a change to caveat venditor will lower the full price of the risky good. See also G. Calabresi and K. C. Bass 'Right Approach, Wrong Implications: A Critique of McKean on Products Liability' (1970) 38 U. Chi. L.R. 74.

5. In principle, impact studies of product and employers' liability are feasible because of the availability of market data. Theory indicates, however, that the allocative effects of changes in the law in this area will tend to be minimized by the ability of those affected to contract around the law. Even when this is prohibited, such as in U.K. where contracts excluding liability in negligence for personal injury are generally unenforceable (Unfair Contract Terms Act 1977, s. 2) market adjustments (such as changes in price levels) in the long run will partially offset the cost reallocation of a change in liability rule. The few empirical studies to date have yielded equivocal results: R. S. Chelius, 'Liability for Industrial Accidents: A Comparison of Negligence and Strict Liability' (1976) 5 J. Legal Stud. 293; R. S. Higgins, 'Producers' Liability and Product-Related Accidents' (1978) J. Legal Stud. 299.

E. Losses

S. SHAVELL

*

Theoretical Issues in Medical Malpractice[9]

A GUIDE TO OPTIMAL COMPENSATION

Whether publicly or privately provided, compensation for a medical accident ought to reflect the insurance coverage against the accident that a rational, well-informed individual with a socially acceptable level of income would have bought. That is, the determination of optimal compensation ought to reflect a hypothetical decision about the purchase of insurance. This point of view certainly does not imply

---

[9] From S. Rottenberg (ed.), *The Economics of Medical Malpractice* (1978), pp. 35–64, with omissions. Copyright © 1978 by the American Enterprise Institute. Used by permission.

that actual compensation should necessarily be left up to individuals and their insurance companies. As . . . stressed below, individuals may not make well-informed decisions about insurance (or may not have socially appropriate incomes).

In the next several subsections, aspects of the insurance purchase decision when made under perfect market conditions are considered. Then characteristics of the decision when made under more realistic circumstances are discussed.

OPTIMAL INSURANCE COVERAGE VERSUS COMPENSATION FOR ECONOMIC LOSSES VERSUS COMPENSATION TO MAKE A PERSON WHOLE

When buying insurance, an individual considers the cost of coverage, the likelihood of an accident, and – what is of particular importance here – the utility he would derive from income if he did not have an accident as compared to the utility he would derive from income if he did have an accident.

Two examples make it clear that the level of coverage which an individual would select does not necessarily correspond to either of two perhaps appealing notions of optimal compensation: (1) the amount of purely economic damages, that is, forgone earnings plus costs of remedial treatment, and (2) the amount required to make a person whole, to restore him to his initial level of well-being, supposing that this were possible. Consider first an individual's decision to buy protection against a permanently disabling medical accident. Assume that the (discounted) costs of treatment, chronic care, and therapy would be $200,000 and that of forgone earnings, another $200,000; assume further than an additional $100,000 would fully compensate pain and suffering. Finally, suppose that the individual has no dependants. In fact, this individual might buy, say, only $275,000 coverage, for money might have very little use to him when disabled yet be very valuable in his current state. In this case, therefore, optimal insurance coverage would not equal the economic damages, much less make the individual whole.

Now consider an individual who is about to buy coverage against the event that his appendix will have to be surgically removed. Assume that the sum of lost wages and medical expenses would be $2,000 and that $1,000 more for pain and suffering would be adequate to make him as well-off as before the contemplated event. If insurance is sold on an actuarially fair basis, this individual might buy only $2,000 coverage because, while he knows that surgery would be unpleasant and could be fully redressed by receipt of an additional $1,000, it may be that the utility he would derive from having the extra $1,000 after surgery is not sufficient to make his paying a higher premium worthwhile. (Equivalently, his need for money after surgery and after the $2,000 compensation for economic losses might be no different from what it had been beforehand.) In this instance, optimal insurance coverage would equal economic damages but fall short of making the individual whole.

In general, optimal insurance coverage would fail to make an individual whole when the marginal utility of income (net of payment of the insurance premium) if he does not have an accident exceeds the marginal utility of income (at the level which would make him whole) if he does have an accident. One guesses investigation would reveal that for most individuals and most accidents, optimal insurance coverage would not be sufficient to make a person whole and would in fact provide little or no benefits beyond the purely economic; furthermore, for accidents which do not involve permanent disability, optimal insurance coverage would probably equal economic losses . . . Of course, in theory almost any amount of insurance coverage could turn out to be optimal.

OBSTACLES TO COMPENSATION

Administrative costs are an obstacle to compensation which would be faced even under perfect market conditions. Two types of administrative costs are noted here . . . The first are fixed costs: the costs of adding an individual's name to the list of insureds and the costs of collecting premiums. It is easy to show that given fixed costs, if it is optimal to purchase any coverage at all, it will be optimal to purchase full coverage (for once one has decided to purchase positive coverage and the fixed costs therefore have to be paid, additional coverage is purchased on actuarially fair terms – in which case full coverage is appropriate). But it will be optimal to purchase coverage only if potential losses are sufficiently high or if they are sufficiently uncertain. The second type of administrative cost is that of processing claims and of making payments. Given this type of cost, the optimal insurance policy is either full coverage against all losses or a kind of deductible (the use of deductibles reduces the number of claims), according to which approximately full coverage is paid if any coverage at all is paid.
. . .

Several well-known obstacles to compensation which arise under less than perfect market conditions need to be mentioned. It will become obvious that these obstacles are due in one way or another to lack of information. The first obstacle, called the *moral hazard*, is the tendency of insurance to reduce the incentive of the insured to avoid losses.

Two types of moral hazard are of potential interest. One is exemplified by the case of a person with insurance who takes less care to avoid a loss than an uninsured counterpart. This happens because the insurer is unable to observe costlessly how careful the insured person is; otherwise the insurer would certainly make the premium or the insurance payment depend on the level of care, thereby giving the insured an incentive to be careful. Insurers have partially offset this kind of moral hazard by spending to acquire information about the level of care or by using deductible and coinsurance schemes. Both practices give the insured an incentive to be careful.

In theory, this type of moral hazard . . . [makes] cause [relevant] to compensation for a medical accident. Suppose that an accident (paralysis) may occur in either of two ways (disease, surgical error). Suppose further that if it occurs in the first way, it is possible that the injured individual may have played a contributory role (failed to seek medical attention when symptoms first appeared). Then, because of the moral hazard, deductibles or coinsurance may be desirable. (Alternatively, the insurer may choose to offset the moral hazard by acquiring information about the level of care and then conditioning the premium or insurance payment on the observation of care; in this case if the information was imperfect, partial coverage would still be desirable.) Optimal compensation, therefore, may be less if the accident occurs in the first way than if it occurs in the second way. . . .

The other type of moral hazard is exemplified by the case of a person with health insurance who (together with his physician) spends more on treatment of a given medical condition than an uninsured individual with a similar condition. This happens because the insurer is unable to observe perfectly the true medical condition; otherwise the insurer would link the premium or the payment to the actual condition. Insurers have attempted to offset this kind of moral hazard in ways similar to those mentioned above.

A second obstacle to compensation is that it may be difficult or impossible for the insurer to distinguish between individuals as to risk. In this circumstance both relatively low- and relatively high-risk individuals have to pay equally for equal amounts of coverage. If risks are pooled, then, the usual consequence is that low-risk individuals pay too much and buy too little insurance (as compared to the optimum under perfect market conditions), while high-risk individuals pay too little and buy too much.

A third obstacle to compensation is that an individual's perception of the risk he faces may be inaccurate. If he overestimates the risk, his purchase of coverage will be too great, while if he underestimates the risk, his coverage will be too small. (A closely related difficulty is that, because an individual may find it distressing to contemplate the possibility of a medical accident, he may buy on an 'irrational' basis.)

This problem may be remedied in several ways by the public sector; the motive and scope for action by private insurers seems limited. On the one hand, individuals can be educated to the true nature of the risk, but this may be very expensive and only partially attainable. Whatever the value of such education, the private sector is unlikely to invest in it sufficiently. An individual insurance firm would find it difficult to appropriate the benefits of its investment, for a better informed customer could just as well buy from the firm's competitors. Although a collective effort on the part of private insurers to inform the public of risks (at least of higher risks) might be worthwhile, such an effort could be hampered by the problem of 'free riders'.

Rather than attempting to educate individuals to the truth, the public sector can provide compensation on a compulsory basis or subsidize the purchase of insurance. (The case considered here is that individuals purchase too little insurance. If they bought too much, the consequences would be less serious; in any event, in this case a tax would be appropriate.) Compulsory protection alone may fail to individualize adequately compensation; and, ideally, compensation ought to be individualized, especially with respect to differences in forgone earnings associated with differences in income earning capacity. However, there are two reasons why compulsory protection may fail to or, as a practical matter, ought not to individualize compensation. First, it may be difficult to determine a good approximation to optimal coverage on an individual basis. Second, it may be difficult to arrange to individualize payments (implicit premiums) to finance the compulsory compensation system; and if payments are not individualized, benefits should not be individualized. Court awards in malpractice cases are financed by physicians and, therefore, ultimately by patients. But the extent to which physicians usually charge patients higher fees when the latter would have wished for greater insurance coverage is unclear.

Subsidization alone would probably help to individualize compensation but still fail to induce individuals – particularly those who were overly optimistic about risk or financially constrained – to purchase correct coverage. Therefore, a compromise between compulsory and subsidized insurance seems attractive.

COURT AWARDS AND INSURANCE PURCHASES AS INDICATORS OF OPTIMAL COMPENSATION

To determine optimal compensation, it is unlikely that one should look to actual court awards. These awards, made after the fact, are apparently often based on the doctrine of making a person whole, a doctrine which, as we have seen, is not justifiable by economic theory. The awards may occasionally be based on payment of economic losses alone, another faulty criterion. Moreover, particularly in cases of malpractice, there is the suspicion that awards may sometimes be inflated to punish the physician or to ensure that the plaintiff is left with his rightful share after deduction of lawyers' fees. . . .

Neither is it clear that the record of actual insurance purchases would furnish the right information. As mentioned above, if individuals misperceive the risks of adverse medical events or if they find the act of insuring against these risks psychologically burdensome, they will not purchase the correct amount of coverage. In addition, if premiums exceed by a large amount actuarial costs (through lack of competition or inordinately high acquisition costs), individuals will not purchase the correct amount of coverage.

SUMMARY

(1) Compensation (the sum of accident benefits from all sources) for a medical accident ought to reflect the amount of insurance coverage an individual (with a socially appropriate income) would have bought against the accident if he were acting rationally and were cognizant of the relevant risks.

(2) Optimal insurance coverage may exclude attributions to pain and suffering and may fail to restore economic losses (costs of treatment plus forgone earnings).

(3) Furthermore, optimal insurance coverage ordinarily depends only on the circumstances of an injured individual. Causal factors such as iatrogenicity or physician negligence are irrelevant to optimal coverage.

(4) There are four major obstacles to compensation: administrative costs, moral hazard (reduced incentive for insureds to avoid loss), pooling of unequal risks, and misperception of risks.

(5) Misperception of risks can be remedied in several ways (education, compulsory or subsidized insurance) by the public sector. The motive and scope for action by private insurers in this regard seems limited.

(6) Neither court awards not the actual record of individual insurance purchases may be good indicators of optimal compensation.

W. D. BISHOP

*

Economic Loss in Tort[10]

The law of torts severely restricts recovery by a plaintiff for financial losses suffered in consequence of the negligent conduct of the defendant. . . . The existing literature does not provide a comprehensive theory to justify the common law restriction of liability for financial loss. The purpose of this paper is to provide one. The theory sketched below will suggest that one important aim of such restrictions is to achieve economic efficiency, or optimal deterrence as it is sometimes called. The combined aims of optimal deterrence and efficient risk distribution will suggest criteria to guide courts in formulating rules for borderline cases.

(A) THE MAIN IDEA

The principal theoretical idea used here is this. In a range of cases private economic loss caused by a tortious act is not a cost to society. Therefore the exclusion of economic loss from the liability which tortfeasors bear will be efficient in such cases . . .

Two examples will help to clarify the main idea. They are based on a railway accident that happened in Canada in November 1979.

Example 1: Imagine two contiguous towns called Mississauga and Etobicoke. A railway runs through them. The railway company is considering installing special equipment to minimize the danger of derailments of trains carrying dangerous chemicals. For simplicity assume that there is no danger to life if people are evacuated in time. Then the main direct effect of any derailment is to induce mass evacuation from the town in which it occurs to the other town, for about a week. The cost of this equipment is $10 million. It has a ten year life. The cost to residents of evacuation is $4 million. About one derailment per decade will be prevented by the equipment. If these were the only relevant costs we would not want the railway to install the equipment. It costs more than it saves.

Now suppose each town is served by a butcher, a baker, a candlestick maker and numerous other tradesmen and merchants. Each businessman has a normal weekly volume of trade. Suppose further, and this is crucial, each can accommodate more than his normal

[10] (1982) 2 Oxford J. Legal Stud. 1, 1–13, with omissions. Reprinted by permission of Oxford University Press.

volume of trade, for a short time at least, at no extra cost beyond cost of raw materials. Assume initially that each businessman is risk neutral.

The effect on businessmen of any derailment and evacuation in Mississauga is this. The Mississauga businessmen make no sales for a week and at the end of the year find their bank balances smaller than they might otherwise have been. The Etobicoke businessmen double sales for a week and have larger bank balances at the end of the year. The effect of the derailment in this respect is to transfer wealth from one set of people to another.

Suppose the Mississauga businessmen have a right of action to recover 'pure economic loss'. They suffer loss (accounting) profits of $8 million during the week. If the railway must pay out this sum as well as direct losses to residents it faces total expected derailment costs of $12 million. This sum is greater than the cost ($10 million) of the special equipment. So the railway will decide to install the equipment. But this would be the wrong decision from the society's point of view. Social welfare calculation still reveals a net loss of only $4 million not $12 million. The $8 million economic loss is not a social cost but rather a transfer payment. It is a loss to one group but a gain to another group.

Example 2: The facts are identical to *Example* 1, except that businessmen cannot easily expand services for a short time to accommodate an upsurge in demand. Each Etobicoke butcher, baker, candlestick maker, must hire extra help who will undertake the work only if paid for the trouble. Further, existing staff are annoyed and overworked and demand extra pay for their trouble. Prices for meat, bread and candlesticks rise for all consumers, both for those who normally buy in Etobicoke as well as for the refugees from Mississauga.

These facts describe a rise in the real costs of production in the short run. . . .

On these facts, 'economic loss' to Mississauga business is *not* merely a transfer to those in Etobicoke. The Etobicoke businessmen incur higher real social costs. Further, some consumers are not now served, because prices have risen too high for them to buy. Their losses are real social costs insofar as the price rise pays for the Etobicoke businessmen's extra costs. Any extra profit to Etobicoke businessmen is only a transfer payment to them. The exact sum of real social loss from the accident depends on the facts . . .

Numerous plausible stories could be told about the Mississauga railway accident. For example if Etobicoke consumers have inventories of goods they may react to the arrival of refugees not by buying more but by running down inventories. Then these are built up gradually after the refugees have gone home. Here there is no sudden sharp rise in demand and the likelihood of cost increases in Etobicoke so much the less.

In Mississauga many firms may find that the lost work compensated for by higher sales in later weeks. This typically will be so for durable goods (e.g. radios) or some services. Here purchase often simply will be delayed rather than lost.

It might be objected on theoretical grounds that the losses to Mississauga businessmen must be real costs. It might be said that if purchases can be accommodated costlessly in Etobicoke then we have no explanation for why the firms exist in Mississauga in the first place. But this argument ignores the $4 million compensation paid to the Mississauga refugees. This is enough to leave them as well off as if they had stayed at home. Any payment to third parties whose market falls in consequence will be a case of *double counting* so long as business costs are not raised in Etobicoke. . . .

(B) RISK AND PORTFOLIO DIVERSIFICATION

The foregoing examples assume that businessmen are risk neutral. That is, they assume that an average weekly income stream is valued equally regardless whether it is a steady stream of (say) $1,000 per week or a variable stream averaging $1,000, but occasionally totalling (say) $2,000 or $0. If businessmen are risk averse then an income variability is a real cost. The sum which correctly measures the social cost is the sum an investor in the butchery business would pay to have the constant stream rather than the variable one, that is, the insurance premium he would pay. For the figures cited above this premium will necessarily be no larger than $1,000 – the maximum deviation below the average. For sums larger than $1,000 the investor simply puts the money in the bank to await the rainy day. . . .

In sum in assessing the value of a less risky over a more risky world we must count forfeiture of unexpected gains as well as compensation for unexpected losses. A world in which accidents occur that cause financial losses is a more risky world. Since men are commonly risk averse it is a more costly world. But the extra cost is at most a fraction, and likely a small fraction, of the sum total of economic loss suffered. . . .

(C) SELF INSURANCE

Next consider a variation on the facts in *Example* 1. Extra demand is accommodated costlessly so that the only cost induced by the tort is increased risk. Suppose that there are two butchers and two bakers in each town. One of each is independent. The other is owned by a chain.

Call the chain Loblaws. If we allow recovery to the independent for lost profit, should we allow recovery to Loblaws as well? That would be very strange since Loblaws has suffered no private loss at all. It merely records in one week larger sales than usual in Etobicoke and smaller sales than usual in Mississauga. In effect, Loblaws is a self-insurer against this type of loss.

If there are only independent butchers then, since risks are for them real costs, part of the loss suffered prima facie should be included. If there are only chain butchers then no part of such loss is a real social cost and prima facie none should be included. But, which rule should be adopted if there are both chain and independent butchers? Here the criterion of 'least cost avoider' or 'efficient risk bearer' as between injurer and victim does not yield a unique result. Awarding such damages to one and not the other would affect incentives in retailing. In effect, it could operate as a subsidy to small-scale distribution. At the margin it would lead to some inefficient retailing patterns. The possibility of efficient self-insurers is one more reason for caution in awarding damages for economic loss.

(D) MALLEABLE AND MOBILE CAPITAL

Suppose next that butchers and bakers have opportunities to avoid losses arising from accidents. They can invest in plant and equipment which can be converted temporarily to some other use when the regular market fails – for example, sharpening tools (for butchers) or baking pies for the frozen food market (for bakers). If such action can be taken in the case of all types of equipment then it is covered in the present law by the requirement of reasonable mitigation. But if this course is open only to some bakers or butchers, those with appropriate equipment, it is not so covered. If no compensation is offered for economic loss, then each butcher or baker, acting in isolation, has an incentive to make the appropriate investment. But if compensation is offered this incentive is absent. Such capital switching if it can be invested in cheaply enough, will be advantageous to society. In the long run, it will reduce to a socially optimal level the total capital needed by society to produce sharp tools, pies, baked goods and meat cutting.

If all capital were perfectly and instantly malleable and mobile, then there would never be any case for awarding lost profit. Or more precisely, there would be no lost profit arising from idle resources. All capital is not malleable and cannot cheaply be made so. But refusal to award economic loss gives the right incentives for firms to undertake such efficient investments as can potentially be made.

(E) MARGINAL AVOIDANCE AND SECOND BEST

However, efficient capital switching may not be the only avoidance possibility open to the firm. To examine possible inefficient avoidance another example is required. ...

Example 3: Martin Construction Ltd negligently cuts a power cable to Spartan Steel's plant. The plant is put out of production for a few days. The lost orders go to Athenian Steel and other firms which can fill the demand easily. Suppose Spartan can take avoidance action (burying a cable deeply in the ground or installing a stand-by generator) for $50. It expects lost profit of $70 (accounting profit, not economic profit). Martin Construction could avoid the accident by spending $30 on extra care.

On these facts, Spartan's private loss is not a social loss but only a transfer to Athenian. Viewed only as a matter of efficiency nothing should be spent on avoidance by anyone and the accident should occur. But on these facts, Spartan has an incentive to spend $50 on avoidance. By doing so, Spartan can avoid private loss to itself. If Spartan could negotiate cheaply with Athenian they would reach an agreement that Spartan would not avoid and Athenian would compensate Spartan $50 or more for its loss out of Athenian's gains of $70. Assume such negotiations are infeasible.

In these circumstances, Spartan will spend $50. This is not only socially inefficient, it is also even more costly than imposing liability on Martin Construction. The possible outcomes can be ranked as follows:

First best – Injurer non-avoidance + Victim non-avoidance
Second best – Injurer avoidance + Victim non-avoidance
Third best – Injurer non-avoidance + Victim avoidance

The 'first best' may be unattainable *where the victim has possibilities for accident avoidance.* In these circumstances, there is an argument for imposing liability for economic loss on the tortfeasor if he has less costly avoidance opportunities. As with the factors which tell in the opposite direction, the cogency of the argument in any particular case depends upon the facts of the particular case, the facts of avoidance possibilities. ...

(F) EACH-WAY LIABILITY RULES AND INSURANCE

So far, attention has been confined to simple liability rules of the sort ordinarily found in legal systems. Now, consider a system which allows more extensive liability rules. Imagine a court which could find costlessly the facts about gains and losses from any accident. This court could then make a tortfeasor liable for losses he causes, but also give him restitution for the fortuitous gains his actions confer on others. . . . Such a system of liability for losses and rights of restitution for gains would preserve correct incentives. Notice that under such a system there would be no incentive for a potential tort victim to take the inefficient avoidance action discussed in the previous section.

In practice, such systems are far too costly to be used. However, the same effect can be achieved by means of insurance. A potential victim who purchases business interruption insurance will, in effect, receive a retransfer of benefits from those who benefit from accidents – if we assume that over time all firms will derive some benefit from some accidents which affect other firms. Where a tort causing economic loss merely shifts income but causes no net social loss then insurance by victims has the important property of *preserving correct incentives to potential tortfeasors.* . . .

(G) RENTS AND LEISURE

Return to *Example* 2 and add the following facts. Jack and Jill work in Mississauga, Jack in the bakery and Jill in the candlestick shop. They are evacuated to Etobicoke. They are compensated for the expense and upset of the move. Jack takes a job in Etobicoke during the week of evacuation. The temporary job pays the same wage but Jack misses his old surroundings and workmates. Jill does not take a temporary job. She very much enjoys her week off despite the lost wages, and she uses the time to knit and to read *War and Peace*.

Jack was earning a rent in his Mississauga job. Rent may be defined as the difference between what a factor earns in its current occupation and the minimum sum its owner would accept to keep it there. Jack would pay something to keep his old job despite the fact that the money wages are equal between it and the new one. This lost rent is a real cost to Jack and to society. It should enter into the cost benefit analysis of people who decide about accident avoidance expenditure.

Conversely Jill loses her full money wage, but has gained leisure. This leisure is valuable. If the tortplanner has to pay this as compensation then he will over-estimate the social cost of an accident and spend too much on avoidance. The cost should include only the difference between Jill's wage and the sum she would accept if offered a week off without wages or work.

(H) PROPERTY RIGHTS PROTECTION: INVESTMENT IN NON-MOBILE CAPITAL

In a world in which tort victims cannot recover for economic loss, that is for frustrated expectations, investors will adjust their behaviour to accord with this legal rule. For example an hotel might be destroyed by fire and might take a year to rebuild. In the meantime profits (quasi rents) are lost. If these profits cannot be recovered in damages then the investor contemplating building an hotel will assess the likelihood of fire and adjust his valuation of the project downward by the expected value of the lost profits. Unless liable, a potential tortfeasor will not include these losses when deciding on his avoidance expenditures.

The analysis above suggested that when losses to the victim are offset by gains to another person then there is no social loss. That proposition was a little too simple. It implicitly assumed either that the levels of investment of potential victims are fixed and so not affected by the recovery rule, or that risk neutral investors would be unaffected by non-recovery because they do not know at the time of investing whether they will be gainers or losers (Athenians or Spartans in the example given). However, it may be that in some cases encountered in the real world neither of these assumptions applies. The first assumption will be appropriate only if accidents are unanticipated or if all investments are 'lumpy', so that there are no alterations at the margin. The second assumption will often be appropriate, but by no means always. Some investments are highly specific to one use and do not benefit from offsetting gains when accidents occur disabling other people's plant. Here property rights might require protection. . . .

(I) DAMAGES FOR PARASITIC ECONOMIC LOSS

The availability of a legal remedy in economic loss cases often turns on whether the loss was suffered by one who also suffered property damage. In particular if the property is that of one person while the financial loss is that of his contractual partner, the courts refuse to consider the interest as one attracting protection. The fact of a property connection in the *legal* sense is in itself arbitrary. . . .

. . . [O]rganizing production by contract or organizing it within a firm (in which case the damage will be suffered by the property owner at law) are often merely two modes of doing the same thing. Each has costs and these costs determine whether some associated activity will be undertaken by the main enterprise or by a contractual partner. When these relative costs change we observe vertical integration or divestiture in industries. The juristic concepts of contract and property ought not to blind us to the real economic relationships. Rigid rules which make recovery depend on the suffering of physical damage to property tend to increase the private costs of contractually organized production relative to intra firm organization. Since there is no underlying social cost difference this tends to bias incentives away from the optimum.

In a world in which courts could fine tune the law to give perfect guidance to investors and others, there would be no merit in a distinction at law between economic loss consequent on physical damage to the victim (parasitic economic loss) and economic loss consequent on damage to a third party (pure economic loss). However, in our world, in which adjudication is costly and very imperfect and in which guidance to tort planners can be at most rough and approximate, there may be some merit in this otherwise quite arbitrary distinction.

First consider the problem of disincentive to investment where economic loss is probable. It may be that there is a systematic correlation between parasitic economic loss and the need to avoid distortion of investment. Certainly . . . potentially large income variation consequent on serious physical damage is much less likely to be ignored by investors in making decisions either about valuation of the investment or about victim avoidance – it is more likely to make a difference at the margin.

Second the general analysis suggested that social cost usually will be some fraction (possibly a large fraction) of private loss, so in general one wants tort planners to face some part, but not all, of private losses. One way to do this is to have courts select only some victims for compensation. They could use physical damage as a rough, even arbitrary, device to select some portion of the victims for compensation.

Third, in practice there normally will be numerous financial gainers and losers from any accident. Courts would not find it easy to discriminate between genuine claims and bogus ones. They could use physical injury as a screening device to sort out good claims from bad. It is very rough – but may be adjudication cost-effective.

The present tort rules allow recovery for financial losses suffered in consequence of damage to an income earning property or chattel. For example if an hotel is destroyed by fire the owner will recover for the profits lost during the period of reconstruction. If a ship is sunk the owner will recover either directly or indirectly for loss of the stream of expected profits from future operation of the ship. In a competitive market this expected profit stream will equal the market value of the ship, which is the normal measure of damages. Such results seem on balance appropriate. When potential investment distortions are large, avoiding them will be the dominant policy consideration, even where there are some off-setting gains to third parties.

(J) SOME TENTATIVE CONCLUSIONS

It is time to draw some tentative conclusions from this theoretical inquiry. The private cost of an accident as seen by plaintiffs need not correspond to the social cost and, in general, it will not. But what exactly is the social cost of an accident is a very complex matter. The answer depends upon innumerable particular facts of interacting markets. Further, there are many complex incentive effects of liability or non-liability that any decision-maker needs to know before he can decide whether imposing liability is efficient or not.

Notes

1. As Shavell shows, the economic measure of damages does not necessarily imply 'full' compensation even for financial loss (cf. R. A. Posner, *Economic Analysis of Law* (2nd edn, 1977), pp. 142–52). In the case of death, legal and economic measures diverge radically. The courts' award of damages is based on the loss to survivors which bears little relationship to the willingness-to-pay measure required for allocative efficiency (E. J. Mishan, 'Evaluation of Life and Limb: A Theoretical Approach' (1971) 79 J. Pol. Econ. 687; M. J. Bailey, *Reducing Risks to Life – Measurement of the Benefits* (1980)). Recent empirical research suggests that the willingness-to-pay measure exceeds gross discounted earnings by between 2 to 10 times (G. Blomquist, 'The Value of Life: An Empirical Perspective' (1981) 19 Econ. Inquiry 197). Hence damages in tort systematically undervalue life and diminish the incentive of potential tortfeasors to reduce death risks.

2. Economists can assist lawyers in calculating legal measures of damages when there is a need to take into account inflation and future earnings, discounting and other offsets: N. K. Komesar, 'Toward a General Theory of Personal Injury Loss' (1973) 2 J. Leg. Stud. 457; S. A. Rea 'Inflation, Taxation and Damage Assessment' (1980) 58 Can. Bar Rev. 280; I. F. Lipnowski, 'The Economist's Approach to Assessing Compensation for Accident Victims' (1979) 9 Manitoba L.J. 319.

3. Not all losses represent social costs. Bishop's explanation of the problematic refusal of the courts generally to impose liability in negligence for 'pure economic loss' builds on the distinction between technological and pecuniary externalities, i.e. pure 'value' changes, referred to earlier (supra, Chapter 1, Section B.). Rizzo, on the other hand, argues that most 'pure economic loss cases' involve social costs, not mere transfers of wealth, and that recovery ought to be allowed if administrative costs do not exceed the value of recovery and the costs if the parties had formed a contract to allocate the risk (M. J. Rizzo, 'A Theory of Economic Loss in the Law of Torts' (1980) 11 J. Legal Stud. 281; also interchange between Bishop and Rizzo (1982) 2 Oxford J. Legal Stud. 197).

4

CONTRACT

A. Nature and Function of Contract

K. LLEWELLYN

*

What Price Contract? – An Essay in Perspective[1]

Bargain is then the social and legal machinery appropriate to arranging affairs in any specialized economy which relies on exchange rather than tradition (the manor) or authority (the army, the U. S. S. R.) for apportionment of productive evergy and of product. It is a machinery which like status, but in contrast to tort, makes it easy to insist on positive, affirmative action. *Contract* in the strict sense is the specifically legal machinery appropriate when such an economy moves into the phase of credit – meaning or connoting thereby future dealings in general; in which aspect the mutual reliance of two dealers on their respective promises comes of course into major importance. This machinery of contract applies in general to the market for land, goods, services, credit, or for any combination of these. . . .

[As] the specialization and credit, and particularly the industrial, aspects of an economy gain ground, it becomes hard to escape the positive case for utility of legal enforcement of promises. Credit or reliance on a purely customary or self-interest basis presupposes for effectiveness either permanence of dealings involving long-run mutual dependence, or an ingrained traditional morality covering the point, or dealings within a face-to-face community (or its equivalent, a close-knit though wandering guild-like interest-group such as the early medieval merchants seem to have made up) in which severe group pressure on delinquent promisors is available. These types of sanction fail in a society mobile as to institutions, mobile as to residence, mobile as to occupation; they fail increasingly as the market expands spatially and in complexity. They fail, in a word, as to long-run, long-range,

---

[1] (1931) 40 Yale L.J. 704, 717–27, with omissions. Reprinted by permission of the Yale Law Journal Company and Fred B. Rothman & Company.

impersonal bargains, as also in cases where death, or transfer of rights, removes from the relation what may at the outset have been a personal aspect.

Whatever the need for legal enforcement of contract in current dealings, then, its place in an *investment* structure is obvious. It is essential to any approach to a market for capital, to any machinery for mobilizing funds or diversifying investments. Equally essential with contract itself is the transferability – which is to say, the depersonalization – of contract rights. The older view of 'privity' as essential to legal action on a contract was connected partly with semi-magical aspects of legal form; partly with a conception of contract as an essentially peculiar, unusual thing; partly with a conception that contractual transactions had no proper importance for non-participants. None of these conceptions fits with an investment market; it is significant that the first free transferability, that of bills of exchange, developed among merchants *apart from law proper*. It is further significant that merchants found no trouble with the concept of suit by a third party beneficiary – which still gives trouble to some courts – and that they shaved the freely transferable contract right down to certain standardized essentials. In business essence, although not so strictly in law, a very similar standardizing and simplifying process occurs in the investment market today. The investor looks for six or seven familiar standard features in a stock or bond, irrespective of the length of mortgage indenture or articles of incorporation. . . . For business purposes, too, a distinction in kind between bonds and stocks tends definitely to disappear. Both, in the same way, are thought of as property – as is also any prospectively profitable contract, whether unilateral or bilateral. Both, in much the same way again, are conceived as in the nature of promises: anticipated performance by 'the corporation' (which is factually viewed as centred in the managing personnel, plus some assets, plus the established management policies) is the essence of the picture; and legal sanction in both cases looms very large. My eyes may be blinded, but to me men do not seem to regard as cutting to the essence (as distinct from questions of *degree* of security and priority in rank) that the legal sanction in the case of bonds goes to payment of certain sums at certain times; while in the case of stocks the legal obligation is built around rather than focussed on payment, built in terms of limiting dissipation of assets and checking manipulation rather than in terms of specified positive performance. And when, finally, even interests in realty are thrown into the bond–stock form, the role of contract and near-contract in the investment field becomes pervasive. Contract, not mere agreement-in-fact. Frequently enough no other sanction than the legal exists at all. Where other sanctions do exist (*e.g.*, desire for continued dealings, or for a business reputation) they show an unfortunate tendency to fail precisely where most needed, *i.e.*, when stress of loss (or gain: management manipulation of the market or merger of the debtor) is strong. . . . It results that even to some extent in short-run face-to-face dealings, and *a fortiori* and importantly in long-run ones, legal enforceability figures as an element of added security in credit matters; a partial insurance against the very case of need: when credit-judgment was misguided, or in the case of death or assignment, or where supervening troubles disrupt either willingness or power to perform.

It has been mentioned that this legal insurance is commonly accompanied by an element of legal risk. What the law official will enforce is what he sees as the legal obligation. An agreement that to a business man calls for shipment of goods as close as conveniently possible to those described, with (as of course) price adjustment for defective deliveries, and return only of unusables, and replacement of those – this agreement means to a court that the seller is to comply with the description precisely, or have no rights at all. What a buyer will curse at not getting, on a rising market, he can then reject with impunity if the market falls; yet this very risk of the market is one which the deal was intended to shift to him. . . . It is true that 'business understanding' of what an agreement means, and indeed of whether an agreement exists, is by no means unambiguous, and not always adjustable. It is not alone wilful default, but honest difference of opinion, which lead to disputes, and which leave some proper room for law officials. Both ways and norms of business practice may be firm at the center, but they are hazy at the edge; they offer little sureness to guide in dealing with the outside and unusual case. . . . The results leave it dark as to how far legal enforceability is in truth a factor in the *initial making* of future commitments and in the giving of short-term credit. They leave it even darker as to how far such influence as is exerted on either is to be regarded as healthy. . . . Nonetheless so much is sure: legal enforceability is sometimes a factor in inducing performance by a debtor; a salvage factor it always is – on bad risks, however, whose badness it may itself have contributed to begetting. Remove the legal sanction and men will give credit with more care.

It is at this point that the law of contract again makes contact with the law of security. From an economic angle, bargaining for 'security' is an intensified case of the security provided by legal enforceability alone. For it looks to cover in part the exact risks mere contract rights leave open. . . . [It] is clear that current future deals themselves, in their effect on the arrangement of economic affairs, lie half-way between mere reliance on the general spot market for either supplies or outlet, and property-wise assurance of either outlet or supply by vertical integration. This, as to goods, whether they be viewed as supplies or as merchandise. On the side of services the situation is quite similar, but rather more complex. Between 'own unit' organization (property plus an ownership and management set-up framed in good part on contract, plus exclusive control of 'agents' under a contract set-up, and of a standing force of labor) and the rather uncommon mere reliance on the general spot market (calling in the plumber or the doctor for immediate action in emergency) lie a short range letting out of individual jobs (contract to roof a house) and a standing-relation contractual letting out of particular types of service (insurance coverage, deposit account, legal or advertising counsel). Perhaps the same can be said as to the supply of and outlet for working funds; yet when one is again tempted to assume legal contract or even factual promises as an utterly essential feature in our economy, it challenges attention that so much of current financing proceeds on flexible and revocable 'understandings' as to line and conditions of credit. And such flexibility is a marked trend in marketing of goods as well, wherever long-range buyer-seller *relations* come to seem more important than exact definition of the risks to be shifted by the particular dicker[2] in terms of quantity, quality, or price. Output and requirement contracts, maximum and minimum contracts, contracts with quality, quantity and kinds to be specified from month to month, and sliding scale price arrangements – these are symptomatic of an economy stabilizing itself along new lines.

C. J. GOETZ and R. E. SCOTT

*

Principles of Relational Contracts[3]

Recent scholarship has demonstrated that a significant proportion of private contracts do not easily fit the presuppositions of classical legal analysis. One reason for this is the pivotal role played in conventional legal theory by the concept of the complete contingent contract. Parties in a bargaining situation are presumed able, at minimum cost, to allocate explicitly the risks that future contingencies may cause one or the other to regret having entered into an executory agreement. Under these conditions, the role of legal regulation can be defined quite precisely. Once the underlying rules policing the bargaining process have been specified, contract rules serve as standard or common risk

---

[2] [*Editors' Note*: bargain]
[3] (1981) 67 Virg. L.R. 1089, 1089–95, with omissions. Reprinted by permission of Fred B. Rothman & Company.

allocations that can be varied by the individual agreement of particular parties. These rules serve the important purpose of saving most bargainers the cost of negotiating a tailor-made arrangement. If the basic risk allocation provided by a legal rule fails to suit the purposes of particular parties, then bargainers are free to negotiate an alternative allocation of risks. All relevant risks thus can be assigned optimally – either by legal rule or through individualized agreement – because future contingencies are not only known and understood at the time the bargain is struck, but can also be addressed by efficacious contractual responses.

In a complex society, however, many contractual arrangements diverge so markedly from the classical model that they require separate treatment. Parties frequently enter into continuing, highly interactive contractual arrangements. For these parties, a complete contingent contract may not be a feasible contracting mechanism. Where the future contingencies are peculiarly intricate or uncertain, practical difficulties arise that impede the contracting parties' efforts to allocate optimally all risks at the time of contracting. Not surprisingly, parties who find it advantageous to enter into such cooperative exchange relationships seek specially adapted contractual devices. The resulting 'relational contracts' encompass most generic agency relationships, including distributorships, franchises, joint ventures, and employment contracts.

Although a certain ambiguity has always existed, there has been a tendency to equate the term 'relational contract' with long-term contractual involvements. We here adopt a very specific construction of the term that is based more precisely on a contrast with the classical contingent contract. A contract is relational to the extent that the parties are incapable of reducing important terms of the arrangement to well-defined obligations. Such definitive obligations may be impractical because of inability to identify uncertain future conditions or because of inability to characterize complex adaptations adequately even when the contingencies themselves can be identified in advance. . . .

Parties enter into relational contracts because such agreements present an opportunity to exploit certain economies. Each party wants a share of the benefits resulting from these economies and consequently seeks to structure the relationship so as to induce the other party to share the benefits of the exchange. Typically, this is accomplished by specifying the performance standard of each party and then selecting a mechanism to ensure compliance with the agreed-upon standard.

In conventional contracts, the parties generally are able to reduce performance standards to rather specific obligations. By contrast, relational contracts create unique, interdependent relationships, wherein unknown contingencies or the intricacy of the required responses may prevent the specification of precise performance standards. Complexity and uncertainty each play conceptually distinct roles, although they frequently operate in combination. For example, suppose a homeowner attempts to write a contract providing for the care of his fine home garden during a summer when he is out of town. Uncertainty is represented by the difficulty of determining in advance the climatic conditions, incursions of the gypsy moth, wind-borne powdery mildew, etc. Complexity is involved in specifying to the gardener exactly what responses should be made in each case: how much to spend on sprays, whether to water, when a diseased plant should be cut down to prevent infection of adjacent ones, and so on.

A typical response to this problem of complexity and uncertainty is to define the performance standard in unusually general terms. The ethical standards of attorneys, brokers, and other agents, the implied fiduciary obligation that attaches to certain relational contractors, and, most typically, 'best efforts' clauses are examples of how performance obligations are articulated in relational contracts. Because these standards are usually described in general terms, it is difficult to apply them in any specific context. Therefore, relational contracts also require more creative control mechanisms than do conventional contingent contracts. In any cooperative contract where performance obligations remain imprecise, there are inevitable costs in ensuring that any particular level of performance is achieved. Parties will bear this cost in various ways. For example, they may grant the principal the right to monitor the agent's efforts. Performance thus can be controlled by direct supervision or by indirect incentive systems designed to encourage the agent to consider fully the principal's interests. Alternatively, in cases where monitoring is relatively costly, the agent may seek to reassure the principal by a 'bonding' agreement.[4] Liquidated damages provisions, covenants not to compete, and unilateral termination clauses are common examples of agent bonding. Ideally, the parties will select that combination of monitoring and bonding arrangements that optimizes the costs of governing the standard of performance.

Parties will enter into relational contracts only after considering alternative methods of achieving their objectives. One obvious alternative is the vertical integration of potentially separable activities, such as manufacturing and distribution, into a single firm. An integrated firm presumably would take all the relevant cost and benefit interactions of the two activities into consideration and would provide the optimal level of manufacturing and distribution inputs so that overall profits are maximized. The vertically integrated firm thus provides a

---

[4] [*Editors' Note*: formal undertaking conferring protection against losses resulting from breach.]

benchmark against which various alternative contractual arrangements can be measured. Vertical integration will be the optimal mechanism so long as the cost of monitoring within the firm is less than the associated gain from internalizing the costs and benefits of the combined activities under integrated management. In many commercial settings, however, vertical integration may not be a feasible alternative. Consider, for example, an industry in which manufacturing and distribution are specialized activities and are, at least potentially, performed much more efficiently by separate firms. Where a single integrated firm is no longer the exclusive decisionmaker, the respective parties need to engage in a form of explicit adjustment in order to ensure that the interactions between the manufacturing and distributing activities will be considered properly.

Notes

1. The simple exchange relationship, in which one good is simultaneously traded for another (often money), has the obvious economic function of conferring gains on both parties; it also enables resources to shift to more highly valued uses (supra, Chapter 1, Section B). While this form of transaction is not insignificant in modern times (cf. consumer shopping and the commercial 'spot' market), legal doctrine has concentrated on the promissory basis of contract: a promise made in return for a benefit or another promise. The reasons for engaging in promises and the justifications for their enforcement by law have been the subject of much recent literature: see, e.g., P. S. Atiyah, *Promises, Morals and the Law* (1981), and C. Fried, *Contract as Promise: A Theory of Contractual Obligation* (1981). Economically, such a contract is a response to the need of individuals and firms to structure patterns of commitment over time: S. T. Lowry, 'Bargain and Contract Theory in Law and Economics' (1976) 10 J. Econ. Issues 1. Constraining choice for the future necessarily involves a cost but this is often outweighed by the benefits of reducing both uncertainty (e.g. greater predictability of cash flow and gains in information as to future levels of demand) and the transaction costs of operating in the 'spot' market. See M. J. Powers, 'Effects of Contract Provisions on the Success of a Futures Contract' (1967) 49 J. Farm Econ. 833; R. L. Sander, 'Innovating by an Exchange: A Case Study of the Development of the Plywood Futures Contract' (1973) 16 J. Law and Econ. 119.

2. As Llewellyn indicates, the future contract is also a risk-allocating device (see E. Patterson, 'The Apportionment of Business Risks Through Legal Devices' (1924) 24 Col. L.R. 335). There are welfare gains when the risk is assigned to the party who can deal with it at least cost, either by an express term or, failing that, by the courts through such devices as implied terms, mistake and frustration (cf. R. A. Posner and A. M. Rosenfield, 'Impossibility and Related Doctrines in Contract Law: An Economic Analysis' (1977) 6

J. Legal Stud. 83). These doctrines avoid the transaction costs incurred in drafting a completely contingent contract (Goetz and Scott, supra; M. R. Cohen, *Law and the Social Order* (1961), p. 100–11; and on standard form contracts, see further infra, Section D) though against the gains must be offset losses arising from the inability of the general law to adapt precisely to the needs of individual contracting parties (cf. Ehrlich and Posner, infra, Chapter 9, Section B). It should also be noted that while *ex ante* it may be in the interests of both parties to allocate risk, *ex post* the process may constitute a zero-sum game in which one party's gain is the other party's loss. By fixing a price at the time of the contract, the buyer is gambling that the market price will rise, and the seller that it will fall, by the time of performance: Lowry, op. cit. p. 141 (undue concern for *ex post* consequences may help to explain the law's apparent readiness to upset bargains on grounds of e.g. unconscionability: infra, Section D.) Economists have employed risk-allocation ideas to analyse agricultural contracts (S. Cheung, 'Transaction Costs, Risk Aversion and the Choice of Contractual Arrangements' (1969) 12 J. Law and Econ. 23) and employment contracts (M. N. Bailey, 'Contract Theory and the Moderation of Inflation by Recession and Controls' [1976] Brookings Papers on Economic Activities 585).

3. Goetz and Scott demonstrate the advantages of the relational contract as an alternative response to the difficulties of formulating completely contingent contracts. In passages omitted from this book their paper focusses on two 'doctrinal lynchpins' of relational contracts, the obligation of one party to use its best efforts to carry on an activity beneficial to the other, and the concomitant right of the latter to terminate the relationship, as 'an optimizing response to the peculiar environmental constraints of complexity and uncertainty'. Exploration of relational contracts has been a central feature of the neo-institutionalist school of law and economics (supra, Chapter 1, Section C); see, especially, V. Goldberg, 'Toward an Expanded Economic Theory of Contract' (1976) 10 J. Econ. Issues 426; O. E. Williamson, 'Transaction Cost Economics: the Governance of Contractual Relations' (1979) 22 J. Law and Econ. 233 and 'Contract Analysis: the Transaction Cost Approach' in P. Burrows and C. Veljanovski (eds.), *The Economic Approach to Law* (1981) ch. 2. The legal implications of this analysis are fully described in the writings of I. R. Macneil; see, e.g., 'Contracts: Adjustment of Long-Term Economic Relations under Classical, Neoclassical, and Relational Contract Law' (1978) 73 Northwestern U.L.R. 854, and in Burrows and Veljanovski, op. cit., ch. 3. For empirical support, see S. Macaulay, 'Non-Contractual Relations in Business: A Preliminary Survey' (1963) 28 Am. Soc. Rev. 55, and H. Beale and T. Dugdale, 'Contracts Between Businessman: Planning and the Use of Contractual Remedies' (1975) 2 Brit. J. Law and Soc. 45.

4. Transaction costs considerations which are seen to justify relational contracts may also explain other legal institutions. In a paper published in 1937 ('The Nature of the Firm' 4 Economica 386), Coase suggested that firms and companies were formed primarily to reduce the information and negotiation costs of individual business transactions. More recent literature in this area has concentrated on limited liability as a method of raising capital –

compare J. M. Landers, 'A Unified Approach to Parent, Subsidiary, and Affiliate Questions in Bankruptcy' (1975) 42 U. Chi. L.R. 589 with R. A. Posner, *Economic Analysis of Law* (2nd edn, 1977), pp. 290–96 – and the relative merits of different legal forms for monitoring performance and thus maximizing production. In the conventional firm, this is achieved by competition between managers as well as by shareholder control (A. A. Alchian and H. Demsetz, 'Production Information Costs, and Economic Organization' (1972) 62 Am. Econ. Rev. 777; H. Manne, 'Mergers and the Market for Corporate Control' (1965) 73 J. Pol. Econ. 110), but in certain environments monitoring costs may be reduced by franchising contracts.

B. Enforcement of Promises and Damages Remedies

C. J. GOETZ and R. E. SCOTT

*

Enforcing Promises: An Examination of the Basis of Contract[5]

I. OPTIMAL ENFORCEMENT OF PROMISES

A. *The Function of Promises: Adaptation by the Promisee*

In analyzing the promisee's reactions to a promise, it is critically important to bear in mind the conceptual distinction between the promise itself and the future benefit that it foretells. By communicating a promise, the promisor informs the promisee about the proposed future receipt of a benefit. The promise itself is merely the production of a piece of information about the future. Normally, advance knowledge of a future transfer will increase the benefit to the promisee because he can more perfectly adapt his consumption decisions to the impending change in wealth. For instance, a person informed of a $25,000 bequest to be made one year hence may revise some of the plans that he otherwise would have followed in the interim twelve months. Because of the revisions in plans, the individual can achieve a higher intertemporal level of satisfaction than if the wealth were transferred without any advance notice. Such adaptive gain from the information embodied in a promise may appropriately be termed

[5] (1980) 89 Yale L.J. 1261, 1266–1309, with omissions. Reprinted by permission of the Yale Law Journal Co. and Fred B. Rothman & Company.

'beneficial reliance'. The problem occurs, however, when the transfer foretold by the promise is not actually performed. In this case, the information conveyed by the promise turns out to have been misleading and the promisee's induced adaptation in behavior makes him worse off than he would have been without the expectation of a future benefit. Losses incurred by ill-premised adaptive behavior are commonly termed 'detrimental reliance.' ...

What happens if the promisee knows that the probability of the promisor's performance is less than certain? In this case, the beneficial results of any adaptive behavior when the promise is performed must be weighed against the detrimental results of the same adaptive behavior if the promise is breached. A prospective gain from an adaptive action is balanced against the risk of loss. Whatever the reasons for the riskiness attached to the performance prospects of any promise, the promisee can protect himself against prospective losses from detrimental reliance by limiting his behavior adjustments. In practice, the attempt to do this is frequently manifested in intermediate courses of action taken by promisees who do not completely ignore the implications of a promise in their planning but do not react as fully as if performance were certain. The price for this self-protection against the risk of detrimental reliance is, therefore, the value of the prospective beneficial reliance that would accrue from full adaptation to the advance knowledge of a promissory performance.

The possibility of self-protection adjustments by promisees undermines the common assumption that detrimental reliance is the only behavior modified by the enforcement choice. This assumption often leads to characterizing certain 'gratuitous' promises as incapable of inducing any reasonable reliance. Once the legal rule is announced, detrimental reliance on such announcements would, it is argued, not be reasonable. But the problem is quite simply that policies that reduce the reliability of promises are likely to reduce both beneficial and detrimental reliance. Thus, legal rules that encourage self-protective adaptation by the promisee achieve desired reductions in detrimental reliance only at the cost of concomitant reductions in beneficial reliance.

B. Making Promises: Actions of the Promisor ...

Potential promisees view promises as beneficial actions and as desirable economic goods. One can thus consider a promisor's willingness to make promises in much the same manner as his willingness to pursue any other economic goal. To predict the level of promise-making activity, the costs of promising must be examined.

1. *The Costs of Promising: The Regret Contingency*

Derivation of the promisor's cost of promising requires consideration of a number of potentially confusing factors. Therefore, we shall begin with the simplest possible environment. First we shall assume that the cost of communicating the promise is negligible. Second, we assume that no legal mechanism exists to enforce promises. Absent a legal compulsion, the promisor remains free to refuse performance. If he does, the making of the promise will have generated costs in the amount of the detrimental reliance imposed on the promisee.

The option of nonperformance also imposes costs on the promisor in two situations. The first case is when the promisor exhibits some welfare interdependence with the promisee; that is, he is to some extent altruistic and cares about costs incurred by the promisee. Then, the detrimental reliance costs imposed by nonperformance become, to some degree, costs to the promisor himself. Intrafamilial promises and promises between close friends are most likely to exemplify this phenomenon. . . .

The second extra-legal sanction arises when nonperformance would produce some post-breach reaction, either from the promisee or others, that is costly to the promisor. The resulting costs may range from hostile, retributive behaviour to a mere loss of others' esteem to foreclosure of future beneficial dealings.

What are the effects of these extra-legal sanctions for breaking promises? To the extent that such sanctions are effective, their prospect acts as a 'cost' of promising and deters promises that are worth less to the promisor than the prospective cost. Thus, extra-legal sanctions are a supplement to, or substitute for, legal sanctions. Given the existence of extra-legal sanctions, under what circumstances might a promisor fail to perform his promise? When a promise is made in good faith, the promisor presumably believes that he is likely to perform. Still, many good-faith promisors would acknowledge the possibility that events may arise that cause them to regret having made the promise. Thereafter, if it were costless to do so, they would indeed breach the promise. Such contingencies may involve a wide range of factors, from changes in personal conditions to disappointment about external considerations that originally made the promise seem desirable. The term 'regret contingency' will be used to denote the future occurrence of a condition that would motivate breach if breach were a costless option for the promisor. Assuming any reliance, the occurrence of a regret contingency necessarily implies that either the promisor or promisee must bear a cost.

When a regret contingency arises, the promisor's options are either to bear the loss attributable to performance, which now costs more than it is worth, or to breach and accept the cost of any corresponding sanction. Presumably the promisor would adopt the cheaper of these regret costs. In any event, someone will suffer a net loss whenever a regret contingency arises, whether in the from of regret costs to the promisor, uncompensated detrimental reliance to the promisee, or both.

2. Adaptation by the Promisor: Precautions and Reassurance

By what means does the promisor adapt to the prospective costs of promising? The promisor can substantially influence the probability of a regret contingency, and thus its prospective costs, by adjusting his behaviour ex ante. One means of mitigating potential costs is by altering the form of the promise. For instance, the promisor may condition performance on the proviso that certain circumstances – potential regret contingencies – not arise. Alterations in the form of the promise will generally entail a cost to the promisor either in terms of direct resource cost – time and trouble – or in the possibility that the benefit of the promise-making to the promisor will be diminished. The second means of avoiding regret costs is simply to make fewer promises. The costs of this option are forgone benefits from unmade promises.

The costs that result from restrictions in the scope or number of one's promises can be termed 'precautionary costs'. It is useful to distinguish these further as either quality precautions or quantity precautions. Quality precautions involve adjustments restricting the scope of promises and impose a cost of decreased reliability. Quantity precautions, which consist of reductions in the number of promises made, result in a loss of benefits from promising. A rational promisor will pursue precautionary adjustments up to the point at which marginal precautionary costs are exactly balanced by marginal reductions in regret costs. . . .

C. Optimizing Promisor–Promisee Interaction

To what extent do legal sanctions optimize the interactions between promisor and promisee? In the present context, optimization is defined as maximizing the net social benefits of promissory activity – that is, the benefits of promises minus their costs. This approach is equivalent to the balancing of prospective costs and benefits under the widely accepted Learned Hand test for the required duty of care in potential tort-producing activities. Indeed, there are strong theoretical parallels between the production of dangerous, but useful, products and the making of promises.

The role of damages or sanctions in generating socially optimal behavior can be focused more sharply by observing the distinction between internal and external effects. Because self-interested maximizing behavior entails consideration of only internal costs and benefits, unfettered individual behavior is incompatible with social optimization in circumstances in which significant external costs or benefits are present. Individuals will oversupply activities with external costs and undersupply those with external benefits. By imposing costs and creating incentives, the law can cause individuals to consider external effects in their decisionmaking and thus 'internalize' them.

Inducing optimal promise-making therefore requires that the promisor's costs of promising be adjusted to reflect any external effects on the promisee. But this adjustment process is complex. Changes in the costs and benefits of promising are highly interactive in two senses. First, an individual's adjustments may substitute one category of his costs for another. Second, the actions of one party may produce reactions by the other and, in turn, feedback responses to the first party. The role of legal damages in optimizing this interaction depends upon whether a promise is reciprocal or nonreciprocal. Nonreciprocal or gratuitous promises, which are not conditioned upon performance of a return promise, do not typically enjoy the presumption of enforceability attached to reciprocal or bargained-for promises. As the analysis below reveals, the critical variable that distinguishes these categories of promises is whether the parties can interactively influence the nature and amount of promise-making through bargaining. It is the existence of effective impediments to interaction in the case of nonreciprocal promises that seems to explain why the law treats these two types of promises in such different fashions.

1. Nonreciprocal Promises

Consider the case of a gratuitous promisor who has adjusted his promise-making to an arbitrarily assumed level of extra-legal sanction so that he cannot further improve his situation. In addition, assume that social considerations effectively prevent the promisee from influencing the promisor's calculations through bargaining. Under these conditions, when does the intervention of the law lead to optimal results?

a. *Legal Enforcement and Reassurance.* Legal enforcement of a particular class of nonreciprocal promises increases the reliability of the promises. This added reassurance increases social benefits in three situations. First, legal enforcement increases the net benefits of promissory reassurance if a legal sanction such as money damages displaces existing extra-legal penalties such as guilt or social pressure. If the total level of the sanction stays the same, the promisor's costs, benefits, and behavior all remain unchanged, while the promisee's benefits are increased by the receipt of the damages. The promisee's self-protection costs also fall. Because the consequences of a regret contingency are reduced by a prospect of legal compensation, the promisee can spend less on mitigating the risk of uncompensated detrimental reliance. . . .

Second, legal enforcement may increase net reassurance benefits regardless of the degree of substitutability of sanctions. Such an opportunity arises when a gratuitous promisor assesses the risk of a regret contingency at zero, because he is certain he will perform. In this case, if the law intervenes by raising the sanction for breach, the promisor's prospective regret and precautionary costs remain at zero. . . .

Third, even the gratuitous promisor who is not totally certain of future performance may prefer more enforcement. This will occur, for instance, when the promisor cares about the welfare or the reaction of the promisee. . . .

Under what circumstances, then, will legally induced increases in the reliability of nonreciprocal promises be socially optimal? When the mutual interests of both parties are furthered by more assured promises, the promisor will voluntarily seek legal mechanisms for providing additional reassurance. However, often it will not be in the self-interest of the promisor to undertake voluntarily a more reliable promise. Even when some benefits to the promisor are produced by additional reassurance, the external benefits from performance may be inadequately communicated to the promisor by self-sanctions. As a general empirical premise, therefore, enforcement will be more likely to optimize promissory reassurance when extra-legal sanctions are relatively ineffective. The social desirability of enforcement, however, ultimately depends upon whether those gains are offset by corresponding costs. Before proposing a sanction for particular nonreciprocal cases, therefore, we must consider the societal effect of the promisors' precautionary adjustments triggered by legal liability.

This analysis suggests that qualitative adjustments by the gratuitous promisor have mixed effects. Increasing these adjustments by legally enforcing nonreciprocal promises is optimal, therefore, only when gains in promisee reliance from improved information exceed the net implementation costs of reallocating the risk of regret to the promisee. This implies, as an empirical generalization, that enforcing nonreciprocal promises will improve outcomes when there exists a substantial prospect of beneficial information exchanges through qualitative adjustments. Conversely, in contexts in which self sanctions are already effective and the prospects of improved information are poor, the social gains from enforcement are negligible and may be exceeded by implementation costs. Nonenforcement of such nonreciprocal promises is thus the optimal choice.

c. *An Optimal Damage Formula.* The effect of a decision to enforce legally any particular class of nonreciprocal promises depends upon the nature of the sanction imposed for breach. Promisors will respond to higher levels of sanction by increasing their qualitative and quantitative precautions, reducing both the reliability of a given volume of promises and the number of promises actually made.

A necessary starting point in determining an optimal damage rule is to specify the external effects of a nonreciprocal promise as the supply of such promises is increased by one marginal unit. The external effects are the prospective detrimental reliance incurred if the promise is broken and the prospective beneficial reliance enjoyed if the promise is performed. Proper reflection of external effects therefore requires not only that the promisor be charged for the harm expected from broken promises, but also that he be rewarded for the prospective benefits of performance. It is helpful to state this condition symbolically. Let p be the promisor's reasonable, subjective assessment of the probability that he will perform a promise under an existing legal rule calling for damages of D in the event of breach. For the damage rule to deter all promises with net social costs and encourage those with net benefits, the amount of damages awarded must satisfy the following equation:

$$(1 - p) \, D = (1 - p) \, R - pB$$

where R and B are the values of detrimental and beneficial reliances, respectively. Assuming that all broken promises are litigated, the left hand side of the equation represents the expected value of the prospective legal sanction. Because only broken promises are affected by the law, the probability $(1 - p)$ of the promise being broken is used to 'discount' the damages D. The values for R and B on the right-hand side of the equation should be understood as those resulting from optimal self-protection by the promisee. Thus, promisees will appropriately minimize the value of the right-hand term, which is the net social cost of the promise. In calculating this prospective net reliance, the magnitudes of the potential detrimental and beneficial reliances are each discounted by their probabilities. When the equation is satisfied through the imposition of optimal damages D, the promisor's internal cost-benefit calculus will reflect the external effects of his promise-making. If the external effects are thus accounted for, the promisor's maximization of his internal net benefits is consistent with supply of the socially optimal quantity and quality of promises. We call this damage rule the 'prospective net reliance' formulation.

In some cases, the prospective beneficial reliance from a promise will exceed its prospective detrimental reliance. Because the net external

effect of such a promise is beneficial, it would be optimal to reward the
making of such promises. However, in the nonreciprocal setting no
practical legal mechanism exists for rewarding promises. This limitation renders true optimization impossible; the situation is necessarily
second-best. At minimum, promises with prospects of net beneficial
reliance should not be the subject of damages if breached. Only
promises with prospective net detrimental external effects should be
enforceable.

The prospective net reliance formulation developed above can be
used to analyze the optimal level of enforcement. By dividing both
sides of the original equation by the probability of breach $(1 - p)$, the
following damage rule emerges:

$$D = R - \left[\frac{p}{(1 - p)}\right] B.$$

The optimal damage rule thus subtracts from the promisee's reliance
cost a fraction of his potential beneficial reliance. This fraction is the
ratio of the ex ante subjective probability of performance to that of
nonperformance. It determines the extent to which the prospect of
beneficial reliance when the promise was made is credited against the
promisee's prospective detrimental reliance. Because this ratio may be
thought of as an index of the promisor's good faith, we call it the
'good-faith ratio'. A damage offset based on the good-faith ratio and
on the amount of potential beneficial reliance will encourage the
optimal quantity and quality of promises by reflecting in the promisor's
decision calculus both the harmful and beneficial effects of his promise-
making. This optimal legal sanction is likely to be unattainable in an
environment of costly legal process and imperfect information. But
specifying an optimal sanction permits more rigorous evaluation of
the error produced by any practical adjustment attributable to process costs. In addition, the good-faith ratio and the damage offset
suggest a possible explanation for the language of the *Restatement of
Contracts*, which conditions both the enforceability and the magnitude of reliance-based sanctions upon the 'requirements of justice'.
This language may reflect the view that the prospective beneficial
effects of a promise should be considered in effecting a remedy for
nonperformance. . . .

. . . [T]he rule penalizes each party for failing to take cost-effective
steps to minimize the social costs of promising. Damages exceeding
those described above will tend to induce the promisor to invest too
much in precautionary adjustments. This phenomenon is analogous to
the excessive level of prudence anticipated if tort victims were awarded
a multiple of their true damages.

2. *Reciprocal Promises*

Promising is reciprocal when the parties can adjust interactively to the nature and amount of promise-making. The prospective net reliance formulation is equally applicable to reciprocal as well as to non-reciprocal promises. But the net reliance damage rule seems in sharp conflict with accepted legal doctrine in the reciprocal promise context, in which damages for breach are typically based on the promisee's full-performance expectation rather than on his detrimental reliance. Upon analysis, the apparent conflict can be dissipated; moreover, reciprocal promises are easier than nonreciprocal promises for the law to address.

This conclusion is buttressed by two independent lines of argument. First, in the case of reciprocal promises, a plausible empirical generalization is that a promisee's acceptance of one promise frequently requires his forgoing a potential substitute promise. The forgone value of the best substitute promise available – the opportunity cost – is key in determining the promisee's detrimental reliance when an accepted promise is subsequently broken. In a well-organized market, alternative promises will be close, if not perfect, substitutes. In that case, detrimental reliance is equal to the full performance value of the breached promise. Similarly, beneficial reliance will be small, because the promisor's pledge, even if performed, will not constitute a very substantial improvement over the potential beneficial reliance from substitute promises. This empirical generalization implies that, in the damage formula developed above, full performance expectation E can be substituted for detrimental reliance R because $E \approx R$. Furthermore, because $B \approx O$, the term of $\left[\dfrac{1-p}{p}\right]$ B drops out. We are left with $D \approx E$; thus, expectation damages are a good proxy for the prospective net reliance damage formulation developed above.

Second, a fundamental theoretical difference exists between reciprocal and nonreciprocal promises. In the case of a reciprocal promise, the principal objective of a promisor is to obtain consideration in the form of a return promise. The value of the return promise elicited is the main element of the promisor's benefit. Therefore, changes in the qualitative aspects of the promise are reflected in commensurate shifts of benefits to the promisor; a higher quality promise motivates a more valuable return promise, and vice versa. In contrast to the case of nonreciprocal promises, qualitative adjustments are internalized in the promisor's cost–benefit calculus by generating a more or less valuable consideration for his promise.

Hence, the bargaining process accomplishes an important part of the behavioral regulation that, for nonreciprocal promises, must be performed by the legal system.

Furthermore, the bargaining process, not available by definition in the nonreciprocal context, can facilitate the optimal allocation of risk for reciprocal promises. Precautionary action is subject to a test of the ability of the promisee to bribe the promisor to make an unconditioned promise. Within any scheme of enforcement, then, the parties can reallocate the risks of regretted promises by buying or selling protection through the terms of their agreement. The least-cost bearer of any risk will presumably agree to absorb that risk in exchange for an enhanced return promise. . . .

II EFFICIENT RULES OF PROMISSORY OBLIGATION

A. *Problems of Proof, Process, and Error Costs*

. . . Because true reliance cost is equal to the opportunity cost of the promise, measurement of the loss requires a comparison of the promisee's behavior in response to the promise with his prospective conduct in the absence of the promise: the promisee's detrimental reliance cost is the difference in satisfaction between these two positions. This calculation entails identifying the value of alternative opportunities forgone because of the promise and the benefits retained from the actions taken in reliance. Generally, these values can be determined solely by evaluating the subjective claims of the promisee. Only when a competitive market generates prices indicating the value of forgone opportunities will there be reliable evidence of the position the promisee would have occupied had no promise been made.

Furthermore, an optimal legal sanction may also include a discount for the effects of extra-legal factors – such as reputational losses or social restraints on breach – that independently reward the performing promisor for taking into account some of the social effects of promising. Thus, any theoretically precise reliance-based damage calculation may require an additional computation of the prospective beneficial effects that performance of the promise would have conveyed. . . . In sum, the administrative and error costs of attempting to apply a theoretically optimal net reliance standard suggest that it may be worthwhile to adopt a surrogate measure that is cheaper to apply. . . .

Introducing the complexities of measurement and proof indicates that the traditional choice between reliance damages and the alternatives of nonenforcement and full performance compensation should be recast as an attempt to select from potential contract rules the best achievable approximation of the optimal enforcement standard.

B. *Reciprocal-Bargain Promises: The Consideration Model*

. . . Evaluating contract rules as cost-reducing surrogates for the theoretically optimal enforcement rule reemphasizes the importance of the distinction between reciprocal and nonreciprocal promises. Promises that satisfy the reciprocal exchange requirement of consideration are presumptively enforceable. Breach entitles the promisee to full performance compensation. . . .

We have pointed out the identity between detrimental reliance and full-performance expectation whenever markets for promises are competitive. Furthermore, bargaining tends to produce the optimal amount of promissory reliance even when the legal rule deviates from the optimal reliance principle. By modifying contractual terms, the parties can vary the standard liability rule in order to maximize net reliance benefits.

What effects can be predicted from full enforcement of reciprocal bargain promises? . . . [A]pplication of sanctions for breach imposes the risk of the regret contingency on the promisor. As the promisor's potential liability is increased, he is encouraged to take precautionary action to minimize the expected liability, by conditioning promises more carefully in negotiations. The promisee, in turn, may bargain for a less restricted promise by paying explicitly for the additional reassurance provided by a compensation award.

Alternatively, a rule denying enforcement of a bargained-for promise reduces precautionary costs incurred by promisors seeking to minimize the risks of regret, because it shifts that risk to the promisee. The promisee may adapt to this increased uncertainty by discounting the price he is willing to pay for the promise. If the promise is actually worth more than the promisee estimates, the promisor will incur costs up to the expected value of the promise in order to assure the promisee of the true worth of the promise. These additional reassurance costs induced by the promisee's adaptive behavior could include the voluntary assumption of legal liability through collateral guarantees or performance bonds.

Thus, because bargainers will attempt to allocate the risk of regret optimally themselves, the effects of enforcement rules depend on the transaction costs of risk allocation. Evaluation of these costs requires an analysis of how bargainers adapt to the risks of regret contingencies. If in certain transactions precautionary efforts by promisors would be more expensive than reassurance, nonenforcement enables the parties to shift the risk of regret more cheaply. Alternatively, when reassurance is more costly fully enforcing promises induces cheaper precautionary conduct. . . . [After examining aspects of the doctrine of consideration in the light of these factors, the authors conclude that] the design of the consideration model can be explained persuasively by an analysis of efficient risk allocation. Manipulation of the liability rule shifts the risk of a regret contingency between promises and promisors. These varying liability patterns can induce interactive adaptations by the parties to allocate the social costs of promising efficiently. This cheapest-risk-allocation design is buttressed by process considerations that justify imposing promissory liability only if agreement upon the basic transaction has been reached. . . . The impact of any enforcement rule ultimately depends on the character of the remedy for nonperformance. Full enforcement compensation is the standard recovery for breach of reciprocal-bargain promises, whenever such an award can be determined accurately. The stated objective of this compensation rule is to place the promisee in the same economic position he would have occupied had the promise been performed. As we have argued above, this rule, by imposing a sanction in excess of the social costs of breach, overdeters socially useful promising, except in competitive markets in which expectation is equivalent to reliance. The bargain context, however, enables the parties to vary, with low transactions costs, the legal rule by agreement and thereby mitigate the effects of any remedial distortion. Moreover, the disparity between compensatory recovery and optimal reliance damages is usually more than offset by gains in the clarity of the rule. . . .

The preceding analysis explains only the basic design of the consideration model. It does not help identify where to draw the line between enforcement and nonenforcement. At common law the category of enforceable bargained-for promises was rigidly narrow. . . . [T]he recent expansion of promissory liability is consistent with the judgment that, for certain types of bargain promises, a larger core of liability can be defined without causing a significant increase in enforcement costs. . . .

C. *Nonreciprocal Promises* . . .

When the promisor is subjectively certain of performance, full enforcement offers the social benefits of increased beneficial reliance without countervailing precautionary costs. Even slightly uncertain promisors may obtain benefits through enforcement that exceed any increased precautionary or regret costs. Thus, the certainty of performance seems critical in distinguishing the enforcement of sham bargains from the legal treatment of other nonreciprocal promises. At common law, the formal contract under seal provided a means for promisors to assure enforcement of gratuitous promises. A sham bargain performs a similar function in encouraging deliberation, preserving evidence, and identifying the promisor's intention. . . .

[The authors then consider the device of promissory estoppel. Section 90 of the Second Restatement of Contracts provides that 'a promise which the promisor should reasonably expect to induce action or forbearance on the part of the promisee or a third party and which does induce such action or forbearance is binding if injustice can be avoided only by the enforcement of the promise. The remedy granted for breach may be limited as justice requires.']

. . .

The optimal damage formula proposed [supra, p. 163] may explain the nature and role of this limited sanction. As we showed earlier, if the ex ante probability of a promisor performing a promise were high, the prospective beneficial reliance from the promise could exceed prospective detrimental reliance, in which case the overall ex ante prospects would represent a net social benefit. Section 90(1) can thus be read to authorize award of optimal damages based upon this calculation of the promisee's prospective net reliance. This may necessitate damages in amounts less than both full performance and full detrimental reliance.

The justification for abandoning the clearer alternatives of non-enforcement and full enforcement is the error cost of using remedies that do not accurately shape optimal promise-making. The advantage of an optimal net reliance rule is lost, however, if the rule cannot be applied accurately without substantial process costs. . . .

R. A. POSNER

*

Economic Analysis of Law[6]

When a breach of contract is established, the issue becomes one of the proper remedy. A starting point for analysis is Holmes's view that it is not the policy of the law to compel adherence to contracts but only to require each party to choose between performing in accordance with the contract and compensating the other party for any injury resulting from a failure to perform.[7] This view contains an important economic insight. In many cases it is uneconomical to induce the completion of a contract after it has been breached. I agree to purchase 100,000 widgets custom-ground for use as components in a machine that I manufacture. After I have taken delivery of 10,000, the market for my machine collapses. I promptly notify my supplier that I am

[6] From *Economic Analysis of Law* (2nd edn., 1977), pp. 88–92, with omissions. Reprinted by permission of Little, Brown and Company.
[7] *Collected Legal Papers* (1920), p. 175.

terminating the contract, and admit that my termination is a breach of the contract. When notified of the termination he has not yet begun the custom grinding of the other 90,000 widgets, but he informs me that he intends to complete his performance under the contract and bill me accordingly. The custom-ground widgets have no use other than in my machine, and a negligible scrap value. Plainly, to grant the supplier any remedy that induced him to complete the contract after the breach would result in a waste of resources. The law is alert to this danger and, under the doctrine of mitigation of damages, would refuse to permit the supplier to recover any costs he incurred in continuing production after my notice of termination.

Let us change the facts. I need 100,000 custom-ground widgets for my machine but the supplier, after producing 50,000, is forced to suspend production because of a mechanical failure. Other suppliers are in a position to supply the remaining widgets that I need, but I insist that the original supplier complete his performance of the contract. If the law compels completion, the supplier will probably have to make arrangements with other widget producers to complete his contract with me. But it may be more costly for him to procure an alternative supplier than for me to do so directly; indeed, were it cheaper for him than for me, he would do it voluntarily in order to minimize his liability for breach of contract. To compel completion of the contract would again result in a waste of resources and again the law does not compel completion but remits the victim to a simple damages remedy.

The problem exposed in the foregoing example is a quite general one. It results from the fact, remarked earlier, that contract remedies are frequently invoked in cases where there is no presumption that an exchange pursuant to the (defective) contract would in fact increase value (for example, cases of defective communication). Here we clearly do not want a remedy that will induce the party made liable to complete the exchange.

The objective of giving the party to a contract an incentive to fulfill his promise unless the result would be an inefficient use of resources (the production of the unwanted widgets in the first example, the round-about procurement of a substitute supplier in the second) can usually be achieved by allowing the victim of a breach to recover his expected profit on the transaction. If the supplier in the first example receives his expected profit from completing the 10,000 widgets, he will have no incentive to produce the remaining 90,000. We do not want him to produce them; no one wants them. In the second example, if I receive my expected profit from dealing with the original supplier, I become indifferent to whether he completes his performance.

In these examples the breach was in a sense involuntary. It was committed only to avert a larger loss. The breaching party would have been happier had there been no occasion to commit a breach. But in some cases a party would be tempted to breach the contract simply because his profit from breach would exceed his expected profit from completion of the contract. If his profit from beach would also exceed the expected profit to the other party from completion of the contract, and if damages are limited to loss of expected profit, there will be an incentive to commit a breach. There should be. The opportunity cost of completion to the breaching party is the profit that he would make from a breach, and if it is greater than his profit from completion, then completion will involve a loss to him. If that loss is greater than the gain to the other party from completion, breach would be value-maximizing and should be encouraged. And because the victim of the breach is made whole for his loss, he is indifferent; hence encouraging breaches in these circumstances will not deter people from entering into contracts in the future. . . .

Thus far the emphasis has been on the economic importance of not awarding damages in excess of the lost expectation. It is equally important, however, not to award less than the expectation loss. Suppose A contracts to sell B for $100,000 a machine that is worth $110,000 to B, i.e., that would yield him a profit of $10,000. Before delivery C comes to A and offers him $109,000 for the machine promised B. A would be tempted to breach were he not liable to B for B's loss of expected profit. Given that measure of damages, C will not be able to induce a breach of A's contract with B unless he offers B more than $110,000, thereby indicating that the machine really is worth more to him than to B. The expectation rule thus assures that the machine ends up where is it most valuable. . . .

One superficially attractive alternative to measuring contract damages by loss of expectation (i.e., lost profits) is to measure them by the reliance loss, especially in cases where liability is imposed not to induce performance but to penalize careless behavior. And even in the case where the breach is deliberate, it is arguable that expectation damages may overcompensate the victim of the breach. Suppose I sign a contract to deliver 10,000 widgets in six months, and the day after the contract is signed I default. The buyer's reliance loss – the sum of the costs he has irretrievably incurred as a result of the contract – is, let us say, zero, but his lost profit $1,000. Why should he be allowed to reap a windfall gain by the use of a measure of damages that does not correspond to any actual social cost?

One answer has already been given: the lost-profit measure is necessary to assure that the only breaches made are those that promote efficiency. But there is another answer: that on average, though not in every case, the lost-profit method will give a better approximation than the reliance measure to the actual social costs of contract breach.

In long-run competitive equilibrium, the total revenues of the sellers in a market are just equal to their total costs; there are no 'profits' in the economic sense. What law and accounting call profits are frequently not profits in that sense at all, but rather reimbursements of the costs of capital, of entrepreneurial effort, and of other inputs. These items of cost are excluded by the reliance measure of damages, which will therefore tend to understate the true social costs of breach.

Notes

1. According to traditional doctrine, the existence of consideration – the bargain element in a contract – provides a good reason for enforcing promises. Superficially, it may seem that in economic terms bargains are distinguishable from gratuitous promises because 'a truly gratuitous, non-reciprocal promise to confer a benefit is not part of the process by which resources are moved, through a series of exchanges, into successively more valuable uses': R. A. Posner, *Economic Analysis of Law* (2nd edn, 1977), p. 69. But as Posner was later to acknowledge ('Gratuitous Promises in Economics and Law' (1977) 6 J. Legal Stud. 411), a gift may be regarded not simply as a transfer payment but rather as a wealth-maximizing transaction, in that it creates utility in the donor as well as the donee (and if the donor is richer than the donee then on conventional assumptions as to diminishing returns, each monetary unit of the gift is worth more to the donee than to the donor). Moreover, the *promise* to make a gift *in the future*, if it is enforceable, is worth more to the promisee than an instantaneous transfer, because he is given information as to his future resources and can plan their use or consumption accordingly (cf. Posner, 'Gratuitous Promises', op. cit., pp. 412–14; Goetz and Scott, supra).

2. The traditional doctrinal explanation for consideration adopts a paternalist stance; it prevents an individual being held to a perhaps rash and overgenerous commitment: L. Fuller, 'Consideration and Form' (1941) 41 Col. L.R. 814. Posner ('Gratuitous Promises', op. cit., pp. 416–17) disavows paternalism and explains consideration on the basis that the administrative costs of enforcing gratuitous promises are typically high, relative to the amount at stake. Goetz and Scott argue, perhaps more convincingly, that the goal of the law is rather to optimize the interacting relationship between promisor and promisee (and therefore also the number and quality of promises) by reducing the costs incurred both by the promisor and the promisee in dealing with the contingency that the promisor might regret his promise. Whether a given type of non-reciprocal promise should be enforced in the light of this objective involes a careful consideration of a number of variables, especially the probability of the promisor keeping his promise, the degree of reliance by the promisee (beneficial and detrimental), the administrative costs of enforcement and the existence of extra-legal sanctions. Such an analysis can also help to elucidate questions concerning the limits of the

doctrine of promissory estoppel, as propounded in *Central London Property Trust* v. *High Trees House* [1947] K.B. 130. Where there is consideration, the matter is much less difficult because the very existence of the reciprocal relationship enables the parties themselves to find the cheapest means of accommodating the regret and reliance costs (cf. R. Coase, supra, Chapter 2, Section C).

3. Posner's economic justification for the expectation interest award (the full value of performance to the plaintiff) as the normal measure of damages for breach of contract should be compared with the optimal damages formula suggested by Goetz and Scott; the nearest equivalent in legal doctrine to this is the reliance interest measure which is, however, only awarded in exceptional cases (cf. A. I. Ogus, *Law of Damages* (1973), pp. 346–54). The difference between the two approaches highlights the difficulty, to which we have already referred (supra, Chapter 3, Section A), of formulating legal rules to achieve two, often conflicting, objectives. The Goetz and Scott formula is designed to encourage the optimal level of promise-making, while Posner and others, explaining the expectation award on the same basis (e.g. J. H. Barton, 'The Economic Basis of Damages for Breach of Contract' (1972) 1 J. Legal Stud. 277), are primarily concerned with efficient behaviour *subsequent* to the contract. In a notable, if also difficult, paper ('Damage Measures for Breach of Contract' (1980) 11 Bell J. Econ. 466) Shavell demonstrates that there does not exist a measure of damages which will be optimal in all contractual situations. The expectation measure will encourage efficient breach (and performance) given the level of reliance but will encourage a greater than optimal level of reliance by the promisee, because the damages will effectively 'insure' him against loss of the benefit to be derived from reliance expenditure, however large. Full recovery of reliance under the reliance measure leads to a similar problem (though not if the award is restricted to reimbursement of *reasonable* expenditure – cf. Ogus, op. cit., p. 348), and, in any event, as Posner shows, may encourage inefficient breach.

4. The problem of excessive reliance may be met, in part at least, by the doctrines which limit recovery for breach of contract. Under the remoteness rule, a promisee cannot recover for the consequences of a special risk known only to him, so that he is induced 'either to take any appropriate precautions himself or, if he believes that the other party might be the more efficient loss avoider, to disclose the risk to that party and pay him to assume it': Posner, op. cit., p. 94; Barton, op. cit., at pp. 293–6. The mitigation doctrine should induce efficient use of resources once a promise has been broken, and because it may require the promisee to accept performance by a third party it may also discourage excessive reliance on performance by the promisor.

5. The enforcement of a liquidated damages clause is easily justified economically. For the given purpose it is simply an example of a completely contingent contract (cf. Shavell, op. cit., pp. 475–8) and may be regarded as an exercise in risk-allocation: with mutual awareness of the risk of non-performance and the losses likely to be incurred, the parties may rationally trade-off the contract price (agreed payment when contract is performed)

against damages (agreed payment when contract is breached) – see Barton, op. cit., p. 286. Under Anglo-American law, however, the clause is not enforceable if the agreed compensation exceeds the anticipated value of performance to the promisee – the so-called 'penalty' doctrine. On the face of it, the traditional argument that penalties are 'extortionate' overlooks their risk-allocating function: the promisee may have been prepared to pay the agreed price only if the promisor offers a substantial guarantee of performance, and this may reflect the high subjective value the promisee has in performance. See C. J. Goetz and R. E. Scott, 'Liquidated Damages, Penalties and the Just Compensation Principle' (1977) 77 Col. L.R. 554; they conclude that the doctrine is either paternalist or is based on the assumption that there was some abnormality (e.g. duress) in the bargaining process. Alternative explanations have been offered by K. W. Clarkson, R. L. Miller and T. J. Muris ('Liquidated Damages v. Penalties: Sense or Nonsense?' [1978] Wisc. L.R. 351), that penalties create an incentive for promisees to spend resources inefficiently to procure breach by the promisor, and by P. H. Rubin, ('Unenforceable Contracts: Penalty Clauses and Specific Performance' (1981) 10 J. Legal Stud. 237), that they impose external costs on society since they typically provoke litigation, the full cost of which is not borne by the parties.

C. Specific Performance

A. SCHWARTZ

The Case for Specific Performance[8]

CONTRACT REMEDIES AND THE COMPENSATION GOAL

Specific performance is the most accurate method of achieving the compensation goal of contract remedies because it gives the promisee the precise performance that he purchased. The natural question, then, is why specific preformance is not routinely available. Three explanations of the law's restrictions on specific performance are possible. First, the law's commitment to the compensation goal may be less than complete; restricting specific performance may reflect an inarticulate reluctance to pursue the compensation goal fully. Second, damages may generally be fully compensatory. In that event, expanding the

[8] (1979) 89 Yale L.J. 271, 274–98, with omissions. Reprinted by permission of the author and the Yale Law Journal Co., and Fred B. Rothman & Company.

availability of specific performance would create opportunities for promisees to exploit promisors by threatening to compel, or actually compelling, performance, without furthering the compensation goal. The third explanation is that concerns of efficiency or liberty may justify restricting specific performance, despite its greater accuracy: specific performance might generate higher transaction costs than the damage remedy, or interfere more with the liberty interests of promisors. The first justification is beyond the scope of the analysis here. The second and third explanations will be examined in detail.

With respect to the second justification, current doctrine authorizes specific performance when courts cannot calculate compensatory damages with even a rough degree of accuracy. If the class of cases in which there are difficulties in computing damages corresponds closely to the class of cases in which specific performance is now granted, expanding the availability of specific performance is obviously unnecessary. Further, such an expansion would create opportunities for promisees to exploit promisors. The class of cases in which damage awards fail to compensate promisees adequately is, however, broader than the class of cases in which specific performance is now granted. Thus the compensation goal supports removing rather than retaining present restrictions on the availability of specific performance. . . .

SPECIFIC PERFORMANCE AND EFFICIENCY

. . . There are two principal ways in which efficiency might suffer as the result of expanding specific performance. First, many parties might prefer to have the specific performance remedy available only in those cases in which the law currently grants it. If the remedy's availability were greatly expanded, these parties would negotiate contract provisions restricting its use. Legal limitations on the availability of specific performance save these transaction costs. Professor Anthony Kronman has argued that limiting specific performance is justified precisely because it avoids such 'pre-breach' negotiations.[9] Second, if specific performance were routinely available, promisors who wanted to breach would often be compelled to 'bribe' promisees to release them from their obligations. The negotiations required might be more complex and costly than the post-breach negotiations that occur when breaching promisors have merely to pay promisees their damages. Professor Richard Posner argues, therefore, that restricting specific performance reduces 'post-breach' negotiation costs.[10] . . .

---

[9] 'Specific Performance' (1978) 45 U.Chi.L.R. 351.
[10] *Economic Analysis of Law* (2nd edn, 1977), pp. 88–9.

A. *Pre-Breach Negotiations*

'Intention justification' theories for restricting specific performance argue that the class of cases in which the parties now can get the remedy, and the class of cases in which the parties would want the remedy to be available, are coextensive. There are two difficulties with this position. First, there is no reason to assume that the parties' preferences are congruent with current law. Second, it is excessively difficult to derive from parties' preferences general legal rules respecting when either remedy should be used.

Both weaknesses are illustrated through an analysis of the most sophisticated intention justification theory, that of Professor Kronman. Kronman classifies as 'unique' those objects for which courts would have great difficulty identifying substitutes. Courts today generally limit specific performance to such cases. Professor Kronman argues that this limitation is consistent with the parties' intentions; if they were to contract as to remedy in the absence of a general rule, they would create a specific performance remedy only for sales of 'unique' goods or services. Kronman's argument starts from the premise that the 'cost of a specific performance provision to the promisor will be determined, in part, by his own estimate of the likelihood that he will want to breach the contract'. This likelihood is primarily a function of 'the probability that he will receive a better offer for his goods or services in the interim between formation of the contract and performance'. This probability is low 'where the subject matter of the contract is unique' because 'there is by definition no developed market [and] transactions are spotty at best. . . .' . . . The promisee in the unique goods case may doubt whether the promisor will actually perform, despite the unlikelihood that the promisor will receive a better offer. Since damage remedies could be undercompensatory, the promisee would probably prefer to have the specific performance remedy available. When the goods are not unique, however, the promisee regards the 'risk [of undercompensation] as slight where there is a developed market generating information about suitable substitutes'. Thus in the unique goods case the parties would be expected to agree to a specific performance remedy; the promisee wants the remedy, whereas the promisor is indifferent. In the non-unique goods case, on the other hand, the parties would negotiate for a damage remedy, because damages would probably adequately protect the promisee, while the promisor would want to be free to accept more favorable offers.

Analysis of the equilibria in 'developed' and 'undeveloped' markets and their reactions to exogenous shocks suggests, however, that the promisors of unique goods care more about retaining the option of breach than do promisors of nonunique goods. Respecting equilibria, Professor Kronman equates an undeveloped market with a market in which unique goods are sold. This is misleading because unique goods markets often are well organized; the antique market provides an example. Such markets have two distinguishing features. First, they are usually characterized by greater price dispersion than obtains in the market equilibria for roughly fungible goods. In addition, sellers of unique goods face a lower 'rate of arrival' of potential buyers than do sellers of roughly fungible goods. These two phenomena are related; a high 'buyer arrival' rate implies extensive comparison shopping among firms, whereas the degree of price dispersion a market can sustain varies inversely with the amount of comparison shopping. Sellers of unique goods face a relatively low buyer arrival rate because each item they sell is highly differentiated; consequently, relatively few potential customers for such items exist. Also, search costs are comparatively higher for unique goods; locating them can be difficult, and the sellers often are geographically dispersed. Further, analyzing the quality of particular unique goods and comparing different goods usually are more time-consuming than searching for roughly fungible goods.

A promisor/seller in an 'undeveloped market' – a market in which unique goods are sold – thus faces a lower arrival rate of potential buyers together with the resultant higher degree of price dispersion than a promisor in a developed market. The promisor of unique goods consequently has grounds to believe that the offers he receives are to some extent random, and that later offers could be much higher than earlier ones. This promisor thus prefers damages to specific performance because the damages remedy preserves his freedom to breach.

This conclusion is reinforced by an examination of the differing reactions of 'developed' and 'undeveloped' markets to exogenous shocks. Exogenous shocks help to explain why promisors might receive better offers between the time they contract and the time they are supposed to render performance. This phenomenon needs explanation because a vendor of goods or services is generally assumed to sell to all of his purchasers on the same terms. Price discrimination is often unlawful and its costs in mass transactions exceed the gains it produces. Customers generally know whether a firm offers the same terms to all and are unlikely to make offers that exceed the going price. In addition, firms that negotiate contracts on an individual basis have a strong incentive not to breach, even if they receive better offers, in order to maintain goodwill. In what circumstances, then, will promisors receive and accept better offers?

The most frequent situation in which these circumstances arise is when there is an unexpected and dramatic increase in demand. The increase in demand will exert an upward pressure on prices. In the case of nonunique goods, this pressure is partially relieved by the ability of sellers to increase output. Unique goods, however, are in inelastic supply; only a few Rembrandts exist, and an increase in demand will not increase their number. In consequence, when buyers demand more of a unique item, the primary response of sellers is to increase the price; they can expand output only slightly, if at all. Therefore, when demand unexpectedly increases, a promisor in a unique goods market could command higher prices than a promisor in a nonunique goods market. The seller of unique goods, when the contract is negotiated, thus has a strong incentive to preserve his freedom to breach. A seller of non-unique goods, by contrast, will probably have to compete with many other vendors for any new business that a demand increase generates, and the resultant price rise will be relatively modest. Thus he will care less about preserving his freedom to breach in response to demand shifts. In sum, if the promisor's preference for specific performance or damages is assumed to be determined solely by whether the performance at issue is unique, the promisor would not choose specific performance in situations in which the law now routinely grants it.

B. *Post-Breach Negotiations*

The second efficiency argument for restricting the availability of specific performance is that making specific performance freely available would generate higher post-breach negotiation costs than the damage remedy now generates. For example, suppose that a buyer (B1) contracts with a seller (S) to buy a widget for $100. Prior to delivery, demand unexpectedly increases. The widget market is temporarily in disequilibrium as buyers make offers at different prices. While the market is in disequilibrium, a second buyer (B2) makes a contract with S to purchase the same widget for $130. Subsequently, the new equilibrium price for widgets is $115. If specific performance is available in this case, B1 is likely to demand it, in order to compel S to pay him some of the profit that S will make from breaching. B1 could, for example, insist on specific performance unless S pays him $20 ($15 in substitution damages plus a $5 premium). If S agrees, B1 can cover at $115, and be better off by $5 than he would have been under the damage remedy, which would have given him only the difference between the cover price and the contract price ($15). Whenever S's better offer is higher than the new market price, the seller has an incentive to breach, and the first buyer has an incentive to threaten specific performance in order to capture some of the seller's gains from breach.

The post-breach negotiations between S and B1 represent a 'deadweight' efficiency loss;[11] the negotiations serve only to redistribute wealth between S and B1, without generating additional social wealth. If society is indifferent as to whether sellers or buyers as a group profit from an increase in demand, the law should seek to eliminate this efficiency loss. Limiting buyers to the damage remedy apparently does so by foreclosing post-breach negotiations.

This analysis is incomplete, however. Negotiation costs are also generated when B1 attempts to collect damages. If the negotiations by which first buyers (B1 here) capture a portion of their sellers' profits from breach are less costly than the negotiations (or lawsuits) by which first buyers recover the market contract differential, then specific performance would generate lower post-breach negotiation costs than damages. This seems unlikely, however. The difference between the contract and market prices is often easily determined, and breaching sellers have an incentive to pay it promptly so as not to have their extra profit consumed by lawyers' fees. By contrast, if buyers can threaten specific performance and thereby seek to capture some of the sellers' profits from breach, sellers will bargain hard to keep as much of the profits as they can. Therefore, the damage remedy would probably result in quick payments by breaching sellers while the specific performance remedy would probably give rise to difficult negotiations. Thus the post-breach negotiation costs associated with the specific performance remedy would seem to be greater than those associated with the damage remedy.

This analysis makes the crucial assumption, however, that the first buyer, B1, has access to the market at a significantly lower cost than the seller; though both pay the same market price for the substitute, B1 is assumed to have much lower cover costs. If this assumption is false, specific performance would not give rise to post-breach negotiations. Consider the illustration again. Suppose that B1 can obtain specific performance, but that S can cover as conveniently as B1. If B1 insists on a conveyance, S would buy another widget in the market for $115 and deliver on his contracts with both B1 and B2. A total of three transactions would result: S–B1; S–B2; S2–S (S's purchase of a second widget). None of these transactions involves post-breach negotiations. Thus if sellers can cover conveniently, the specific performance remedy does not generate post-breach negotiation costs.

The issue, then, is whether sellers and buyers generally have similar cover costs. Analysis suggests that they do. Sellers as well as buyers have incentives to learn market conditions. Because sellers have to 'check the competition', they will have a good knowledge of market prices and quality ranges. Also, when a buyer needs goods or services tailored to his own needs, he will be able to find such goods or services

---

[11] [*Editors' Note*: See infra, Chapter 5, Section B.]

more cheaply than sellers in general could, for they would first have to ascertain the buyer's needs before going into the market. However, in situations in which the seller and the first buyer have already negotiated a contract, the seller is likely to have as much information about the buyer's needs as the buyer has. Moreover, in some markets, such as those for complex machines and services, sellers are likely to have a comparative advantage over buyers in evaluating the probable quality of performance and thus would have lower cover costs. Therefore, no basis exists for assuming that buyers generally have significantly lower cover costs than sellers. It follows that expanding the availability of specific performance would not generate higher post-breach negotiation costs than the damage remedy.

C. *Efficiency Gains from the Routine Availability of Specific Performance*

. . . Further expanding the availability of specific performance would produce certain efficiency gains: it would minimize the inefficiencies of undercompensation, reduce the need for liquidated damage clauses, minimize strategic behavior, and save the costs of litigating complex damage issues.

First, if only a damage remedy is available, promisors may sometimes breach when their gains from breach exceed the damages a court will assess, though not the full costs breach imposes on the promisees. Such breaches may be inefficient for they make promisors better off but promisees worse off.

Second, under current law, parties have an incentive to create a 'contractual' specific performance remedy in cases in which specific performance is now prohibited or its availability is uncertain by negotiating liquidated damage clauses. This is because these clauses perform the same function as specific performance – ensuring adequate compensation or performance when damage rules provide neither. If specific performance were routinely available, much of the costs to the parties of negotiating liquidated damage clauses would be saved.

Third, commentators have argued that liquidated damage clauses that require relatively high payouts would create incentives for the promisee to breach when changed circumstances cause the promisee to prefer the payout to performance. Resources spent on inducing breach or on countering this conduct constitute deadweight efficiency losses. If specific performance were made widely available, however, contracting parties would have an incentive to choose it rather than liquidated damage clauses because, as we have seen, specific performance and liquidated damages are often substitutes. Since the gains to the promisee from inducing breach are greatly minimized when large damage payouts do not accompany it, such strategic behavior would rarely occur.

Finally, specific performance often is sought when damages would be difficult to establish. Granting the remedy in such cases would save the resources that would otherwise be devoted to exploring complex damage questions.

D. *Administrative Cost Objections to Specific Performance*

. . . One final efficiency objection remains – that the remedy increases the administrative costs of the parties and the courts because of the expense entailed in creating and implementing specific performance decrees. This objection is at present the basis for a defense to a specific performance action: a court can deny the remedy on the ground of 'difficulty of supervision' even if a plaintiff otherwise establishes a right to specific performance. An analysis of the administrative cost objection, however, establishes that the difficulty of supervision defense should be available much less frequently than current law permits. . . . First, . . . it is often difficult to know whether the costs to courts of allowing a specific performance remedy would exceed the gains resulting from increased availability of the remedy. In situations in which a cost comparison between specific performance and damages is not possible, the more accurate remedy, specific performance, should be granted. Second, the administrative costs that the specific performance remedy imposes on the parties should not count against its wider use, because those costs will be incurred only when the parties perceive them to be lower than the gains from equitable relief.

Notes

1. The choice between damages and specific performance is closely analogous to that between damages (the liability rule) and injunction (the property rule) in nuisance and other tort claims: see Calabresi and Melamed, supra, Chapter 2, Section D. In the present context there is a stronger prima facie case for the property rule since (a) contractual arrangements, unlike land use conflicts, typically only involve two parties; and (b) the parties have already formed a legal relationship. Both of these facts suggest that the transaction costs problem, which arises where it is necessary on grounds of efficiency for the parties to negotiate a waiver of the specific performance order, is less acute: see A. Kronman, 'Specific Performance' (1978) 45 U. Chi. L.R. 351, 352.

2. Schwartz makes out a powerful case for the general availability of specific performance, at least where the benefits are not outweighed by the transaction costs, and he is thus critical of the traditional reluctance of Anglo-American courts to order this remedy. He appears, however, to overlook a fundamental difficulty with this solution, that specific performance unlike

damages cannot accommodate the doctrines of remoteness and mitigation which limit damages awards and which, as has been seen (supra, notes to Section B), may set appropriate incentives for efficient behaviour by the promisee. (See also E. Yorio, 'In Defense of Money Damages for Breach of Contract' (1982) 82 Col. L.R. 1365). The same problem arises in relation to rules enforcing the payment of a debt, as is evidenced by the much criticized decision in *White & Carter* v. *McGregor* [1962] A.C. 413.

3. There is, it should be noted, a remedy which is analogous to that of specific performance but which may avoid the difficulties referred to in the last paragraph. This is where the court awards the cost of alternative performance by a third party – often called the 'reinstatement' measure (see T. J. Muris, 'Cost of Completion or Diminution in Market Value: The Relevance of Subjective Value' (1983) 12 J. Legal Stud. 379). The fact that the plaintiff is not compelled to use the money to secure the alternative performance obviates the need for the court to supervise performance and thus, in comparison with specific performance, reduces the transaction costs. It is sometimes objected that this may lead to the plaintiff gaining a 'windfall', if the amount awarded exceeds the value of performance to him, and he does not in fact secure performance from a third party. This explains why the English courts apparently require the plaintiff to show that he has a 'sufficient intention' to spend the money in this way. But it should be observed that if the award is refused on a failure to satisfy this condition and the defendant is relieved from paying for the cost of performance, then it is he who is gaining the 'windfall': D. R. Harris, A. I. Ogus and J. Phillips, 'Contract Remedies and the Consumer Surplus' (1979) 96 L.Q.R. 581, 592–4.

D. Unequal Bargaining Power and Unconscionability

M. J. TREBILCOCK

*

An Economic Approach to the Doctrine of Unconscionability[12]

In fashioning economically defensible criteria of unconscionability, it is submitted that two criteria are central. First, if the market in which the transaction occurs is *structurally impaired*, this may provide grounds for judicial intervention by way of preventing the enforcement of such a transaction. Secondly, even in cases where the trans-

---

[12] From B. J. Reiter and J. Swan (eds.), *Studies in Contract Law* (1980), ch. 11, with omissions. Reprinted by permission of Butterworth & Co. (Canada) Ltd., the author and editors.

action in question is entered into in a structurally sound market, the market may be *informationally impaired*, thus rendering the transaction suspect. It is proposed to examine each of these two concepts in turn.

STRUCTURALLY IMPAIRED MARKETS

What is contemplated here is the case of a market which is so structurally impaired as to preclude the behaviour of one or other of the parties to a contract being effectively disciplined in his behaviour towards the other party by market (competitive) forces. Two subsets of circumstances can be identified in this respect. . . .

(i) Situational Monopolies

This class of case is approximately conterminous with those circumstances often considered as falling under the doctrine of duress. The doctrine of duress has historically been assigned a highly circumscribed role in the Anglo-Canadian common law of contracts, with the scope of the doctrine being confined mostly to cases of physical threats to the person or unlawful detention of another person's goods, inducing a contract. The doctrine has occasionally been cast more widely, and the beginnings of a concept of 'economic duress' seem discernible in some of the case law. . . .

It is submitted that the relevant test in all of the so-called duress cases is whether the conduct of the party against whom the doctrine is pleaded was such as to remove from, or to take advantage of the absence of, effective access by the other party to a workably competitive range of alternative choices. For example, in the salvage cases, what may be objectionable about the terms exacted by a tug owner from the owner or captain of a sinking ship is that the latter faces no realistic alternative suppliers of the demanded service. Similarly, in cases where one contracting party threatens to suspend performance unless the other party agrees to a variation in the contract. . . .

The extension of the doctrine of duress to any form of monopolistic threat would seem a promising and defensible line of development for the doctrine to take. Beyond rationalizing all the various classes of cases hitherto subsumed under the doctrine of duress, a doctrine so functionally defined has the advantage of posing a relatively realistic inquiry for the courts to embark upon. In cases of situational monopolies, the circumstances directly surrounding the particular transaction between the two parties in question will generally yield reliable inferences as to the extent of the monopoly power possessed by one in relation to the other. This is in sharp and significant contrast to the problems posed in cases of market-wide monopolies, discussed below. On the other hand, several cautions need to be added.

First, despite the monopoly that exists in these cases some of the transactions may be value maximizing; what has happened is that the monopolist has taken all or almost all the consumer surplus in rents (*e.g.*, in the salvage cases). Thus, these transactions may not be so much allocatively inefficient as distributively 'unfair'. What makes them distributively unfair cannot avoid a value judgment, although economic analysis might suggest some caution in intervention where excessive profits merely signal a transition to a new equilibrium or where excessively blunt intervention may eliminate incentives to supply the product or service in question. Second, in a number of the standard duress cases, the circumstances are more accurately characterized, economically, not as simple monopolies but as bilateral monopolies. For example, even in the salvage cases, depending on the circumstances, it may be the case that both the owners of the tug and the vessel in distress each possess abnormal market power in relation to the other. That is to say, the tug owner may be the only supplier of salvage services readily accessible to the distressed vessel, but in turn, the distressed vessel may be the only readily available demander of the tug's services. As economic theorizing has shown, in bilateral monopoly situations the outcomes of the resulting bargaining processes are somewhat indeterminate in terms of a competitive market benchmark. The implications of this for a judicial doctrine of unconscionability is that it will sometimes be difficult to determine whether resulting contracts are optimal in any relevant economic sense. However, apart from 'fairness' considerations, one potential advantage of a properly fashioned intervention here is that the social waste (inefficiency) that is often generated by strategic behaviour in bilateral monopoly situations might be reduced. . . .

(ii) Market-Wide Monopolies

Here, the case differs from situational monopolies because of the difficulty facing a court in making reliable determinations of abnormal market power simply by looking at the relationship and interactions between the two parties to a contested contract. Claims of abuse of market power can only be validated by extensive enquiry into the structure of the entire market in which the transaction has taken place. The difficulties facing a court in this context are well illustrated by the decision of the House of Lords in *Macaulay v. Schroeder Publishing Co. Ltd.*[13] . . .

The judgment of Lord Diplock is particularly instructive in its

[13] [1976] 1 W.L.R. 1308.

treatment of the alleged abuses of market power flowing from the use of standard form contracts. His Lordship said that standard forms of contract are of two kinds. The first, of early origin, are widely used in commercial transactions, are the result of extensive prior negotiations by the parties, and are adopted because 'they facilitate the conduct of trade'. Examples cited were bills of lading, charter parties, insurance policies, and contracts of sale in the commodity markets. Here, his Lordship said, there is a strong presumption that the terms of these contracts are fair and reasonable because they are used by parties 'whose bargaining power is fairly matched'.

As to the second class of standard form contracts (essentially consumer-type transactions) such a presumption was said not to apply. These were said to be of comparatively modern origin and are *the result of the concentration of particular kinds of business in relatively few hands*'. Said to exemplify this category were the ticket cases. The identifying characteristics of contracts falling into this category were described as follows:

The terms of this kind of standard form contract have not been the subject of negotiation between the parties to it, or approved by any organization representing the interests of the weaker party. They have been dictated by that party whose bargaining power, *either exercised alone or in conjunction with others providing similar goods and services,* enables him to say: 'If you want these goods or services at all, these are the only terms on which they are obtainable. Take it or leave it.' To be in a position to adopt this attitude toward a party desirous of entering into a contract to obtain goods or services provides a classic instance of superior bargaining power.

His Lordship went on to point out that the fact that the defendants' bargaining power vis-a-vis the plaintiff was strong enough to enable them to adopt this take-it-or-leave-it attitude raised no presumption that they had used it to drive an unconscionable bargain but that special vigilance on the part of the court was called for to see that they had not. The fact that in the result the court struck down the contract means, of course, that in the court's view the defendants' superior bargaining power had in fact been abused in the terms it had exacted from the plaintiff.

While recognizing that the assumptions underlying this analysis of the use of standard form contracts have enjoyed considerable academic currency, it is submitted that they are fallacious. First, the proposition that the use of consumer standard-form contracts is the result of the concentration of market power is entirely without factual foundation. The reason why such contracts are used is exactly the same as for their use in the commercial context, that is to 'facilitate the conduct of trade', or in economic terms, to reduce transaction costs. . . . Moreover, it is a matter of common observation that standard forms are used (for this reason) in countless contexts where no significant degree of market concentration exists. . . . [E]ven the presence of dickering between parties, standing alone, is ambiguous as between the presence or absence of competition. Dickering may, for example, be merely a reflection of attempts by a monopolist to price discriminate among consumers by ascertaining and exploiting different demand elasticities. The use of standard forms is a totally spurious proxy for the existence of market power. The real measure of market power is not whether a supplier presents his terms on a take-it-or-leave-it basis but whether the consumer, if he decides to 'leave it', has available to him a workably competitive range of alternative sources of supply. . . . If the market is workably competitive, any supplier offering uncompetitive standard-form terms will have to reformulate his total package of price and non-price terms to prevent consumers (at least consumers at the margin, which are the decisive consideration in such a market) from switching their business to other competitors.

It is, of course, true that general use of common standard-form contracts throughout an industry may, on occasion, be evidence of cartelization. But here one must be discriminating. If a reasonable choice of different packages of price and non-price terms is available in the market, albeit all through the medium of different standard-form contracts, then obviously the allegation of a 'fix' will not stand up. Even where all contracts are the same, in perfectly competitive markets where the product is homogeneous, commonality of terms is what one would expect to find (for example, the wheat market). Every supplier simply 'takes' his price and probably other terms from the market and is powerless to vary them. In a perfectly competitive market, with many sellers and many buyers each supplying or demanding too insignificant a share of total market output to influence terms, all participants, sellers and buyers, are necessarily confronted with a take-it-or-leave-it proposition. . . .

The intent of the doctrine of inequality of bargaining power, at least as it emerges from *Macaulay*, is clearly to redistribute contractual incidents between contracting parties, for example, to make it less costly for songwriters to secure publishers' services and more costly for publishers to provide them, in other words to adjust the relative values exchanged. What will be its effect?

. . . By assumption, in a perfectly competitive market both for the final product and for intermediate inputs, no excess profits are being made (that is, no profits beyond a reasonable return on capital), so that any reduction in industry profits will also induce a reduction in output and thus intermediate inputs (for example, the work of unknown songwriters). The response of firms in such a market to a cost-increasing rule . . . will be to offset this cost increase with an appropriate reduction in the prices they are willing to pay for song-writers' services as a factor input in the production of music or records. . . . Alternatively, or in addition, because of the reduced prospect now of returns on successful composers' efforts (because of greater ease of contractual termination) publishers in their turn will presumably find it no longer rational to make the same investment in promoting unknown songwriters. Probably they will 'carry' high risks for shorter periods before setting them adrift. . . . Indeed, at the limit, music publishers may demand that composers compensate them directly for their promotional efforts on a composer's behalf, thus inducing a composer (rather than a publisher), in effect, to make an investment in human capital by securing at his own expense the services of an agent (a common arrangement in other contexts). . . . The lesson of economics, in this context, is that legal liability rules are unlikely to be able to affect the broad balance of advantage between buyers and sellers.

If the market for the final products of songwriters' service is mon-opolized, the analysis changes little. A single music-publisher acting as a monopolist in the sale of a songwriter's output is also likely to respond to a cost-increasing rule (for example, termination on non-publication) by reducing royalties or 'carry' periods. He has limited ability (depending on the price elasticity of demand and supply for his product) to pass on increased costs to consumers of the final product, and thus has an incentive to minimize costs similar to firms in a competitive industry. Even assuming supra-competitive profits, further rules which proscribe reductions in royalty rates or other contract variations (that is, increase the full wage to songwriters) will generate similar economic incentives to those facing firms in a competitive industry to make substitutions of other factors. . . .

INFORMATIONALLY IMPAIRED MARKETS

(i) Lack of Normal Information-Processing Capacity . . .

. . . Setting aside the problems associated with the over inclusive nature of current rules on capacity and instead focussing on their under inclusive character, it is useful to 'decompose' the concept of infancy into some set of physiological characteristics which might then be extrapolated into a set of guidelines for the courts in applying the doctrine of unconscionability to transactions involving adults.

Rules which deny contractual capacity to infants probably reflect a concern over vulnerabilities flowing from factors such as: illiteracy, lack of education, and experiential factors such as the absence of reasonable acquaintance with market bench-marks against which to evaluate proposed contractual offerings. Thus, an inability to reason about a proposed contractual offering in a reasonably mature adult fashion, as a result of some fairly precisely identifiable physiological disability, or an inability resulting from lack of experience to evaluate proposed contractual offerings against prevailing market bench-marks, seem to lie at the heart of the current rules on contractual incapacity, at least as they relate to infants. Thus, it seems reasonable to accept that similar physiological characteristics which might impair the ability of adults to reason about proposed contractual offerings, or experiential factors which impair the ability to relate those offerings to market norms, are useful indicators in shaping the doctrine of unconscionability as it might be applied in this context.

The doctrine of unconscionability, as it applies to the foregoing cases of impaired ability to process information, seems to be playing a very useful and defensible role. The scope of the inquiry posed for the courts by the doctrine in this context seems a relatively manageable one, given that typically the courts need only to examine the circumstances immediately surrounding the particular transaction in question, the characteristics of the parties, and the nature of the relationship between them. They are not called on to embark upon extensive inquiries into conditions generally in the relevant market beyond establishing, where possible, a market norm against which the values exchanged in the transaction in question can be measured.

However, it is important that the doctrine be seen as a constrained tool of intervention and not the basis for unfettered judicial second-guessing of market participants. The constraints that ought to be particularly noted are: first, the courts, wisely, have generally insisted on a conjunction of a substantial divergence between the consideration received by the party seeking relief and the consideration available from elsewhere in the market and some quite specifically identifiable source of impairment in the information-processing powers of the party seeking relief which prevented him from capturing the benefits of those market alternatives. . . . Second, even where this conjunction of circumstances is present, it should probably be treated as doing no more than raising a strong presumption of unconscionability which the other party to the transaction should be at liberty to attempt to rebut. . . . Third, to the extent that the party seeking relief is not able to identify any precise source of impairment to his information-processing capabilities, to that extent the court should insist on more rigorous proof of the market norm against which the applicant seeks to have the inadequacy of consideration provided under the impinged transaction measured. . . . Fourth, it is axiomatic that if a person who would otherwise be entitled to relief under the criteria outlined above nevertheless has the advantage of independent legal or similar advice, the presence of an agent with presumably normal information-processing capabilities fully answers any claim for relief by the applicant.

(ii) Material Non-Disclosure

If resources are efficiently allocated by private exchange when both parties to the exchange are optimally informed as to its costs and benefits, then liability rules conducive to that end may have a useful role to play. On the demand side, a consumer will be making a rational investment in information if he invests resources in search and evaluation of information to the point where the expected marginal benefits from further search and evaluation are equal to the marginal costs of further such activity. On the supply side of the market in information, a supplier will be producing for consumers of his products and services a socially optimal amount of information about them if the price which consumers are prepared to pay for the marginal benefits of this information is equal to the marginal social costs (in terms of real resources consumed) of producing it.

There seem to be good reasons for supposing that in many markets this latter condition will not hold. Consumer ignorance in such markets, even following economically rational search, may permit non-competitive price-quality dispersions to persist for reasons such as the following. Even in competitive markets, a firm offering non-competitive terms may occupy too insignificant a share of the market to attract disparagement from competitors, particularly when a competitor who engages in justified disparagement has no way of confining the gains from such disparagement to himself alone. While the marginal social costs to the non-competitive firm of disclosing information to consumers that makes clear the inferiority of its terms may be trivial, the marginal private costs to the firm of disclosure (in terms of lost sales) will induce suppression of the information even though consumers may be willing to pay the marginal social costs of its production. In this sense, market outcomes will not be allocatively efficient, in a Pareto optimal sense. This problem may be particularly severe in markets involving expensive and complex goods and services which consumers purchase infrequently and of which they have little 'experience' information. Given limited innate ability to make accurate price/quality comparisons, extensive search, evaluation, self-education, or purchased expertise may be necessary to generate even modest marginal returns and would be an economically irrational investment on the part of a consumer. On the other hand, firms in the market may be able to provide the desired information at a much lower marginal social cost. In other words, in this respect sellers may have a lower-cost production function for information than consumers and, provided consumers are prepared to pay for more information, should be required to provide it. Again, in markets characterized by monopolization and therefore a lack of competitive incentives to produce countervailing information about alternative contractual offerings, a firm may produce less information about its terms than is socially optimal. In addition, in markets characterized by a high level of instability, that is, a rapid turnover of buyers and sellers and therefore a high information depreciation rate, less than socially optimal amounts of information may be produced by the market.

Markets in information are probably flawed in a more general sense by another factor – the public goods characteristic of much information. Once information has been produced, it will be difficult to prevent those who do not buy a product or service (and therefore the information that accompanies it), but who nevertheless derive value from the information, from using it although they do not pay for it. This will leave consumers who do buy such products or services (and the accompanying information) facing a disproportionately large part of the costs of the information while others who also value it are able to pay nothing. Market mechanisms will therefore not accurately reveal to suppliers the true demand function of consumers for information and are likely to lead to its systematic under-production.

If this analysis is correct in theory, then the practical question that follows is how does one move the production of information on the supply side of the market closer to the socially optimal?

One context in which the courts might be more forthcoming than they have been historically is in the treatment of material non-disclosure. With some important qualifications, the general contract rule has been that one party to a contract is not under any obligation to inform the other party to the contract of some factual circumstance of which the first party is aware and which may be of significance to the second party in his decision to enter into the contract and on what terms.

Canadian courts have recently begun to make substantial modifications to the rule against liability for non-disclosure, principally by using tort and contract law on misrepresentation as the basis of liability. . . .

The most important caveat with respect to this evolution in the case-law is to distinguish the treatment of casually acquired information from that which has been deliberately acquired. . . . [To] impose a duty of disclosure on a party who has deliberately, and presumably at some cost, sought out information in the market which will enable him to participate in market activity more effectively (*i.e.*, more profitably) would be to eliminate incentives to engage in this information acquisition and generation process, thus rendering even more imperfect, on

account of informational deficiencies, the functioning of such markets.
. . .

(iii) Information Problems with Standard Form Contracts

Courts and commentators alike have commonly taken the view of
standard form contracts that the party who draws them up has a
disproportionate bargaining power in terms of his ability to impose
terms involuntarily on the other party. . . . We have already examined
the market structure argument in this respect, and rejected it. However, the issue remains whether information imperfections afflicting a
consumer in this context are such as to lead to unconscionable
contractual outcomes even in structurally sound markets. . . . A
number of difficult conceptual issues are raised by the question of the
abuse of bargaining power through differential information about the
content of standard form contracts.

First, . . . it does not follow that the supplier has unconstrained
bargaining power to impose any terms that he wishes on a consumer.
One of the most important determinants of whether contract terms in
such circumstances might be considered fair, in the sense of having
been effectively disciplined by market forces, is whether at the *margin*
of the market, there are *enough* consumers who are sensitive to the
content of these clauses to bring effective pressure to bear on suppliers
to modify them in an acceptable way. . . .

A recognition of the importance of the marginal consumer confronts
a court with intractable factual issues pertaining to how 'thick' the
margin of sophisticated consumers is in the relevant market and how
well a supplier is able to discriminate in favour of those consumers and
against the inframarginal consumers. Both issues are difficult. As in the
case of market-wide monopolies, the first issue requires evidence and
analysis of conditions prevailing throughout the market in question.
. . .

Goldberg[14] has argued that in the case of standard-form insurance
policies, the costs to the consumer of obtaining, processing, and
evaluating information about the implications of 'hidden', subsidiary
clauses in such contracts will tend to direct competitive forces, even in
workably competitive markets, away from the subject-matter of these
clauses and towards broader price-quantity comparisons. The result of
such a process may be harsh-term-low-price policies, whereas many consumers, in the absence of information and transaction costs, may have
preferred an easier-term-higher-price combination. Thus, bargaining
processes are distorted. This may be so, Goldberg argues, even though

[14] 'Institutional Change and the Quasi-Invisible Hand' (1974) 17 J. Law and Econ. 461.

the industry is making no supra-competitive profits. Therefore, the argument goes, the industry would be made no worse off, and many consumers might be made better off, by liability rules designed to produce the mix of terms that would have been reached by the parties in a world without information or transaction costs. Unlike rules designed to improve the quality of available information discussed below, these rules would take information markets as given and simply regulate the substantive contents of contracts.

There are several difficulties with Goldberg's argument. First, even assuming that information and transaction costs relative to the stakes involved in matters dealt with in subsidiary terms . . . are as high as Goldberg asserts, how does one determine whether more or fewer consumers will be advantaged under a legal reallocation of risks which produces an easier-term-higher-price contract and displaces previous harsher-term-lower-price combinations, given that on Goldberg's hypothesis, information costs are such that consumers' true preferences can never be revealed? . . .

A further factor unaccounted for in Goldberg's analysis, as in that of other critics of standard-form contracts who point to the absence of subjective consumer consent to all contractual terms, is the price that most consumers attach to uncertainty. Making the usual assumption that most consumers are risk-averse, consumers who sign contracts containing clauses which have been drafted by the other party with his advantage obviously in mind and which they do not understand will reflect their aversion to the assumption of undetermined, but intuitively adverse, risk allocations by discounting the consideration they are prepared to offer for entering into such contracts.

Finally, if courts were to impose liability rules on parties to standard form contracts on Goldberg's rationale, then *ex post ad hoc* judicial interventions cannot fairly take the form simply of invalidating 'harsh' clauses. In addition, other clauses will have to be reworked to compensate the supplier for the expanded package of contractual benefits which he is now providing to the consumer. In effect, this form of judicial policing of standard-form contracts should strictly involve reformulating whole contracts. If substantive intervention is to occur, this may argue for general, *ex ante*, legislative intervention where 'harsh' terms are invalidated and the market is permitted to take care of consequential adjustments to other terms. . . .

Thus, if in a standard form contract context, prohibiting or substituting clauses may or may not move us closer to optimality, given the absence of a revealed preference by consumers, . . . what role can the courts usefully play in policing transactional fairness through the instrumentality of the unconscionability doctrine?

A modest proposal would be for the doctrine of unconscionability to penalize contractual documents which in their wording or organization are apt to mislead consumers. . . .

A more expansive formulation of a rule against unfair surprise might impose conspicuousness, intelligibility, and specific assent requirements with respect to clauses creating substantial divergences from the reasonable expectations of the consumer as reflected in terms available to other consumers at the margin of the market. Such a rule would of course avoid outright prohibitions of such clauses but instead would attach conditional prohibitions which could be avoided by compliance with the required standards of conspicuousness, etc. Thus, such a rule would avoid imposing preferences on the parties while at the same time improving, hopefully, the quality of information in the market, or at least the thickness of the margin of sophisticated consumers whose actions 'make' the market.

The courts would need to apply this second formulation of the rule against unfair surprise with a great deal of caution, if only to avoid the problems associated with assuming non-cost justified discrimination between two classes of consumers without really investigating why different contractual offerings for each of the two groups might in fact be justified. . . .

Subject to similar cautions, in limiting cases a yet more substantial form of judicial intervention may be justified than that contemplated by rules against unfair surprise directed at the contents and format of the initial contract. Recalling the importance of examining not only the contents of standard-form contracts but performance in fact rendered thereunder, it may be that an infra-marginal consumer should be able to upset a transaction where he can show a very substantial divergence between the value of the performance he has received from a supplier and the value of the performance typically realized by marginal (sophisticated), but otherwise similar, consumers in the same market. In other words, non-cost justified forms of performance discrimination, where very substantial and clearly proven, may properly raise a strong presumption of unconscionability even though there may be no discrimination in the initial contract terms.

DISTRIBUTIVE CONSIDERATIONS IN THE APPLICATION OF THE DOCTRINE OF UNCONSCIONABILITY

In the course of this essay, circumstances have been identified where lack of endowments might well lead to circumstances which justify intervention by the courts to prevent contract enforcement. For example, . . . poverty may in some cases be conducive to the creation of situational monopolies. Secondly, poverty as it manifests itself in illiteracy, lack of education, or lack of experience with market activity may provide grounds for intervention on the grounds of impaired information-processing ability. However, outside limited cases of this kind, this essay has not suggested distributive considerations as a major underpinning for a judicial doctrine of unconscionability. It is important to elaborate on why this view has been taken.

First, while it is clear that poor people often will be compelled, *e.g.*, to enter into consumer credit transactions at very high rates of interest, or to rent accommodation of very low quality, it is not at all clear that this apparently differential treatment of poor people in the market-place is in any way attributable to objectionable behaviour on the part of the suppliers who deal with them. Even though the demand on the part of poor people for certain necessities of life may be highly inelastic, *i.e.*, unresponsive to price, given their resources, it does not follow from that fact alone that they will be exploited. Exploitation will only occur, in the sense of a charging of supra-competitive prices etc., if there are restrictions on supply in the relevant markets.

Notes

1. A major theme of the literature of contract law has been the problem of reconciling classical principles, under which the courts have no power to control for unfairness or unconscionability, with the widespread phenomena of agreements between parties of unequal bargaining power, especially standard form contracts: see, especially, F. Kessler, 'Contracts of Adhesion – Some Thoughts about Freedom of Contract' (1943) 43 Col. L.R. 629; W. Friedmann, *Law in a Changing Society* (2nd edn, 1972), ch. 4; V. Goldberg, 'Institutional Change and the Quasi-Invisible Hand' (1974) 17 J. Law and Econ. 461. The response to the demand for intervention has been to extend protection to the 'weaker' party at a general level, both by judicial doctrine (e.g. *Lloyds Bank* v. *Bundy* [1975] Q.B. 326; *Schroeder Music Publishing* v. *Macaulay* [1974] 1 W.L.R. 1308) and by legislation (Unfair Contract Terms Act 1977; Supply of Goods and Services Act 1982), and at a specific level, by detailed regulation of contract-types (e.g. employment, landlord-tenant, consumer credit). Much of the thrust of the economic analysis – Trebilcock's paper provides an excellent example – has been to show that these developments are often based on unsound theory and inadequate empirical data.

2. Where intervention is based on the content of the contract, as opposed to the environment in which it was made, the critics focus not only on the difficulty of the determining what is 'fair' or 'reasonable', but more importantly also on the consequences of intervention: see, e.g. R. H. Coase, 'The Choice of the Institutional Framework: A Comment' (1974) 17 J. Law and Econ. 77; A. Schwartz, 'A Reexamination of Nonsubstantive Unconscionability' (1977) 63 Virg. L.R. 1053, 1056–63. If one term of the contract is

regulated, the seller can often adapt by changing other terms, so that the object of the control is subverted. If the control is effective and an allegedly unfavourable term is banned, it will impair the buyer's ability to choose between a contract with that term at a lower price and a contract without that term at a higher price (see further, on regulation, infra, Chapter 7.) Some have, however, argued that sound intervention is to be explained, and perhaps justified, on paternalist grounds: D. Kennedy, 'Distributive and Paternalist Motives in Contract and Tort Law, with Special Reference to Compulsory Terms and Unequal Bargaining Power' (1982) 14 Maryland L.R. 563.

3. The existence of legal controls on 'procedural unconscionability', where the law assumes that through personal incompetence (e.g. infancy or mental handicap) a party is not in a position to make a utility-maximizing decision, is less controversial (cf. R. A. Epstein, 'Unconscionability: A Critical Reappraisal' (1975) 18 J. Law and Econ. 293, 300–1), though difficulty does arise in determining the limits of these doctrines (A. Schwartz, op. cit., pp. 1076–82). As Trebilcock observes, cases of so-called 'economic duress' are best rationalized in terms of 'situational monopolies', the restriction of access to alternative choices. Where the access to choice is limited for both parties – bilateral monopolies – the position is more complicated because the risk of either party extracting an extortionate price must be balanced against the cost of discouraging the formation of an agreement: W. M. Landes and R. A. Posner, 'Salvors, Finders, Good Samaritans, and Other Rescuers: An Economic Study of Law and Altruism' (1978) 7 J. Legal Stud. 83.

4. Conventional analysis suggests that much of the problem of unequal bargaining power is in reality a problem of unequal access to information. As has been shown by A. Schwartz and L. Wilde in a penetrating study, 'Intervening in Markets on the Basis of Imperfect Information: A Legal and Economic Analysis' (1979) 127 U. Penn. L.R. 630, there is a need both to balance the benefits of information-producing obligations against their costs (which inevitably will be reflected in the price of the goods or services) and to focus on how markets behave when characterized by imperfect information. If the market is competitive, then it only requires that a certain number of customers at the margin are sufficiently informed for a socially efficient set of products and contract terms to be made available. What constitutes a 'certain number' for this purpose will depend on the nature of the market; and, as Goldberg has indicated, firms may 'renegotiate terms for the few aggressive customers while keeping the high information barrier for other customers virtually intact' (op. cit., p. 485). The paradox which emerges is that standard form contracts which do not discriminate between buyers may result in greater protection for consumers as a whole than the individualized transaction: Schwartz and Wilde, op. cit., pp. 663–6. For a broader discussion of the information problem, see infra, Chapter 7, Section D.

PART III

*

Public Law

5

COMPETITION AND MONOPOLY

A. Introduction

The economics and law of monopoly and restrictive trade practices is a subject with a large and at times demanding literature. It is not possible here to cover adequately the institutional features of competition policy and the more specific topics. In this chapter, we concentrate instead on the broad conceptual issues surrounding market power and its control. For texts on the legal and economic issues raised by market power and restraints, see: G. C. Allen, *Monopoly and Restrictive Practices* (1968); D. A. Hay and D. J. Morris, *Industrial Economics – Theory and Evidence* (1979); D. Swann, *Competition and Consumer Protection* (1979). For analysis of American approaches, see, especially, R. A. Posner, *Antitrust Law: An Economic Perspective* (1976) and E. Gellhorn, *Antitrust Law and Economics in a Nutshell* (1981).

B. Welfare Economics of Competition and Monopoly

F. M. SCHERER

*

Industrial Market Structure and Economic Performance[1]

Competition has long been viewed as a force that leads to an optimal solution of the economic performance problem, just as monopoly has been condemned throughout recorded history for frustrating attainment of the competitive ideal. To Adam Smith, the vital principle underlying a market economy's successful functioning was the pursuit of individual self-interest, channelled and controlled by competition. . . .

[1] From *Industrial Market Structure and Economic Performance* (2nd edn., 1980), ch. 2. Copyright © 1980 by Houghton Mifflin Company, Boston. Adapted by permission.

COMPETITION DEFINED

... In modern economic theory, an industry is said to be competitive (or more precisely, purely competitive) only when the number of firms selling a homogeneous commodity is so large, and each individual firm's share of the market is so small, that no individual firm finds itself able to influence appreciably the commodity's price by varying the quantity of output it sells. In mathematical jargon, price is a *parameter* to the competitive seller – it is determined by market forces, and not subject to the individual seller's conscious control. The parametric character of price to the competitive firm is fundamentally a subjective phenomenon. If industry demand curves are smooth and continuous, it is not strictly true that a small seller's output changes have *no* effect on the market price. They simply have such a minute effect that the influence is *imperceptible* to the seller, who can therefore act as if the effect were in fact zero.

This technical definition of competition differs markedly from the usage adopted by business people who ... are apt to perceive competition as a conscious striving against other business firms for patronage, perhaps on a price basis but possibly also (or alternatively) on nonprice grounds. Failure to recognize these implied semantic distinctions has often led to confusion in policy discussions. To keep such confusion at a minimum, we adopt the term 'rivalry' to characterize much of the activity business people commonly call 'competition'. The essence of rivalry is a striving for potentially incompatible positions (e.g., if Firm A sells 100 units of output to Mr. X, Firm B cannot satisfy that part of X's demand) combined with a clear *awareness* by the parties involved that the positions they seek to attain may be incompatible. ...

Violations of the principal structural preconditions for pure competition give rise to a rich variety of sellers' market types. For present purposes it suffices to identify the five most important types, using the two-way classification based upon the number of sellers and the nature of the product presented in Table 1. The distinction between homogeneity and differentiation in this classification hinges on the degree

Table 1 Principal seller's market structure types

	One	A Few	Many
Homogeneous product	Pure monopoly	Homogeneous oligopoly	Pure competition
Differentiated product	Pure monopoly	Differentiated oligopoly	Monopolistic competition

of substitutability among competing sellers' products. Homogeneity prevails when, in the minds of buyers, products are perfect substitutes. Products are differentiated when, owing to differences in physical attributes, ancillary service, geographic location, information, and/or subjective image, one firm's products are clearly preferred by at least some buyers over rival products at a given price. The distinguishing trait of a differentiated product is the ability of its seller to raise the product's price without sacrificing the entire sales volume. Obviously, infinite gradations in the degree of product differentiation may exist, and it is difficult in practice to draw a precise line where homogeneity ends and differentiation begins. Similarly, although pure monopoly ends and oligopoly begins when the number of sellers rises from one to two, it is difficult to specify on a priori grounds exactly where oligopoly shades into a competitive market structure. The key to the distinction is subjective – whether or not the sellers consider themselves conscious rivals . . . If the sellers are sufficiently few in number to have each believe (a) that its economic fortunes are perceptibly influenced by the market actions of other individual firms, and (b) that those firms are in turn affected significantly by its own actions, then the market can be said to be oligopolistic.

Pure monopolists, oligopolists, and monopolistic competitors share a common characteristic: Each recognizes that its output decisions have a perceptible influence on price or, in other words, each can increase the quantity of output it sells under given demand conditions only by reducing its price. All three types of firms possess some degree of power over price, and so we say that they possess *monopoly power* or *market power*.

Homogeneity of the product and insignificant size of individual sellers and buyers relative to their market (i.e., *atomistic* market structure) are sufficient conditions for the existence of pure competition – the only basic structural type under which sellers possess no monopoly power. It is conventional, however, to add several additional characteristics in describing the 'ideal' competitive market of economic theory. When these are present, competition is said to be not only *pure* but also *perfect*. The most important is the absence of barriers to the entry of new firms, combined with mobility of resources employed or potentially employable in an industry. Conversely, significant entry barriers are the *sine qua non* of monopoly and oligopoly, for . . . sellers have little or no enduring power over price when entry barriers are nonexistent . . .

THE CASE FOR COMPETITION

. . . Why is a competitive market system held in such a high esteem by statesmen and economists alike? Why is competition the ideal in a market economy, and what is wrong with monopoly?

Political arguments

We begin with the political arguments for competition, not merely because they are sufficiently obvious to be treated briefly, but also because, when all is said and done, they and not the economists' abstruse models have tipped the balance of social consensus toward competition. One of the most important arguments is that the atomistic structure of buyers and sellers required for competition decentralizes and disperses power. The resource allocation and income distribution problem is solved through the almost mechanical interaction of supply and demand forces on the market, and not through the conscious exercise of power held in private hands (e.g., under monopoly) or government hands (i.e., under state enterprise or government regulation). Limiting the power of both government bodies and private individuals to make decisions shaping people's lives and fortunes is one of the oldest and most fundamental goals in the liberal ideology. . . .

A [second] political merit of a competitive market system is its freedom of opportunity. When the no-barriers-to-entry condition of perfect competition is satisfied, individuals are free to choose whatever trade or profession they prefer, limited only by their own talent and skill and by their ability to raise the (presumably modest) amount of capital required.

The efficiency of competitive markets

Admitting the salience of these political benefits, our main concern nonetheless will be with the economic case for competitive market processes. Figure . . . 1(b) reviews the conventional textbook analysis of equilibrium in a competitive industry and Figure . . . 1(a) portrays it for a representative firm belonging to that industry. Suppose we begin observing the industry when the short-run industry supply curve is S_1, which in turn embodies the horizontal summation of all member firms' marginal cost curves. The short-run market equilibrium price is OP_1, which is viewed as a parameter or 'given' by our representative firm, so the firm's subjectively perceived demand curve is a horizontal line at the level OP_1. The firm maximizes its profits by expanding output until marginal cost (MC) rises into equality with the price OP_1. It produces OX_1 units of output and earns economic profits – that is, profits above the minimum return required to call forth its capital investment – equal to the per-unit profit GC_1 times the number of units OX_1.

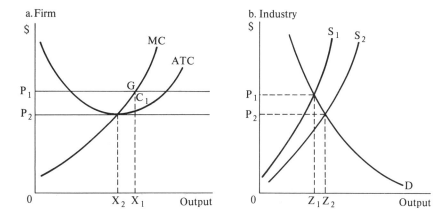

Figure 1 Equilibrium under pure competition

Because economic profits are positive for the representative firm, this cannot be a long-run equilibrium position. New firms attracted by the profit lure will enter the industry, adding their new marginal cost functions to the industry's supply curve and thereby shifting the supply curve to the right. Entry will continue, expanding industry output and driving the price down, until price has fallen into equality with average total cost (ATC) for the representative firm. In the figures shown, this zero-profit condition emerges with the short-run supply curve S_2, yielding the market price OP_2. The representative firm maximizes its profits by equating marginal cost with price OP_2, barely covering its total unit costs (including the minimum necessary return on its capital) at the output OX_2.

The long-run equilibrium state of a competitive industry has three general properties with important normative implications:

a. The cost of producing the last unit of output – the marginal cost – is equal to the price paid by consumers for that unit. This is a necessary condition for profit maximization, given the competitive firm's perception that price is unaffected by its output decisions. It implies efficiency of resource allocation in a sense to be explored momentarily.

b. With price equal to average total cost for the representative firm, economic (i.e., *supra-normal*) profits are absent. Investors receive a return just sufficient to induce them to maintain their investment at the level required to produce the industry's equilibrium output efficiently. Avoiding a surplus return to capital is generally considered desirable in terms of the equity of income distribution.

c. In long-run equilibrium, each firm is producing its output at the minimum point on its average total cost curve. Firms that fail to operate at the lowest unit cost will incur losses and be driven from the industry. Thus, resources are employed at maximum production efficiency under competition.

One further benefit is sometimes attributed to the working of pure competition, although with less logical compulsion. Because of the pressure of prices on costs, entrepreneurs may have especially strong incentives to seek and adopt cost-saving technological innovations. Indeed, if industry capacity is correctly geared to demand at all times, the *only* way competitive firms can earn positive economic profits is through leadership in innovation. We might expect therefore that technological progress will be more rapid in competitive industries. . . .

The inefficiency of monopoly pricing

Monopolists . . . differ from purely competitive firms in only one essential respect: They face a downward-sloping demand curve for their product. Given this fact of its economic life, the firm with monopoly power knows that to sell an additional unit (or block) of output, it must reduce its price to the customer(s) for that unit; and if it is unable to practice price discrimination (as we shall generally assume, unless otherwise indicated) the firm must also reduce the price to all customers who would have made their purchases even without the price reduction. The net addition to the . . . monopolist's revenue from selling one more unit of output, or its *marginal revenue*, is equal to the price paid by the marginal customer, minus the change in price required to secure the marginal customer's patronage multiplied by the number of units that would have been sold without the price reduction in question. Except at prices so high as to choke off all demand, the monopolist always sacrifices something to gain the benefits of increased patronage: the higher price it could have extracted had it limited its sales to more eager customers. Marginal revenue must therefore be less than the price paid by the marginal customer. Or, to state this critical condition more generally, when demand functions are continuous and smooth, *marginal revenue under monopoly is necessarily less than price* for finite quantities sold. . . .

Now the profit-maximizing firm with monopoly power will expand its output only as long as the net addition to revenue from selling an additional unit (marginal revenue) exceeds the addition to cost from producing that unit (the marginal cost). At the monopolist's profit-maximizing output, marginal revenue equals marginal cost. But as long as output is positive, marginal revenue is less than the monopoly

price. Price therefore exceeds marginal cost. This equilibrium condition for firms with monopoly power differs from the competitive
firm's equilibrium position. For the competitor, price equals marginal
cost; for the monopolist, price exceeds marginal cost. . . . This seeming
technicality, so trivial at first glance, is the basis of the economist's
most general condemnation of monopoly: It leads to an allocation of
resources that is inefficient in the sense of satisfying consumer wants
with less than maximum effectiveness.

To see this, we must think more deeply about the meaning of price as
it affects the decisions of a consumer just on the margin between
buying one more unit of a product and not buying it. A numerical
illustration is especially helpful, so let us consider Figure [2]. It
assumes that the production of a composite commodity 'manufactured
goods' with the demand curve D is monopolized. The industry is
assumed (for simplicity) to produce under constant cost conditions,
with long-run average total cost and marginal cost equal to $5.00 per
unit at any output level chosen. The manufactured goods monopolist
maximizes its profits by setting marginal cost [labelled LRMC in
Figure 2] equal to marginal revenue [labelled MR] which for the
assumed cost and demand conditions requires producing 2 million
units and setting a market-clearing price of about $9.70 per unit.

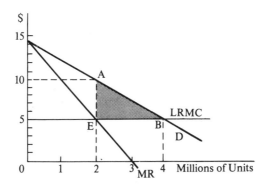

Figure 2 Resource allocation with . . . monopoly

Now in setting this price, the monopolist chokes off the demand of
consumers who would have been willing to purchase units (or
additional units) at prices below $9.70. Consider some consumer who
would purchase an extra unit at $9.60, but not at $9.70. We say that
$9.60 is her *reservation price* – the price just low enough to overcome
her reservations about purchasing an extra unit. She buys the extra
unit at $9.60 because it is worth that much to her; she refrains from

purchasing at $9.70 because she considers the unit not worth the higher price. The consumer's reservation price for any incremental unit of consumption indicates in monetary terms how much that unit is worth to her; it is an index of the value of an extra unit of consumption from the consumer's viewpoint and hence, in a social system honoring consumer sovereignty, from the viewpoint of society.

The extra unit of manufactured goods required to satisfy the demand of this marginal consumer can be produced with resources costing $5.00. The marginal social value of the extra unit is $9.60. Marginal value exceeds marginal cost, so it would appear eminently worthwhile to produce that unit. The same can be said for all other units of manufactured goods that would be demanded at prices from $9.60 down to $5.00; their value to the marginal consumers exceeds their marginal cost, so they ought to be produced. They are not produced – that is, output is unduly restricted – because the monopolist is unwilling to sacrifice the profits it can secure by charging the higher price ($9.70) and selling fewer units.

For virtually all units of manufactured goods the monopolist does supply, the value to consumers of those units . . . exceeds the monopolist's $9.70 price. On all but the 2 millionth (i.e., marginal) unit supplied and demanded, therefore, there is a surplus of value to consumers over the price paid. This is called *consumers' surplus*. With a monopoly price of $9.70, the total consumers' surplus realized is defined by the triangular area in Figure [2] bounded by the vertical axis, the horizontal line at the $9.70 level, and the demand function from its vertical intercept to point *A*. By analogy, the monopolist's profit is called a producer's surplus. It is measured as quantity sold times unit profit, or in Figure [2] as the rectangular area between 0 and 2 million units and between the $9.70 price and the $5.00 cost. If, contrary to its profit-maximizing instincts, the monopolist reduced its price to $5.00, its profit or producer's surplus would be converted into consumers' surplus on the 2 million units that would have been consumed even at the $9.70 price. This is essentially a redistribution of income. But in addition, 2 million more units will be demanded, virtually all (given the demand function's slope) at reservation prices exceeding $5.00. Satisfying that demand would add consumers' surplus equal to the triangular area *ABE* between the demand curve and the $5.00 price line. At the $9.70 monopoly price, this surplus is realized neither by the monopolist nor by consumers. It is in effect lost, and therefore it is called a *dead-weight welfare loss*. It provides a first indication of the inefficiencies associated with monopolistic output restriction. Only through an expansion of manufactured goods output to 4 million units, where price equals marginal cost, does some segment of society realize the surplus *ABE*. . . .

. . . Quite generally, when all sectors of an economy are in competitive equilibrium, with price equal to marginal cost for each firm, the total value of the output, measured in terms of each commodity's equilibrium price, is at a maximum. It is impossible to make any small resource reallocations that yield a higher output value. Because it maximizes the social value of output, a fully competitive market system is said to allocate resources efficiently. Conversely, a system shot through with monopoly elements is inefficient because it fails to do so. This, in a nutshell, is the heart of the economic theorist's case for competition and against monopoly. . . .

[E]liminating monopoly [has] another effect . . . more difficult to assess. Income will have been redistributed, with former monopoly profit recipients losing and other claimants (such as workers) gaining. Whether this is good or bad cannot be decided without a value judgment over which reasonable persons may disagree. There are at least two reasons for thinking that the competitive equilibrium may be preferred to the monopolistic one on equitable grounds, but the case is not airtight. First, society may object to monopoly profits as unearned gains and place a high ethical value on seeing them eliminated. The trouble with this objection is that the monopoly's original builders may already have reaped their gains by selling out their ownership interests at high capitalized values, leaving secondary and tertiary stockbuyers, who are receiving no more than a normal return on their money investment, holding the bag if the monopoly is atomized. Second, the ownership of industrial enterprises is concentrated among a few hundred thousand wealthy individuals. If all persons have similar income utility functions, the marginal utility of income must be higher for the multitudes who supply only their labor services to industry than for the wealthy few with monopoly shareholdings. A redistribution of income away from monopolists and toward labor suppliers will therefore add to total societywide utility. Still, however appealing this may appear intuitively, there is no scientific way of making the interpersonal utility comparisons required to support the assertion. Therefore, we tread warily when we say that competition is beneficial not only because it allocates resources efficiently, but also in terms of income distribution equity.

This completes the case based upon orthodox economic theory against monopoly and for competition. Some other more institutional criticisms of monopoly can be mentioned briefly. Monopolists' price-raising propensities may stimulate imports and complicate individual nations' balance of payment problems. In the absence of competitive pressure, firms may not exercise diligence in controlling their costs and therefore waste resources. As Adam Smith observed, 'Monopoly . . . is a great enemy to good management.' For similar reasons, monopolists may display a lethargic attitude toward technological innovation, although contrary suggestions [have been made]. And finally, enterprises with monopoly power may sustain superfluous advertising, excess production capacity, or other types of waste; or they may maintain pricing systems that encourage inefficient geographic locations and unnecessarily high transportation costs. These alleged flaws, . . . may be even more serious than the resource misallocation problem.

Notes

1. Scherer emphasizes an important feature of the economist's model of perfect competition which is frequently confused. Perfect competition does not imply rivalry; it is an analytical notion defined by the outcome of price equal to marginal cost or the inability of individual sellers and buyers unilaterally to determine price (or other conditions of sale). In perfect competition price is said to be parametric, i.e. individual market participants cannot influence prices. (For an application, see M. S. Trebilcock, 'The Doctrine of Inequality of Bargaining Power; Post-Benthamite Economics in the House of Lords' (1976) 26 U. Toronto L.J. 359.) Moreover, perfect competition does not necessarily require a large number of firms or buyers, provided entry and exit into the market is costless. In such situations, the *threat* of competition may be sufficient to encourage competitive market outcomes. It should be noted that not all economists define competition in this way. So-called 'Austrian economics' regards competition as a process of active rivalry and discovery among individual buyers and sellers that gives them maximum freedom for initiative, experimentation and innovation and to respond flexibly and quickly to changes in market conditions (see I. M. Kirzner, *Competition and Entrepreneurship* (1973); S. C. Littlechild, *The Fallacy of a Mixed Economy* (1978).

2. Market power can manifest itself in a multitude of ways other than by price exceeding marginal cost. Such practices as resale price maintenance, exclusive dealing, tie-in sales, predatory pricing and cartels and mergers may all be attempts to restrain trade. (G. C. Allen op. cit.; R. H. Bork, *The Antitrust Paradox* (1978); Swann, op. cit., ch. 5). The economic analysis of these practices provides a rich field of study, often yielding, unfortunately, ambiguous implications for public policy. This is because many 'restraints on trade' can frequently be justified on the ground that they enhance efficiency by reducing costs or else responding to a market deficiency (such as risk and uncertainty) assumed away in the textbook model of perfect competition (O. E. Williamson, 'Economics as an Antitrust Defence: The Welfare Tradeoff' (1968) 58 Am. Econ. Rev. 18; Rowley infra, Sect. D).

3. Another concept not discussed by Scherer is a natural monopoly. It exists 'when a single firm can produce at lower cost than any . . . two or more firms in a market' that is otherwise free from restrictions on competition (W. M. Sharkey, *The Theory of Natural Monopoly* (1982), p. 55; also

A. Kahn, *Economics of Regulation* (Vol II, 1976) pp. 119–23). The monopoly is 'natural' in the sense that the market is supplied at lowest cost by one firm and only one firm – the financially strongest or best-managed – would profitably survive in the market. Examples of such industries are electricity, gas, water and some forms of telecommunications. In the USA, natural monopolies have tended to be privately owned and controlled by rate-of-return regulation administered by independent commissions (Rowley, infra, Section D.; M. Crew and P. R. Kleindorfer, *Public Utility Economics* (1979)), whereas in the UK they are publicly owned: W. Friedmann (ed.), *Public and Private Enterprise in Mixed Economies* (1974).

4. The social costs resulting from monopoly pricing are qualified by at least four important factors. First, if the monopolist can charge each consumer a different price (i.e. practise price discrimination) then the misallocative effects will be less severe and, if he can charge each consumer the price that he is prepared to pay (called perfect price discrimination), the competitive level of output will be produced. (In the latter case, the marginal revenue curve (MR) in Scherer's Figure 2 will be coincident with D, resulting in the production of 4 million units). However, price discrimination (i.e. price differences unrelated to differences in costs) will place more wealth in the monopolist's hands and, may, for this reason alone, be deemed undesirable. Secondly, the theory of the second best (Scherer, op. cit., pp. 22–7; Veljanovski, supra, Chapter 1, Section B) indicates that correcting monopoly in one sector of the economy may not improve allocative efficiency if other sectors are uncompetitive. The optimal policy will require 'second best' prices that depart from the marginal cost pricing rule. Thirdly, it is sometimes argued that monopolists undertake more research and development, thus contributing to technological progress that partially (or fully) offsets the shortrun inefficiency of monopoly prices (J. A. Schumpeter, *Capitalism, Socialism and Democracy* (1942), pp. 83–103). The validity of this view has, however, been questioned: M. I. Kamien and N. L. Schwartz, 'Market Structure and Innovation: A Survey' (1975) 13 J. Econ. Lit 1. Finally, elements of monopoly are often necessary for efficiency when there are difficulties in appropriating the full rewards of invention and new information, e.g. patents (see Bowman, supra, Chapter 2, Section A; H. Demsetz, 'Barriers to Entry' (1982) 72 Am. Econ. Rev. 47).

5. Measuring the social costs of monopoly (Scherer's 'deadweight loss') is fraught with difficulties. First, the costs of the monopolist may be higher than under competition. Part of the potential monopoly profits may be used to provide well-appointed offices, generous expense accounts, and excessive support staff, thus inflating costs above the minimum required for production. This is frequently referred to as X-inefficiency (H. Leibenstein, 'Allocative Efficiency vs. X-Efficiency' (1966) 56 Am. Econ. Rev. 392; C. K. Rowley, *Antitrust and Economic Efficiency* (1973), ch. 5). If this is the case the consumers' surplus measure will underestimate the true social costs of monopoly. Secondly, prospective monopoly profits may also be used to acquire market power either in the market place or by lobbying for govern-

ment regulations that restrict competition. This activity is referred to by economists as *rent seeking* – 'the study of how individuals compete for artificially contrived transfers' of wealth (R. D. Tollison, 'Rent Seeking: A Survey' (1982) 35 Kyklos 575, 601). See also G. Tullock, 'The Welfare Costs of Tariffs, Monopolies and Theft' (1967) 5 Western Econ. J. 224; R. A. Posner, 'The Social Costs of Monopoly and Regulation' (1975) 83 J. Pol. Econ. 807; Posner infra, Chapter 6, Section B). If rent seeking is widespread, the social costs could well equal the monopoly profits plus the lost consumers' surplus.

C. Defining Market Power

C. W. BADEN FULLER

*

Article 86 EEC: Economic Analysis of the Existence of a Dominant Position[2]

INTRODUCTION

In three recent judgments, namely those of *United Brands — Bananas (UBC)*[3] *Hoffmann-La Roche — Vitamins (Roche)*[4] and *Hugin,*[5] the European Court has ruled that a company has held a dominant position in the EEC for the purposes of Article 86. Economists who have studied monopoly would not agree with all the elements of the Court's reasoning. In this paper I shall . . . explain the methodology that would be used by economists. . .

THE COURT'S METHODOLOGY

Definition of dominance

Dominance means economic power over a customer (or supplier), or a group of customers (or group of suppliers). This idea seems simple to comprehend. In one respect, however, it is not commonly understood:

---

[2] From (1979) 4 Eur. L.R. 423, with omissions. Copyright © 1979 Sweet & Maxwell and the author. By permission.
[3] Case 27/76, *United Brands* v. *Commission* [1978] E.C.R. 207; [1978] 1 C.M.L.R. 429, hereafter referred to as *UBC.*
[4] Case 85/76, *Hoffman-La Roche* v. *Commission* [1979] E.C.R. 461; [1979] 3 C.M.L.R. 211; hereafter referred to as *Roche.*
[5] Case 22/78, *Hugin Kassaregister and Hugin Cash Register Ltd.* v. *Commission* [1978] 3 C.M.L.R. 45 hereafter referred to as *Hugin.*

dominance is economic power over a period of time, and not transient power. Let me explain by example. Consider a London neighbourhood where only one shop opens on Sunday. Next Sunday, if it were to double its prices without warning, it would not lose many customers initially. Is this store dominant? The answer must be 'No', since in London there are many entrepreneurs who would open their shops on Sunday if they discovered that the existing firm had raised its prices in this way. The new competition would quickly drive prices down, and the existing shop might suffer badly, especially if its customers were to cease to patronise it even when its prices were lowered to meet the new competition. . . . In contrast, a shop located in an isolated community such as a Scottish island, may have real economic power. Its community may be so small that it cannot support more than one such shop. Of course, its potential monopoly may be very small, as its community may be few and poor. . . . Nonetheless, such a store enjoys a position which is almost unassailable, and the prices it charges may be higher than if competition were to prevail.

In *UBC* the European Court defined dominance for the purpose of Article 86 as follows:

The dominant position referred to in this article relates to a position of economic strength enjoyed by an undertaking which enables it to prevent effective competition being maintained on the relevant market by giving it the power to behave to an appreciable extent independently of its competitors, customers and ultimately of its consumers.

It reiterated the definition in *Roche*, and went on to say that dominance does not exclude the existence of certain competition, but that a dominant firm can decide or at least influence the conditions under which competition will develop, and that a dominant firm can behave in its market without needing to take account of the competition and without suffering damage as a result.

Economists would agree with the Court in so far as a firm does not need to supply all the market to be dominant. . . . Economists, however, would like the Court to make it quite clear that dominance is a concept related to time. . . . Dominance is a position of power over time. . . .

The relevant market

The Court has said that it is necessary to define a market: economists would agree – for to point out dominance, one must say upon what market a firm is dominant. In *Roche* (para. 28) and *UBC* (para. 22), the Court defined the extent of a market by reference to the existence of substitutes on the demand side . . . For example, in *Roche* the defendants disputed whether Vitamins C and E should each be considered as part of one market. According to the Court (paras. 28 and 29), Vitamins C and E had two usages, one as additives to foodstuffs (called the bio-nutritive use), and the other as anti-oxydants, fermentation agents and additives (called the technological usage); in their first usage, C and E performed different functions and in this usage neither could be substituted for the other, and there was no other product which could perform as substitutes for either; in their second usage, C and E were not only interchangeable with each other, but there was a variety of other products which could also be interchanged with them. The notable aspect of the case was that it was not always possible for Roche to distinguish between customers who wanted Vitamins C and E for the different uses, because some buyers who used C or E in foodstuffs also required anti-oxydants for which C and E could be used interchangeably. An economist would argue that there were three markets defined from the demand side: the two separate bio-nutritive usage markets of C and E, and the technological usage market which included C, E and other anti-oxydants. It is obvious that a change in price of (say) Vitamin C would have little effect on the quantity of E sold for its bio-nutritive use. Economists would say that there is a low cross elasticity between C and E, and that these products were not substitutes (*i.e.* they were in different markets). But a change in price of C would have a substantial effect on the quantity of E sold for its technological use, indicating a high cross elasticity, and that these products were substitutes (*i.e* in the same market). The Court ruled that Vitamins C and E were separate markets stressing their bio-nutritive uses. Here economists would agree with the Court, but would note that any analysis of these markets must also consider the technological market for reasons which will be explored. . . .

Test of dominance

In *Roche* (para. 41) the Court said:

Furthermore although the importance of the market shares may vary from one market to another the view may legitimately be taken that very large shares are in themselves, and save in exceptional circumstances, evidence of the existence of a dominant position.

However, it is quite clear from the Court's pronouncements in *Roche* and *UBC* that it believes that the existence of large market shares cannot by itself prove dominance: to prove dominance there must be both large shares of the market and other factors which are called 'indicators'. In *Roche* and *UBC* the following factors have (among others) been considered to be indicators by either the Commission or the Court: large investment requirements; surplus capacity; profit-ability; production of a range of products; efficiency; and vertical integration.

Comment

The major disagreement between economists' methodology and that of the Court is in their attitude to the question of the relevant market. Contrary to what many people have suggested, the disagreement is not so much in the way the relevant market is defined but rather in the way in which the Court restricts the scope of its analysis to that market. As will be explained in the next section, dominance presupposes barriers to entry. Its proof requires an analysis of all the factors influencing the firm – for factors outside the relevant market can affect competition in that market . . .

HOW ECONOMISTS WOULD IDENTIFY DOMINANCE

There are potentially two methods of identifying dominance. The first is to examine whether a firm has monopoly power, that is, whether it has the power to raise prices without competition materialising (in a relatively short period of time). The second is to examine whether the firm is receiving the benefits of monopoly, one of which might be the earning of monopoly profits. Economists focus attention on the former.

Economists define dominance in a number of different ways. Perhaps the clearest definition is that dominance is the power of the firm to raise prices to above supply cost without existing rivals or new entrants taking away its customers in due time. This definition uses a concept of supply cost which may not be familiar. Supply cost can be conveniently seen as the minimum cost that an efficient firm would have to incur to produce the product in question. Included in such costs are not only raw materials and labour, but also opportunity costs of using scarce resources such as management, and a normal rate of return to providers of capital funds. The importance of time has been mentioned already – for a firm can have the whole market and have only temporary power which is not dominance if, upon raising prices (above supply cost), a new firm would appear and undercut prices. In contrast, if there are 'barriers to entry', then a firm can raise prices without rivals appearing. Economists would describe all 'barriers to entry' as 'indicators', for a firm cannot exercise monopoly unless there are barriers to entry for new competitors.

By far the most obvious barriers to entry are those prescribed by law, such as patent rights or exclusive government licences. Moreover, from the earliest studies of economics, all have agreed that if economies of scale are such that the minimum efficient scale of operation is large in comparison to the market, then there can be a barrier to entry . . .

DOMINANCE AS A CONSEQUENCE OF ECONOMIES OF SCALE

'Economies of scale' is a phrase describing the changes in unit costs that result from operating a process at different outputs. The term does not describe the actual cost differences in operating a given plant at different outputs, nor the benefits of vertical integration. The process under consideration can be a production operation, or a distribution system, or a research laboratory or even a whole firm. It is also assumed that the process adopted uses the best available techniques. There are two dimensions usually discussed, the minimum efficient scale (MES) and the slope of the scale curve. MES is defined intuitively as the smallest sized plant which achieves the lowest unit cost, and the slope of the curve can be approximated by the amount by which costs rise when a plant of half MES is used. . . .

In . . . the monopoly case . . . the MES is large in comparison to the size of the market . . .

THE CRITICAL MARKET SHARE TO PROVE DOMINANCE

. . . [E]conomists do not believe that there is a magic number for the critical market share which a firm must possess in order for it to be dominant. It would, however, seem very unlikely that a firm with less than 50 per cent of the market could be dominant. (For, supposing the existing firm to be efficient, then MES would be less than 50 per cent of the market and any attempt by the firm at raising prices would encourage competitors to challenge the firm's position. Likewise, if the firm were inefficient in the sense that the MES was larger than the firm's market-share, then a new entrant would most probably arrive and be able to undercut the existing firm's prices – which is what we want).

The Court, like economists, does not believe that there is any magic number for market share. However, in *UBC* (para. 109) and *Roche* (paras. 50, 51), it has ruled that (together with other indicators) market shares of around 45 per cent are sufficient. Again, in *UBC* (para. 111) and *Roche* (paras. 51 and 58), it has also used the criterion of whether the shares of the firm's next two largest competitors combined exceed the firm's share. In the proceedings against *Roche* (paras. 54–56), where the question arose whether market share should be measured by sales value, quantities sold or productive capacity, the Court used several of these tests. Economists prefer quantities sold, because economies of scale (the source of monopoly power) is an engineering concept which relates to output in units and not values.

THE NECESSITY FOR A FULL MARKET ANALYSIS

It is obvious from the preceding analysis that if the MES is small in relation to the market, then it would be impossible for a firm to be dominant unless there were some additional entry barriers. But it might seem that if the MES is large in relation to the 'relevant market', then a firm with a large market share would be dominant; this latter presumption should be restated, for there are four cases where MES may be very large and yet a firm is not dominant, even if it supplies all the 'relevant market'.

The first case is fairly obvious. It is where . . . although the MES is very large relative to the market the disadvantages of operating at a small scale may be slight.

The second case is where the 'relevant market' as defined from the point of view of the Court, is in a sense too small. To take a topical example, if the relevant market were silicon chips in the EEC, and if the MES were 100 per cent of this market, then in the absence of a high tariff or a quota, a firm having 100 per cent of the European market is unlikely to be dominant because silicon chips are easily transported. From the point of view of EEC buyers, suppliers outside the EEC are potentially excellent alternatives to the existing firm. Because the Court is concerned only with the EEC, it is understandable (but possibly misleading) that it does not define the relevant market as broadly as the economic market.

The third case is where the market is correctly defined from the demand side, but the existence of alternative uses for the product causes the significance of MES to be overstated. For example, consider a chemical compound which has two uses, X and Y. . . . Suppose that in its X use, the product has no substitutes, but in the Y use it competes with many other products. If the 'relevant market' is defined as use X and not uses X + Y, and if the MES of production is as large as the size of the X market, then a firm may command the whole of the X market and yet not be dominant. To see this, suppose that the firm were to raise prices to its X customers, then a new firm may be able to set up production, devoting most of its output to the Y market (where the influence, even of a plant of MES, on price may be very small due to Y being a much larger market),and devote a small part of its output to the X market in competition with the existing firm. If prices fall in the X market, the new firm may still be able to survive by devoting its output to the Y market.

It might be thought from these examples that a better definition of the relevant market, in particular a recognition of substitutes in supply, would allow one to show a clear connection between dominance and MES, size of the market and market share. This is not so, for, as I shall show in the fourth example, it is the existence of common costs that makes this tinkering with definitions such an unsatisfactory alternative to a proper analysis.

For the fourth example, consider the market for wool. Let us suppose (hypothetically) that technology were to advance so that sheep-rearing were to exhibit economies of scale, and that as a result there were only one farmer in the market rearing sheep. (Let us further assume that tariff barriers were to prevent import competition and that there were no alternative uses for wool beyond its present uses.) Would this farmer be dominant? The answer is no, not necessarily. Suppose that the farmer were to raise the price of wool. Now, the raising of sheep yields two outputs: fleeces and meat. If (as is probable) mutton competes on reasonable terms with other meat, in particular beef, and if the price of meat were sufficiently high, then a new farmer could enter into sheep production at a level where all economies of scale would be exhausted and just cover the costs by the sale of mutton. Wool fleeces would be a by-product of this process, and so this new farmer could compete with the existing farmer, driving down the price of fleeces and, hence, would eliminate the first farmer's dominance over wool. From this example, it can most clearly be seen that the price of beef would affect the ability of the sheep farmer to monopolise the market for wool and yet, by no stretch of the imagination, could beef and wool be considered as part of the same market, as they are not substitutes in either demand or supply. . . .

In short, the proof of dominance lies not in the definition of the 'relevant market' but, rather, in a full analysis of all the factors which influence the power of a firm.

THE RELEVANCE OF TIME

In several places I have alluded to the importance of time. Economists have noted that few monopolies other than those prescribed by law have lasted more than a decade or two, as, even without anti-monopoly laws, the process of competition is very powerful. But those applying the EEC Treaty may have (rightly or wrongly) shorter time horizons. [Economists] distinguished the short time period from the long period. In the short period, productive capacity is fixed – in the long period it is variable. As was said earlier, firms may have some power in the very short run – but such power does not define monopoly. Monopoly is the power to raise prices without entry taking place in time. Relevant indicators which might be useful in defining the time period are the time required to build, and the life of, a new plant of minimum efficient scale, the rate of technical change in the industry, and ease with which customers can switch from one supplier to another. Clearly, when time required to build a plant is long, as with, say, aluminium smelting, then competition is a slower process than when the time period is short, as with, say, garment fabrication.

THE CONCEPT OF EFFICIENCY

In *Roche* (para. 48) the Court alleged that Roche's technological lead and highly developed marketing facility was an indicator of its dominance. (The technological lead was not protected by patents – see *Roche*, para. 42). It is not quite clear what is the cause of such superiority. If it is better management, better labour relations and a harder working labour force, but not economies of scale – then such superiority is a trait which competition law is seeking to foster. It is hardly a barrier to entry – if an entrant were equally efficient, then it could compete on equal terms. It is here that the question of time is most important, for if a firm commands a large market share because of superior efficiency, then such a command will be temporary unless it continually augments its position by increasing its efficiency faster than its competitors. . . . [T]he Court may not have meant that this superiority was the consequence of effort only, but rather that it meant that the existing firm has lower costs than any new firms by the very fact that it was the largest in its market and had been there for a long time. This popular view, that existing firms have some absolute cost advantage, can only be explained if there are benefits of learning by doing or, in other words, that costs of production not only depend on the rate of output but also on cumulative output, and that new firms do *not* have access to this 'experience'. . . . The possibilities of lowering costs as a consequence of 'learning by doing', *i.e.* experience, are well recognized but many economists and managers point out that such 'experience' effects unless patented can be copied by new firms, and so the advantage does not create a barrier to competitors.

INDICATORS OTHER THAN ECONOMIES OF SCALE

In *UBC* (para. 122) the Court said that the need for new firms to enter with large investments was an indicator (barrier to entry). If this means that MES is large relative to the market, then the question has already been discussed . . . If, however, the Court means only that a new firm needs substantial capital funds to enter, then this is not a barrier to entry. Most economists believe that capital markets are fairly efficient and, even if they are not, there are many firms in the world who have access to very large amounts of capital.

A number of economists believe that the existence of cost advantages conferred through economies of scale is the only barrier to entry aside, of course, from legal barriers such as licensing or patents; and they believe that the discussion of whether large promotion expenditures or product differentiation can be a barrier to entry, can usually be considered as a discussion as to whether there are economies of scale in brand names or in research and development. In contrast, some economists would include under-utilised capacity as a barrier to entry . . . and others would argue that other factors such as brand loyalty, predatory pricing, tying, can act as a barrier to entry, for reasons besides economies of scale in promotion. . .

Earlier, I said that potentially there is another method of identifying monopoly, and that is to examine whether a firm is receiving monopoly profits. These monopoly profits may be given to the firm's owners in the form of increased dividends or retained earnings, or may be captured by the workers and managers in the form of higher wages, or better work conditions, or else consumed in organisational slack. Because accounting records register disbursements and receipts and do not record opportunity costs, economists universally recognise that accounting records are at best a poor guide, and more likely to be quite wrong in showing whether a firm is making monopoly profits. High accounting profitability is compatible with competition, for instance, if a firm buys some valuable vineyard cheaply, its profits from the sale of wine will seem very high in relation to its investment. Accounting losses are compatible with monopoly: for instance, a firm may buy a dominant position (*e.g.* a patent) at a price which is greater than the value of the future stream of profits. In *UBC* (para. 126) the Court rightly rejected the Commission's arguments that UBC's high accounting profitability was an indicator.

In *Roche* (paras. 48, 49, 54 and 55) the Court cited the large amounts of unused capacity held by Roche as an indicator of dominance. Economists draw an important distinction between 'idle' capacity and 'excess' capacity. 'Idle' capacity is capacity whose incremental cost of usage is greater than the ruling market price. 'Excess' capacity is the opposite: the existence of excess capacity for a long period of time is clear evidence of monopoly power being exercised. 'Idle' capacity, in contrast, is observed in both competitive and uncompetitive industries. 'Idle' capacity is usually a symptom of an unforeseen contraction in demand, or the advent of new firms or new technologies to an industry. 'Idle' capacity is also observed in industries whose demand is cyclical. Distinguishing between 'idle' capacity and 'excess' capacity is almost impossible (because accounting data are inappropriate for this purpose) and, for this reason, economists are very wary indeed of drawing any direct connection between the existence of unused capacity and monopoly. The Court should also be wary.

Some economists argue that capacity of either an 'idle' or 'excess' nature can be a barrier to entry. They would argue that the existence of unused capacity could deter entry, as the entrant fears a price war rendering its investment unprofitable. . . . But would it be threatening if the entrant came in with a plant of MES or larger? Probably not, for the argument tends to overlook the costs to the existing firm of conducting a price war. Because the entrant's costs are as low as those of the existing firm, it may be impossible for the existing firm to drive the entrant out. (If the existing firm uses operationally expensive idle capacity to flood the market with goods, then its costs may be greater than those of the entrant, who does not have to increase supply). For these reasons, most economists believe that only 'excess' as opposed to 'idle' capacity can act as a deterrent to entry. Some others hold a more extreme view, which is that entrants ignore unused capacity and enter in belief that the existing firm will not start a price war, but rather contract output to accommodate the entrant. Therefore, in deciding whether unused capacity acts as a barrier to entry, the Court should proceed with great caution and, where possible, look at the facts: *a priori* reasoning is dangerous.

VERTICAL INTEGRATION: AN INDICATOR OR AN ABUSE?

In *UBC* (para. 122) the Commission alleged that vertical integration (including vertical contracts) was an indicator of UBC's dominance. The Court neither agreed nor disagreed with the Commission, but drew attention to the marked degree of ownership or control over the banana plantations, the packing stations, the transportation system (railways and ships), as well as a marketing network which included the advertised brand name 'Chiquita'. Economists usually argue that vertical integration does not increase existing barriers to entry. For example, if I were to hold a patent for a wooden mousetrap, I could prevent anyone using such a mousetrap. Now, if I were to integrate vertically backwards into timber, could I increase the barriers to entry? The answer is clearly, no, unless there are barriers to entry to the timber trade. Economists usually argue that by integrating vertically, the barriers to entry are only added up and not multiplied.

Vertical integration nearly always accompanies monopoly, not because it raises barriers to entry, but because it gives the monopolist greater power to extract more favourable prices from its customers. A monopolist usually wishes to charge higher prices to those customers for whom its product has fewer substitutes. It cannot do this if its customers inter-trade. Vertical integration takes place to prevent inter-trading. For example, electricity generating companies own their own distribution systems (among other reasons) so that they can practice price discrimination between residential and commercial customers. When, in an early paragraph, I stated that abuse can extend beyond the relevant market, I was referring to such a situation. It will not be long before the Court realises that vertical integration is not a method by which monopoly power is created, but rather a method by which monopoly profits can be extracted. But, vertical integration although it accompanies monopoly, is not an indicator of monopoly. Many firms operating in competitive industries are vertically integrated because such actions bring greater control over quality of inputs or outputs, and because of other cost savings.

CONCLUSIONS

In applying Article 86 EEC, the European Court has said on several occasions that it is necessary to examine the economic power of the undertaking concerned. For more than two hundred years, economists have been concerned with this difficult question. Their deliberations have revealed several points. *First*, dominance is only possible when there are barriers to entry into the industry, and that the chief barrier is where the minimum efficient scale of operation is large compared to the market. *Secondly*, proof of dominance requires an analysis of all factors influencing the firm, and not just of the relevant market – because factors outside the relevant market may be very important. *Thirdly*, dominance is a concept which is related to time. It is not the power that a firm has in a short period (for most firms, large and small, have power in the short term) but the power that the firm has over a longer period. That power is the power to raise prices above supply costs without competition materialising. The longer time period should be defined as that period in which one would expect competition to materialise if it were not hindered or fettered either by actions of the existing firm, or by the nature and technology of the market.

Notes

1. Perfect competition and monopoly lie at the opposite extremes of a continuum of market structures which give rise to different degrees of market power. The identification of market power in practice is rarely a simple matter. It requires foremost an economically correct definition of the product and geographical markets. Two or more products are part of the same

product market if consumers regard them as close substitutes, even though they may be physically dissimilar or supplied by firms in different industries. Economists measure the degree of substitutability between products by the *price cross-elasticity* of demand. This shows the percentage change in the quantity demanded of a good X resulting from a given percentage change in the price of a related good Y or, more formally:

$$\frac{\%\text{ change in quantity of } X}{\%\text{ change in price of } Y}$$

According to this method of classification, goods X and Y are said to be substitutes if the price cross-elasticity is positive so that, for example, an increase in the price of pork will, all other things being held constant, increase the quantity demanded of beef. The larger the cross-elasticity, the more substitutable the products. The boundary of a market may also be defined by the distance between sellers. Transport costs, for example, may render a seller immune from direct competition, enabling him to charge above competitive prices even though many firms supply the same product elsewhere.

2. Another factor which complicates the task of identifying market power is *potential* competition, i.e. the threat of new firms entering the industry. The intensity and effectiveness of potential competition depend crucially on the height of barriers to entry. A barrier to entry can be defined as 'a cost of producing (at some or every rate of output) which must be borne by a firm which seeks to enter an industry but is not borne by a firm already in the industry' (G. J. Stigler, *The Organisation of Industry* (1968), p. 78; see, also, J. Bain, *Barriers to New Competition* (1956)). An extreme example is a licence to operate a TV station awarded to only one firm by the government. If barriers to the entry of new firms are negligible then this will cause existing firms in the industry to behave competitively. The mere *threat* of entry created by monopoly profits will be sufficient to induce even a single firm to price at marginal cost to forestall competition. Thus, to determine whether firms in an industry have *market power* one must also consider 'indicators' of potential competition, and barriers to entry in particular. (See W. M. Landes and R. A. Posner, 'Market Power in Antitrust Cases' (1981) 94 Harv. L.R. 987.) This also suggests that it is inadvisable to rely on quantitative estimates of industry concentration, such as a firm's market share (cf. Fair Trading Act 1973, ss. 6–8, 64) as measures of market power. (H. J. Goldschmid *et al.* (eds.), *Industrial Concentration: The New Learning* (1974).)

D. Alternative Approaches to Controlling Market Power

C. K. ROWLEY

*

Antitrust and Economic Efficiency[6]

The merits and demerits of market power will clearly vary, both in character and degree, from one case to another, and for this reason a pragmatic cost-benefit approach to public policy might seem essential. Yet the cost-benefit approach to the market power problem has its critics as well as its advocates, and a range of alternative policies merits consideration. This survey restricts attention to four separate approaches to market power, all of which have been practised or are currently operational in the economies of the U.S.A. and the U.K., namely (1) *laissez-faire*; (2) fair-rate-of-return regulation; (3) cost-benefit analysis; and (4) non-discretionary antitrust . . . Throughout the discussion three separate aspects of the market power problem are carefully distinguished, namely (i) restrictive agreements; (ii) horizontal mergers and acquisitions; and (iii) single-firm monopolisation.

LAISSEZ-FAIRE

Essentially, the *laissez-faire* approach to the market power problem is one (*a*) of denying that the problem in fact exists, or (*b*) of rejecting the notion that it can be corrected by the available instruments of public policy, or (more usually) some combination of the two approaches. The basis of this policy approach is the view that market forces can be relied upon, without outside intervention, to maximise social welfare subject to irremovable constraints of the environment . . .

   In part, the *laissez-faire* case rests upon the view that the market economy is fundamentally competitive and, indeed, that the most intractable pockets of market power are those which exist as a consequence of state intervention. For in the absence of massive scale economies, monopoly profits serve as a signal for new firms to enter the market and/or for existing competitors to expand their output. Other entry barriers – often state-induced – are not expected to obstruct competitive forces in the longer haul, at least where the profit incentives are at all marked. Even market power based upon scale

---

   [6] From *Antitrust and Economic Efficiency* (1973), pp. 72–90, with omissions. Reprinted by permission of Macmillan, London and Basingstoke.

economies is susceptible to technical progress and, in the last event, market power grounded upon such economies would be endorsed even by a fully-fledged cost-benefit analysis. Those who advocate the *laissez-faire* approach are equally agreed that scale economies are less significant and less pervasive, that restrictive agreements are less widespread and less effective, and that the merger movement is less monopolistic than proponents of state intervention would allow ...

In part, moreover, the case for the *laissez-faire* approach is grounded upon a view of the state itself which is less charitable than that customarily represented in the economic theory of public policy. For in assessing the social welfare impact of state intervention ... advocates of *laissez-faire* reject the notion of the state as impartial and omniscient servant of the public good in favour of a more realistic view of vote-maximising politicians operating on an environment characterised by uncertainty and riddled with pressure-group activities, within the context of a two-party, majority-voting political system ... Advocates of *laissez-faire* take a pessimistic view of any antitrust programme weathering successfully the combined pressures of uncertainty in the political market-place and sustained producer lobbying. Better, they argue, an imperfect market solution than an emasculated antitrust alternative.

FAIR-RATE-OF-RETURN REGULATION

Regulation of the rate of return on capital of specific firms, whether of a continuous or an *ad hoc* variety, is designed to prevent firms with significant market power from exploiting their position by charging monopoly prices. This approach allows market power to take place without antitrust intervention. In the U.S.A., continuous fair-rate-of-return regulation is a prevalent feature of the public utilities. In the U.K. such regulation is predominantly *ad hoc* in character ...

Regulatory commissions are usually authorised to establish prices which will provide a fair rate of return on capital for the monopolist firm, taking account of all relevant circumstances. In this way it is hoped to combine the cost-saving benefits from large-scale production with the minimum possible loss of consumer benefits. .... The regulatory commission is usually given access to the accounting records of the regulated firm and must rely substantially upon such information in establishing fair-rate-of-return prices. ...

If firms always combined their factor inputs efficiently and produced at minimum cost, if the prices of factor inputs always reflected their opportunity cost, and if the accounting ledgers of the firm accurately reflected the costs incurred, the task of the regulatory commission, though difficult, would be manageable. Merely to indicate these requirements is to underline the immensity of the real-world problems faced by regulatory commissions.

For in practice there is little reason to suppose, in the absence of competition, that the regulated firms will combine their factor inputs efficiently and produce at minimum cost. There is perhaps even less reason to suppose that the accounting ledgers will provide an accurate reflection of company activities. The regulators are rarely in a position to confront the firms' accountants with alternative cost estimates. In such circumstances, the discretionary power of the regulated firm is considerable. In periods of inflation there are additional problems in the selection of the most appropriate measure of profit and of capital, and there is no necessary reason why fair rates of return assessed in terms of historic cost measurements should coincide with fair rates of return assessed in terms of replacement or reproduction cost measurements . . .

There is, however, a yet more pernicious problem raised by the regulatory approach to the market power problem, which becomes evident in cases where the fair-rate-of-return solution provides profits which are less than those which an unregulated firm could extract from its market, and where the regulators are not omniscient with respect to cost information. For in such circumstances the regulated firm has every incentive to increase its X-inefficiency, taking out in the quiet and more comfortable life the very discretionary profits which the regulators are intent on eliminating . . .

One such response to regulatory intervention, first noted by Averch and Johnson,[7] is that of increasing capital employed beyond the efficient level as a means of raising total profit (since the fair rate of return is calculated as a percentage on the rate base) as well as raising costs above the minimum level theoretically available. In such circumstances, regulation would actually create X-inefficiency in the use of capital inputs, however successful the application of fair-rate-of-return criteria . . .

More generally, however, firms subjected to fair-rate-of-return regulation, . . . are likely to respond by allowing costs to drift upwards via X-inefficiency of a non-specific nature, i.e. not tied to capital inputs alone . . . The regulatory authorities would have to be extremely vigilant to protect against this outcome. . . . Profit incentives for regulated firms to pursue X-efficiency would seem essential, even though they do imply some deviation from the fair-rate-of-return principle, if regulation is not entirely negated by firm responses.

There can be no certainty, of course, that the regulatory authority will in fact pursue fair-rate-of-return regulations as assiduously as

---

[7] 'Behavior of the Firm Under Regulatory Constraint' (1962) 52 Am. Econ. Rev. 1053.

textbooks conventionally assume. . . . [T]he possibility [exists] that the regulated firms might successfully subvert the regulation machinery to their own ends, thereby extending rather than diminishing their pre-regulation market power . . . This outcome is more likely in the case of firms which encounter continuous regulation by a single commission than in the case of firms which periodically face regulation following *ad hoc* investigations . . .

The foregoing discussion emphasises the deficiencies and limitations of the regulation approach to the problem of market power. It should not be assumed, however, that there is no case and no public sympathy for this form of state intervention . . . For it does represent a serious attempt to combine the achievement of scale economies with a minimum loss of consumer benefits, and as such it is tolerated, if not indeed welcomed, as a widespread form of intervention both in the U.K. and in the U.S.A. . . .

COST–BENEFIT ANALYSIS

The cost–benefit analysis approach to the market power problem recognises that restrictive agreements, mergers and existing monopoly positions may result in both welfare gains and welfare losses, and requires that the expected performance of the company or companies concerned should be fully investigated before a verdict is passed. In principle, a thoroughgoing cost–benefit analysis is impossible in the absence of a carefully defined social welfare function which determines what is to be treated as a welfare gain and what as a welfare loss, and which assigns appropriate weights to these various categories. . . . Despite the evident advantages of such an approach in clarifying the welfare issues, no such formal social welfare function has ever been applied in practice by countries which endorse the pragmatic, cost–benefit analysis approach to the market power problem. Rather, a set of ill-defined and sometimes contradictory guidelines have supported pragmatic investigation.

Nevertheless, the . . . approach, clearly merits serious consideration at a time when cost-benefit and cost-effectiveness techniques have assumed such importance in public-sector decision-making generally. . . . [A] brief assessment of the task encountered by those responsible for such an exercise is . . . necessary.

The first task, inevitably, would be that of determining the degree of market power which would exist following the application of appropriate antitrust instruments and comparing this with the degree of market power which would exist in the absence of such intervention, taking full account of market reactions. It is important to recognise that this task is a *sine qua non* for a realistic cost–benefit analysis, since the differential market power under consideration is of quite central significance for the measurement of welfare gains and losses.

The second task would be that of determining the objectives of the company or the companies concerned under each of the relevant market organisation alternatives. Profit maximisation can no longer be taken for granted . . . Yet in the absence of some judgement on motivation, attempts to isolate the price–output implications for cost–benefit analysis are practically meaningless.

In the light of this information, the task of assessing the relevant consumer and producer benefits at issue could be set in motion. It would not be simple . . . As a prerequisite for assessing the loss of consumer benefits from allocative inefficiency in the market power solution, it would be necessary (a) to identify the relevant portion of the market demand curve . . . (b) to identify the likely price–output implications of the market power solution; and (c) to identify the corresponding price–output implications of the antitrust solution (complex indeed in oligopolistic cases). As a prerequisite for assessing the welfare loss from X-inefficiency, it would be necessary to define the functional relationship between X-inefficiency and market power and to determine just which components of X-inefficiency constituted a welfare loss. No easy task this, since accounting data are practically useless and the exercise almost entirely hypothetical. As a prerequisite for assessing the welfare gain from scale economies in the market power solution, it would be necessary to determine the likely scale of operation both of the monopolist and of the rival firms in the competitive solution, and to define the functional relationship between average cost and the scale of activity. Once again this is no easy task, since accounting data at best defines a single point on the production function and there are serious limitations . . . in alternative approaches to the measurement of scale returns.

This exercise is sufficiently daunting in the most stable of market environments and on assumptions of instantaneous adjustment. In the real world, characterised by volatile market conditions and significant time-lags in the adjustment process, the task appears daunting in the extreme, especially since the analysis could not be once-for-all but would necessarily have to be periodically renewed as market conditions altered. At best the estimated net benefit or net loss associated with the market power solution would be subject to wide error bars, and where the judgement was at all close, the error bars might be wider than the net benefit or loss thrown up by the analysis. Nor should the resources devoted to the cost–benefit analysis be treated as free goods. For the opportunity cost of pragmatic inquiry – which includes not only the cost of the resources committed to the inquiry by the state, but also the cost of the resources committed by the companies concerned –

is often extremely high. The question must be asked, therefore, whether in economic terms cost–benefit analysis is justified even when unambiguous results are obtained. In a perverse sense, what is needed is a cost–benefit analysis of the cost–benefit analysis approach to the market power problem!

Further problems arise, in cases where antitrust intervention appears justified, of ensuring that suitable policy instruments are available. For there is little point in engaging in costly analysis when there is no prospect of obtaining an effective antitrust solution should it be required. In this respect merger proposals present the least problem, since they can be rejected without any significant institutional problems arising . . .

Restrictive agreements, it is true, can be banned, and indeed noncompliance with a prohibition could be made a serious offence in criminal as well as in civil law. This could raise the costs of noncompliance to an uneconomic level. But this is to beg the question as to what precisely constitutes a restrictive agreement, and indeed opens the door to all sorts of information agreements and understandings which company lawyers devise as a means of maintaining market power without falling foul of the law. The problems encountered in applying antitrust intervention to single-firm monopolists would seem to be yet more serious. For whatever measures are applied to the firm itself – and prohibitions on further expansion and divestiture of assets spring readily to mind – they are bound to disrupt market performance with perhaps serious short-term consequences for social welfare. Equally, measures designed to increase competition from outside sources – for example, tariff reductions and state-subsidised competition – raise perhaps quite serious problems for the balance of payments and the fiscal activities of central government. These costs of enforcement are especially relevant in comparing the antitrust with the *laissez-faire* approach to the market power problem, and they will come under scrutiny again in evaluating non-discretionary antitrust. . . .

NON-DISCRETIONARY ANTITRUST

Of the four principal approaches discussed in this survey, this is the only approach to the problem of market power which can fairly be called an antitrust policy . . . Non-discretionary antitrust rejects the notion that market power can best be treated by pragmatic cost–benefit analysis in favour of a more dogmatic treatment based upon rules. The characteristic of this approach is that it equates social welfare with the maintenance or reinvigoration of competition and that it attempts to achieve this latter objective via a set of non-discretionary rules enforceable through the judicial and/or the administrative process. In principle, at least, this is the market power approach currently operative in the U.S.A., though in practice significant deviations from non-discretionary antitrust are tolerated even by the U.S. antitrust authorities.

At first sight, at least, an approach based upon rules appears at once less complicated and less ambiguous than either the regulation or the cost–benefit approach, and also more easily enforceable, on the assumption that the penalties for non-compliance can be higher in the presence than in the absence of clear-cut policy guidelines. For those who value economy and unambiguity in market power policy, therefore, the non-discretionary approach would seem to have much to commend it. What form, then, might an approach based upon rules take in practice?

Firstly, there would be a cogent case for prohibiting all agreements in restraint of trade, on the principle that scale benefits can very rarely be significant in such circumstances since the participating firms retain their independent identities, and that the benefit side of a cost–benefit analysis in any event would be lightly weighed. . . . A prohibitory approach of this kind would still present problems for the antitrust authorities on issues such as the precise definition of restraint of trade and the precise definition of the term 'agreement'. . . . For the most part, however, this branch of non-discretionary policy presents few really serious problems of interpretation (though detection procedures are necessarily costly and sophisticated). . .

The use of non-discretionary rules in handling merger proposals presents less tractable problems, however, . . . since the scale economies sacrificed by such a policy might well be considerable. For the essence of a non-discretionary policy towards mergers is the prohibition of all mergers which would raise the market share of the resulting combine above an acceptable limit, irrespective of the net benefits which might be bestowed by such a merger. There are evident problems in deciding just what is the precise market under consideration and just what the acceptable market-share limits shall be. . . .

The problem of market definition in antitrust investigations is a very real one . . . Despite the plethora of criteria (often quite impracticable) showered upon the courts by economists – including coefficients of cross-elasticity of demand and/or supply beloved by the textbook writers, who never sully their hands on the real world – the . . . antitrust authorities have fallen back upon . . . somewhat crude criteri[a] . . . that . . . does not really direct their attention to precise issues. . . .

. . . [T]he difficulty of market definition in merger cases is an important weakness in the non-discretionary approach, . . . In particular, it is a relative disadvantage of non-discretionary antitrust when compared with the *laissez-faire* and the regulation approaches to the market power problem, where issues of market definition really do not arise. But it is in a sense a relative advantage of non-discretionary antitrust when compared with the cost–benefit analysis approach, since the latter approach encounters the market definition problem at the outset and must resolve it before proceeding to yet thornier issues.

Given some definition of the market, the non-discretionary antitrust approach must next resolve the issue of what is an acceptable market-share limit beyond which mergers should be prohibited. This is no easy task, since features other than the number and relative size of the firms in a market (most notably the level of entry barriers and the degree of product differentiation) affect the incidence of competition in specific commodity markets and the precise relationship between market structure and market performance is not known at the present time. Moreover, market-share rules cannot be formulated without any reference whatsoever to the size of the economy under consideration, unless scale issues are to be given zero weights in the formulation of rules . . .

It is the essence of non-discretionary antitrust, . . . that any merger proposal which fails to satisfy the e[st]ablished rules on market share must be condemned. No discussion is allowed on the possible welfare gains and losses consequent upon such a prohibition. For this reason, non-discretionary antitrust has been criticised as being excessively dogmatic . . . There are two ways of viewing this criticism. The first is to accept that non-discretionary antitrust cannot be justified by strict reference to economic theory, that not enough is known about the relative significance of scale economies and X-inefficiency, about the relationship between market structure and market performance, or even about company motivation, to justify taking such a dogmatic standpoint on the market power issue. In such circumstances, those supporting non-discretionary antitrust must do so for reasons that are not strictly economic, but derive from their particular political and social philosophy . . .

There is, however, an alternative way of viewing the non-discretionary approach to merger policy which squares more closely with the dictates of economic analysis . . . This viewpoint rests upon the acknowledged uncertainty and high transaction costs surrounding the cost–benefit investigations into merger proposals. A case is arguable on these grounds that the pragmatic approach is neither the most economical nor the most effective method of dealing with the merger problem. This is in no sense to deny that benefits may flow from pragmatic investigation. Rather it is to suggest that the benefits derived therefrom are unlikely in practice to outweigh the costs . . .

The non-discretionary approach to single-firm monopolisation presents additional problems which are largely avoided in dealing with merger proposals, since existing institutional arrangements must be disrupted where antitrust measures are applied to existing monopolists. Once again, the non-discretionary approach would emphasise structural rather than performance criteria, and any firm which enjoyed a greater share of properly defined market than the rules allowed . . . would expect antitrust intervention. A range of instruments would be available, including attacks on entry barriers by lowering tariffs, controlling sales promotion, etc., subsidising new entry, prohibitions on the absolute growth of the monopolist in a growing total market, and so on. In extreme cases, and where the technique of production so allowed, divestiture decrees might be imposed, though action of this severity would be the exception rather than the rule, and would be imposed only where alternative methods seemed inopportune. Only where completely intractable problems existed (as for example in the case of public goods and chronic production indivisibilities) might antitrust intervention be waived in favour of regulatory or public enterprise alternatives.

Notes

1. There are two additional approaches to controlling market power which are not considered in this extract. The first is public ownership, which under UK legislation has been applied particularly to natural monopolies or public utilities. By itself, public ownership does not control market power; indeed, it may have been instituted primarily to achieve other, notably distributional purposes, e.g. the cross-subsidization of services: L. De Alessi, 'On the Nature and Consequences of Private and Public Enterprise' (1982) 67 Minn. L.R. 191. Rather it places the ability to control the consequences of market power in an institution which is legally or politically answerable. The activity of the public enterprise should, therefore, be subjected to constraints both as to pricing policy and to efficient management (R. Rees, 'The Pricing Policies of the Nationalised Industries' (1979) 122 Three Banks Rev. 3; Report of Monopolies and Merger Commission on Central Electricity Generating Board (1980–81 H.C. 315).

2. The second technique, again used predominantly to control public utilities, is franchising (see, e.g., Report of Inquiry Into Cable Expansion and Public Broadcasting (1982, Cmnd. 8679)). It has been argued by Demsetz ('Why Regulate Utilities?' (1968) 11 J. Law and Econ. 55) that awarding franchises to a natural monopolist who promises to sell his goods or services at the lowest price will result in a competitive outcome, despite the existence of only one supplier. The efficacy of competitive-bid franchises as a complete solution to market power problems has, however, been questioned

(O. E. Williamson, 'Franchise Bidding for Natural Monopolies – in General and with Respect to CATV' (1976) 7 Bell J. Econ. 73; C. G. Veljanovski and W. D. Bishop, *Choice by Cable – The Economics of a New Era in Television* (1983) chs. 6, 7).

6

THEORIES OF REGULATION

A. Introduction

1. The subject-matter of chapters 6 and 7 is problematic for British students because, though vital to an appreciation of the role of law in a mixed economy, it has been neglected by academic lawyers (see A. I. Ogus, 'Economics, Liberty and the Common Law' (1980) 15 Jo. S.P.T.L. 42). Critical analysis has tended to focus either on the sociological framework (e.g. E. Kamenka and A. E. Tay (eds.), *Law and Social Control* (1980)) or on specific areas of regulation (e.g. R. Cranston, *Consumers and the Law* (1978)). British economists, too, have been reluctant to provide a general overview (though see J. D. Tomlinson, 'Regulating the Capitalist Enterprise: The Impossible Dream?' (1983) 30 Scot. J. Pol. Econ. 54); they have concentrated on particular forms of intervention, especially public ownership (cf. G. L. Reid and K. Allen (eds.), *Nationalized Industries* (1973)), or on specific areas (e.g. P. Burrows, *The Economic Theory of Pollution Control* (1979); A. J. Culyer, *The Political Economy of Social Policy* (1980)). In contrast, there is a considerable American literature on the general topic see, especially, A. E. Kahn, *The Economics of Regulation* (1970); B. M. Mitnick, *The Political Economy of Regulation* (1980); S. Breyer, *Regulation and its Reform* (1982); and B. M. Owen and R. Braeutigam, *The Regulation Game* (1978).

2. There is no universally accepted definition of 'regulation.' For the purposes of this book, we regard it as covering all forms of legal control which are primarily enforced by a public institution, often an administrative agency created for that specific purpose. We focus on the justifications for regulation and the instruments available to the policymaker, drawing on studies of particular regulatory systems to illustrate the general problems.

B. Traditional Justifications for Regulation

S. BREYER

*

Analyzing Regulatory Failure: Mismatches, Less Restrictive Alternatives, and Reform[1]

The framework for analysis suggested in this Article assumes that an unregulated marketplace is the norm and that those who advocate government intervention must justify it by showing that it is needed to achieve an important public objective that an unregulated marketplace cannot provide. This assumption, and the traditional 'market failure' analysis that it suggests, are sometimes justified by appealing to basic societal values such as freedom of individual action and minimization of governmental coercion. The justification for the assumption here, however, lies in its ability to generate demonstrably desirable results by identifying regulatory problems, predicting regulatory failures, and suggesting alternatives. Because the assumption that an unregulated marketplace is the norm does not rest on the adoption of a particular set of values, the analysis should point to conclusions and proposals which would be accepted by persons holding a broad range of political values and beliefs.

Of course, the intrinsic advantages offered by a well-functioning competitive marketplace also help to support a presumption in favor of a free market system. These advantages have traditionally been identified as the market's tendency to minimize economic waste by allowing for continuous individual balancing of economic costs and benefits by consumers and producers, the 'carrot and stick' incentive the market provides for greater production efficiency, and the incentives it provides for innovation and the channelling of these innovations into socially desired directions.

In achieving these ends, competitive markets reduce the need for the central collection of information. Their price signals allow producers and consumers to adapt quickly to change. And the impersonality of the decisionmaking process in competitive markets prevents those injured in the process (because, for example, their goods are no longer in demand) from obstructing change. To these advantages may be

[1] (1979) 92 Harv. L.R. 547, 552–60, with omissions. Copyright © 1979 by the Harvard Law Review Association. Reprinted by permission of the author and the Harvard Law Review.

added a competitive market's tendency to decentralize power and to make decisions that are 'fair' in the sense of being impersonal. . . .

The most important justifications for government regulation of the economy are well described as instances of classical market failure. Most of the market defects that give rise to a demand for regulation can be classified as follows:

1. Control of Monopoly Power. A traditional, persistent rationale for price and profit regulation is based on the need to control the exercise of power by a 'natural monopolist.' . . .

2. Rent Control. Sudden increases in price may allow those who hold interests in a commodity to earn a windfall profit, one kind of economic 'rent'. For example, those who owned large stocks of oil earned huge rents when the Arabs raised the price of new oil; owners of old natural gas earned rents when the costs of finding new natural gas rose; and those who own existing housing earn rents as long as construction costs rise faster than other costs. Rents exist throughout the economy, in competitive and noncompetitive industries alike. Any firm that finds a more efficient production process, that finds an unusually cheap supply source, that luckily buys machines when they are cheap, or that has unusually effective managers – but which cannot expand to satisfy all industry demand – will earn a rent. Ordinarily rents are not regulated, but when rents are great in amount and do not reflect any particular talent or skill on the part of producers, there is sometimes a demand for regulation. The object of the regulation is to transfer these 'undeserved windfall profits' from producers or owners of the scarce resources to consumers or taxpayers.

3. Correcting for Spillovers. Regulation is frequently justified as needed to compensate for the fact that the price of a product does not reflect certain major costs that its production and use impose upon the economy. . . .

. . . Regulation must therefore rest on a judgment that some extra production cost . . . is warranted by the resulting reduction of . . . harm. . . . Regulation in the presence of spillover costs can be seen as a way of correcting for the fact that bargaining among affected parties is difficult.

4. Correcting for Inadequate Information. For competitive markets to function well consumers must have information sufficient to evaluate competing products. This information is itself a commodity, the supply of which will reflect costs and demand. Government regulation is sometimes designed to correct for inadequate consumer information or to lower the costs to the consumer of obtaining adequate information. . . .

5. *Excessive Competition.* A commonly advanced justification for the regulation of airlines, trucks, and ships is the need to control 'excessive competition'. In fact, this notion refers to several different sorts of justification, all of which assume that if prices fall too low, firms will go out of business, and products will end up being too costly. This particular set of justifications is an 'empty box', because no existing regulatory program can be justified by reference to it. Analysis of the different problems to which this rationale for regulation refers makes it clear how empty the box is.

This rationale may refer to an historical problem. For example, when airlines originally received large government subsidies (from the 1920s through the 1950s), they had an incentive to cut prices well below costs to increase their size, while making up the additional losses through additional subsidy. Though the problem was caused by government intervention (through subsidization), it required additional intervention to counteract it. . . .

The rationale may refer to problems faced by an industry with large fixed costs and cyclical demand. The firms in the industry, pricing at incremental cost in the downswing, may find they have insufficient revenue to maintain full capacity. To reduce capacity during slack periods is inefficient, for it is more expensive to increase it during the next upswing than to maintain it continuously. . . .

The rationale might refer to the possibility of 'predatory' pricing – a dominant firm's setting prices below variable costs in order to drive its rivals out of business, then raising its prices, and recouping lost profits before new firms, attracted by the higher prices, can enter the industry. There is little evidence, however, that this problem exists in any of the highly regulated industries. Where predatory pricing might exist, it can be dealt with through application of the antitrust laws.

In a related vein, the excessive competition rationale may be an argument against allowing new firms to enter a 'natural monopoly' industry, where the existence of more than one firm would lead to higher costs per unit of output. But if the industry is truly a natural monopoly, thus presenting economies of scale and high barriers to entry, it is not clear why or how another firm would enter the market.

6. *Moral Hazard.* The term 'moral hazard' is used to describe a situation in which someone other than a buyer pays for the buyer's purchases. The buyer feels no pocketbook constraint, and will purchase a good oblivious to the resource costs he imposes upon the economy. When ethical or other institutional constraints or direct

supervision by the payer fail to control purchases, government regulation may be demanded.

The most obvious current example is escalating medical costs. As medical care is purchased to an ever greater extent by the government or by large private insurers (with virtually no constraint on the amount demanded by the individual user), medical costs have accounted for an ever greater proportion of the national product. The fact that purchases are paid for by others frees the individual from the need to consider that using more medical care means less production of other goods; thus he may 'unnecessarily' or 'excessively' use medical resources. . . .

7. *Rationalization.* Occasionally government intervention is justified on the ground that, without it, firms in an industry would remain too small, or would lack sufficient organization, to produce their product efficiently. One would ordinarily expect such firms to grow or co-operate, and unit costs to decrease. But often social or political factors act to counteract this tendency. In such circumstances, agencies have sought to engage in industrywide 'planning'. . . .

8. *Minor Justifications.* Several additional justifications have on occasion been advanced for government regulation. While not in themselves persuasive, these justifications often provide partial support for regulatory action.

(*a*) *Unequal Bargaining Power.* The assumption that the 'best' or most efficient allocation is achieved by free market forces rests in part upon an assumption that there is a 'proper' allocation of bargaining power among the parties affected. Where the existing division of such bargaining power is 'unequal' in this sense, it may be thought that regulation is justified in order to achieve a better balance. It is sometimes argued, for instance, that the 'unequal bargaining power' of small sellers requires special legislative protection. While in principle one might regulate the 'monopoly buyer' in order to protect these sellers, the more usual congressional response is to grant an exemption from the antitrust laws, thus allowing the sellers to organize in order to deal more effectively with the buyer. This rationale underlies the exemption granted not only to labor, but also to agricultural and fishing cooperatives.

(*b*) *Scarcity.* Regulation is sometimes justified in terms of scarcity. Regulation on the basis of this justification reflects a deliberate decision to abandon the market and use regulatory allocation to achieve a set of (often unspecified) 'public interest' objectives, such as in the case of licensing television stations. Sometimes regulatory allocation is undertaken because of sudden supply failures which would work too serious a hardship on many users who could not afford the resulting dramatic price increases, as in the case of the Arab oil boycott. It must be remembered, however, that the 'shortage' may be the result of the workings of an ongoing regulatory program, as when natural gas must be allocated because of rent control or an agency awards licenses to enter an industry.

(c) *Paternalism*. Although in some cases the full and adequate information needed to reach a rational decision may be available to the decisionmaker in the marketplace, some may argue that he will nevertheless make the wrong decision and therefore government regulation is needed. This justification is one of pure paternalism: the government knows better than the individual what he wants or what is good for him. The distrust of the ability of the purchaser may be based on the inability of the lay person to evaluate the information, as in the case of purchasing professional services, or the belief that, although the information could be accurately evaluated by the lay person, irrational human tendencies prevent this. The latter may be the case where small probabilities are involved, such as small risks of injury, or where matters of life and death are implicated, such as when those suffering from cancer will purchase a drug even though all reasonably reliable information indicates that it is worthless or even harmful. Whether the brand of paternalism based on mistrust of the rationality of the consumer is consistent with notions of freedom of choice which underlie the free market assumption is questionable. But it seems to play an important role in some government decisions.

Many existing regulatory programs rest upon not one but several different rationales. Thus, for example, one might favor regulation of workplace safety for several reasons. One might recognize that employers and employees can bargain for improved workplace safety (greater safety expenditures), but argue that accidents impose costs on others who are not represented at the bargaining table; thus bargaining alone will produce inadequate expenditure upon safety devices. This is a *spillover* rationale. Or one might believe that the worker does not know enough about the risks or consequences of accidents so he will not insist upon added safety expenditures. This is to argue that there is an *informational defect* in the market. Or, one might feel the worker is too poor or too weak to bargain for the safety he needs – that he has *unequal bargaining power*. Finally, one might claim that workers (indeed, all persons) are simply incapable of understanding their likely future feelings about accidents that hurt them. They inevitably underestimate the risk. If regulation is an effort to give them what they 'really' want (contrary to their expressed views), a *paternalistic* rationale is at work. The importance of distinguishing rationales lies in the extent to which doing so suggests different remedies. Thus, one who believes the primary problem is informational will tend to favor government efforts to provide more information, not classical regulation. Although one who accepts a paternalistic rationale may disagree with one who believes the problem is informational, the clear statement of their points of difference can lead to empirical work that will lead them toward agreement upon the basic rationale and thus help choose the regulatory weapon best suited to the problems at hand.

Notes

1. The growth of the state and the imposition of centralized controls either to correct or supplant market mechanisms have been broadly treated in the sociology of law literature (see J. T. Winkler, 'Law, State and Economy' (1975) 2 Brit. J. Law and Soc. 103; E. Kamenka and A. E. Tay (eds.), *Law and Social Control* (1980), the basis of which is to be found in the classic German texts of M. Weber, *The Theory of Social and Economic Organization* (trans. A. M. Henderson and T. Parsons 1947) and F. Tönnies, *Community and Association* (trans. C. P. Loomis 1955)).

2. While traditional welfare economists have, almost from the beginning, been ready to justify these controls on the basis of 'market failure', they have tended to isolate and concentrate on particular forms of such failure, e.g. imperfect competition (J. Robinson, *The Economics of Imperfect Competition* (1930) or externalities (A. C. Pigou, *The Economics of Welfare* (1924)). The Breyer paper conveniently and succinctly gathers together the various justifications advanced to support regulation; for a fuller treatment, see his *Regulation and its Reform* (1982), ch. 1, and for alternative surveys, R. B. McKenzie and G. Tullock, *Modern Political Economy* (1978), chs. 11–12; G. M. Richardson, A. I. Ogus and P. Burrows, *Policing Pollution* (1983), ch. 1.

3. Breyer's list is not comprehensive. Perhaps surprisingly, he does not include the problem of public goods. These are goods for which consumption by one person does not reduce the level of consumption by others. The classic examples are defence and law and order, but many other resources contain public good aspects, e.g. highways; clean environment; information; education. If individuals cannot easily be excluded from the benefits of these goods, the market is unlikely to achieve an efficient allocation of resources: who would be willing to pay, and thus specifically to formulate his demand, for a good, from which he will in any event be able to benefit as a 'free rider'? Some collective, non-market means of determining supply and prescribing payment is, therefore, justified. See, generally, A. J. Culyer, *Political Economy of Social Policy* (1980), pp. 43–54, and M. Olson, 'On the Priority of Public Problems' in R. Marris (ed.), *The Corporate Society* (1974), ch. 10.

4. Breyer offers no more than a hint that regulation may serve a redistributional purpose, while others lay great emphasis on this theoretical goal:

cf. Culyer, op. cit., ch. 4 and A. Okun, *Equality and Efficiency: The Big Tradeoff* (1975). The legislature may impose the control primarily to redistribute resources from one group in society to another, or, where regulation is considered desirable for other reasons, e.g. market failure, may prefer one form of control to another because it is thought likely to have distributional effects which accord with current social and moral values.

5. There is a wide choice of regulatory instruments available to government, ranging from the effectively non-interventionist self-regulation, through taxes and subsidies, information controls, price controls and quality standards, to licensing and public ownership. Most of these will be considered in Chapter 7. For more general discussions of the choice, see: the dated but exhaustive analysis in E. Freund, *Legislative Regulation* (1932); R. F. Cranston, 'Reform through Legislation: the Dimensions of Legislative Technique' (1978) 73 Northwestern U.L.R. 873; Breyer, op. cit., (1982), ch. 8; and L. J. White, *Reforming Regulation: Processes and Problems* (1981), ch. 3. There is a useful distinction between so-called 'economic regulation', concerned primarily with prices charged in individual industries and with entry into such industries, and 'social regulation' (e.g. safety and environmental health) which cuts across broad areas of the economy and which typically lays down standards enforceable by government agencies.

C. The 'Economic Theory' of Regulation

R. A. POSNER

*

Theories of Economic Regulation[2]

A major challenge to social theory is to explain the pattern of government intervention in the market – what we may call 'economic regulation'. Properly defined, the term refers to taxes and subsidies of all sorts as well as to explicit legislative and administrative controls over rates, entry, and other facets of economic activity. Two main theories of economic regulation have been proposed. One is the 'public interest' theory, bequeathed by a previous generation of economists to the present generation of lawyers. This theory holds that regulation is supplied in response to the demand of the public for the correction of inefficient or inequitable market practices. It has a number of deficiencies that we shall discuss. The second theory is the 'capture' theory . . . Espoused by an odd mixture of welfare state liberals,

---

[2] (1974) 5 Bell J. Econ. 335–51, with omissions. Copyright © 1974 by the American Telephone and Telegraph Company. Reprinted by permission.

muckrakers, Marxists, and free-market economists, this theory holds that regulation is supplied in response to the demands of interest groups struggling among themselves to maximize the incomes of their members. There are crucial differences among the capture theorists. I shall argue that the economists' version is the most promising, but shall also point out the significant weaknesses in both the theory and the empirical research that is alleged to support the theory.

THE PUBLIC INTEREST THEORY OF REGULATION

The original theory

Two assumptions seem to have typified thought about economic policy (not all of it by economists) in the period roughly from the enactment of the first Interstate Commerce Act in 1887 to the founding of the *Journal of Law and Economics* in 1958. One assumption was that economic markets are extremely fragile and apt to operate very inefficiently (or inequitably) if left alone; the other was that government regulation is virtually costless. With these assumptions, it was very easy to argue that the principal government interventions in the economy – trade union protection, public utility and common carrier regulation, public power and reclamation programs, farm subsidies, occupational licensure, the minimum wage, even tariffs – were simply responses of government to public demands for the rectification of palpable and remediable inefficiencies and inequities in the operation of the free market. Behind each scheme of regulation could be discerned a market imperfection, the existence of which supplied a complete justification for some regulation assumed to operate effectively and without cost.

Were this theory of regulation correct, we would find regulation imposed mainly in highly concentrated industries (where the danger of monopoly is greatest) and in industries that generate substantial external costs or benefits. We do not. Some fifteen years of theoretical and empirical research, conducted mainly by economists, have demonstrated that regulation is not positively correlated with the presence of external economies or diseconomies or with monopolistic market structure. . . . The conception of government as a costless and dependably effective instrument for altering market behavior has also gone by the boards. Theoretical revision has both stimulated and been reinforced by a growing body of case studies demonstrating that particular schemes of government regulation cannot be explained on the ground that they increase the wealth or, by any widely accepted standard of equity or fairness, the justice of the society.

A reformulation

The empirical evidence is sometimes challenged on the ground that the disappointing performance of the regulatory process is the result not of any unsoundness in the basic goals or nature of the process but of particular weaknesses in personnel or procedures that can and will be remedied (at low cost) as the society gains experience in the mechanics of public administration. Thus reformulated, the public interest theory of regulation holds that regulatory agencies are created for bona fide public purposes, but are then mismanaged, with the result that those purposes are not always achieved.

This reformulation is unsatisfactory on two grounds. First, it fails to account for a good deal of evidence that the socially undesirable results of regulation are frequently desired by groups influential in the enactment of the legislation setting up the regulatory scheme. . . .

Second, the evidence that has been offered to show mismanagement by the regulatory agency is surprisingly weak. Much of it is consistent with the rival theory . . . that the typical regulatory agency operates with reasonable efficiency to attain deliberately inefficient or inequitable goals set by the legislature that created it. . . .

Third, no persuasive theory has yet been proposed as to why agencies should be expected to be less efficient than other organizations. The motivation of the agency employee to work diligently and honestly is similar to that of the employee of a business firm. Both want to obtain advancement (not necessarily within the employing firm or agency) and to avoid being fired, demoted, or humiliated. . . .

A further reformulation of the public interest theory

The idea that regulation is an honest but frequently an unsuccessful attempt to promote the public interest becomes somewhat more plausible if we introduce two factors often ignored. The first is the intractable character of many of the tasks that have been assigned to the regulatory agencies. . . . The agencies are asked to do the impossible and it is not surprising that they fail, and in attempting to succeed distort the efficient functioning of the regulated markets. But this does not explain why legislatures assign such tasks to agencies.

The second factor is the cost of effective legislative supervision of the agencies' performance. In a recent article on legal rulemaking, Isaac Ehrlich and I point out that legislative bodies are a type of firm in which the costs of production are extremely high and, moreover, rise very sharply with increases in output.[3] The reason is that legislative

---

[3] Infra, Chapter 9, Section B.

'production' is a process of negotiation among a large group, the legislators, and the analysis of transaction costs in other contexts suggests that bargaining among a number of individuals is a costly process (and explains why legislatures require only a majority and not a unanimous vote in the conduct of their business). Because costs of bargaining rise rapidly with the number of bargainers, a legislature cannot respond efficiently to a growth in workload by increasing the number of its members. Hence, as the business of a legislature rises, it can be expected to delegate more and more of its work to agencies, and to exercise progressively less control over those agencies. . . .

Behavioral assumptions of the public interest theory

A serious problem with any version of the public interest theory is that the theory contains no linkage or mechanism by which a perception of the public interest is translated into legislative action. In the theory of markets, it is explained how the efforts of individuals to promote their self-interest through transacting bring about an efficient allocation of resources. There is no comparable articulation of how a public perception as to what legislative policies or arrangements would maximize public welfare is translated into legislative action. . . .

SOME VERSIONS OF THE CAPTURE THEORY

The Marxists and the muckrakers

The theory that economic regulation is not about the public interest at all, but is a process by which interest groups seek to promote their (private) interests, takes several distinct forms. One, which is put forward by Marxists and by . . . muckrakers can be crudely summarized in the following syllogism. Big business – the capitalists – control the institutions of our society. Among those institutions is regulation. The capitalists must therefore control regulation. The syllogism is false. A great deal of economic regulation serves the interests of small-business – or nonbusiness – groups, including dairy farmers, pharmacists, barbers, truckers, and, in particular, union labor. Such forms of regulation are totally unexplained (and usually either ignored or applauded) in this version of the interest-group or 'capture' theory.

The political scientists' formulations

A more interesting version of the 'capture' theory derives from political science. . . . A few political scientists have proposed the rudiments, at least, of a usable theory. This theory – which the term 'capture' describes particularly well – is that over time regulatory agencies come to be dominated by the industries regulated. This formulation is more specific than the general interest group theory. . . .

Unfortunately, the theory is still unsatisfactory. First, it is confusingly similar to, and in practice probably indistinguishable from, some versions of the public interest theory discussed [above]. Second, while I have generously called it a 'theory', it is actually a hypothesis that lacks any theoretical foundation. No reason is suggested for characterizing the interaction between the regulatory agency and the regulated firm by a metaphor of conquest, and surely the regulatory process is better viewed as the outcome of implicit (sometimes explicit) bargaining between the agency and the regulated firms. No reason is suggested as to why the regulated industry should be the only interest group able to influence an agency. Customers of the regulated firm have an obvious interest in the outcome of the regulatory process – why may they not be able to 'capture' the agency as effectively as the regulated firms, or more so? No reason is suggested as to why industries are able to capture only existing agencies – never to procure the creation of an agency that will promote their interests – or why an industry strong enough to capture an agency set up to tame it could not prevent the creation of the agency in the first place.

The 'theory' answers none of these questions. In addition, it is contradicted by three important bodies of evidence. First, not every agency is characterized by a pristine virtue; often there is no occasion for conquest. . . .

Second, the theory has no predictive or explanatory power at all when a single agency regulates separate industries having conflicting interests. . . . Third, the capture theory ignores a good deal of evidence that the interests promoted by regulatory agencies are frequently those of customer groups, rather than those of the regulated firms themselves. . . .

The economic theory of regulation

What I shall call 'the economic theory of regulation' was proposed by George Stigler in a pathbreaking article.[4] The theory seems at first glance merely a refined version of the capture theory just discussed. It discards the unexplained, and frequently untrue, assumption of pristine legislative purpose; it admits the possibility of 'capture' by interest groups other than the regulated firms; and it replaces the 'capture' metaphor, with its inappropriately militaristic flavor, by the

---

[4] 'The Theory of Economic Regulation' (1971) 2 Bell J. Econ. 3.

more neutral terminology of supply and demand. But it insists with the political scientists that economic regulation serves the private interests of politically effective groups.

More is involved, however, than merely a recasting of the work of the political scientists. The economic theory is more precise and hard-edged – easier to confront and test with a body of data – than the political theory . . . Moreover, the economic theory is committed to the strong assumptions of economic theory generally, notably that people seek to advance their self-interest and do so rationally. A political scientist can argue that regulation is more likely to be imposed in a declining industry because adversity is a greater spur to effort than opportunity (an example that assumes that regulation is normally obtained for the benefit of the regulated firms). The economist is reluctant to accept such an explanation. He does not distinguish between a profit foregone and a loss incurred – the former is a cost too, indeed the same kind of cost. . . . The economic theory insists that regulation be explained as the outcome of the forces of demand and supply. . . .

A CLOSER LOOK AT THE ECONOMIC THEORY OF REGULATION

The theory

. . . The theory is based on two simple but important insights. The first is that since the coercive power of government can be used to give valuable benefits to particular individuals or groups, economic regulation – the expression of that power in the economic sphere – can be viewed as a product whose allocation is governed by laws of supply and demand. The second insight is that the theory of cartels may help us locate the demand and supply curves.

Viewing regulation as a product allocated in accordance with basic principles of supply and demand directs attention to factors bearing on the value of regulation to particular individuals or groups, since, other things being equal, we can expect a product to be supplied to those who value it the most. It also directs our attention to the factors bearing on the cost of obtaining regulation. The theory of cartels illuminates both the benefit and the cost side. The theory teaches that the value of cartelization is greater, the less elastic the demand for the industry's product and the more costly, or the slower, new entry into the industry (or cartelized markets within the industry) is. The theory identifies two major costs of cartelization (besides punishment costs, which are relevant only where cartelization is forbidden by law). The first is the cost to the sellers of arriving at an agreement on the price to be charged by and the output of each seller. This agreement determines the profits of each cartel member. The second cost is the cost of enforcing the cartel agreement against nonparticipants or defectors. Cartels are plagued by 'free rider' problems. After the sellers agree to charge the price that maximizes their joint profits, each seller has an incentive to sell at a slightly lower price, because his profits are likely to be higher at the much greater sales volume that a slightly lower price will enable him to obtain. If enough sellers submit to the temptation, the cartel will collapse. . . .

Since the effect of typical regulatory devices (entry control, minimum rates, exemption from the antitrust laws) is the same as that of cartelization – to raise prices above competitive levels – the benefit side of cartel theory is clearly relevant. The cost side also seems relevant. The members of the industry must agree on the form of regulation. And just as the individual seller's profits are maximized if he remains outside of the cartel (as long as his competitors remain inside), so any individual or firm that would be benefited by regulation will have some incentive to avoid joining in the efforts of his group to obtain the regulation. If the regulation is forthcoming, he will benefit from it – he cannot be excluded from the protection of a general regulation, just as a seller cannot be excluded from the benefits of his competitors' charging a monopoly price – but, unlike the active participants in the coalition, he will benefit at no cost.

The theory of cartels teaches that the reluctance to cooperate in maintaining a monopoly price is most likely to be overcome if the number of sellers whose actions must be coordinated is small, which tends to reduce the costs of coordination and of policing, and if the interests of the sellers are identical or nearly so, which should reduce the cost of securing agreement. Likewise in the regulatory sphere, the fewer the prospective beneficiaries of a regulation, the easier it will be for them to coordinate their efforts to obtain the regulation. Also, it will be more difficult for one of them to refuse to participate in the cooperative effort without causing the effort to collapse. Thus, all will tend to participate, knowing that any defection is likely to be followed promptly by the defection of the remaining members of the group, leaving the original defector worse off than if he had not cooperated. The homogeneity of the interests of the members is also significant. The more homogeneous their interest in the regulation in question, the easier (cheaper) will it be for them to arrive at a common position and the more likely will it be that the common position does not so disadvantage one or more members as to cause them to defect from the group.

The analysis of cartels is plainly relevant to the development of an economic theory of regulation, but it is not that theory. If it were, we would observe the same industries obtaining regulatory protection as form durable cartels. We do not. . . .

There are two reasons why the pattern of regulation and the pattern of private cartelization are different. First, the demand for regulation (derived from its value in enhancing the profits of the regulated firms) is greater among industries for which private cartelization is an unfeasible or very costly alternative – industries that lack high concentration and other characteristics favorable to cartelizing. They lack good substitutes for regulation. . . .

Second, whereas cartelization is the product purely of the co-operative action of the firms, favorable regulation requires, in addition, the intervention of the political process. Some industries may be able to influence that process at lower cost than others and these may not be the same industries that are able to cartelize at low cost. In particular, the political dimension of regulation requires two modifications of the theory of cartels as applied to regulation. First, . . . each member of an industry will have an interest in participating in the coalition seeking protective regulation when there is significant asymmetry among the positions of industry members. Protective regulation can take a variety (greater than in the case of private cartelization) of forms – limitation of entry, cash subsidy, tariff, etc. – and the choice of the form may, assuming asymmetry among the positions of the industry's members, affect differentially the welfare of those members. If so, each will want to participate in the industry campaign for regulation so that the choice of the form of regulation to seek will reflect his views. The free-rider problem will still be easiest to overcome where the number of firms in an industry is small, but if the asymmetry condition is fulfilled, even the presence of many firms may not erect an insurmountable obstacle to the formation of an effective coalition. This suggests that it may be cheaper for large-number industries to obtain public regulation than to cartelize privately.

Second, the determinants of political influence must be worked into the supply side of the market in regulation. But before this can be done it is necessary to specify the character of the political system under discussion . . .

One can distinguish three distinct forms of political system, all of which play some role in the actual political systems of democratic countries . . . One system I shall call 'entrepreneurial': favorable legislation is sold to the industries that value it most. For the reason just mentioned, these would not be the same industries that form private cartels. The costs of cooperative action are irrelevant under this system: the government can use its taxing or other powers of coercion to enable the industry to overcome any free-rider problem it might have, in order that the industry can raise the maximum purchase price for the legislation.

The next system to be considered is the 'coercive': legislation is awarded to groups that are able to make credible threats to retaliate with violence (or disorder, or work stoppages, or grumbling) if society does not give them favorable treatment. We lack good theories of threats or violence but as a first approximation it would seem that the number of people in the group would be an important determinant of its ability to make credible threats of *serious* disorder or violence (as opposed to threats of minor sabotage, annoying and costly but not deeply threatening).

The third system is the 'democratic': legislation is awarded by the vote of elected representatives of the people. This system, like the coercive, emphasizes the importance of numbers: not of threateners but of voters. The groups are not identical, but there is great overlap, so we are led to predict that the economic legislation of dictatorial regimes will broadly resemble that of democratic ones – as seems on casual observation to be the case. Willingness to pay is also important in the democratic as in the entrepreneurial political system, since legislators are elected in campaigns in which the amount of money expended on behalf of a candidate exerts great influence on the outcome. However, unlike the case of an entrepreneurial system, in a democratic system the free-rider problem remains a serious one: it may limit the ability of an industry or other interest group to make substantial campaign contributions.

The foregoing analysis suggests that while the characteristics that predispose an industry to successful cartelization may also help it to obtain favorable government regulation, one characteristic that discourages cartelization – a large number of parties whose cooperation is necessary to create and maintain the cartel – encourages regulation. Large numbers have voting (and, potentially, coercive) power and also increase the likelihood of an asymmetry of interests that will encourage broad participation in the coalition seeking regulation. In addition, large numbers, and other factors that discourage private cartelization, increase the demand for protective legislation.

The economic theory can thus be used to explain why we so often observe protective legislation in areas like agriculture, labor, and the professions, where private cartelization would hardly be feasible. This is an important advance over the other theories that we have examined. However, the economic theory has not been refined to the point where it enables us to predict specific industries in which regulation will be found. That is because the theory does not tell us what (under various conditions) is the number of members of a coalition that maximizes the likelihood of regulation. Formally, this is the number beyond which the loss of group cohesiveness caused by adding another member would outweigh the increase in the feasibility and attractiveness of becoming regulated produced by greater voting power and by greater demand for regulation due to greater difficulty of cartelizing privately. . . .

. . . [T]he economic theory is still so spongy that virtually any observations can be reconciled with it. . . .

As part of the search for a harder-edged theory of regulation, it has been suggested that the geographic concentration of the people who would benefit from favorable regulation is an important element since a legislator will exert greater efforts on behalf of a voter bloc large enough to influence the outcome of an election materially. But it has not been demonstrated that this is a generally valid proposition. If the same number of voters are more widely dispersed, no legislator will pay as much attention to their demands, but more legislators will pay some attention, and the net effectiveness of the interest group in the legislature *may* (it is an empirical question whether it *will*) be greater. . . . Thus we are at a loss to say whether observing a geographically concentrated – or dispersed – group obtaining – or failing to obtain – regulation confirms or refutes the economic theory of regulation. And this illustrates the essential deficiency of the economic theory of regulation in its present form. At best it is a list of criteria relevant to predicting whether an industry will obtain favorable legislation. It is not a coherent theory yielding unambiguous and therefore testable hypotheses.

Another sort of weakness is that the theory, pushed to its logical extreme, becomes rather incredible, because it excludes the possibility that a society concerned with the ability of interest groups to manipulate the political process in their favor might establish institutions that enabled genuine public interest considerations to influence the formation of policy. One can certainly argue that . . . the many features of law and public policy designed to maintain a market system are more plausibly explained by reference to a broad social interest in efficiency than by reference to the designs of narrow interest groups. One can of course say that on some issues the relevant interest group consists of everyone, or almost everyone, in the society. But this usage robs the interest group concept of its utility by collapsing it into the public interest theory.

Notes

1. Lawyers have traditionally accepted the 'public interest' theory of legislation; indeed, it is incorporated in the principles of statutory interpretation: R. Cross, *Statutory Interpretation* (1976), pp. 44–52. The social historian O. MacDonagh has developed a model, proceeding from a public interest hypothesis, to explain nineteenth-century law reform: 'The Nineteenth

Century Revolution in Government – A Reappraisal' (1958) 1 Historical
J. 56.

2. As is revealed in the Posner paper, the 'public interest' theory of regulation
has been increasingly regarded as inadequate, in so far as it fails to explain the
motivation of legislators or administrators in imposing and enforcing the
controls (though recent developments towards deregulation have prompted
some to revive it in a modified form: M. E. Levine, 'Revisionism Revived?
Airline Deregulation and the Public Interest' (1981) 44 Law and Contemp.
Problems 179). More specifically, it was found to be difficult to reconcile with
the practice of regulation, as studied through empirical research (the
literature accumulated by American scholars is considerable; for convenient
summaries, see e.g., P. W. MacAvoy (ed.), *The Crisis of the Regulatory
Commissions* (1970); B. M. Mitnick (1982), op. cit. The problematic
findings were: (a) the introduction of some regulatory controls could not be
justified on the traditional 'public interest' grounds; (b) some regulatory
controls *might* have been justifiable on this basis, but legislators did not seek
to procure such evidence; (c) regulation often does not achieve its desired
effect, or does so inefficiently (i.e. the administrative costs exceed the social
costs resulting from unregulated market behaviour); (d) some regulation,
particularly where it creates barriers to entry, turns out to be in the interests
more of those whose activities are being regulated rather than those for whose
benefit it was ostensibly introduced.

3. By way of response, economists felt compelled to posit a theory of
'government failure' as the counterpart to the more traditional analysis of
'market failure'; see, e.g., G. Stigler, *The Citizen and the State* (1975), and
B. A. Weisbrod, 'Problems of Enhancing the Public Interest: Toward a
Model of Government Failures' in B. A. Weisbrod, J. F. Handler and
N. K. Komesar (eds.) *Public Interest Law: An Economic and Institutional
Analysis* (1978), ch. 3. The implication that for certain problems there is no
'first best' solution has led some to engage in a comparative institutional
analysis and to suggest methods of determining which arrangement, market
and private law or regulation and public law, is likely normatively to offer the
'second best' solution (see, e.g., N. K. Komesar, 'In Search of a General
Approach to Legal Analysis: A Comparative Institutional Alternative' (1981)
79 Mich. L.R. 1350). But there has been a more sustained, if also more
controversial, effort to explain legislative behaviour – more exactly, the
behaviour of *legislators* – by economic, utility maximizing theory. In simple
terms, groups in society compete to 'buy' legislative favours through a 'price
mechanism' which consists primarily in voting behaviour. See, S. Peltzman,
'Towards a More General Theory of Regulation' (1976) 19 J. Law and Econ.
211 and infra, Chapter 9, Section A.

4. It is, of course, striking that the protagonists of this theory and the
subject-matter of their analysis are almost exclusively American. Does the
approach hold an equally persuasive force for British institutions? An initial
response is that the question cannot be answered since British regulatory
institutions have not been scrutinised in the same way, or to the same degree.

It should, however, be noted that a rudimentary and impressionistic thesis to a similar effect was advanced by Dicey in 1905: *Law and Public Opinion in England During the Nineteenth Century*. The influence of the American literature may be observed in C. K. Rowley and A. T. Peacock, *Welfare Economics – A Liberal Restatement* (1975), esp. ch. 8, and C. K. Rowley and G. K. Yarrow, 'Property Rights, Regulation and Public Enterprise: the Case of the British Steel Industry 1957–75' (1981) 1 Int. Rev. Law and Econ. 63, but what Posner refers to as 'the Marxists and the muckrakers' (e.g. P. A. Baran and P. M. Sweezy, *Monopoly Capital* (1966)) have had a greater impact on legal writers (cf. N. Gunningham, *Pollution, Social Interest and the Law* (1974); R. B. Ferguson, 'Legal Ideology and Commercial Interest' (1977) 4 Brit. J. Law and Soc. 18). Though comparisons are difficult, it seems clear that there are significant institutional differences between American and British regulation: see B. Schwartz and H. W. R. Wade, *Legal Control of Government* (1972), especially ch. 2. In Britain there is a sharp cleavage between government departments, subject to ministerial control and responsibility and independent tribunals, while in the USA the regulatory agency which combines judicial and legislative activities but which is not responsible to the executive is, by British criteria, a 'constitutional monstrosity' (Schwartz and Wade, op. cit., p. 37). Secondly, the British notion of parliamentary omnipotence has never been accepted in the USA and this may have had an impact both on the legislative process itself and on the manner in which it has been treated by social scientists (cf. E. Freund, *Standards of American Legislation* (Phoenix edn, 1965), pp. 188–93).

5. Whether or not it is directly applicable to British institutions, it may be that the 'economic theory of regulation', as conventionally formulated, pays insufficient heed to the ideological commitment of politicians (cf. J. B. Kau and P. H. Rubin, 'Self-Interest, Ideology and Logrolling in Congressional Voting' (1979) 22 J. Law and Econ. 365) and the altrustic motivation of those who work in the public interest; see B. Weisbrod, 'Conceptual Perspective on the Public Interest: An Economic Analysis' in Weisbrod, Handler and Komesar, op. cit., ch. 2 (though this is primarily concerned with the public interest motivation of those who work in the private sector).

7

TECHNIQUES OF REGULATION

A. Economic Incentives or Control by Standards

LORD ZUCKERMAN and W. BECKERMAN

*

The Case for Pollution Charges[1]

[W]hat is required, ideally, is some incentive to polluters to reduce pollution up to the point where the costs to them of further pollution abatement would be greater than the damage done (at the margin) by the pollution. By and large the price mechanism provides just such an incentive. . . . [I]f the polluter were charged £1 per unit of pollution he would have an incentive to reduce pollution, thereby saving himself the payment of pollution charges, only up to the point where it would cost him £1 per unit to achieve a further reduction. For beyond that point, he would have to spend more in pollution abatement costs than he would save through paying less pollution charges. He would tend not to go beyond this point, and so would not incur, say, £2 in abatement costs where the pollution charge (set to equal the gain to society from the further abatement) was only £1. And, conversely, he would have an incentive not to stop short of this optimum point. For if he could reduce pollution at a cost of, say, £0.5 per unit he would have an incentive to incur this cost thereby saving himself a pollution charge of £1 per unit, and he would, in fact, have an incentive to continue reducing pollution up to the point where his abatement costs and hence, roughly speaking, the costs to society, would rise to equal the pollution charge. This is why the ideal means of avoiding excessive pollution at least in principle, is to make the polluter pay a charge corresponding to the damage done (at the margin) by his pollution. Who he pays it to does not really matter from the narrow point of view of giving him an incentive to abate pollution, but, in practice, it would

[1] From Minority Report to Third Report of Royal Commission on Environmental Pollution (Cmnd. 5054, 1972), paras. 2–22, with omissions. Reprinted by permission of Her Majesty's Stationery Office.

usually be necessary for the pollution charge to be determined by, and paid to, a public authority.

Almost all taxes, whether on goods, on factors of production, or even on work, tend to mis-allocate resources. By contrast, a pollution charge tends to correct an existing mis-allocation of resources by making polluters bear the true social cost of the clean resources that they are using up. . . .

[S]ome form of financial disincentive to pollute already exists, up to a point, in this country, namely the charges for the treatment of trade (that is, non-domestic) effluent discharged to municipal sewers. The Public Health (Drainage of Trade Premises) Act 1937 and the Public Health Act 1961, provide drainage authorities with adequate authority to control the discharges into their sewerage systems and to 'charge for the reception of the trade effluent into the sewer regard being had to the nature and composition and to the volume and rate of the discharge of the trade effluent so discharged . . .' (Public Health Act 1961). A large number of local authorities do, in fact, charge for trade effluent according to formulae which take account of some indicators of pollution (notably the BOD and the amount of suspended solids in the effluent.) In arriving at our conclusion to the effect that greater use should be made of pollution charges rather than direct regulation, we are not, therefore, advocating the introduction of some entirely novel policy instrument on account of purely theoretical considerations. . . . Whilst recognizing the many limitations on the price mechanism as a means of achieving all society's objectives, notably those concerned with income distribution or the provision of public goods, as a means of achieving the appropriate levels of output of other goods, (and 'bads') the price mechanism is likely to be more efficient, and hence cheaper, than the use of direction. . . . By contrast, the imposition of production quotas or 'norms', according to which different firms are given production targets in the form of direct quantitative regulations is generally unlikely to ensure that goods are produced by the firms best able to do so and by the most economical methods. With certain exceptions, it is not the type of economic policy instrument used in this country. The use of direct regulations for the control of pollution amounts precisely to such a system of production quotas and norms.

The same forces which tend to make the price mechanism a cheaper means of producing most goods apply to the production of pollution. If a uniform pollution charge is imposed at any particular stretch of river or estuary all polluters will tend to abate their pollution up to the point where it would cost them more to abate further than the charge they pay per unit of pollution. In other words, at the margin, the cost of pollution abatement is equal in all firms, since it is equal to the charge in all firms. Contrast this with the use of some direct control, such as a regulation to the effect that all firms must reduce their pollution by a uniform percentage, or to some uniform amount. This will obviously involve very high marginal costs of pollution abatement for some firms and low marginal costs for others. Clearly, the same total amount of pollution abatement could have been obtained if some of the abatement had been switched from the former firms, where it is costly, to the latter, where it is cheap; and savings of this kind could be made by the switching up to the point where the marginal costs of further abatement were equal for all firms. This is precisely the situation to which the pollution charge system tends to lead. In saying this we are not under any illusions to the effect that all firms are ruthless profit maximisers making careful rational calculations of the optimal degree to which they should reduce pollution. Most firms do not make the theoretically ideal calculations of their investment needs, for example, but even those who are opposed to pollution charges would not argue, on this account, that firms' investment projects should be determined by direct regulation. Hence, our argument no more depends on a very simple view of the way that firms operate than would arguments in favour of using the price mechanism rather than direct regulation to allocate labour and capital and raw materials between different firms rather than allocate supplies to them according to some quantitative plan.

Direct regulation of pollution also imposes costs on firms, and hence, on society. The great advantage of the charge method is that it enables firms to find the cheapest means of reducing their pollution. Some may change their raw material inputs, others may carry out more re-cycling, others may institute more effluent treatment plant inside the firm, and so on. Also, as explained above, a pollution charge allocates total abatement in the cheapest manner between firms.

Thus we do not subscribe to the objection . . . to the effect that the right to pollute will pass into the hands of a few wealthy buyers. On the whole, large firms also tend to employ more labour, capital, and raw materials than do small firms, and this is not generally regarded as a reason for using direct regulation in order to share out available resources of labour, capital and raw materials more evenly. In the same way it should not constitute a reason for not allowing the scarce resource 'clean water' to be allocated by any principle other than that which reflects the value placed on its use by different firms. Similarly, more profitable firms are not noticeably less anxious to respond to price incentives than unprofitable firms; if anything the reverse is presumably the case, so there is no reason to fear that very profitable firms will tend to ignore the pollution charge and continue to pollute as much as before. On the whole, firms that find it very costly to reduce pollution considerably will have to pay heavier charges, and those that can easily reduce pollution at relatively low cost will have an incentive to reduce it considerably instead of merely to some maximum level set by a direct regulation. And this is precisely the way that society obtains any given output at lowest cost. . . .

Secondly, the introduction of a charge system will require that some body or authority has full-time and permanent responsibility for collecting the necessary information. But with direct regulation there can be some unevenness in the extent to which the regulations are implemented and enforced. In fact, direct regulation is also a form of tax, in the sense that a small fine may be imposed if breaches of the regulations are identified and proved to the satisfaction of the courts. But its incidence is often uncertain, subject to delays, and usually too small anyway. The implementation of direct regulations on pollution may vary with the extent to which pollution happens to be a live, popular and fashionable issue. As a rule, no such vagaries apply to a machinery for collecting charges. . . .

IS POLLUTION A SPECIAL CASE FOR WHICH THE PRICE MECHANISM IS NOT APPROPRIATE?

First, it is often argued that pollution charges can have no effect since the polluters will merely pass them on in higher prices. But producers normally try to cover all their costs in their prices – otherwise they would soon go out of business – and one does not, therefore, say that they do not bear the costs of the labour or capital that they employ, and that they are indifferent to how much of it they use. Firms will still try to employ each factor of production up to the point where further use would not add to their revenues more than they add to their costs. In general, it is the more profitable firms that carry out this process more efficiently. To assume that by paying a 'licence to pollute' firms have no incentive to economise on pollution is like assuming that firms do not economise in their use of other factors of production. . . .

Secondly, it is often maintained that a charge scheme is unworkable because we do not have the data needed to decide on the appropriate charge in all cases, making full allowance, for example, for variations in the conditions (such as, state of river flow, air temperature, tidal conditions) that determine the amount of damage done by effluent at any point in an estuary. This is true, but the same data limitations mean that one does not know the correct amount of pollution abatement to be imposed by direct regulation either. . . .

Thirdly, it is often claimed that charges are impracticable because data are not available to permit an accurate calculation of the amount of pollution that should be taxed. For example, it may be feared that monitoring difficulties preclude the observation of the pollution which is to be charged. This is true but, again, precisely the same problems apply to the surveillance and implementation of direct controls. The imposition of direct control implies that whatever is controlled can be measured — otherwise it is pointless to institute the control, since it would be impossible to check whether it is respected. Hence, if whatever is controlled can be measured it can also be made the basis for a tax. . . .

Fourthly, it is often believed that the great advantage of the direct regulation is that the regulating authority knows exactly whether or not the abatement target will be achieved, whereas with a charge system they will not know in advance how far firms will respond to the charge and hence how far pollution will be reduced to the optimum amount. . . . But this objection to the charging system is rather like arguing that the great advantage of direct regulation in centrally planned economies is, for example, that they can be sure that the target for clothing output will be produced whereas if they had left it to the market mechanism actual clothing output might have fallen below or above the target. Now this is quite true, but the accuracy with which one hits any target is not, in itself, a desirable objective of policy irrespective of the extent to which it is the appropriate target. The advantage of the price mechanism is precisely that if the output of clothing is too high its price will fall, thereby discouraging its production (and encouraging its consumption) until the correct amount is produced. But with a production quota, and, in addition, no market anyway (as would be the case with pollution), producers would continue to produce the target level of pollution and nobody would know whether or not it is the correct target. By comparison, with the charge method, if the charge failed to produce the level of pollution at which the marginal social damage is equal to the charge, this would itself constitute evidence for the fact that the initial estimate of optimum pollution could not have been correct, so that some adjustment in the charge would be appropriate in due course.

J. BRAITHWAITE

The Limits of Economism in Controlling Harmful Corporate Conduct[2]

I. INTRODUCTION

Corporations in unprincipled pursuit of profits can do great social harm. Countless workers die each year because their employers reduce costs by cutting corners on safety. The environment suffers at the hands of companies which put production ahead of environmental protection. Criminalizing irresponsible acts of pollution and other unsafe practices has been the most favored solution to this social problem. This is reinforced by the fact that the doctrines of deterrence, rehabilitation, and incapacitation – largely discredited for controlling common crime – can be shown to have considerable force with corporate crime.

On the other hand, the law has limited control over the complex affairs of powerful corporations. Typically, neither the political will nor the prosecutorial resources exist to prove beyond a reasonable doubt that the complex activities of a large company constituted a crime. Powerful actors consistently exploit the complexities of the law, the books, and decision making in large organizations to evade the spirit of the law.

These limits of legalism are one reason for a shift to economism as the favored model for controlling harmful corporate conduct. Instead of punishing wrongdoers, responsible conduct is to be encouraged with economic incentives and disincentives. Punishing illegal pollution, for example, is replaced by taxes based on the quantity and quality of effluent released. The underlying idea is that the state should intervene to create a contrived approximation of the 'invisible hand of the market', which will guarantee responsible corporate conduct without costly judicial processes.

This article will argue that the regulatory limits of economism are more profound than the limits of legalism. . . .

Legalism . . . turns on the condemnation both of illegal means and ends, while economism is morally neutral about means. Even the moral definition of ends is more qualified under economism; while

[2] (1982) 16 Law and Soc. Rev. 481–4, 488–90, 492–3, 495–500. Copyright © The Law Society Association. Reprinted by permission of the Law and Society Review, the official publication of the Law and Society Association.

legalism delineates certain categories of conduct as wrong, economism defines a continuum of harm. Legalism condemns and punishes wrongs; economism imposes disincentives for harm and incentives for good which must be weighed among other incentives and disincentives which exist in the society. In a legalistic system, the severity of punishments is determined by a society's imprecise and confused concept of what constitutes justice. The magnitude of disincentives in an economistic system is decided mathematically by inserting the output of social harm into an equation to calculate tax liability. Economistic sanctions against individual firms therefore tend to be imposed by clerks with calculators, while legalistic sanctions are imposed by courts with a paraphernalia of due process protections.

There is no need to labor the fact that real-world enforcement fails to conform precisely to either ideal type, that taxation decisions will often be litigated in courts of law, and so on. Indeed, this analysis begins with an explicit recognition that economism-legalism is a continuum. We will now move from the legalism to the economism end of the spectrum by considering in turn specification standards, performance standards, marketable rights, and taxes on social harm.

II. THE NEW REGULATION

. . . The first victories for the new regulation have been in the replacement of many government specification standards by performance standards. . . . Rather than specify that ladders have rungs at least one inch in diameter, the performance standard states that the rungs must be capable of withstanding 400 pounds. The latter example illustrates how specification standards stultify innovation more than performance standards. A new type of ladder made out of lighter but stronger material might be impermissible under the specification standard but acceptable under the performance criterion. . . .

Perhaps the most spectacular example of the disadvantages of the technological forcing which follows from specification standards is . . . how the Environmental Protection Agency's forcing of a scrubbing technology to reduce sulfur oxide emissions from power plants resulted in some companies switching to high sulfur coal (so that their aggregate output of pollution increased). . . .

We have seen that performance standards can serve to foster flexibility and innovation, cut down red tape, and thereby reduce costs. These advantages for efficiency and growth are taken one step further by the notion of 'marketable rights' in social harms like pollution. Each plant can be given a 'right' to emit a certain amount of pollution (e.g., so much sulfur oxide) per unit of production. Alternatively, the state can issue a finite number of rights to pollute a given basin, and let companies bid for the rights. The idea is that economic efficiency can be promoted by allowing companies to buy and sell these governmentally conferred rights to pollute. Firms with antiquated plants occasionally find that they would be better off shutting the plant down than retooling to meet new environmental standards. However, if they could buy some of another plant's pollution rights, they might survive in economically viable form. In contrast, a company building a new plant from scratch might find it economically sound to incorporate a design which will put its emissions well below the quota; it can profit from selling the excess pollution rights to another old plant which it owns, or even to a competitor. Again, the total output of pollution is kept below the aggregate level which the government deems unacceptable by introducing abatement programs at the points where these will be cheapest and threaten the fewest jobs. . . .

The high-water mark of economism is the tax on social harm. Rather than punish companies for culpable acts which cause social harm, they pay a tax in proportion to their output of the harm. Sanctioning of occupational safety and health violations is replaced with 'injury taxes' whereby the company pays the government so much for each worker-related injury of a given severity which occurs in the course of the financial year. Culpability is not an issue. The tax is paid in proportion to the number and severity of injuries, irrespective of corporate fault. . . . There are reasons why the traditional enforcement of legalism is inferior, at least in principle, to an injury tax. There is considerable evidence that the majority of industrial injuries are not attributable to violations of the Occupational Safety and Health Act and other enforcement standards . . . The great advantage of the injury tax is that it gives an incentive for prevention programs which would reduce injuries of all types, regardless of whether they involve violations of law. Moreover, the incentives for improvement continue when sanctionable dangers have been brought well below the levels specified by laws. In contrast, a legalistic approach gives manufacturers an incentive to reduce noise, carcinogens, or pollutants to the level required by law, but no lower. They may introduce a waste treatment technology required by law, but then fail to maintain it properly and utilize it fully because there is no incentive to do so.

Under the injury tax proposal, finite resources for the reduction of industrial injuries would be deployed in ways which would minimize taxable injury rates. A less than optimal deployment of injury abatement resources results under the traditional enforcement of legal standards, because resources are concentrated on ensuring compliance with regulations, to the neglect of alternative means which would have greater impact on injury rates. . . . The fundamental advantage of economism is that it encourages the minimizing of social harm, whereas legalism encourages the minimizing of culpability. Management strategies to minimize social harm will save more lives and limbs than strategies to stop law violations. Moreover, economism permits the company to find the cheapest way of minimizing harm; legalism may force more expensive means to the same end. For instance, it may be that the cheapest way to ensure that workers do not lose fingers in a machine is to put them through an extra training course rather than to enforce a rule or a technology which inhibits productivity.

III. THE LIMITS OF PERFORMANCE STANDARDS

The rigidity of specification standards is needed in many areas critical to human and environmental health. It would be intolerable to regulate a nuclear power plant according to the performance standard of how much, if any, radiation escapes the plant. The risks of nuclear accidents are so profound that after-the-event monitoring of radiation output is simply not good enough. Governments justifiably specify that nuclear plants incorporate the most modern and effective technologies, standard operating procedures, in-process controls, and checks and balances to avert malfunctions. Similarly, uniform rigid standards are justified in many areas of the regulation of the pharmaceutical industry to ensure that patients do not die from hazardous drugs. . . .

A profound advantage of direct regulation is that it can change corporate conduct within a short time frame. A new regulation can be enacted overnight to stop manufacturers from spilling into waterways a product which new research has shown to be carcinogenic. A redesigned tax schedule, in contrast, would take months or years to bring about the adjustment of industry behavior in realignment with the new incentives. This is especially true if trial and error has to be used until a tax rate is found which actually begins to cause changes to filter through to industry behavior.

The retrospectivity of performance standards is their great defect. It makes them inappropriate in areas where society is prepared to tolerate even very high levels of economic inefficiency to build in guarantees that disasters are prevented *before* they occur. . . .

Most of us obey the law not because we are afraid of punishment but simply because it seems the right thing to do. Society gets more protection from the habit-forming value of law than from its deterrent value. A critical deficiency of economism is that it fosters a moral relativism which undermines the moral authority of law. . . .

Another advantage of specification standards is that government monitoring and enforcement is easier than under performance standards. While it is easy to enforce a design standard – one need only look at the equipment – it is often hard to monitor performance. . . .

IV. THE LIMITS OF TAXING HARM

All of the foregoing deficiencies of performance standards as an alternative to specification standards are also applicable to proposals to control corporate conduct by taxing harm. But because taxes on harm take economism a step further, there are some additional deficiencies to be considered.

Before weighing the problems of such taxes in effectively controlling corporate harm, it must be pointed out that they would have adverse effects in other areas. Taxes on social harm would further complicate tax codes which are already so hopelessly complex as to constitute one of the major problems confronting western societies. With increasing complexity the difficulties and costs of tax collection increase. Moreover, because wealthy and powerful actors are better able to exploit complexity than are the powerless, measures which increase complexity tend to widen inequities. . . .

The whole idea of taxes on harm presupposes that companies are always rational economic actors: all we need do is set an effluent tax at a high enough level, and the invisible hand of the market will force firms to reduce environmental damage. But companies are not always economically rational. How does economism deal with the crusty general-manager who believes that the old ways of disposing of toxic wastes are the best and that no new-fangled effluent tax is going to change his tried and true practices? Legalism does have a way of dealing with this not-so-uncommon menace to the public health; it takes him to court and threatens to shut his plant down . . .

One of the attractions of taxes on harm to its advocates is that it is supposed to avoid the need for government inspectors to swarm over factories checking every little thing. But the rub is that the inevitability of widespread evasion would mean that government environmental and safety inspectors would be replaced by tax investigators checking that effluents and injuries were being accurately reported. . . .

Indeed, the problem is worse than a simple substitutive regress back to the old inspectorial mode: the new evasion inspectors would be less constructive servants of the public interest than old-style inspectors who directly monitor environmental and safety performance. The latter play an important educative role. . . .

A tax on social harm can never totally substitute for the enforcement of standards, because the concept is fundamentally unworkable with small firms. A motor workshop with six mechanics might go for years without a single injury and then suddenly have an accident which causes a death on the job. Any viable tax rate would have to impose a massive tax on a firm which had one sixth of its workforce die from industrial accidents in one year. . . .

. . . There are critical thresholds for many pollutants: thresholds beyond which fish species do not have enough dissolved oxygen to survive, thresholds at which treatment of just a little extra biological waste would eliminate a terrible stench. In theory, it should be possible to adjust tax rates when they fail to keep pollution below the threshold. But since pollution control so often involves massive capital investment, changes will not be rapid in response to tax adjustments. Moreover, frequently fluctuating effluent tax rates may cause pollutors to adopt a wait-and-see attitude before embarking on pollution control investment. . . . Even when charges are set at an economically 'optimal' level to trade off the benefits of pollution control against the costs of pollution abatement, some firms would be shut down by the expense of pollution taxes when, in fact, the damage they caused would not warrant this action. In other words, because effluent taxes are set at levels that are optimal in aggregate, but not necessarily so in the individual case, firms may be forced to close 'even when they could have remained in business if they were required to pay only the social cost imposed by the untreated portion of their waste'.[3]

. . . In the real world of politics charge levels would not follow from rational calculations of benefits and costs. They would arise from compromises forged out of conflicts between pro-business low-tax advocates on one side and 'make business pay' high-tax advocates (or revenue-hungry treasuries) on the other. Even if economically optimal tax rates did fortuitously result from this political process, there would be pressures to grant exemptions which would undermine economic rationality. . . .

V. TOWARDS A LIMITED ROLE FOR ECONOMISM

A bland summary of the foregoing would be to say that while the weaknesses of economism outweigh its strengths, the opposite is true of the direct enforcement of rules regulating hazardous corporate practices. For most areas of regulation, full-fledged economistic solutions such as effluent taxes cannot replace law enforcement because of insurmountable transaction costs. Less extreme forms of economism could in many areas be useful so long as legalism is available as a backstop to catch the many abuses which will slip through the coarse mesh of economism's net. The replacement of many specification standards with shorter and simpler performance

---

[3] S. Rose-Ackerman, 'Effluent Charges: A Critique' (1973) 6 Can. J. Econ. 572, 573.

standards by agencies such as OSHA has undoubtedly in many cases made for more cost-effective regulation.

Notes

1. The extracts reflect a lively debate which has taken place in the last decade or so on the relative merits of economic incentives and standards enforced by the criminal law as techniques of regulation. Most economists prefer the use of pecuniary incentives to achieve resource allocation goals. The idea of a tax or charge to correct misallocations resulting from externalities is derived from Pigou (*Economics of Welfare* (1924)). The advantage of this technique, as revealed by Zuckerman and Beckerman, is that it should achieve policy objectives in the least restrictive and most cost-effective way: see also W. J. Baumol, 'On Taxation and the Control of Externalities' (1972) 62 Am. Econ. Rev. 307; A. M. Freeman and R. H. Haveman, 'Residual Charges for Pollution Control: A Policy Evaluation' (1972) 177 Science 322.

Braithwaite's paper challenges this conclusion, at least in certain environments. For additional criticisms by economists, see S. Rose-Ackerman, op. cit.; P. Burrows, 'Pricing versus Regulation for Environmental Pollution' in A. J. Culyer (ed.), *Economic Policies and Social Goals* (1974), ch. 13; J. G. Head, 'Public Policies and Pollution Problems' (1974) 32 Finanzarchiv. 1.

2. Policy objectives can be achieved by the 'carrot or the stick'. An alternative economic instrument to the corrective tax is the payment of a subsidy to an individual or firm to behave so as to avoid net social costs, for example by installing pollution abatement or industrial safety equipment (there are, in addition, broader macro-economic justifications for subsidies: see, generally, A. Whiting (ed.), *The Economics of Industrial Subsidies* (1978)). Provided that the marginal subsidy rate is identical to the marginal tax rate, the subsidy will produce the same allocative results as the tax: A. V. Kneese and K. G. Mäler, 'Bribes and Charges in Pollution Control: An Aspect of the Coase Controversy' (1973) 13 Nat. Res. J. 705. But the distributional consequences are, of course, profoundly different: a tax on a firm increases its costs of production and also generates revenue which can be used to compensate those adversely affected, while to finance a subsidy scheme the government must increase taxation or reduce expenditure in other areas. Moreover, subsidies may create perverse incentives by, for example, inducing firms to increase inefficiencies in order to attract further subsidies: see, generally, J. L. Migué, 'Controls Versus Subsidies in the Economic Theory of Regulation' (1977) 20 J. Law and Econ. 213; C. J. Schultze, *The Public Use of Private Interest* (1977), pp. 57–64.

3. Legal control through standards, supported by criminal sanctions and often enforced by a specialist agency, is the most traditional and widely used form of regulation. Despite this, there is a paucity of literature on the general issues. A notable exception is S. Breyer, *Regulation and its Reform* (1982). There are useful discussions of some aspects in E. Freund, *Standards of*

American Legislation (Phoenix edn, 1965); D. J. Gifford, 'Communication of Legal Standards, Policy Development and Effective Conduct Regulation' (1971) 56 Cornell L.R. 409; and R. F. Cranston, 'Reform through Legislation: the Dimension of Legislative Technique' (1978) 73 Northwestern U.L.R. 873. For particular regimes in Britain, see T. C. Sinclair, *A Cost-Effective Approach to Industrial Safety* (1972); R. G. Cranston, *Consumers and the Law* (1978), chs. 8, 10; G. M. Richardson, A. I. Ogus and P. Burrows, *Policing Pollution*, (1982) ch. 3.

4. The objectives of the control should be the minimization of three sets of costs: (a) the costs arising from the given product or activity (damage costs); (b) the costs of complying with the standard; and (c) the costs of administering the standard, including formulation and enforcement. Breyer, op. cit., ch. 5, highlights some of the problems, theoretical and pragmatic, in meeting these objectives, particularly with imperfect information. The assessment of damage costs is notoriously the most difficult, not only because of the problem of attributing a monetary value to such subjective matters as life, good health and aesthetics (cf. supra, Chapter 3, Section E), but also because of the time dimension; some estimate must be made of the impact on future generations. See, e.g., Schultze, op. cit., pp. 35–42. While compliance costs vary as between firms (particularly having regard to their size – K. W. Chilton and M. C. Weidenbaum, *Small Business Performance in the Regulated Economy* (1980)), there is a marked reluctance to differentiate standards on this basis. There are two main exceptions to this: first, the variable may be taken account of at the enforcement stage (for evidence, see Richardson *et al.*, op. cit., pp. 152–70); secondly, the law often imposes a new or stricter standard only prospectively, i.e. it exempts existing products or activities (ibid., pp. 45–55) – here the degree of capital expenditure in the latter will mean that the costs of compliance are greater than those incurred by firms only at the planning stage.

5. The degree of specificity desirable is a problem general to rulemaking (see Ehrlich and Posner, infra, Chapter 9, Section B): a balance has to be struck between the costs of an imperfect fit arising from a uniform standard, and the higher administrative costs generated by a very specific standard (cf. Richardson *et al.*, op. cit., pp. 40–8; P. Burrows, *The Economic Theory of Pollution Control* (1979), pp. 124–36). It should also be noted that the more individualized the standard, the greater the likelihood that the standard setting will be delegated to an administrative agency (e.g. Health and Safety Executive; Regional Water Authorities), thus giving rise to problems of accountability.

6. The decision to impose standards and the type of standard chosen should take account of enforcement costs, notably those arising from the monitoring of firms, prosecutions, and countering avoidance behaviour: see, generally, W. K. Viscusi and R. J. Zeckhauser, 'Optimal Standards with Incomplete Enforcement' (1977) 17 Pub. Policy 437; R. N. McKean, 'Enforcement Costs in Environmental and Safety Regulations' (1980) 6 Policy Analysis 269. We shall see infra, Chapter 8, that there is in theory an optimal level of

enforcement. The low rate of prosecutions relative to the number of standard contraventions in several areas of regulatory control (see, especially, R. F. Cranston, *Regulating Business: Law and Consumer Agencies* (1979), ch. 7; Richardson *et al*, op. cit., pp. 62, 134–5) might be invoked to support the 'capture theory', that enforcement agencies operate more to protect the regulated industries than the public interest (cf. E. Cox, R. Fellworth, J. Schultz, *The Consumer and the Federal Trade Commission* (The 'Nader Report') (1969); P. J. Quirk, *Industry Influences in Federal Regulatory Agencies* (1981)). On the other hand, the traditional justification offered, that persuasion is more effective than confrontation in dealing with recalcitrant firms (see e.g. Annual Report of the Alkali Inspectorate 1971, p. 13) may be consistent with the economic model on the ground that substantial costs may arise from generating friction between government and industry: C. Stone, *Where the Law Ends* (1975), pp. 103–5.

7. Despite the problems of cost–benefit analysis in this area, considerable efforts have been made by American scholars to evaluate the effects of standards. There is evidence of a reduction in the number of consumer complaints (S. Oster, 'Product Regulations: A Measure of the Benefits' (1981) 29 J. Ind. Econ. 395), but also of rises in the price of regulated products (S. Peltzman, 'An Evaluation of Consumer Protection Legislation: the 1962 Drug Amendments' (1973) 81 J. Pol. Econ. 1042). Quality controls on housing have resulted in a decrease of the supply of low-cost rentable premises (W. Z. Hirsch, J. G. Hirsch, S. Margolis, 'Regression Analysis of the Effects of Habitability Law upon Rents: An Empirical Observation on the Ackerman–Komesar Debate' (1975) 63 Calif. L.R. 1098). Some safety regulations have been shown not to have been effective in reducing injuries (S. Peltzman, 'The Effects of Automobile Safety Regulation' (1975) 83 J. Pol. Econ. 677): this may result from suboptimal enforcement, consumers taking less care, or producers spending less on unregulated safety equipment (cf. W. J. Oi, 'On the Economics of Industrial Safety' (1974) 38 Law and Contemp. Prob. 669). More broadly, there are claims that standards have created disincentives for innovation (H. G. Grabowski, J. M. Vernon, L. G. Thomas, 'Estimating the Effects of Regulation on Innovation: an International Comparative Analysis of the Pharmaceutical Industry' (1978) 21 J. Law and Econ. 133; Symposium, 'Regulation and Innovation' (1979) 43 Law and Contemp. Prob. 1) and help to explain the general decline in industrial productivity in the period 1973–77 (G. B. Christinsen and R. H. Havemann, 'Public Regulations and the Slowdown in Productivity Growth' (1981) 71 Am. Econ. Rev. 312).

8. Given these findings and the economists' general preference for the corrective tax, the question arises why the latter technique has been adopted so rarely. Two answers may be suggested. First, taxes and pricing schemes are frequently associated with a pro-market, anti-government ideology which makes them unattractive to regulators and some governments (S. Kelman, 'Economists and the Environmental Muddle' (1981) 64 Public Interest 106). Secondly, taxes lower the profits of the polluting industry. Polluting firms can thus be expected to oppose tax and pricing schemes and support a standards

approach that enhances the wealth of politically influential segments of the industry (J. S. Buchanan and G. Tullock, 'Polluters' Profits and Political Response: Direct Controls Versus Taxes' (1975) 65 Am. Econ. Rev. 139).

B. Licensing

T. MOORE

*

The Purpose of Licensing[4]

NON-PROFIT RATIONALES FOR LICENSING

Three rationales based on public welfare arguments are generally advanced as to why certain occupations should be licensed: lack of information or misinformation, society's knowing better than the individual what is best for the individual, and social costs being higher than private costs.

Lack of information and misinformation

Licensing, it is argued, increases information by establishing minimum standards for entrants. In effect, all practitioners must meet certain minimum qualifications, for no unlicensed practitioners are permitted. The consumer therefore knows that practitioners of the licensed occupation possess a given degree of competence.

However, licensing establishes minimum qualifications only for entrants. In the years immediately following the enactment of the licensing law, there will probably be many practitioners who do not meet these requirements, since the original statute invariably grants licences to all those already practicing, irrespective of their training. Nor does licensing give any information concerning the difference between practitioners above the minimum entrance requirements. A system of certification, it can be argued, would furnish at least as much information as licensing. Under such an arrangement, those practitioners who desired to be certified and who could meet certain standards, including the passing of an examination, would be given a certificate of approval. Such certificates could even be graded much as restaurants are in France. Certification would therefore appear to satisfy the lack of information hypothesis better than licensing.

[4] (1961) 4 J. Law and Econ. 93, 103–17, with omissions. Copyright © 1961 by the University of Chicago. All rights reserved. Reprinted by permission of the University of Chicago Press and the author.

If licensing were costless, then there would be no reason to expect the price of the licensed service to rise above the price of the unlicensed service. In that case, if licensing did reduce the probability of disappointment, the consumer would be better off. But a system of certification would increase information to the same extent as or more than a system of licensing and consequently would benefit the consumer at least as much. Licensing, however, does have a cost; the imposition of standards for entering an occupation can be expected to raise the cost of the service. For some consumers it is possible that the price of the licensed service will be higher than what they feel the information is worth. Other consumers will gain by purchasing the licensed service, but they would have benefited to the same extent under a system of certification without imposing welfare losses on those consumers who will lose by licensing. Hence, if there is a lack of information in the market, certification is preferable to licensing on consumer welfare grounds.

Consider the argument that licensing is designed to prevent or to reduce fraud. While it is clear that compulsory licensing helps to produce more information for the market, it is less clear that it helps to prevent fraud. There seems to be less reason to believe that practitioners' having met certain conditions helps the consumer evaluate the probability of being defrauded. It is possible that practitioners, having learned a particular 'system', will be less likely to try selling a fraudulent 'system'. It is also possible that the licensing regulations, which usually require that the practitioner 'be of good character and temperate habits', will decrease the number of people who might practice fraud.

Another argument for compulsory licensing is that it establishes a cheaper remedy than going to the courts in cases of fraud. It may also aid the police in tracking down fraudulent practitioners.

Certification would apparently give similar assurance that the practitioner would not defraud the consumer. True, it would be of little assistance in police work and would not give no cheap remedy in case of fraud. But to accomplish these two purposes, it is unnecessary to establish standards for entering the occupation. Registration would achieve the same results. Moreover, a system of registration could be combined with a system of certification.

Implications

For which occupations will certification be cheaper than consumer search? Since certification spreads the cost of investigating practitioners over many consumers, the higher the cost of consumer search in time, money, and energy, the cheaper certification will be relative to consumer search. The cost of consumer search will be greater, the more the variance in the quality of the service furnished by the practitioner, the more important the variance, the more skill needed to evaluate the service offered, and the less the consumer is exposed to the practitioner. Thus certification will be used more frequently, *ceteris paribus*, the greater the possible variation in the service, the greater the possible harm from poor service, the more training necessary to evaluate the service, and the less the contact of the consumer with the practitioner.

In all likelihood, medicine is a field in which certification would be cheaper for most individuals than consumer search, since it takes considerable training to evaluate the worth of the treatment and since the possible harm from poor treatment is great. Here, even after being treated by a physician, many consumers are unable to judge the ability of the physician. Consequently, for a consumer to check on the ability, training, and degree of past success of practitioners, while still possible, would probably be expensive. A public or private board for the certification of practitioners, however, could rate physicians by amount of training, success on examinations, and past cure rate. Such information could then be sold to the public, either by selling the information directly to the consumer or by charging physicians for being rated and allowing them to advertise their scores.

Hence, if licensing is designed to add more information and thus to reduce uncertainty (the function of certification), licensing could be expected for the same occupations as those one would expect to be certified. Under this simple version of the lack of information theory, however, certification and registration meet all requirements while preserving freedom of choice.

Society knows best

Another rationale offered for licensing certain occupations is that society knows better than the individual what is best for the individual. This rationale takes two forms. According to one, the individual, if he had perfect knowledge of past, present, and future, would know what was best for himself. This rationale differs from the lack of information rationale discussed above only in that it says that the individual does not know the future and that society may have a better idea of the future than the individual. According to the other form of this rationale, the individual, even if he did have perfect knowledge of past, present, and future, would still not be the best judge of his own welfare. . . .

The proponents of the thesis that society knows the future better than the individual claim that individuals are overly optimistic in evaluating the expected results of their actions. In other words, they claim that individuals have, subjectively, a higher probability expectation of a desired result than is statistically warranted for society as a whole. Hence, while an individual may agree that, if n people go to unlicensed practitioners, there is a probability α that any one of these persons will be disappointed or harmed, the individual himself will base his course of action on the assumption that there is a smaller probability than α that he personally will be harmed. Therefore, the proponents of this thesis argue, welfare of individuals will be greater in the long run under licensing.

As a consequence, licensing is justified for those occupations most subject to certification under the lack of information hypothesis. In other words, licensing can be expected when the variance in the quality of the service furnished by the practitioner is high, when the import-ance of that variance is great, when the amount of training necessary to evaluate the service is large, and when the degree of exposure of the consumer to the practitioner is small. . . .

The second form of this rationale says that the consumer may not know what is best for him, even if he has perfect knowledge of past, present, and future. This approach raises great philosophical problems. If the individual is not the best judge of what is best for him, then what is best and who is to decide? According to this approach, all activity can and should be regulated by the body that does know what is best for the individual. Not only the purchasing of services but all other 'important' economic activity carried on by the individual should be controlled. While this hypothesis explains the total income correlation, it does not account for the level of education correlation. Thus the first form of this rationale – individuals do not know the future as well as society does – better fits the facts.

Social costs exceeding private costs

The last non-profit rationale to be considered holds that licensing may sometimes be necessary when social costs are greater than private costs. What does it mean to say that social costs are greater than private costs? Social costs comprise all the costs that arise from a transaction. Private costs are those costs which are borne by the parties to the transaction. Therefore, to say that social costs are larger than private costs means that others besides the parties to the transaction bear part of the costs. (By 'the parties to the transaction' is meant not only the buyers and sellers but also all persons who have voluntarily entered into arrangements with them which in effect delegate auth-ority to make these transactions.)

Registration and certification of practitioners would be useless in repressing practices by some practitioners which might lead to social costs being larger than private costs. To justify licensing by this rationale, it is necessary to argue that others besides the buyers of the service are harmed by purchasing the service from 'incompetent' practitioners. However, if the less well-trained practitioners are prevented from practicing, the average price of a unit of service will rise and will rise especially for those who would have purchased the service from the less highly skilled practitioners. Some of those who would have purchased the service from those with little training may decide to forego the purchase entirely. It is therefore necessary to argue as well that the harm done through purchasing from 'incompetent' practitioners is greater than the possible harm done through not purchasing the service at all.

The medical profession is often cited as a case where social costs are greater than private costs. It is usually said that 'incompetent' physicians may diagnose a disease incorrectly and thus start an epidemic. To complete the argument, it is necessary to contend that this is more likely or more damaging than the possibility that, if the inexpensive medical practitioner is made unavailable, the consumer will neglect to consult a physician at all, thus starting an epidemic.

Only in the case of a few occupations, such as physicians, veterinarians, and pharmacists, is it possible to argue that social costs are greater than private costs. For a great many of the occupations that are licensed, it is unlikely that social costs are larger than private costs. . . .

LICENSING FOR PROFIT

Having analyzed . . . the hypothesis that occupations are licensed in the public interest, we now consider an alternative proposition, that they are licensed in the interest of the practitioners themselves. In support of this hypothesis it will be shown that licensing raises the cost of entry, which, in turn, benefits practitioners already in the occupation at the time of licensing. Practitioners of an occupation will therefore have every reason to attempt to convince the legislature of the need for licensing. . . . As the first step, let us consider the effect of licensing upon the cost of entry.

Cost of entry

The licensing legislation for the self-regulating occupations usually requires the entrant to have completed successfully a formal program of education, to have spent a specific period in apprenticeship, to have passed an examination, to be a citizen, to have good character, and to be above a minimum age. For entering an occupation, these requirements establish a minimum cost consisting of: (1) the opportunity costs of the entrant while he is being formally schooled; (2) his opportunity cost, minus his pay as an apprentice, during his apprenticeship; (3) the risk that, after paying part or all the cost of entering, he will be denied entry; (4) that part of any entrance fees never recaptured as a member of the occupation; and (5) that part of his expenditure on tuition and books also never recaptured as a member of the occupation. Parts (1), (2), and (3) of the cost of entering are relatively simple, but parts (4) and (5) require further consideration.

If many of the books the potential entrant is required to buy have been written by members of the occupation he is entering, part of his expenditure on books goes back into the occupation. A portion of the funds spent on tuition will be converted into salaries for the members of the occupation hired to teach. The demand for the services of this occupation is consequently increased by the imposition of training requirements. The potential entrant will therefore consider not only the cost of books and tuition to him as a student but also his future gain as a member of the occupation from this requirement.

Part of the expenditure on books and tuition is equivalent to an entrance fee which is distributed among the practitioners of an occupation. This raises the cost of entry; however, since part of the entrance fee will be recovered in the future from the entrance fees of others wishing to start practice, the rise in the cost of entry is smaller than the fee.

If licensing imposes a cost on an entrant above what he would have borne in its absence it raises the cost of entry. . . .

To the entrant the rise in the cost of entry is equivalent to an entrance fee. Such an entrance fee can best be regarded as an investment from which the entrant expects a return. When the cost of entry rises, income must rise in the occupation. For the same number of practitioners to be willing to enter the occupation, *ceteris paribus*, the discounted value of the rise in income must equal the rise in the cost of entry. . . .

The larger the rise in the cost of entry, the greater will be the return to practitioners already in the industry, *ceteris paribus*. This is true because the amount by which the supply curve of practitioners shifts upward is a function of the rise in the cost of entry. Since supply and demand must tend toward equality, the price of the service and consequently the income of the licensed practitioners must rise until equilibrium is reached. . . .

The return to each practitioner is a direct function of the length of time the practitioner will remain in the occupation. Those who enter the occupation just prior to the licensing, assuming all practitioners remain in the occupation the same length of time, will benefit the most.

Those who have been in the occupation for years and are about to retire or die will benefit the least. Therefore, the longer the working life, the more benefit the average practitioner will receive from the licensing. . . .

The return also depends on how easily the regulations can be avoided. The more easily unlicensed persons can compete, the smaller the return to licensed practitioners. . . .

Becoming licensed

In the preceding section, the return to practitioners from licensing has been discussed. Licensing which raises the cost of entry benefits the practitioners already in the industry. How, then, can practitioners get themselves licensed?

Most legislators probably vote most of the time for what they consider to be in the public interest. When in doubt, however, they are likely to consider what they believe the majority of the voters support and what will net the greatest return in campaign funds. Even though an assumption that legislators are interested only in becoming re-elected is clearly untrue, as a working premise it will be assumed that, all other things being equal, the legislators will vote for the bill that gives them the best chance of being re-elected.

Therefore, for a given level of expenditure, the larger the number of practitioners in the occupation, the more votes; ergo, the stricter will be the entrance requirements enacted and the larger will be the rise in the cost of entry. The larger the expenditure for a given size of occupation, the greater the amount by which the cost of entry will be raised. . . .

Each occupation can vary only its expenditures on lobbying. If the legislation can be considered as being bought once and for all, it may be treated as an investment. Each practitioner will wish to invest in legislation up to the point at which the marginal return from the investment to the practitioner equals the interest rate.

Notes

1. On the face of it, licensing appears to be one of the most stringent instruments of regulation in so far as it involves the total prohibition of an activity by those who fail to satisfy the specified conditions for the grant of a licence. On the other hand, the specified conditions are typically confined to educational qualifications and the absence of manifest abuses, e.g. fraudulent or immoral conduct, and so in practice it provides only for *minimum* standards (although more rigorous standards may be imposed independently). Moore contrasts licensing with (a) certification, the process by which an

individual is accredited with the necessary skills but which does not prohibit others from practising, and (b) registration which simply provides an official list of those practising but which does not stipulate any conditions which must be fulfilled. See also M. Friedman, *Capitalism and Freedom* (1962), pp. 144–9 and M. J. Trebilcock, C. J. Tuohy and A. D. Wolfson, *Professional Regulation*, Staff Study of Ontario Law Reform Commission (1979), pp. 72–82.

2. It should be noted that while the literature has concentrated on licensing of the professions, the technique has been applied to a broader range of activities, for example moneylending and the driving of motor vehicles. The UK Parliament has adopted licensing less frequently than in some other countries, notably USA and Germany (see C. H. Fulda, 'Controls of Entry into Business and Professions – A Comparative Analysis' (1978) 8 Texas Int. Law J. 109), but the areas so governed have not been uncontroversial: see, especially, Report of the Monopolies Commission on the General Effect on the Public Interest of Certain Restrictive Practices (1970) Cmnd. 4463 and G. Borrie, 'Licensing Practice under the Consumer Credit Act' [1982] J. Bus. L. 91. American economists and lawyers have been most forthright in their criticisms, arguing that licensing generally results from rent-seeking behaviour by the profession concerned and generates more social costs than social benefits: e.g., Friedman, op. cit., ch. 9; W. Gellhorn, *Individual Freedom and Government Restraints* (1956), ch. 3; and D. B. Hogan, *The Regulation of Psychotherapists* (1978), ch. 6, with bibliography. More recently, the British Director General of Fair Trading has concluded that the restriction on sales of optical appliances to licensed opticians has resulted in excessive prices: Office of Fair Trading, *Opticians and Competition* (1982).

3. In passages omitted from the extract, Moore subjects to empirical verification the two hypothetical explanations of licensing that we considered in Chapter 6 (see also K. B. Leffler, 'Physician Licensure: Competition and Monopoly in American Medicine' (1978) 21 J. Law and Econ. 165) but finds that the evidence does not unequivocally support either. The lack of information – or misinformation – aspect of the first, public interest, explanation is generally regarded as the most important (cf. G. A. Akerlof, 'The Market for Lemons: Qualitative Uncertainty and the Market Mechanism' (1970) 84 Q.J. Econ. 488 and infra, Section D). The apparent greater readiness to impose licensing where the consumer places at risk his life or health (cf. Monopolies Commission Report, op. cit.) may reflect the additional problem of the individual evaluating life or health (on which see supra, Chapter 3, Section E) or may rather be an example of Moore's second paternalist rationale. His third rationale, social costs exceeding private costs, may be more important than his discussion implies: the service or product may be of higher quality than would be the case with unrestricted competition and some of the analysis overlooks that there are often important external benefits involved (see Trebilcock *et al.*, op. cit., pp. 56–60). For example, faulty architecture and engineering may have adverse consequences both for safety and for the general environment; and there are publicly financed schemes, notably social security and the social services, which come to the aid of those who are

disabled or rendered penniless. Whether these social costs outweigh any additional costs which licensing itself generates naturally varies from case to case. A number of studies are available on this, e.g., L. Shephard, 'Licensing Restrictions and the Cost of Dental Care' (1978) 21 J. Law and Econ. 187.

4. The alternative, rent-seeking, explanation was developed by Friedman (op. cit.) and others on the public choice basis that the professions form a politically more concentrated group than their clients and thus can more easily 'purchase' legislative votes. To be contrasted with Moore is a paper by Maurizi ('Occupational Licensing and the Public Interest' (1974) 82 J. Pol. Econ. 399), which, on the basis of similar data, alleges that for about one half of the licensed occupations examined there was a significant correlation between the tendency to license and the monetary return to the profession.

5. The risk of licensing generating consumer losses by creating barriers to entry and imposing other restrictive practices, such as non-advertising, is clearly greater when the profession itself, either formally or informally, determines the entry conditions and standards of behaviour. The traditional argument that only members of the profession are competent to formulate and apply appropriate standards may be simply a cover for self-interest and in any event should not imply the total exclusion of public representatives from the decision-making process. See the Monopolies Commission Report, op. cit., para. 352, and more generally G. Williams, 'Control by Licensing' [1967] Current Legal Problems 81, and R. Cranston, *Consumers and the Law* (1978), ch. 12. It should be noted, however, that the problem of barrier to entry exists only where it reduces the supply of potential entrants; in some cases it is alleged that there is no excess supply.

C. Price Controls

K. HARTLEY

*

Price Controls, Markets and Income Distribution[5]

INTRODUCTION

The state frequently intervenes in the market price-setting process. In the UK in recent years, various prices and incomes policies have been used to control the prices of goods and services and of factor incomes. The state also fixes prices in such markets as agriculture, air travel, health, housing, foreign exchange, North Sea oil and gas, roads,

[5] From *Problems of Economic Policy* (1977), ch. 8, with omissions. Reprinted by permission of George Allen & Unwin (Publishers) Ltd.

university admission and sectors of the labour market (for example, minimum wages and equal pay). . . . This chapter considers why governments attempt to control prices and shows how the basic demand and supply framework can be used to analyse regulation. The analysis is straightforward but the frequency with which governments attempt to set prices and incomes and subsequently express concern about the perverse effects of controls suggests that the message cannot be repeated too often. . . .

WHY DO GOVERNMENTS CONTROL MARKET PRICES?

A government might use price controls to 'correct' market failure. Such controls can be introduced as a means of regulating private monopoly power (for example, NHS drugs). In addition, state control of monopoly prices in product and labour markets has formed the micro-economic foundations of pay policies. Elsewhere, prices might be controlled because of externalities as in the case of the domestic agricultural and defence equipment sectors. Here it is believed that, if left to themselves, private markets will provide 'too little' of the desired commodity, namely *home* supplies of food and weapons. In each instance, a two-stage exercise is involved which distinguishes the technical and policy aspects of the problem. First, significant market failure and its causes have to be identified. Secondly, from the range of possible alternative policies, it has to be recognised that the choice of price controls to 'correct' a market deficiency represents the policy-maker's preference for market-displacing measures. However, an additional argument is frequently used to justify state control of prices, namely, inequalities in income distribution. It is often claimed that with free market prices, those on relatively low incomes will experience hardship and be unable to purchase the 'basic essentials of life', such as food, clothing and accommodation. Markets are criticized because the 'wrong people get the goods': the rich can buy second homes and fresh meat and clothing for their pets, whilst the poor are homeless and unable to feed and clothe their children. Not surprisingly, it has been concluded that these are the 'faults' of markets and that price ceilings and wage floors will 'solve' the problem by redistributing income from rich to poor. . . . [M]arket prices are *one* mechanism for allocating scarce commodities and resources. In their absence, alternative allocative mechanisms are required. The alternatives include allocation by voting, bureaucracy, dictatorship, bargaining, queuing, force, fraud and deceit, as well as by gifts, inheritance and chance. Certainly, the allocation problem is not automatically solved by preventing market prices from reflecting relative scarcities: there are no costless solutions. At the same time, market prices have never been presented as devices for ensuring that the 'right' people (for example, not the rich?) receive the goods. Such an interpretation misunderstands the essential allocative function of markets. This is not to deny the existence of a poverty problem of concern to policy-makers but rather to suggest that the cause is the existing distribution of income and wealth and not the operation of markets. On this basis, income inequality is regarded as a separate and distinct policy problem and not as an *additional* source of market failure.

WHAT HAPPENS WHEN A GOVERNMENT INTRODUCES MAXIMUM PRICE CONTROLS?

Consider the market for petrol: it could equally well be bank loans, clothing, eggs, football or theatre tickets, houses, meat, sugar, refrigerators or TVs. Suppose that the government decides to introduce maximum price controls which legally restrict the price of petrol below its market-clearing level. If the price control is effective, the result will be excess demand at the regulated price. . . .

Excess demand raises a fundamental problem. If the price mechanism is not allowed to allocate the available quantity of petrol, other methods of allocation must be found. The excess demand will reveal itself in the formation of queues at petrol stations. In the absence of state intervention, garages may decide to allocate the available quantity . . . on the basis of 'first come, first served' or, say, three gallons per customer. Other forms of informal seller rationing might include allocation on the basis of the pump attendant's personal feelings towards his customers or on the basis of his customers' past purchases and behaviour. However, in the case of petrol and commodities such as meat, eggs and butter, it might be deemed socially undesirable to leave the choice of rationing method to the seller. Considerations of equity, need and income distribution will probably dictate a state rationing scheme in which the government would issue ration coupons to each household. Even so, government officials have to ensure that the number of ration tickets issued exactly equals the available quantity of the commodity: an exercise which is not without its costs!

'Black markets' are likely to emerge with maximum price controls. The development of a black market simply means that the price system re-emerges illegally and takes over part of the allocation function outside of the law. For example, petrol might be sold outside the legal market and ration coupons are likely to be traded for cash. . . . To prevent black markets, the state might have to impose severe penalties, such as heavy fines, imprisonment and even firing squads for those who undertake transactions outside the legal market: this will involve substantial 'policing' costs.

Over time, the market will adjust to the price regulation. Smaller quantities of petrol will be forthcoming. Refining companies will have every incentive to transfer supplies to any unregulated markets, such as domestic central heating. Garages will not be maintained and repaired and some will be converted into units not subject to price controls, such as shops, restaurants and car repairs.

The analysis of maximum price controls shows that in a world of scarcity, the basic forces of demand and supply cannot be eliminated by passing a law. A price ceiling simply transfers the allocative task to some other channel. Whether the allocation is performed by official state rationing, informal seller rationing or by black markets, someone or something has to decide who is to obtain the available quantity of a commodity when a price ceiling is imposed below the market equilib-rium. In the case of statutory maximum wage policies, the excess demand will be reflected in unfilled vacancies at employment agencies, with labour being allocated more on non-wage criteria. Black market pressure will be created in the form of illegal payments above the statutory limits ('backhanders') or through legal substitutes, such as the provision of cars, holidays, promotion or second jobs. . . .

RENT CONTROL

Rent control is an example of government maximum price controls. . . . If the general model of price controls is valid, it should be revealed in evidence of excess demand for rent-controlled property, black market pressures and landlords transferring their property and new investments to the unregulated and more profitable activities. These predictions are consistent with the facts.

Excess demand for rent-controlled accommodation in both the private and public sectors has been reflected in 'waiting lists'. Indeed, the length of waiting lists measures the extent to which the controlled rent is *below* the market rent. Waiting lists for council houses are a well-known fact, with allocation frequently based on a points system determined by such factors as size of family, number of years on the list, age, health and current accommodation. Size of waiting lists has also been used as an indicator of society's 'need' for housing (for example, homeless, shortages). When accommodation becomes avail-able in the rent-controlled private sector, it is not unknown for rent collectors to require 'key money' from the prospective tenant. The excess demand in the private sector results in the re-emergence of the price mechanism in such black market forms as key money. Further evidence of excess demand and black markets was provided in the

Francis Report which examined the operation of the 1965 Rent Act.[6] Evidence was found of harassment and illegal eviction in the private sector. Whilst the law provides penalties for these offences, the Francis Report felt that, at the time, these were inadequate. Clearly, offences such as illegal eviction are not really surprising in a market situation where there were possibilities of cash gains to landlords if they could change their tenants and obtain higher rents for their property.

The existence of waiting lists and queues in the controlled sectors means that some of the unsatisfied demand 'spills over' into the remaining substitutes, especially the market for house purchase. This spillover effect together with rising real incomes and the availability of cheap mortgage finance have resulted in an increasing demand for house purchase. Theory predicts rising house prices in a situation of increasing demand: a prediction which is supported by the evidence. The average purchase price of both new and used houses has generally followed an upward trend throughout the post-war period.

Rent control results in a reduction in the rate of return on private investment in rent-controlled property compared with the return on an investment in similar markets which are not subject to price regulation. As a result, it must be expected that rent control will reduce the long-run supply of *new* buildings for the rent-controlled private sector. One UK survey has concluded that 'private building for rent has virtually disappeared due partly to rent control, partly to competition from local authorities and partly to increased and more attractive opportunities for investment in industrial and commercial undertakings'. Table 1 provides the supporting evidence.

Table 1. The Total British Housing Stock, 1914–72

Type	1914 %	1947 %	1972 %
Private-rented	88	55	14
Owner-occupied	10	26	52
Local authority	1	12	31

Source: Alex Henney, 'The Housing Situation in the UK', in *Moorgate and Wall Street* (Autumn 1974); also NIESR, 'The Price of Accommodation', in *Economic Review* (August 1964).

Note: Figures are approximations. 'Others' account for residuals.

But rent control also provides every incentive for landlords to transfer their *existing* property and any new investments from the regulated to the uncontrolled sectors, such as shops, offices and luxury

[6] Report of the Committee on the Rent Acts (Cmnd. 4609, 1971).

flats. Until 1974, regulation was restricted to unfurnished accommodation. Many landlords responded by transferring their property to
the furnished sector of the market. The 1974 extension of regulation
and security of tenure to furnished accommodation predictably led to
an immediate and substantial diminution in the supply of this type of
rented property. Finally, landlords have also adjusted by selling their
rent-controlled property to tenants so contributing to an increase in
the stock of owner-occupied dwellings and a further decline in
privately rented houses.

Rent control adversely affects the quality of privately rented houses
and this is seen in the existing stock of dwellings. Controls reduce the
relative rate of return on rented property. Landlords receive lower
incomes which might be expected to reduce both their *ability* and the
incentives to maintain and repair accommodation. This has happened
on a substantial scale, with obvious implications for slums. The
eventual demolition of these slums will further reduce the stock of
private rented houses! A government White Paper succinctly described
the problem when it stated that rent control had accelerated '. . . the
deterioration of Britain's older houses. A landlord who receives only a
controlled rent cannot be expected to maintain, let alone improve, his
house. If the present system [of rent control] is continued, slum clear-
ance will be neutralised by the drift into "slumdom" of controlled
houses.'[7]

MINIMUM WAGE LEGISLATION

Minimum price controls in product and labour markets are the
opposite of maximum prices. The state establishes a price or wage
above the market-clearing level. In the case of, say, the British agricultural and aircraft industries, such a policy aims to support a larger
domestic industry than would otherwise exist. Support might be
justified for balance of payments, technology or defence reasons.
Similarly, in the labour market the state might pursue distributional
objectives and try to raise the incomes of the lower paid by increasing
wages above the equilibrium level. Minimum prices create excess
supply which will be revealed in stocks and surpluses in goods markets
and unemployment in labour markets. Excess supply situations lead to
downward pressures on prices which might be reflected in illegal
price-cutting or in state intervention to support the controlled price
level. Once again, 'successful' state intervention in markets is not
costless. Who bears the costs and are there any perverse effects of
minimum price and wage controls? . . . Minimum wage legislation and
equal pay show some of the perverse effects of policy. . . .

---

[7] *Fair Deal on Housing* (Cmnd. 4728, 1971).

Minimum wage legislation *appears* to be an attractive solution to the problem of poverty due to low pay. Where the low paid are concentrated in specific industries, politicians frequently argue that workers' incomes can be raised simply by introducing a (higher) legal minimum wage. Demand and supply analysis shows the fallacy of this argument and that the policy leads to perverse results: some of those who are supposed to benefit find themselves without jobs!

An effective legal minimum wage will raise wage rates above the market equilibrium level. Using the competitive model, it can be predicted that there will be a reduction in the quantity of labour demanded or less employment and a rise in the amount supplied, the net effect being unemployment at the new legal minimum price. Those who remain employed receive higher wages, which was the original policy objective. However, others who are supposed to benefit from the policy actually lose their jobs, an outcome which is clearly inconsistent with the aim of poverty-reduction! The market is likely to react in a variety of ways. Some of the unemployed will be willing to undercut the legal minimum or encourage other members of the household to seek work. Others will enter unregulated markets so further reducing relative wages in such occupations. Employers will respond by substituting machines for men, by changing working conditions and, where possible, by re-defining jobs so as to be exempt from the legislation. Whether the introduction of a legal minimum will cause the industry's total wage bill to rise or fall depends on the elasticity of demand for labour. An inelastic demand over the relevant range will result in an increase in the industry's total wage bill. . . .

Notes

1. In accordance with conventional analysis, as Hartley demonstrates, price controls lead to an excess of demand over supply and thus to the rationing of goods and services by costlier and less efficient methods. Where queuing ensues, savings in pecuniary expenditure are replaced by time costs which, as measured by opportunity cost – the forgone earnings in the next best use – may exceed such savings and thus result in aggregate social losses: G. S. Becker, 'A Theory of the Allocation of Time' (1965) 75 Econ. J. 493; Y. Barzel, 'A Theory of Rationing by Waiting' (1974) 17 J. Law and Econ. 73. On distributional grounds, it should be noted, queuing may not be inequitable in that the time costs will be greater for higher earners than for lower earners, but the weakness of this justification is that typically the same degree of redistribution can be achieved by cheaper methods.

2. Hartley also points to some of the secondary effects of price controls, most importantly that sellers will attempt to maintain the return on their goods or services by other means. They may be induced to deal in the 'black market', to

reduce the quality of the product, or to alter the nature or terms of the contractual undertaking. The price control will therefore have to be buttressed by other regulation which consumes resources in its formulation and enforcement. Rent controls provide an excellent illustration. One consequence was that landowners sought to evade them by offering accommodation under a licence rather than a tenancy agreement (see A. Arden, 'Defending Rent Act Evasions' [1979] L.A.G. Bull. 87); subsequent legislation had therefore to extend protection to licensees (e.g. Housing Act 1980, s. 48). Another was that landlords allowed controlled premises to fall into disrepair, thus necessitating the imposition of quality controls: see T. Hadden, *Housing: Repairs and Improvements* (1979) and, more generally, D. C. Stafford, *The Economics of Housing Policy* (1978) and R. Robinson, *Housing Economics and Public Policy* (1979).

3. The discussion so far assumes an environment of a competitive market. Some have argued that in concentrated industries firms are able to overreach the forces of supply and demand and 'administer' prices. Price controls are therefore necessary to maintain efficiency of production; for example, a monopoly firm which can only charge a maximum price for its goods or services will have to intensify production to increase its revenue. See, generally, J. K. Galbraith, *Economics and the Public Purpose* (1973).

4. In recent times, experiments in price controls have been designed to restrain inflation (for the British legislation, see P. Smith and D. Swann, *Protecting the Consumer: An Economic and Legal Analysis* (1979), pp. 103–18). The technique typically adopted is either to freeze prices for a given period, or allow them to be raised by only a percentage of increased costs (cf. S. Breyer, *Regulation and its Reform* (1982), ch. 3). This form of regulation gives rise to a set of apparently insuperable problems (cf. R. A. Kagan, *Regulatory Justice: Implementing a Wage–Price Freeze* (1978)). First, the price caught by the freeze may, as a result of seasonal or abnormal market conditions,be inappropriate for the period governed by the control. Secondly, account has to be taken of the interdependence of different industries. If, for example, exceptions have to be made for the impact of the increased cost of raw materials, perhaps imported, on the cost of manufacturing a given product, allowances have to be made for any subsequent process incorporating that product. Thirdly, enforcement requires a large bureaucratic machinery with time and competence to scrutinize highly complex statistics and accounts. In consequence, the policing costs may well exceed the social benefits of the control. Finally, unless the controls are universal, covering all goods and services – a practical impossibility – there will be distortions in the allocation of, and investment in, resources. See R. W. Evely, 'The Effects of the Price Code' (1976) 88 Nat. Inst. Econ. Rev. 50.

D. Information Controls

H. BEALES, R. CRASWELL, AND S. SALOP
*

The Efficient Regulation of Consumer Information[8]

The importance of information to the operation of efficient markets is, by now, fairly well accepted. Information about price, quality, and other attributes allows buyers to make the best use of their budget by finding the product whose mix of price and quality they most prefer. In turn, buyers' ability to locate preferred products gives sellers an incentive to compete to improve their offerings by allowing buyers to find and reward (with patronage) the seller whose offer they prefer. Without such information, the incentive to compete on price and quality will be weakened, and consumer welfare will be reduced. . . .

INFORMATION MARKETS AND MARKET FAILURES

Although consumers may desire information for its own sake, most demand for product information is derived from the demand for products themselves. That is, consumers desire information in order to improve the level and likelihood of satisfaction derived from commodities purchased in the marketplace. To satisfy this demand, a diverse set of information sources have arisen in the economy. Consumers produce prepurchase information themselves from direct inspection of commodity attributes. These attributes may be desired for their value in consumption, their utility as signals of other unobserved attributes, or both. Information gleaned from past experience influences purchase decisions and is essential for constructing signals. Experience may also be used to define conditions of contingency payments after more information is available, as with warranties or trial periods. Consumers also purchase information, certifications, and warranties from a variety of intermediaries like journalists, termite inspectors, attorneys, and other consultants. Consumers are also given information by interested sellers who may substantiate it themselves or purchase certification from intermediaries . . . Finally, consumers may benefit from the information-gathering activities of others, either directly, in the form of recom-

[8] (1981) 24 J. Law and Econ. 491, 492–527, with omissions. Copyright © 1981 by the University of Chicago. All rights reserved. Reprinted by permission of the University of Chicago Press and the authors.

mendations, or indirectly, in the form of reputation and other market signals. . . .

At the same time, sellers have a substantial economic incentive to disseminate information to consumers. Indeed, if information dissemination were costless to sellers, theory suggests that disclosure would be complete. It is reasonable to suppose that, in the absence of additional information, consumers would view all brands as equivalent (for example, average), though the brands differed in fact. In this case, sellers of above-average brands have an economic incentive to disclose the status of their brands in order to distinguish from below-average competitors. Given these disclosures, consumers might begin to perceive that the average value of nondisclosing sellers is lower. The process does not end here. This consumer perception creates, in turn, a new incentive for those of the remaining nondisclosing sellers who are above the average to disclose their advantage. This would again lower the average of nondisclosing sellers, and so on, until every seller discloses.

Thus, one might argue that the overall richness and competitiveness of information markets imply that it is *never* efficient to mandate the generation or dissemination of currently undisclosed information. However, market failures may prevent an efficient quantity and quality of product information from being provided, even if there are no artificial impediments to competition in the information market. Such market failures are virtually inherent in information provision. Yet, at the same time, this does not mean that every deviation from perfect information should be corrected. Information is costly to produce and to disseminate, and at some point the provision of additional information is no longer socially optimal. . . .

A. Possible Information Failures

(a) *Market-perfecting Benefits.* The first and most ubiquitous market failure arises from the fact that information has *public good* properties. The purchase, production, and use of information by consumers generate a market – perfecting external benefit to uninformed consumers. Additional information induces sellers to compete for the patronage of informed consumers by offering better values – either lower prices or higher qualities. This induced competition also benefits those uninformed consumers who purchase randomly. Although perfect markets do not require all consumers to be perfectly informed, this externality implies that too little product information will generally be produced, even in an otherwise competitive information market.

(b) *Natural Monopoly and Free-Rider Problems.* Two other

characteristics of information generation and dissemination are that, once generated, information can be disseminated at low marginal cost (natural monopoly), and buyers can resell purchased information to others (free-rider externality). Either factor may lead to an under-supply of information. These have often been cited as a cause of shortages of third-party information providers. . . .

(c) *False Claims.* Disseminating false information and with-holding negative information about a brand are obviously profitable in the short run, if the claims are believed and not countered by others. Although repeat purchases based on experience and reputation provide some market check on this strategy, some attributes may be learned only after long experience, if at all. Competitiors may also have an insufficient incentive to counter false or limited information, for at least two reasons. First, competitors may share the same negative attribute, as with the health hazards of cigarettes. Second, in a competitive market, the increased patronage from the corrected consumer beliefs must be shared with other competitors, leading to the free-rider problems discussed above. In this sense, oligopolistic markets may provide a superior flow of counteradvertising than competitive ones, since the benefits are better internalized. . . .

[I]t should also be noted that consumers may not always protect themselves by gathering and rationally evaluating the optimal amount of product information. For example, consumers may underestimate the value of additional information simply because they lack other data that would tell them of their need to learn more. Consumers' information-processing skills are also imperfect. Consumers, like any-one else, can make false deductions or errors of judgment. Moreover, consumers can also be poor negotiators and may be persuaded by insistent salesmen to 'buy the product now' without waiting to acquire additional information. While these problems can be formally (and tautologically) analyzed as a change in consumers' preferences for information, it seems more sensible to treat them as factors which lead the market to generate less information than informed consumers would 'really' prefer.

(d) *Signal Competition.* Information may be valued not only for itself but also as a signal for other product attributes. For example, Nelson has shown that one function of high advertising expenditures is to provide a credible (self-enforcing) signal of product value.[9] Because superior products obtain more repeat purchases by satisfied pur-chasers from a given trial rate, these brands have a greater incentive to advertise to obtain trial. Similarly, market share may itself be a signal of value to an uninformed consumer, since relative market shares indicate the relative valuations of other buyers.

[9] 'Information and Consumer Behaviour' (1970) 78 J. Pol. Econ. 311.

Although such signals can often provide valuable information at low cost, they are not without limitations. First, these signals may be highly imperfect. For example, the first entrant in a product class may maintain its high share solely from the force of its historical monopoly, rather than from superior value, if a market share signal is used. Second, the validity of the signal will depend on the other functions of the attribute. For example, suppose advertising has the dual role of providing objective product information and serving as an indirect signal of value. In that advertising is a substitute for information diffusion by satisfied buyers, lower-valued brands may have an incentive to advertise more, even if this results in a negative signal being implied. Third, signaling competition generally leads to over-investment in the signal. Given that the market provides too little information because of other problems, though, this signal over-investment may provide a partial offset. Finally, signal competition may be self-destructive. As sellers overinvest in the signal to exploit its information value, they may destroy its information content in the process. . . .

(e) *Market Power.* . . . [O]nce the existence of firms with market power is admitted into the analysis, additional complexity occurs. As a general matter, imperfectly competitive sellers may provide either too much or too little product information, according to the particular type of information, the market structure of the industry, and the distribution of consumer preferences. Efficiency in the information market requires equality between the expected marginal social benefits and marginal cost of information gathering or information provision — where the marginal social benefit of the information includes the increment to consumer surplus plus the gain in sellers' net revenues. In contrast, profit-maximizing sellers will provide presale information up to the point where marginal net revenue equals the marginal cost of providing the information. Thus, it follows that sellers provide too little information if the marginal social benefit exceeds the marginal net revenue, and vice versa. Unfortunately, this comparison depends on a number of conflicting economic forces.

On the one hand, we have a generalization of the free-rider analysis of generic product information discussed earlier. A tendency for inefficient information undersupply results when the seller providing information does not capture (as additional profit) the entire social benefit of that additional knowledge. . . .

On the other hand, there are other forces that may lead to a non-optimal oversupply of information. In contrast to the previous analysis, brand-specific information will typically increase the market share of the provider at the expense of competing brands; that is, advertising diverts customers. However, if competitors have some degree of market power, these lost sales represent a net revenue loss to them. Turning the previous analysis around, the seller who provides information does not count these losses to its competitors as a loss to itself; yet they represent losses to society in the social benefit calculation. If these losses to competitors exceed uncaptured gains in consumer surplus (that the information providers also ignore), the result is an overprovision of information. . . .

Finally, in an imperfectly competitive product market, sellers' incentives to supply brand information may result in an imperfect provision of product variety. Information that induces product differentiation may raise prices in equilibrium by more or less than the social value. This is a simple extension of the well-established result that monopolistically competitive industries do not generally provide the optimal degree of variety. . . .

B. Product Market Failures and Institutions

Information problems may also prevent the underlying *product* markets from working properly in various ways. First, if consumers are imperfectly informed, even small sellers can achieve a degree of *informational market power* over price, leading to monopolistic rather than perfect competition. For example, because the bereaved cannot easily shop among funeral homes, the industry is fragmented (each seller averages only 100 funerals per year), and prices are high. . . . If information is poor, price dispersion for identical products also occurs, even in unconcentrated markets. Similarly, poor information about the quality of competing brands may lead to spurious product differentiation and reputation premiums, raising prices for some or all functionally equivalent brands.

Taking a more general equilibrium view, the marketplace responds by channelling competition toward more easily observable product attributes and signals of unobservable product characteristics. . . . [I]f price is more easily observed than quality, competition may be skewed toward less expensive, lower-quality products. If consumers cannot easily obtain information about a product's safety (but can easily observe its price), price competition may reward those who cut their price by offering a less safe product. . . .

It should be apparent from this survey that virtually no consumer product market or associated information market meets the textbook ideal of perfect information and perfect competition. As long as information is not perfectly free or products perfectly simple, there are almost certain to be some forms of market imperfections present. This does not imply that government intervention is always warranted to correct every instance of incomplete information in the marketplace or every market failure discovered. Given the difficulties of separating imperfections from the fact that information is costly, intervention must be limited to those instances in which information imperfections demonstrably lead to significant consumer injury and which can be corrected in a cost-effective manner – without creating serious distortions or side effects which lead to even greater injury. . . .

INFORMATION REMEDIES

The focus on information remedies in this paper reflects the belief that, where inefficient outcomes are the result of inadequate consumer information, information remedies will usually be the preferable solution. Remedies which simply adjust the information available to consumers still leave consumers free to make their own choices, thus introducing less rigidity into the market. Such remedies leave the market free to respond as consumer preferences and production technologies change over time. For the same reason, information remedies pose less risk of serious harm if the regulator turns out to have been mistaken. For example, if consumers are not really interested in increasing the quality or safety of certain product attributes, an information remedy will not force the market to make an inefficient change (where a mandatory product standard would). Similarly, information remedies allow different consumers to strike different balances between price and product quality, while direct quality regulation almost necessarily imposes a single choice on all consumers.

A. Removing Information Restraints

Perhaps the information remedy most compatible with the interests of individual sellers (if not their collective interest) is the removal of private or governmental restraints on the free flow of information. Such restrictions often tend to inhibit competition, with consequent efficiency losses. . . .

B. Prohibiting Misleading Claims

Remedies which prohibit misleading claims, unlike the other remedies discussed here, work by *reducing* the amount of information available to consumers. The rationale for such remedies, obviously, is that misleading claims do more harm than good, and that consumers are therefore made better off by their prohibition. However, because such prohibitions do work to restrict the information communicated to consumers, the prohibitions should be treated with some care.

Careful analysis is particularly important because prohibiting misleading claims is not nearly as simple a matter as might appear at first glance. [There are] difficulties involved in determining when an advertisement has made a 'claim', and whether it is possible to draw any useful distinction between the advertisement's claim and the consumers' beliefs concerning the advertised product. In addition, even when it is clear what the advertisement is claiming (and that the claim is believed by consumers), defining 'truth' is also a far from trivial issue.

This latter problem arises because it is often impossible to determine with certainty whether a given claim is true or false. . . . All that can be done is establish that the claimed performance level is likely with some probability. Moreover, for most claims, an array of tests are available, each of which sheds varying degrees of light on this probability. Such tests are costly, though, and the most precise tests (that is, those which leave the least uncertainty about the claim's truth or falsity) are usually the most expensive to conduct. Given this cost of testing, requiring perfect certainty may not be cost-effective, even if it is technically feasible. The question which then arises is: What probability of truth should be required if a claim is not to be considered misleading? . . .

Consider an advertising claim which in fact is either true or false. As a first approximation, the value of testing to any individual consumer depends on three factors: (1) the net benefits of using the product if it performs as advertised; (2) the net costs of consuming it if it does not; and (3) the consumer's *a priori* estimate of the likelihood of each of these two outcomes. For example, suppose that a consumer is agnostic in his prior assumption about the truth of the claim, believing (in the absence of further information) that there is a 50 per cent probability that the claim is true and a 50 per cent probability that it is false. If no further testing is done, such a consumer will maximize his expected benefits by purchasing the product only when the benefits of consumption if the claim is true exceed the costs of consumption when it is not. However, further testing of the claim allows the consumer to improve his *a priori* estimate of the claim's truth, thereby permitting finer decisions. If the tests show an increased probability that the claim is true (that is, an increase over the *a priori* estimate), then the consumer can purchase even when the benefits if the claim is true are relatively low or the costs if the claim is false are relatively high. If the tests show an increased probability that the claim is false, the converse is true. In short, testing is valuable because of the chance that it will improve the consumer's purchase decision from that which would be made on the basis of the consumer's *a priori* estimate.

Of course, testing will not always be sufficiently valuable to be justified, especially once a fourth factor – the cost of the tests – is taken into account. . . . In general, further testing will be cost-effective only when the test is sufficiently precise that its outcome may change the decision to buy or not to buy but sufficiently inexpensive that the costs of testing do not exceed the expected value of the benefits to be gained by this correction.

While the analysis so far has examined the value of testing to an individual consumer, the same considerations apply to testing decisions for consumers in the aggregate. The benefits of testing depend on the possibility that the information revealed by the test will change (some) consumers' purchase decisions, but tests must also be sufficiently cheap that the testing costs do not exhaust the potential savings. Aggregating consumers' testing decisions does shift the optimum in the direction of a higher level of testing, since the costs of testing remain the same while the benefits are shared by a larger number of consumers. . . .

Of course, the parameters that determine the optimal level of testing – the potential gains and losses from purchasing, the costs of testing, the number of consumers who receive the claim, and their prior estimates of the claim's truth – will almost certainly vary from product to product and from claim to claim. It is thus unlikely that there will be a single level of testing which it will be optimal to require in all circumstances. Because consumers differ in their prior expectations, relative degrees of risk aversion, and potential gains and losses from consumption, the optimal amount of testing may also be different for each consumer. As a result, decisions about how much testing is adequate must be made on a case by case basis. What constitutes a reasonable basis for one claim may be either inadequate or excessive for another.

The analysis cannot stop here, however, for it must also consider the effect of the testing requirement on the number of testable claims that are made. If the costs of testing are borne by the advertiser (as under current law), increases in the required level of testing will increase the cost of any advertising claim whose truth can be subjected to objective tests, thus giving firms an incentive to avoid such claims. The exact effect of testing requirements will depend on the relative costs of substantiating different kinds of claims and on the relative benefits of those claims to the firm making them. If 'puffery' and other subjective claims (that is, those which cannot even be tested) are perfect substitutes for objectively testable claims as far as the advertiser is concerned, then any testing requirement will induce firms to completely abandon the testable claims. . . .

C. INCREASING CONSUMER INFORMATION

Traditionally, this has usually taken the form of a requirement that sellers disclose certain standardized information to consumers. Cigarette manufacturers are required to disclose on packages and in advertising the general warning that smoking may be hazardous to health; automobile manufacturers are required to disclose a standard miles per gallon rating (as well as the fact that actual mileage may differ depending on individual driving habits); light bulb manufacturers are required to disclose the bulb's average light output as measured in lumens. This form of required disclosure is not the only method of increasing consumer information. Two additional methods which are also considered are: (a) stopping at the establishment of a standardized scoring system for measuring product attributes; and (b) consumer education efforts. Depending on the circumstances, any of these three techniques (or some combination of them) may represent the most efficient remedy.

Before discussing these specific techniques, however, we should note one general point. Consumers' information will always be incomplete to some extent, as perfect or total information would cost far more to obtain than it would be worth. . . .

1. *Establishing a Scoring System.* A scoring system measures the quantity of one or more product attributes across brands. The score may be dichotomous, as with a definition (for example, 'walnut' means solid walnut, as opposed to veneer), or it may be continuous (for example, gasoline mileage ratings).

However devised, scoring systems are intended to reduce the costs of communicating about measured attributes. Before firms can compete for consumers on the basis of different amounts of some attribute, it is necessary for consumers to be able to observe the amount of the attribute in different products. When a scoring system provides a new measure where none existed previously, consumer comparisons (and hence competition) on the attribute become possible. Where the system substitutes a new, standardized measurement for a host of conflicting ones, the costs of comparing quantities of the attribute are also reduced, and competition on the basis of the attribute becomes easier.

Two factors may limit the emergence of scoring systems in the absence of government intervention. First, when an attribute is relatively complex, there frequently is no unambiguously best measure of it. As a result, nearly any measure can be challenged as false or misleading, at least by competitors. Since any system is likely to disadvantage some competitors, those firms will have an incentive to challenge it. Thus, firms may simply choose not to use it rather than bear the cost of defending their method.

Second, informational measures may be particularly vulnerable to deceptive usage. If cigarette 'tar' measurements were not standardized, a manufacturer could generate a lower measured tar content for his cigarette by basing the measure on fewer or smaller puffs of smoke wihout being discovered by most consumers. In this sense, measurement is a credence good. . . .

Whether a new scoring system actually reduces the costs of communicating about an attribute depends on the costs of using it. The costs of scoring products arc likely to increase with the precision of the measurement. At some level, the required precision may be so great that the new system may be too costly to be efficient. For example, the costs of actually having to determine the mileage for each individual automobile would surely make the cost of communicating about gasoline mileage prohibitive.

The decision to impose a new scoring system must also consider the possible side effects of that index in addition to the ongoing costs of testing products to calculate their scores. Side effects stem from the fact that inevitably only a few product attributes are scored. Because this eases the costs of communication about these attributes relative to others, the scoring system may increase the market's emphasis on them at the expense of the unscored attributes. . . .

2. *Required Disclosures.* The need for requiring disclosure, in general, depends on the completeness of the total information environment and sellers' incentives to disclose voluntarily. If information is readily available from another source, or if firms have their own incentives to disclose whenever disclosure would be useful, required disclosure is unnecessary.

Mandatory disclosure is least likely to be necessary for information that differentiates one brand from another. In such cases, the producer of the brand with an advantage has every incentive to convey that fact. . . .

Conversely, disclosure is most likely to be appropriate when information affects an entire product class without differentiating the brands within that class. In such cases, no one firm may have sufficient incentive to disclose the information on its own, whether the information is positive or negative. If the information is positive, the firm's competitors will share in the benefits as free riders. If the information is negative, it will reduce the sales of each firm, and thus no firm will have an incentive to convey it. . . .

Notes

1. It is only relatively recently that economists have directed their attention to the problem of information: G. Stigler, 'The Economics of Information' (1961) 69 J. Pol. Econ. 213; and for a general survey, E. Mackaay, *Economics of Information and Law* (1982). See also in the context of contract law, supra Chapter 4, Section D, and A. Schwartz and L. L. Wilde, 'Intervening in Markets on the Basis of Imperfect Information: A Legal and Economic Analysis' (1979) 127 U. Penn L.R. 630. As these discussions indicate, the questions of what level of market imperfection may justify intervention, and what form such intervention should take, are not easy to resolve.

2. Consider, first, market failure in the provision of information on prices. The cost of comparison shopping to the individual may exceed the benefit to be derived from a transaction at a lower price. At the extreme, this enables sellers to charge a monopoly price (i.e. the price charged if there were no competition for the product) which may substantially exceed the equilibrium price (the price charged in a setting of perfect information and competition). If there is a sufficient number of consumers who do engage in comparison shopping, notwithstanding the cost, suppliers will have the appropriate incentive to offer at the equilibrium price (Schwartz and Wilde, op. cit., pp. 649–51). But it should be noted that there will be a suboptimal supply of such consumers, because their activity generates an external benefit (the gain in welfare to non-comparison consumers), and, secondly, that firms may be able to offer more favourable prices or terms to the comparison shoppers, thus discriminating against those who do not compare prices: ibid., pp. 662–6. For evidence of price discrimination in the used car market, see K. McNeil *et al.*, 'Market Discrimination against the Poor and the Impact of Consumer Disclosure Law: the Used Car Industry' (1979) 13 Law and Soc. Rev. 695.

3. Imperfect information as to quality is even more problematic. If consumers are insufficiently informed of the relative costs and benefits of products, they cannot effectively express their preferences and there will be a misallocation of resources. If sellers anticipate that consumers will be unable effectively to verify the quality of goods they will have incentives to attract consumers by low prices to purchase products of a quality inferior to that which, with perfect information, they would have preferred: G. A. Akerlof, 'The Market for "Lemons": Quality Uncertainty and the Market Mechanism' (1970) 84 Quart. J. Econ. 488. The problem is acute in relation to 'experience' goods, the quality of which cannot be evaluated prior to purchase: see P. Nelson, 'Information and Consumer Behaviour' (1970) 78 J. Pol. Econ. 311, contrasting them with 'search' goods. Traditionally, economists regard advertising as an efficient means of communicating information on quality, and some argue that the unregulated market is capable of disciplining misrepresentations, on the ground that if, without substantial cost, consumers can validate advertisers' claims through their experience of goods, market pressures will render false advertising ineffectual

(see Stigler, op. cit., and L. Telser, 'Advertising and Competition' (1964) 72 J. Pol. Econ. 537). In markets characterized by oligopoly, advertising increases demand for a good and, by stimulating brand loyalty, reduces demand elasticity. This exacerbates the anti-competitiveness of the market and is socially wasteful: A. Dixit and V. Norman, 'Advertising and Welfare' (1978) 9 Bell J. Econ. 1. There is, however, a marked reluctance to admit that advertising can change consumers' tastes (though see J. K. Galbraith, op. cit., ch. 14), primarily because economic analysis can only operate within the parameter of stable preferences (cf. Veljanovski, supra, Chapter 1, Section B). See, generally, Y. Kotowitz and F. Mathewson, 'Advertising, Consumer Information and Product Quality', (1979) 10 Bell J. Econ. 566.

4. Granted that a case for intervention exists, there are advantages in this focusing on information rather than e.g. quality controls (supra, Section A) or the non-enforcement of contracts (supra, Chapter 4, Section D), for it preserves choice for both purchasers and suppliers; in short, it supports rather than hinders the competitive market (cf. Breyer, op. cit., p. 161). There is an extensive literature evaluating the various forms of regulation discussed by Beales *et al.* On the removal of information restrictions, see L. Benham, 'The Effect of Advertising on the Price of Eyeglasses' (1972) 15 J. Law and Econ. 377. The problems involved in controlling advertising claims are well documented in S. Peltzman, 'The Effect of FTC Advertising Regulation' (1981) 24 J. Law and Econ. 403; cf. R. Pitovsky, 'Beyond Nader: Consumer Protection and the Regulation of Advertising' (1977) 90 Harv. L.R. 661. The case for a centralized information service (e.g. 'scoring system') would seem to be strong when regard is had to the external benefit problem, but it generates high administrative costs and some writers are sceptical of the ability of bureaucracies to provide reliable and valuable information (e.g. M. P. Darby and E. Karni, 'Free Competition and the Optimal Amount of Fraud' (1973) 16 J. Law and Econ. 27). Imposing disclosure requirements on firms increases the price of goods and may generate undesired secondary effects, raising the question whether such costs are exceeded by the welfare gains accruing from increased information. On this, see R. Urban and R. Mancke, 'Federal Regulation of Whiskey Labels: from the Repeal of Prohibition to the Present' (1972) 15 J. Law and Econ. 411; and S. A. Rhoades, 'Reducing Consumer Ignorance: An Approach and its Effects' (1975) 20 Antitrust Bull. 309.

PART IV

*

Legal Institutions

8

CRIME AND LAW ENFORCEMENT

A. Deterrence

I. EHRLICH

*

The Economic Approach to Crime – a Preliminary Assessment[1]

The fundamental hypothesis in the economic approach to crime is that offenders and those who attempt to control crime on the whole respond to measurable opportunities, or incentives. It is the verification and estimation of the extent of offenders' responsiveness to, and the cost of producing and meting out, such incentives that are posed as central targets of scientific investigation.

THE DETERRENCE HYPOTHESIS

. . . [T]he 'economic' approach to crime is heavily predicated on the 'deterrence hypothesis'. By its direct connotation the latter expression conveys the belief that the threat of a criminal sanction, or any other form of punishment, has some moderating or restraining effect on the willingness of actual or potential offenders to engage in criminal activity. But, to interpret this hypothesis so narrowly runs the risk of missing the basic idea on which it is founded, for the basic idea has to do with the moderating effect on criminal behaviour of *all* commonly recognized incentives, *positive* as well as negative. Properly construed, the hypothesis is that *all potential offenders – even the perpetrators of 'crimes of passion' – on the whole respond to costs and gains, prices and rewards, in much the same way, although not necessarily to the same extent, as do individuals who pursue legitimate or socially approved activities.*

[1] From S. Messinger and E. Bittner (eds.), *Criminology Yearbook*, Vol. 1 (1979), pp. 25–60, with omissions. Copyright © 1979 by Sage Publications Inc. Reprinted by permission of the publisher and the author.

THE ECONOMIC MODEL: OFFENSE AND DEFENSE

Assumptions

... [R]ecent work by economists has developed in broad outlines a model of crime and the criminal justice system that applies the basic principles of supply and demand analysis in explaining 'equilibrium' in the criminal sector of the economy. Underlying the model are five basic assumptions.

1. *Maximizing Behavior.* Offenders, actual and potential, are assumed to behave as if they are interested in maximizing their personal welfare, or preferences, subject to the opportunities available to them in alternative legitimate and illegitimate pursuits. ...

2. *Stable Preferences.* ... The assumption that lends the economic approach its explanatory or predictive power ... is that the distribution of individual preferences for crime – penchant for violence, preference for risk, benevolence, malevolence, or envy, to mention a few – is, to a significant degree, stable across different communities at a point in time or in a given community over reasonable periods of time. At the very minimum, the assumption is that changes in preferences for crime are uncorrelated with the observed changes in measurable opportunities for criminal endeavors.

3. *Unbiased Expectations.* Because criminal decisions are made under uncertainty, maximizing behavior involves the assessment of probability of 'success'. Such assessment is subjective to the offender, however, whereas the risk measures utilized in empirical research are based on objective observations. To provide a link between subjective and objective assessments, the economic approach implicitly assumes that, on average, the two tend to be identical or, at least, systematically related. This assumption can be defended in large measure by the basic maximizing-behaviour postulate discussed above. Although information pertaining to criminal sanctions or probabilities of their imposition is incomplete, in the same way that information pertaining to government taxes, probabilities of employment in specific industries, or the supply of money is not fully available, and assumptions of unbiased (or 'rational') expectations concerning the actual magnitudes of these variables is justifiable on the ground that any systematic gaps between perception and reality would generate incentives to revise the former in the direction of the latter. The incentives would be particularly strong when the consequences of misperception would be quite costly to the actor, as may be the case in connection with most felonies.

4. *Market Equilibrium.* The economic approach is based on the assumption that an implicit 'market' for criminal activity exists, that

coordinates the behavior of offenders, potential victims, and law enforcement authorities, and makes it mutually consistent through the effect of explicit prices (as in some illegal transactions) and implicit, or 'shadow', prices (as in most law enforcement and private protection activities), and that the ensuing market equilibrium is stable . . .

5. *The Concept of Crime.* Whereas the concept of crime relevant for the theoretical analysis of offenders' behavior can be defined as any unlawful activity punishable by a legal sanction, in the theoretical analysis of the demand for public enforcement crime is defined as an activity that imposes external diseconomies in either wealth or utility. External diseconomies (or negative externalities) are said to arise in all those circumstances where an activity by one person imposes costs on other persons, for which it is not feasible to make him compensate them – an activity which cannot be controlled through voluntary exchanges between the parties involved. An illegal activity is thus conceived of in the analysis as one which imposes costs on society in excess of the direct costs borne by the perpetrator.

These assumptions have provided the foundation for the development of a . . . model of crime and defense against crime. The basic components of the model are defined below.

Basic Components of the Model

The Supply of Offenses. Central to the economic approach is the assumption that despite the diversity of activities defined as illegal, all such activities share some common characteristics, which form the basis for a general analysis of individual participation in crime. Any violation of the law can be conceived of as yielding a potential increase in the offender's pecuniary wealth, his psychic well being, or both. In violating the law one also risks a reduction in one's pecuniary and nonpecuniary well being: conviction entails paying a penalty (a monetary fine, probation, the discounted value of time spent in prison, and related psychic disadvantages, net of any direct benefits received by the offender), acquiring a criminal record (and thus losing earning opportunities in legitimate activities), and other disadvantages. As an alternative to violating a specific law one could violate another, or participate in an alternative legitimate (wealth or consumption generating) activity, which may also be subject to specific hazards.

The model of participation in illegitimate activities proceeds in this general context of decision making under uncertainty by treating the offender's relevant choice as one that involves the optimal allocation of time and other resources to competing legal and illegal activities. The factors identified as the basic determinants of that choice are the marginal probabilities of punishment for the relevant set of crimes, the discounted real value of the marginal penalties imposed upon conviction, the marginal 'wage rates' in the competing illegitimate and legitimate activities, the probability of unemployment in the legitimate labor market and the value of individual assets net of current earnings. Note that the analysis does not suggest, nor does it require, that pecuniary considerations are the sole or even the predominant motive in the decision to participate in crime. The latter decision is viewed as being affected by both pecuniary and nonpecuniary or psychological considerations, including the capacity to tolerate risk. For methodological convenience, and in order to stress the distinct role played by attitudes toward risk, all other psychic costs and benefits may be defined in terms of monetary equivalents and incorporated in the definitions of the marginal costs and gain variables discussed above.

Of central importance from the viewpoint of the positive analysis are the behavioral implications of the model concerning the effects of specific incentives on the decision to participate in specific crimes. An increase in the probability and severity of the marginal punishment for any offense . . . is expected to lower the incentive to enter a criminal activity unambiguously, and generally also the frequency of offenders' participation in that activity. . . .

Although the basic model of participation in illegitimate activity is formulated at the individual level of the analysis, its behavioral propositions apply at the aggregate level as well. The response of the aggregate supply of offenses to the various incentives elaborated upon in the preceding discussion can be shown to depend, however, not only on the extent of responsiveness of individual offenders, but also on the homogeneity of potential offenders insofar as criminal proclivities and abilities to generate returns from crime is concerned. The more homogeneous offenders are, the greater the elasticity of the aggregate supply of offenses to changes in specific incentives . . .

The Demand for Protection and Law Enforcement. Because criminal behavior results in losses to victims which, by a social consensus, are larger than the gains to offenders, potential victims have an incentive to protect themselves against the risk of victimization both privately and collectively. Private protection involves expenditures of resources on locks, guards, watchdogs, safes, burglar alarm systems, and a myriad of other precautionary steps which generally aim at reducing the probability of victimization (self-protection), the private loss if victimized (self-insurance), or both. In addition, there is the incentive to buy insurance against theft and other losses in the conventional market for insurance. As was the assumption for potential offenders, potential victims are assumed to choose an optimal mix of market insurance, self-insurance, and self-protection by maximizing their expected utility from protection, subject to their private opportunities.

Private protection against crime has direct relevance for the analysis of 'equilibrium' in the general criminal sector because it imposes limits on the profitability of criminal activity to offenders. By limiting the opportunities for profitable targets, raising the cost of successfully carrying out an offense, and increasing the likelihood that an offender will be apprehended and punished through the reporting of a crime and collaborating with enforcement agencies, potential victims help modify the net returns from crime to offenders in a fashion similar to that of public protection. Moreover, an increase in the threat of victimization is likely to increase the incentive to provide private protection against crime. This expectation is shown below to apply to public defense against crime as well.

If private protection and its effects on security were free of any externalities or 'public goods' aspects, all protection against crime would be provided through private endeavors, including the enforcement of criminal laws. Indeed, prior to the 19th century, this was the prevailing method in England. . . . Since the 19th century, however, public enforcement of laws constitutes the lion's share of all enforcement and protective activities in society – a fact suggesting that private protection alone would have resulted in a socially suboptimal level of criminal activity. The aim of public enforcement can be understood as effecting a socially optimal level of crime prevention through provision of optimal criminal rules and procedures, penal policy, law enforcement, and the general administration of justice.

In its essential form the economic model of optimal public defense against crime, . . . abstracts from any consideration of vengeance, moral 'justice', or any distributional aspects of law enforcement and criminal penalties. Instead, it seeks to explain the behavior of the relevant authorities as an implicit attempt to minimize the total losses to society due to crime. Social losses, measured in terms of potential aggregate wealth foregone, are present even in cases of thefts involving a pure transfer of property from victim to offender where no destruction of property or loss of efficiency in the utilization of property takes place, because the real resource devoted by offenders to carry out crimes represent a pure loss of resources from a social point of view – resources that could be utilized to increase society's potential product. Society is assumed to set up an optimal criminal justice system that would maximize that product.

More specifically, the aggregate social loss functions from crime are defined to incorporate three principal sources. The first is the net harm to victims, including the cost of private protection, minus the net gain to offenders from committing crimes. Both the average and the marginal net social loss arising from these activities are assumed to increase with the aggregate level of crime. The second source of social losses is the expenditure of real resources on apprehending, charging, and prosecuting suspected offenders. The third source incorporates the net social loss resulting from the imposition of criminal sanctions on all convicted offenders – guilty, as well as innocent. . . . Counted here are both the private losses to the offenders' net of gains to society if any exist, and the cost of meting out and administering the penalties. By this formulation gains and losses to both victims and offenders are assigned equal weight in calculating the social losses from crime.

What is the socially optimal level of public law enforcement? In terms of the social optimization rule defined above, optimal enforcement occurs at the point where the reduced social income due to the cost of additional enforcement equals the increased social income due to the resulting decrease in crime: social policy is assumed to be conducted according to the basic proposition that severity and certainty of sanctions deter crime. Since the marginal social costs of enforcement are assumed to rise with the level of enforcement and its marginal social benefit is expected to fall as the frequency of victimization declines, however, optimal enforcement will not be compatible with the elimination of all crime. Put differently, it would be optimal for society to allow some crime to take place not because crime itself serves any useful social function, but because the additional costs of combating crime beyond a certain finite level exceed the resulting additional benefits to society. In fact, because public enforcement is an activity organized through an effective state *monopoly*, its actual level may be expected to be lower than the level that might have been produced under a competitive market for enforcement free of any externalities or other imperfections due to the public good aspects inherent in specific law enforcement activities.

The same analysis leads to specific propositions concerning the optimal certainty and severity of punishment for specific crimes. Optimal sanctions require a measure of 'proportionality' between crime and punishment not because abstract justice requires that the more serious crimes be more seriously avenged, but because the more 'serious' crimes inflict greater social damages. Aside from consideration of the potential damages to society from crime, however, optimal penalties must also be determined in view of their effectiveness in moderating the level of the criminal activity itself; that is, in view of the expected responsiveness of prospective offenders to changes in penalties. For example, if crime is committed by various groups of offenders, optimal penal policy would require that punishment will be used in greater moderation when imposed on members of groups whose responsiveness to incentives is believed to be relatively low. . . .

Market Equilibrium. In equilibrium, the quantity supplied of any object of choice equals the quantity demanded. Likewise in the general equilibrium pertaining to the criminal sector in society: the frequency of offenses supplied at an average net return from crime to offenders equals the quantity 'demanded' by society as determined by private and public defense against crime. Because optimal private and public protection from crime is expected to rise with an exogenous increase in offenses, and because these activities lower the net returns to offenders from crime, the effective 'demand' by society for crime will be negatively associated with the net return from crime to offenders. In contrast, the supply of offenses is generally expected to be positively associated with an offender's net return from crime. These responses by offenders and by society act as stabilizing factors in the general criminal market because they are crucial in ensuring the stability of the equilibrium attained in this market. . . .

Finally, a crucial lesson to be learned from the preceding equilibrium analysis in the context of an empirical implementation of the economic model of crime concerns the simultaneity relations between offense, defense, and the production of means of enforcement and crime prevention. The analysis emphasizes that while the crime rate depends, in part, on probability and severity of punishment, both the production and social demand for the latter may be affected by the level of crime itself. In addition, arbitrary changes in specific deterrence variables – such as the severity of a sanction – may lead to opposite modifications in the level of substitutable means of enforcement, such as the probability of apprehension and conviction. Proper statistical testing of any of the basic propositions of the model therefore requires that the empirical analysis account for the multiple set of theoretically relevant variables, and that appropriate . . . estimation techniques be employed to 'identify' the relevant causal relationship underlying the observed association between crime and punishment in specific samples.

R. CARR-HILL and N. STERN

*

More Police, More Crime[2]

The Conservative government is pledged to increase the numbers and effectiveness of the police. 'Law and order', long prominent in the party's political platform, has been stressed increasingly as the crime rate has risen – from 'only' 472,489 recorded indictable offences in

[2] New Statesman, 18 January 1980, 85–7. Reprinted by permission of The New Statesman.

England and Wales in 1946 and 479,710 in 1956, to 1,199,859 in 1966 and 2,135,700 in 1976. During that time the clear-up rate (the proportion of offences solved) has oscillated between 40 and 50 per cent. Would more police officers have resulted in a slower rise in the number of recorded offences, or in an improved clear-up rate? Our analysis of recent criminal statistics suggests that the answer may be no.

Of course, it is difficult to distinguish cause from effect. For example, a larger number of police officers in one area would be likely to increase the expectation that more offenders would be caught. That might act as a deterrent and so reduce the number of offences. On the other hand, the more police officers there were, the more offences would be likely to be recorded. But an increased number of recorded offences would stretch the resources of the police force and possibly reduce the clear-up rate. Finally, a larger number of recorded offences and a lower proportion of crimes solved might lead the Home Office to allocate more police to the area.

In our analysis, we were particularly interested in the (unmeasured) number of *real* offences, so we tried to disentangle this from other factors. We examined the level of recorded offences per capita, the clear-up rate and the number of police per capita for each of the police districts in England and Wales for the three most recent census years – 1961, 1966 and 1971. We also looked at the proportion of young males in each area, the class balance, the severity of punishment (measured by the proportion of those convicted sent to prison) and the likelihood of detection. The Table shows our findings for urban police districts in 1966.

We can see that an increase in the severity of punishment and in the likelihood of detection do indeed reduce recorded offences – but only slightly. In 1966, for example, we estimate that a ten per cent increase in the clear-up rate (say from 40 to 44 per cent) would have reduced the level of recorded offences by eight per cent, while a ten per cent increase in the proportion of convicted offenders imprisoned (say from 20 to 22 per cent) would have reduced recorded offences by only three per cent – some support, perhaps, for the old adage that the certainty of punishment is more important than its intensity. (Of course, a harsh deterrent may not only reduce the level of actual offences, but may also encourage individuals to take more care that their actions are not recorded as offences.)

A more striking link was found between the increased numbers of police per capita and increased expenditure per police officer on the one hand, and an increase in the number of recorded offences on the other. This does not necessarily suggest that police commit offences. More or better-equipped police are likely to see, hear of, and record

How would a *one per cent increase* in the factors listed in the vertical columns affect the number of recorded offences per capita, the clear-up rate and the number of police per capita?

1% increase in:	% change in recorded offences per capita	1% increase in:	% change in clear-up rate	1% increase in:	% change in police per capita
Clear-up rate	− 0.79	Recorded offences per capita	0.45	Clear-up rate	− 0.28
Severity of punishment	− 0.28	Number of police per capita	− 1.57	Proportion of middle-class in population	− 0.56
Proportion of males aged 15−24 in population	0.40	Proportion of males aged 15−24 in population	− 0.51	Population density	0.04
Proportion of working-class in population	0.42	Proportion of working-class in population	− 0.10	Rate of unemployment	0.06
Total rateable value per unit area	0.20	Proportion of violent offences	0.12		
Expenditure per police officer	0.45				

Urban police districts, 1966. (Figures have been omitted where the impact would be insignificant.)

more incidents as offences. They may also lead the public to report minor offences which are difficult to solve, or not worth solving: this would help to explain our finding that increased numbers of police have a *negative* effect on the clear-up rate. But if that is the case, how can the clear-up rate be increased? It certainly improves where violent offences are concerned, since violent offenders are more easily identified, but one cannot seriously argue for more violent offences so that clear-up rates can be boosted. Smaller police districts seem to do better than larger ones, which casts doubt on the wisdom of the amalgamations of police districts which took place in the late 1960s.

As for the numbers of police to be found in any one area, this seems best understood in terms of the ease with which officers can be recruited, rather than a positive allocation policy: there were more police per capita in areas where unemployment was high and fewer where it was low. The more middle-class an area, the fewer police there were per capita − contrary to what one might expect, given the strong wish of the well-heeled to have their property adequately defended.

It is not true that areas with more young males always had more offences: in fact, they had fewer offences than other areas in 1961, more in 1966 and about the same in 1971. This may reflect a shift in relations between the police and young people, from paternalistic attention in the Fifties (so that fewer of their offences were officially recorded) to antagonism by the mid-Sixties, moving on to a more general formalisation of police relations with the public as a whole.

What are the implications of our analysis? First, deterrence is not a serious policy option if its aim is to reduce the level of recorded indictable offences. The possible 'benefit' of reducing recorded offences by two or three per cent would hardly justify the 'cost' of a ten per cent increase in the prison population. And while an increase in the detection rate might look more promising as a means of reducing offences, it is very hard to see how this might be achieved. Certainly one cannot assume that extra or better-equipped police will increase the overall proportion of crimes solved; if anything it would seem to have the reverse effect.

Second, we should expect that if the government carries out its policy of spending more on a larger and better-equipped force, the result will be more recorded offences, not less. And we must watch out for the argument that the still higher level of recorded offences will require still more expenditure on police. . . .

Notes

1. The economic analysis of crime begins with G. Becker's 'Crime and Punishment – An Economic Approach' (1968) 76 J. Pol. Econ. 169 which casts the earlier utilitarian approach of Beccaria and Bentham into a more rigorous framework (C. Bonesara-Beccaria, *Essays on Crimes and Punishment* (1764); J. Bentham, *An Introduction to the Principles of Morals and Legislation* (J. H. Burns and H. L. A. Hart (eds.), 1970) pp. 165–74).

2. The positive branch of this literature (I. Ehrlich, 'Participation in Illegitimate Activities: A Theoretical and Empirical Analysis' (1973) 81 J. Pol. Econ. 521) is the principal example of the economists' attempt to determine the effects of legal sanctions on individual behaviour. The empirical literature on the deterrence of crime is vast. See anthologies by G. Becker and W. M. Landes (eds.), *Essays in the Economics of Crime and Punishment* (1974); J. M. Heineke, *Economic Models of Criminal Behaviour* (1978); also P. J. Cook, 'Punishment and Crime: A Critique of Current Findings Concerning the Preventative Effects of Punishment' (1977) 41 Law and Contemp. Prob. 164. This is in marked contrast to other areas of law, notably contract and tort, where attempts to 'test' the economic model using quantitative data have been meagre. For studies of crime statistics using UK data, see R. Carr-Hill and N. Stern, *Crime, the Police and Criminal*

Statistics (1979); K. I. Wolpin, 'An Economic Analysis of Crime and Punishment in England and Wales, 1894–1969' (1978) 86 J. Pol. Econ. 815.

3. Economists also treat the criminal justice system as part of the model and responsive to changes in crime-related variables. These models postulate that society (i.e. police, the courts and prospective victims) seeks to deploy resources so as to minimize the social loss caused by criminal activity. (W. M. Landes, 'An Economic Analysis of the Courts' (1971) 14 J. Law and Econ. 61; R. Adelstein, 'The Plea Bargain in Theory: A Behavioural Model of the Negotiated Guilty Plea' (1978) 44 So. Econ. J. 488.)

B. Punishment and Enforcement

G. BECKER

*

Crime and Punishment: an Economic Approach[3]

THE CASE FOR FINES

Just as the probability of conviction and the severity of punishment are subject to control by society, so too is the form of punishment: legislation usually specifies whether an offense is punishable by fines, probation, institutionalization, or some combination. Is it merely an accident, or have optimality considerations determined that today, in most countries, fines are the predominant form of punishment, with institutionalization reserved for the more serious offenses? This section presents several arguments which imply that social welfare is increased if fines are used *whenever feasible*.

In the first place, probation and institutionalization use up social resources, and fines do not, since the latter are basically just transfer payments, while the former use resources in the form of guards, supervisory personnel, probation officers, and the offenders' own time. . . .

Moreover, the determination of the optimal number of offenses and severity of punishments is somewhat simplified by the use of fines. A wise use of fines requires knowledge of marginal gains and harm and of marginal apprehension and conviction costs; admittedly, such knowledge is not easily acquired. A wise user of imprisonment and other punishments must know this too, however; and, in addition, must

[3] (1968) 76 J. Pol. Econ. 169, 193–8, with omissions. Copyright © 1968 by the University of Chicago. All rights reserved. Reprinted by permission of the University of Chicago Press and the author.

know about the elasticities of response of offenses to changes in punishments. As the bitter controversies over the abolition of capital punishment suggest, it has been difficult to learn about these elasticities.

Fines provide compensation to victims, and optimal fines at the margin fully compensate victims and restore the status quo ante, so that they are no worse off than if offenses were not committed. Not only do other punishments fail to compensate, but they also require 'victims' to spend additional resources in carrying out the punishment. It is not surprising, therefore, that the anger and fear felt toward ex-convicts who in fact have *not* 'paid their debt to society' have resulted in additional punishments, including legal restrictions on their political and economic opportunities and informal restrictions on their social acceptance. Moreover, the absence of compensation encourages efforts to change and otherwise 'rehabilitate' offenders through psychiatric counseling, therapy, and other programs. Since fines do compensate and do not create much additional cost, anger toward and fear of appropriately fined persons do not easily develop. As a result, additional punishments are not usually levied against 'ex-finees', nor are strong efforts made to 'rehabilitate' them.

One argument made against fines is that they are immoral because, in effect, they permit offenses to be bought for a price in the same way that bread or other goods are bought for a price. A fine *can* be considered the price of an offense, but so too can any other form of punishment; for example, the 'price' of stealing a car might be six months in jail. The only difference is in the units of measurement: fines are prices measured in monetary units, imprisonments are prices measured in time units, etc. If anything, monetary units are to be preferred here as they are generally preferred in pricing and accounting.

Optimal fines . . . depend only on the marginal harm and cost and not at all on the economic positions of offenders. This has been criticized as unfair, and fines proportional to the incomes of offenders have been suggested. If the goal is to minimize the social loss in income from offences, and not to take vengeance or to inflict harm on offenders, then fines should depend on the total harm done by offenders, and not directly on their income, race, sex, etc. In the same way, the monetary value of optimal prison sentences and other punishments depends on the harm, costs, and elasticities of response, but not directly on an offender's income. Indeed, if the monetary value of the punishment by, say, imprisonment were independent of income, the length of the sentence would be *inversely* related to income, because the value placed on a given sentence is positively related to income. . . .

Another argument made against fines is that certain crimes, like murder or rape, are so heinous that no amount of money could compensate for the harm inflicted. This argument has obvious merit and is a special case of the more general principle that fines cannot be relied on exclusively whenever the harm exceeds the resources of offenders. For then victims could not be fully compensated by offenders, and fines would have to be supplemented with prison terms or other punishments in order to discourage offenses optimally. This explains why imprisonments, probation, and parole are major punishments for the more serious felonies; considerable harm is inflicted, and felonious offenders lack sufficient resources to compensate. Since fines are preferable, it also suggests the need for a flexible system of instalment fines to enable offenders to pay fines more readily and thus avoid other punishments.

This analysis implies that if some offenders could pay the fine for a given offense and others could not, the former should be punished solely by fine and the latter partly by other methods. In essence, therefore, these methods become a vehicle for punishing 'debtors' to society. Before the cry is raised that the system is unfair, especially to poor offenders, consider the following.

Those punished would be debtors in 'transactions' that were never agreed to by their 'creditors', not in voluntary transactions, such as loans, for which suitable precautions could be taken in advance by creditors. Moreover, punishment in any economic system based on voluntary market transactions inevitably must distinguish between such 'debtors' and others. If a rich man purchases a car and a poor man steals one, the former is congratulated, while the latter is often sent to prison when apprehended. Yet the rich man's purchase is equivalent to a 'theft' subsequently compensated by a 'fine' equal to the price of the car, while the poor man, in effect, goes to prison because he cannot pay this 'fine'.

Whether a punishment like imprisonment in lieu of a full fine for offenders lacking sufficient resources is 'fair' depends, of course, on the length of the prison term compared to the fine. For example, a prison term of one week in lieu of a $10,000 fine would, if anything, be 'unfair' to wealthy offenders paying the fine. Since imprisonment is a more costly punishment to society than fines, the loss from offenses would be reduced by a policy of leniency toward persons who are imprisoned because they cannot pay fines. Consequently, optimal prison terms for 'debtors' would not be 'unfair' to them in the sense that the monetary equivalent to them of the prison terms would be less than the value of optimal fines, which in turn would equal the harm caused or the 'debt'. . . .

COMPENSATION AND THE CRIMINAL LAW

Actual criminal proceedings in the United States appear to seek a mixture of deterrence, compensation, and vengeance. I have already indicated that these goals are somewhat contradictory and cannot generally be simultaneously achieved; for example, if punishment were by fine, minimizing the social loss from offenses would be equivalent to compensating 'victims' fully, and deterrence or vengeance could only be partially pursued. Therefore, if the case for fines were accepted, and punishment by optimal fines became the norm, the traditional approach to criminal law would have to be significantly modified.

First and foremost, the primary aim of all legal proceedings would become the same: not punishment or deterrence, but simply the assessment of the 'harm' done by defendants. Much of traditional criminal law would become a branch of the law of torts, say 'social torts', in which the public would collectively sue for 'public' harm. A 'criminal' action would be defined fundamentally not by the nature of the action but by the inability of a person to compensate for the 'harm' that he caused. Thus an action would be 'criminal' precisely because it results in uncompensated 'harm' to others. Criminal law would cover all such actions, while tort law would cover all other (civil) actions.

Notes

1. The normative economic theory of crime is merely a generalization of the theory of externalities to include enforcement costs. Crimes, like torts, are treated as loss-imposing events and the objective is to minimize social losses. There is disagreement among economists whether the utility the offender derives from crime should be included in the economic calculus (see Ehrlich supra, cf. G. Stigler, 'The Optimum Enforcement of Laws' (1970) 78 J. Pol. Econ. 526), or whether more nebulous 'costs' reflecting the general outrage of the community can be properly included. (R. P. Adelstein, 'Information Paradox and the Pricing of Crime: Capital Sentencing Standards in Economic Perspective' (1979) 70 J. Crim. L. and Criminology 281). Also see I. Ehrlich, 'On Positive Methodology, Ethics, and Polemics in Deterrence Research' (1982) 22 Brit. J. Criminol. 124; T. Gibbons, 'The Utility of Economic Analysis of Crime' (1982) 2 Int. Rev. Law and Econ. 173.

2. Becker's 'case for fines' is designed to achieve maximum deterrence at minimum enforcement costs. He is not describing the actual system of fines, which are the most frequently used sanctions (R. Morgan and R. Bowles, 'Fines: The Case for Review' [1981] Crim. L.R. 203) but the economically ideal system. One major difference between the latter and current practice is that fines are not paid as compensation to victims. Another, not evident from Becker's discussion, is that draconian penalties may be implied by the

economic model. This is because detecting, prosecuting and convicting offenders are expensive, whereas the threat of a large penalty deters almost costlessly. Thus, the same level of deterrence can be gained by trading-off higher penalties for lower detection and prosecution rates, thereby saving enforcement costs. This implies almost sole reliance on fines, with very severe penalties imposed on the occasional offender caught, in order to deter other potential offenders. Several factors limit the effectiveness (and efficiency) of this strategy. (See generally, M. K. Block and J. G. Sidak, 'The Cost of Antitrust Deterrence: Why Not Hang a Price Fixer Now and Then?' (1980) 68 Georgetown L.J. 1131.) First, fines equal to the 'harm' would only make the criminal indifferent between the criminal act and voluntary lawful transactions. Such a fine therefore would not be sufficient to deter inefficient offences (G. Calabresi and A. M. Melamed, 'Property Rules, Liability Rules and Inalienability: One View of the Cathedral' (1972) 85 Harv. L.R. 1089, 1124–7). Secondly, fines which do not bear a reasonable relationship to the gravity of the offence are liable to be nullified by jury, prosecutor and/or judge (J. Hall, 'Strict or Liberal Construction of Penal Statutes' (1935) 48 Harv. L.R. 748, 750–1 points to the nullification of the death penalty imposed for lesser offences in the early 1880s in England). Thirdly, and related to this, such a sanctioning system may be regarded as unfair. Those offenders unfortunate enough to be caught can legitimately complain that their punishment does not fit the crime and that they are being sacrificed in order to deter other offenders that the enforcement agency has decided not to catch because of a policy of minimizing its expenditure.

3. Becker suggests that crime and tort, and by implication private and public law, are analytically identical in that the laws governing the 'harms' they seek to control can be reduced to a general damage remedy. The boundary between crime and 'social' tort would be determined solely by the inability of the offender to pay the optimal fine. It is interesting that historically Anglo-Saxon law knew no distinction between crime and tort – both were the subject of the same civil action for pecuniary compensation. See F. Pollock and F. Maitland, *The History of English Law*, Vol. II (2nd edn, 1968), p. 451; J. Hall, 'Interrelations of Criminal Law and Tort' (1943) 43 Col. L.R. 753. On the other hand, scholars have suggested that the boundary between tort and crime is defined by the relative efficiency of public enforcement for the latter because the 'concealability' of crime generates economies of scale in detection. (H. V. Ball and L. M. Friedman, 'The Use of Criminal Sanctions in the Enforcement of Economic Legislation: A Sociological View' (1965) 17 Stan. L.R. 197; W. M. Landes and R. A. Posner, 'Private Enforcement of Law' (1975) 4 J. Legal Stud. 1.) There is, however, an important difference between crime and tort. Tort law simply involves definitions of rights and as such can (typically, but subject to legislative prohibition) be modified by agreement (see Coase supra, Chapter 2, Section C); one cannot contract-out of criminal law obligations.

4. In the area of regulatory enforcement, 'optimal deterrence' often does not appear to be the practical objective. Instead, the enforcement agencies appear to seek compliance from individual offenders and often adopt highly selective

enforcement procedures which rely on direct negotiation between inspectors and offenders to induce conformity with the law (K. Hawkins, *Environmental Pollution – The Social Construction of Pollution* (1984); G. M. Richardson, A. I. Ogus and P. Burrows, *Policing Pollution* (1983)). Such a bargaining strategy can partly be explained as a device to fine-tune overinclusive legal rules (see Ehrlich and Posner, infra, Chapter 9, Section B) and to minimize enforcement costs: C. G. Veljanovski, 'Regulatory Enforcement – An Economic Study of the British Factory Inspectorate' (1983) 5 Law and Policy Q. 75.

9

LEGAL SYSTEM AND PROCEDURE

A. Constitutions

J. M. BUCHANAN

*

The Limits of Liberty[1]

TWO-STAGE CONTRACT

. . . Conflict between A and B in the state of nature will . . . arise over the disposition of all of those goods that are not superabundant. . . .

[A] natural distribution will emerge from actual or potential conflict. This distribution . . . will be influenced by the initial disposition of the goods, and by the relative personal characteristics and behavior patterns of each person. . . . In attaining his share in this natural distribution, each person finds it necessary to invest effort (time and energy) in predatory and/or defense activity. There is no difference in this respect between this and the one-good model. And, . . . the natural distribution provides the base from which contractual agreements become possible. Agreement will . . . take the form of some mutual acknowledgment of rights. Gains are secured from the reductions in predation-defense effort. This contract, which becomes the initial leap from Hobbesian anarchy, is the first stage of a two-stage contractual process. For purposes of convenience, I shall, here and later, refer to this as 'constitutional contract'.

It is the existence of two stages or levels of agreement that distinguishes the many-good from the one-good model. In the latter, the initial agreement on shares in the single scarce good represents the limit to trade. No further contracts between the two persons will offer mutual gains. The two-person group attains the Pareto-frontier through its initial agreement on rights of disposition. The many-goods

[1] From *The Limits of Liberty* (1975), pp. 28–180, with omissions. Copyright © 1975 by the University of Chicago. All rights reserved. Reprinted by permission of the author and the University of Chicago Press.

model differs sharply at precisely this point. If individual tastes differ, there may be potential gains from trade over and beyond the initial 'trade' of agreements on individual rights. The trading process at this second, or *postconstitutional* stage is, of course, the domain of traditional economic theory. Individual participants are assumed to enter the potential trading arena with identifiable endowments and/or capacities, and their rights to these initially held endowments are assumed to be mutually accepted by all members of the community and to be enforced by the state. . . .

MARKET FAILURE AND THE FREE-RIDER PROBLEM

If individual rights are well defined and mutually accepted by all parties, persons will be motivated voluntarily to initiate trades in partitionable goods and services, those that are characterized by full or quasi-full divisibility among separate persons or small groups. That is to say, markets will emerge more or less spontaneously out of the self-interested behavior of individuals, and the results will be beneficial to all members of the community. The potential gains-from-trade will be fully exploited, and all persons will be better off than they would have been by remaining in their initial postconstitutional positions, with well-defined endowments and capacities imbedded in a structure of legally binding human and property rights. . . .

The thrust of the modern theory of public or collective-consumption goods is the demonstration that markets fail to emerge and to produce tolerably efficient results when potential contracts require the simultaneous agreement of many parties. Neither of the efficiency-generating elements of private-goods markets is present in the pure public-goods model. Agreement or transactions costs are much higher because of the large number of persons who must be brought into the same bargain or exchange. And this inclusiveness itself tends to eliminate potential alternatives for participants, alternatives which narrow the range over which terms of trade might settle. . . .

Each person has an incentive, therefore, to try to become a 'free rider', one who secures the benefits of the jointly consumed good or service without participating fully in the sharing of its costs. . . .

A 'natural equilibrium' in which some coalition of persons provides some of the public good and in which some other members of the community remain outside as free riders may emerge spontaneously in particular instances, but these results will tend to be inefficient. Careful analysis suggests that if efficiency criteria are to be met, some 'social contract' among *all* persons must be made, a contract that requires all members of the community to participate in collective decisions which are, in turn, made under a unanimity rule. There is an apparent paradox here worth noting. A rule of unanimity will insure to each individual that he will not be harmed or damaged by collective action. But individuals, until and unless they are specifically organized under a 'social contract' like that indicated, will not, privately and independently, attain efficient outcomes through voluntary trades or exchanges. . . .

INDIVIDUAL RIGHTS UNDER NONUNANIMITY RULES

On grounds of institutional efficiency, departure from unanimity in the reaching of collective decisions seems necessary. . . .

Under a unanimity rule, decisions if made at all are guaranteed to be efficient, at least in the anticipated sense. Individual agreement signals individual expectation that benefits exceed costs, evaluated in personal utility dimensions, which may or may not incorporate narrowly defined self-interest. With a purely public good, the individually secured benefits, as evaluated, must exceed the individually agreed-on share of costs, measured in foregone opportunities to secure private goods. From an initial imputation of endowments or goods, the multiparty exchange embodied in public-goods provision moves each individual to a final imputation, which includes public goods, that is evaluated more highly in utility terms. Each person in the collectivity moves to a higher position on his own utility surface, or thinks that he will do so, as a result of the public-goods decision reached by unanimous agreement.

No such results are guaranteed when collective decisions are made under less-than-unanimity rules. Under simple majority voting, for example, a person may find that a majority decision for public-goods provision shifts him to a lower rather than a higher position on his utility surface. What are his 'rights' in such a postconstitutional change? It would seem that, for the person in question, this sort of change could hardly be called a 'contract'. Goods that he values are taken from him against his expressed desire. Coercion is apparently exercised upon him in the same way as that exerted by the thug who takes his wallet . . .

This is one of the major sources of confusion in modern discussion of social policy . . . If, as we have postulated, individual rights are defined as rights to do things with respect to some initial set of endowments or goods, *along with* membership in a collectivity that is empowered to act by less-than-unanimity rules, and, further, *if* these rights should be mutually accepted, it becomes inconsistent and self-contradictory for a person to claim that his 'rights' are violated in the mere working out of the collective decision rules that are constitutionally authorized. At this point it is worth recalling once again that the analysis remains timeless. We are assuming that the *same* persons participate in the conceptual constitutional contract and in post-constitutional adjustments. From this it follows that, if a constitutional contract is made that defines separate persons in terms of property rights, and if these rights are widely understood to include membership in a policy that is authorized to make collective decisions by less-than-unanimity rules, each person must have, at this prior stage, accepted the limitations on his own rights that this decision process might produce. (Note that this statement need not imply that the prior constitutional contract was itself optimal or efficient. Note further that the justice or injustice of this contract is irrelevant here.) . . .

The distinction between the constitutional and the postconstitutional stages of social contract allows us to interpret the state, the collective agency of the community, in two separate roles. . . . At the constitutional stage, the state emerges as the enforcing agency or institution, conceptually external to the contracting parties and charged with the single responsibility of enforcing agreed-on rights and claims along with contracts which involve voluntarily negotiated exchanges of such claims. In this 'protective' role, the state is not involved in producing 'good' or 'justice', as such, other than that which is embodied indirectly through a regime of contract enforcement. Explicitly, this state cannot be conceived as some community embodiment of abstract ideals, which take form over and beyond the attainment of individuals. This latter conception is and must be foreign to any contractarian or individualistic vision or model of social order. Nonetheless, because of each person's interest in the security of his agreed-on rights, the legal or protective state must be characterized by precepts of neutrality. Players would not consciously accept the appointment of a referee who was known to be unfair in his enforcement of the rules of the game, or at least they could not agree on the same referee in such cases. 'Fairness' or 'justice' may emerge, therefore, in a limited sense from the self-interest of persons who enter the enforcement contract. It will not emerge from the acceptance of overriding ideals for society at large.

This legal or protective state, the institutions of 'law' broadly interpreted, is *not* a decision-making body. It has no legislating function, and it is not properly represented by legislative institutions. This state does not incorporate the process through which persons in the community choose collectively rather than privately or independently. The latter characterizes the functioning of the conceptually separate productive state, that agency through which individuals provide themselves with public goods in postconstitutional contract. In this latter context collective action is best viewed as a complex exchange process with participation among all members of the community. This process is appropriately represented by legislative bodies and the decision-making, choosing process is appropriately called 'legislation'. By sharp contrast, the protective state which carries out the enforcement task assigned to it in constitutional contract makes no 'choices' in the strict meaning of this term. Ideally or conceptually, enforcement might be mechanically programmed in advance of law violation. The partici-pants agree on a structure of individual rights or claims that is to be enforced, and violation requires only the findings of fact and the automatic administration of sanctions. . . . In its postconstitutional role, what we may call the 'productive state' is the constitutional process through which citizens accomplish jointly desired objectives, a means of facilitating complex exchanges *among* separate citizens, each of whom enters the contractual or exchange process with rights assigned in the more fundamental legal structure. In this role, govern-ment is *internal* to the community, and meaningful political decisions can only be derived from individual values as expressed at the time of decision or choice. . . . In such a context, current participation in collective choice becomes a desirable attribute. And, as noted, . . . unanimity offers the idealized rule for the reaching of decisions. Departures from this benchmark are justifiable only because of the excessive costs of attaining genuine consensus. Even when the practicably acceptable departures from unanimity are acknowledged, however, the decision-making process is properly conceived as a surrogate for a full consensus model.

In this role or capacity, the state is not 'protecting' defined individual rights. Government is a *productive process*, one that ideally enables the community of persons to increase their overall levels of economic well-being, to shift forward the efficiency frontier. Only through governmental-collective processes can individuals secure the net benefits of [public] goods. . . . In this capacity, government decision-making involves agreements on quantities and cost-sharing. Outcomes are reached by compromising among conflicting desires, by making full use of various devices for compensation, by facilitating and promoting indirect trade-offs among persons and groups. . . .

It may be argued that, in carrying out its enforcement role, the state should employ 'experts', 'scientists', 'truth seekers', 'fact finders' – persons who are particularly trained in the law. If confined to its appropriate limits there seems to exist a logical and rational basis for delegation of enforcing power to a judicial elite. The problem is, of course, that of keeping any such elite confined within any limits that might be specified, and it is in recognition of this problem that much of the modern ambiguity arises. Democratic procedures, including representation of interests, may be explicitly incorporated into the structure of the enforcer state because these seem to offer the only means of exercising ultimate control over the experts to whom enforcing tasks are delegated. . . .

By a converse chain of reasoning, expert or scientific judgments become wholly inappropriate in generating outcomes in the productive state, and democratic procedures become necessary. The question of 'form' becomes all important here, and, of course, the productive state is that aspect of government that spends billions, allegedly in promoting the 'general welfare'. The ambiguity in attempts to incorporate democracy directly into government's enforcer role is matched by that which holds that government should provide goods and services for citizens in accordance with 'social goals' or 'national priorities' rather than in accordance with citizens' own expressed desires. This latter view is, in part, fostered by the practical necessity of bureaucratic discretion and by the intellectual failure to distinguish procedural and substantive norms.

The costs of decision-making guarantee that wide discretionary powers rest with bureaucratic personnel. Representative assemblies, themselves already one stage removed from constituency demands, can scarcely vote separately on detailed items in a multipurpose budget. Allocative decisions are necessarily shifted to the executive branch, to the bureaucracy, and without criteria for determining citizenry evaluation, the temptation to introduce 'experts' is strong. For those allocative decisions within his power, how is the bureaucrat to choose? On his private, personal preferences? Or, on the introduction of some presumed judgment of 'general welfare' or 'public interest'? . . . As noted, governmental process here must be interpreted as a surrogate for a complex exchange among all citizens in the community. To the extent that this interpretation mirrors reality, all outcomes that are reached through agreed-on and efficient procedures for decision-making become equally acceptable. When it is recognized, however, that governmental process must include departures from any rules that would be fully analogous to voluntary exchanges, it is difficult to maintain a stance of full neutrality as among possible alternatives. . . .

MAJORITY VOTING UNDER BENEFIT–COST CONSTRAINTS

The most familiar decision rule, both in the analytical models of political process and in existing historical structures that are appropriately classified as 'democratic', is that of majority voting. We may assume that some constitutional structure exists, a structure that defines individual property rights and enforces contracts among persons and, further, requires that all collective or governmental decisions secure the majority of the representatives of citizens in some legislative assembly. Even in this formulation we have, by assumption, already bypassed a significant part of the issue being discussed. At the stage of constitutional contract, when individual rights are initially defined, few persons would conceptually agree to wholly unconstrained departures from a unanimity rule for collective decision-making. The reason is, of course, that once an individual's consent is not required for a decision that will be enforced upon him, the individual holds no protection of his own nominal assignment of claims, no guarantees that his rights will not be exploited on behalf of others in the name of governmental objectives. At the same time that a collective decision rule, say that of majority voting, is adopted, procedural limits on the exercise of this rule may be incorporated into the constitutional document or understanding. Experience indicates, however, that the procedural limits incorporated in constitutional structures historically have not been very effective in curbing the appetites of majority coalitions.

Nonetheless, it will be useful for analysis to develop the argument in two stages. In the first, we assume that an economically meaningful constraint on majority decision exists. Assume that a constitutional provision requires that all proposals for public or governmental outlay satisfy a benefit–cost criterion; gross benefits must exceed gross project costs, regardless of the array of votes in the legislative assembly.

We want to look at public-goods proposals that do not benefit all members of the group sufficiently to offset fully tax costs, but which do, nonetheless, meet the benefit–cost criterion imposed. If, for example, in a three-person group there should be only two beneficiaries of a project costing $100, and if each of these beneficiaries expects to secure a value of $51, the proposal would meet the benefit–cost criterion no matter how costs are distributed. If the costs are equally distributed among all members, say, by a general tax, the proposal would secure majority approval. The effect would be to impose net losses on the minority. The benefit–cost constraint guarantees, however, that if compensation should be required, the majority could arrange to secure minority acquiescence with appropriate side payments. Another way of saying this is to state that the benefit–cost criterion insures that all spending projects are 'efficient' in the strict economic meaning of this term. . . .

If each and every proposal for spending funds governmentally is required to meet the efficiency criterion, . . . it would seem that the test could also be met by the aggregate of all projects. . . .

MAJORITY VOTING WITHOUT BENEFIT–COST CONSTRAINTS

If we drop the arbitrary requirement that all proposals for spending publicly collected revenues meet criteria of economic efficiency, it is evident that majority voting rules for reaching collective or group decisions will produce at least some budgetary components that are inefficient in net. Some projects that will secure majority approval will yield less in total benefits than they cost. The minority will suffer net losses from these projects, and these losses will exceed the benefits secured for members of the majority. In a regime with costless side payments, the minority could bribe the majority so as to prevent the approval of all such projects. But when the absence of effective side payments is acknowledged, the existence of inefficient spending projects can hardly be questioned. . . .

. . . The majority voting model discussed above suggests that inefficient budgetary projects may secure approval if considered separately, but that, at a minimum, the estimated value of benefits from any proposal to the members of an effective majority coalition must exceed the tax costs borne by those members. Even this minimal constraint on budgetary inefficiency is not operative, however, when logrolling[2] can take place among divergent minorities to produce effective majority coalitions on a subgroup of budgetary items. . . .

INDIVIDUAL RIGHTS IN DEMOCRACY

A necessary step in the process of genuine constitutional revolution is a *consensual redefinition* of individual rights and claims. Many of the interventions of government have emerged precisely because of ambiguities in the definition of individual rights. The central issue here concerns the reconciliation of nominally expressed claims by individuals to private property, to human as well as nonhuman capital, and the equalitarian distribution of the 'public property rights' through the voting franchise. Whether treated as value or as fact, modern democracy incorporates universal adult suffrage. From this elementary base, several questions arise. How can the poor man (with 'poor' defined in terms of private-property claims) exert his putative claims to the wealth nominally held by the rich man except through exercise of his voting franchise? Acknowledging this, how can the rich man (or the libertarian philosopher) expect the poor man to accept any new constitutional order that severely restricts the scope for fiscal transfers among groups? Consensual support for such restriction could scarcely be predicted to be forthcoming. This need not, however,

[2] [*Editors' note*: the process of trading votes, so that a coalition agrees to vote 'insincerely' on a number of issues: see R. Sugden, *The Political Economy of Public Choice* (1981), pp. 182–5.]

suggest that all attempts at renegotiation of the basic constitutional structure should be abandoned before they commence. There may well exist potential gains-from-trade for all participants, but the existing as well as the prospective distribution of rights and claims must inform the bargaining process. The rich man, who may sense the vulnerability of his nominal claims in the existing state of affairs and who may, at the same time, desire that the range of collective or state action be restricted, can potentially agree on a once-and-for-all or quasi-permanent transfer of wealth to the poor man, a transfer made in exchange for the latter's agreement to a genuinely new constitution that will overtly limit governmentally directed fiscal transfers. . . .

THE CREATION OF RIGHTS

Assume that the problems of income and wealth distribution among persons could be satisfactorily settled in a renegotiated constitutional contract, one that would redefine individual rights and reduce the scope for collectively determined coercive activity. Would this basic step be sufficient to allow for the implementation of laissez-faire principles? If property rights should be redefined so that distributional results are acceptable to all participants, would the operations of private markets, with minimal collective enforcement of contracts, be sufficient to insure efficient outcomes, to remove the social dilemma? A negative answer is immediately suggested with reference to the many problems summarized under the rubrics: congestion, pollution, environmental quality. Here the issues are specifically not distributional, or at least not exclusively or predominantly so. The alleged failures of existing social arrangements in many of these situations cannot legitimately be attributed to markets or to government, if we think of these as alternative processes of postconstitutional contracting. The social dilemma reflected in apparent results here stems from incomplete constitutional agreement, from first-stage failure to define and to limit individual rights. Resolution of this dilemma lies not in any explicit redistribution of rights among persons, not in some reshuffling of claims, but in the *creation* of newly defined rights in areas where none now exist, at least none that can offer a basis for predictability and exchange. In essence, congestion and pollution describe settings analogous to that generalized in Hobbes's model of anarchy. Individuals find themselves in conflict over the use of scarce resources, with results that are desired by no one because there is no agreed-on and enforced set of rights. The constitutional revolution suggested involves mutual agreement on those restrictions on behavior that are required to achieve tolerably efficient outcomes. . . .

Idealized constitutional revolution here would require that limits be placed on behavior with respect to *all* scarce resources, whether this be in the form of assigning individual ownership titles or of imposing restrictive behavioral limits under common titles. Much of the dilemma summarized under the pollution rubric finds its origins in the presumption made by the founders of our constitutional-legal order that certain resources were in permanent abundance. Growth and technological advance have converted once-free resources into scarce resources, but existing property assignments have failed to keep pace. The resulting dilemma was predictable. This alone suggests that genuine constitutional change must take place as population grows, as technology develops, and as demand shifts through time.

Notes

1. The study of constitutions and politics has become an important new branch of economics; its origins can be traced to the study of public finance by continental scholars (cf. R. Musgrave and A. Peacock, *Classics in the Theory of Public Finance* (1958)). For a survey of the literature, see D. C. Mueller, 'Public Choice: A Survey' (1976) 14 J. Econ. Lit. 395, and *Public Choice* (1979). It has been slower to develop in Britain (though see Institute of Economic Affairs, *The Economics of Politics* (1978); A. Peacock, *The Economic Analysis of Government* (1979); and R. Sugden, *The Political Economy of Public Choice* (1981)). Buchanan has attributed this neglect to the continuing strength here of Benthamite utilitarianism with its 'idealised objectives' for government policy and its disregard of institutional structure. 'In Britain', he concludes, 'you surely held on longer than most people to the romantic notion that government seeks only to do good in some hazily defined Benthamite sense, and, furthermore, to the hypothesis that government could, in fact, accomplish most of what it set out to do' (Institute of Economic Affairs, op. cit., pp. 3–4).

2. The public choice literature proceeds, as does conventional economic analysis, from an assumption of individuals as self-interested utility-maximizers (cf. G. Brennan and J. Buchanan, 'The Normative Purpose of Economic "Science": Rediscovery of an Eighteenth Century Method' (1981) 1 Int. Rev. Law and Econ. 155): 'common interest' cannot motivate choice except where small groups, such as clubs, are involved (M. Olson, *The Logic of Collective Action* (1971)). It has been suggested that a basis for rational preferences may be found in the idea of *commitment*, where individuals identify with the aims of a particular group or movement (A. K. Sen, 'Rational Fools: A Critique of the Behavioural Foundations of Economic Theory' (1977) 6 Philosophy and Public Affairs 317), but even this extension of the traditional self-interest hypothesis falls well short of providing a framework for public decisionmaking. Given the huge variety of, and contradiction between, individual preferences, it would seem to be impossible institutionally to arrange social choice in such a way as to maximize social

welfare: K. J. Arrow, 'Values and Collective Decisionmaking' in P. Laslett and W. G. Runciman (eds.), *Philosophy, Politics and Society* (1967).

3. Buchanan's method of escaping from the impasse is by reference to contracts, the technique used with apparent success in a market context – the notion is similar to that employed by Rawls in his *Theory of Justice* (1971), and by Posner in his efforts to justify ethically efficient, non-consensual rules of law by the notion of 'ex-ante compensation': 'The Ethical and Political Basis of the Efficiency Norm is Common Law Adjudication' (1980) 8 Hofstra. L.R. 487, 492–9. The device is intended to offer protection against the weaknesses of typical democratic constitutions which emerge from the public choice analysis of the 'political market' (see, with applications to the British system, G. Tullock, *The Vote Motive* (1976)). From this perspective, legislation is the commodity supplied in response to demand by those individuals and groups who can pay for the commodity by electoral votes and other forms of political support. The simple-majority voting rule of the legislature not only enables the majority to impose costs on minorities but also may lead to excessive public expenditure, when the benefits which accrue to interests represented by the majority are exceeded by the losses imposed on those represented by the minority (G. Tullock, 'Problems on Majority Voting' (1959) 67 J. Pol. Econ. 571). Buchanan's 'ideal' constitution would involve a protection of rights to scarce resources against expropriation by the legislature. See, further, J. M. Buchanan and G. Tullock, *The Calculus of Consent: Logical Foundations of Constitutional Democracy* (1962).

4. The implications of public choice theory of this kind for British constitutiuonal law (cf. Peacock, op. cit., ch. 5 and pp. 114–16 and C. K. Rowley, in *The Economics of Politics*, op. cit., pp. 39–40) has led to proposals for: (a) proportional representation; (b) political decentralization; (c) the institution of some general rule requiring that public expenditure should not exceed a fixed percentage of the gross national product; (d) a Bill of Rights to protect minorities.

5. There are a number of difficulties to which these theories give rise. (a) As a *positive* analysis of the political process, are they convincing? Can the very existence of the Welfare State be explained without regard to a notion of 'caring' or 'social concern'? (cf. A. Culyer, *The Political Economy of Social Policy* (1980), pp. 57–71.) (b) It is hard to conceive of unanimous consent being given to a 'constitutional contract' which defines rights and lays down procedural limits on interference with those rights; even if such unanimity were to exist, why should future generations feel bound to accept the principles laid down by their ancestors? (cf. T. Nagel, 'Rawls on Justice' (1973) 82 Philosophical Rev. 220). (c) The entrenchment of rights of this kind in a constitutional form would give rise to acute problems of interpretation and enforcement which would confer considerable power on the judiciary. Public choice theorists express faith in the independence and impartiality of judges, primarily because, unlike legislators (and, it is assumed, bureaucrats) they do not stand to gain materially from the outcome of decisions: see R. Posner, *Economic Analysis of Law* (2nd edn, 1977), ch. 19. But this fails

to take account of the fact that, at least in Britain, the structure of the legal professions may lead to judges being selected from only a narrow section of the community, with a consequent risk of ideological bias (cf. J. Griffith, *The Politics of the Judiciary* (2nd edn, 1981)) and their very insularity from political pressures may enable that bias to be reflected in the decisionmaking process.

B. Legal Rulemaking

I. EHRLICH and R. A. POSNER

*

An Economic Analysis of Legal Rulemaking[3]

If we want to prevent driving at excessive speeds, one approach is to post specific speed limits and to declare it unlawful per se to exceed those limits; another is to eschew specific speed limits and simply declare that driving at unreasonable speeds is unlawful. Any choice along the specificity-generality continuum will generate a unique set of costs and benefits. This article discusses the conditions under which greater specificity or greater generality is the efficient choice and makes a preliminary effort to appraise the efficiency of the choices actually made by the legal process. . . .

I. PRELIMINARY ISSUES

To facilitate exposition, we will sometimes treat the specificity-generality continuum as if it were a dichotomy between 'rules' and 'standards'. The term 'standard' denotes in our usage a general criterion of social choice; efficiency (and its counterparts in legal terminology, such as reasonableness) is an example. A standard indicates the kinds of circumstances that are relevant to a decision on legality and is thus open-ended. That is, it is not a list of all the circumstances that might be relevant but is rather the criterion by which particular circumstances presented in a case are judged to be relevant or not. . . .

A rule withdraws from the decision maker's consideration one or more of the circumstances that would be relevant to decision according to a standard. . . . The simplest kind of rule, then, takes the form: if X, then Y, where X is a single, simple, determinate fact (*e.g.*, the car's

---

[3] (1974) 3 J. Legal Stud. 257–80, with omissions. Copyright © 1974 by the University of Chicago. All rights reserved. Reprinted by permission of the authors and the University of Chicago Press.

speed) and Y is a definite, unequivocal legal consequence – a judgment of liability or nonliability – that follows directly from proof of X (*e.g.*, driver has violated traffic code). It should be clear, therefore, that we are using the term 'rule' in a somewhat special sense; 'general rule' would be a contradiction in our usage.

The difference between a rule and a standard is a matter of degree – the degree of precision. The efficiency standard itself could be regarded as a rule of social choice designed to implement a broader standard (the greatest happiness of the greatest number of people), while a rule that required the weighing of many circumstances (unlike our hypothetical . . . rule, which required the weighing of only one, distance) would be like a standard. Our fundamental concern is with precision of law rather than with choosing between rule and standard as such.

II. THE OPTIMUM PRECISION OF LEGAL OBLIGATION: A STATIC ANALYSIS

We shall consider in this part the benefits and costs associated with different choices along the continuum between the highly specific rule and the highly general standard and discuss the optimum choice – the choice that maximizes the excess of benefits over costs. . . .

Several points should be kept in mind throughout the analysis.

Rules are addressed to two audiences: people who might violate (or be accused of violating) the law, and participants in the process of determining whether a violation has occurred (judges, lawyers, etc.). The effects of the choice between rule and standard on the first group we shall call effects on 'primary behavior', as contrasted with the effects of the choice on law enforcement and other activities of the legal system.

The legislature's choice whether to enact a standard or a set of precise rules is implicitly also a choice between legislative and judicial rulemaking. A general legislative standard creates a demand for specification. This demand is brought to bear on the courts through the litigation process and they respond by creating rules particularizing the legislative standard. Thus an appraisal of the efficiency of a legislative decision to enact a standard requires consideration of the differences in costs and benefits between legislative rules and judge-made rules (precedents). . . .

A. Elements of the Model

Benefits of Rules. a. *Primary behavior.* A perfectly detailed and comprehensive set of rules brings society nearer to its desired allocation of resources by discouraging socially undesirable activities and encouraging socially desirable ones. This is because detailing the law efficiently (the importance of this qualification will become clear later) results in an increase in the expected gain from engaging in socially desirable activity relative to that from engaging in undesirable activity.

It does this by increasing the (subjective) probabilities that the undesirable activity is punishable and that the desirable is not. The cost of an activity includes any expected punishment costs. The expected punishment cost of engaging in an activity is the product of (1) the subjective probability of the participant's being apprehended and convicted and (2) the cost to him of the penalty that will be imposed if he is convicted. The probability of apprehension and conviction, in turn, is the product of (1) the probability that the activity in which the person is engaged will be deemed illegal and (2) the probability that, if so, he will be charged and convicted for his participation in it. The more (efficiently) precise and detailed the applicable substantive standard or rule is, the higher is the probability that the activity will be deemed illegal if it is in fact undesirable (the kind of activity the legislature wanted to prevent) and the lower is the probability that the activity will be deemed illegal if it is in fact desirable. Thus the expected punishment cost of undesirable activity is increased and that of desirable activity reduced. . . .

The 'chilling' of socially valuable behavior by an uncertain law is a potentially serious problem whenever criminal penalties are involved. This may explain why the Constitution has been interpreted to require greater specificity in criminal than in civil statutes. Not only do criminal sanctions tend to be severe (costly) but it is normally impossible to purchase insurance against criminal liability. The average individual can avoid the risk of being subjected to a criminal penalty only by avoiding criminal activity. But if what constitutes criminal activity is uncertain this is not enough: he can eliminate the risk only by avoiding, in addition to clearly criminal behavior, all other behavior that is within the penumbra of the vague standard. And he may very well do this, even though the penumbral activity is quite valuable privately as well as socially: a rational individual, especially if he is risk averse, may incur heavy costs to avoid even a slight risk of criminal punishment. Thus the social costs of vague criminal standards might be high.

b. *Legal-system behavior.* Here we consider the benefits of greater precision of legal obligation in terms of its effects on behavior within the legal system.

(1) An increase in precision increases the probability of convicting the guilty and of acquitting the innocent ('guilty' here meaning engaged in socially undesirable activities and 'innocent' engaged in

socially desirable activities). Stated differently, it increases the marginal productivity of expenditures by the law enforcer (public or private) on prosecuting the guilty, reduces the marginal productivity of his expenditures on prosecuting the innocent, reduces the marginal productivity of the guilty defendant's litigation expenditures, and increases the marginal productivity of the innocent defendant's litigation expenditures. The combination of these effects should induce an increase in prosecutorial resources in cases involving guilty defendants, a decrease in defendants' expenditures in those cases, an increase in defense expenditures in cases where the defendant is in fact innocent, and a decrease in prosecutorial expenditures in those cases. The net result should be a further increase in the probability of convicting the guilty and of acquitting the innocent, resulting in a further increase in the efficiency of primary behavior.

(2) The reduction in the amount of socially undesirable activity brought about both directly and (through the greater efficiency of law enforcement expenditures) indirectly by rule precision should reduce the total number of cases brought and hence the total amount of resources devoted to legal dispute resolution. In addition, fewer cases will be brought that arise out of socially desirable activities. Also, the sum of the parties' expenditures in those cases that are litigated may be lower. This is because a rule withdraws from a lawsuit many of the issues that would have been litigable were the case decided under a standard and it seems likely that there are diminishing – often very rapidly diminishing – returns to proof of a point.

(3) If a legal dispute occurs, the fact that the outcome of the dispute, if it is litigated, will be determined by application of a rule rather than a standard should make it easier for the parties to predict the outcome. According to the economic analysis of the settlement of legal disputes out of court, an increase in the predictability of the outcome of litigation should result in an increase in the settlement rate. Since the costs of litigating are generally higher than the costs of settling a dispute out of court, an increase in the settlement rate (at least within a broad range) should reduce the total costs of legal dispute resolution. . . .

When the rules in question are judicial rather than statutory, our conclusion that decision by rule reduces the costs of the legal process must be qualified. Precedents are produced by activity of lawyers and judges in court. This is a costly activity, and although the rules produced yield, as we have seen, reductions in outlays on the courts, the net cost of judicial rulemaking must be positive – otherwise the optimum number of such rules would be infinite.

(4) The choice of rule versus standard affects the speed, and hence indirectly the costs and benefits, of legal dispute resolution. Because of

the sequential character of a trial, an increase in the number of issues to be litigated will lengthen the trial. Decision by standard therefore increases the interval between an incident giving rise to a legal dispute and final judicial resolution of the dispute. The principal effects, so far as relevant here, are to increase the costs of legal error through the effect of delay in causing evidence to decay and to foster settlements in some classes of cases.

(5) Rules reduce the costs of organizing and communicating information for use in resolving legal disputes. A rule that the driver of the following car is liable in a rear-end collision amounts to saying that since experience has shown that the driver of that car can usually avert the collision at moderate cost, the benefits of determining the question still another time are likely to be less than the costs of doing so. The rule summarizes what has been learned in the prior adjudications. . . .

(6) Decision according to rule facilitates the social control of decision makers. Where the correct outcome of a litigation is highly uncertain due to the number of circumstances that must be weighed and the uncertain weight of each, detection of an incompetent or corrupt outcome is more difficult. . . .

The Costs of Legal Rules. Several different sorts of cost are associated with greater precision of legal obligation. Some of these costs arise from the fact that making law more precise often involves making it more detailed in order to minimize the costs of overinclusion and underinclusion, which, as we are about to see, are generated by precise rules.

a. Obtaining and correctly evaluating information concerning the various combinations of events or circumstances under which the general standard that the set of rules is designed to implement should be activated are costly. The cost is presumably greater the more heterogeneous the conduct sought to be regulated. . .

b. Formulating a rule, once the appropriate scope of the desired prohibition has been determined, involves a cost. This cost, we conjecture, is greatest when the rule is a statutory rule and the conduct to be regulated is politically controversial. The formulation of a statutory rule requires negotiation among the legislators. This makes legislative production an extremely expensive form of production . . . The costs of negotiation will be even higher when a proposed rule is controversial, that is, costly to a politically effective segment of the community.

Transaction costs tend to increase rapidly with the number of parties whose agreement is necessary for the transaction to occur. This suggests that there are practical limits to increasing the size of a legislature. Hence . . . as the amount and complexity of social activity increase over time, we can expect to find that legislatures, rather than expanding, will delegate more and more of the legislative function to bodies that do not produce rules through negotiation among a large number of people – *i.e.*, to executive and administrative agencies and to courts – as has in fact happened. We are similarly led to predict that delegation will be less common in systems (such as the British) where party discipline in the legislature is tight and the legislature is (effectively) unicameral; both circumstances reduce the costs of arriving at agreement on legislation. A related prediction, one also supported by at least casual observation, is that over time judicial interpretation of statutes will become more flexible. As the costs of legislative enactment increase, courts will be more reluctant to apply principles of strict statutory construction, which have the effect of confining to the legislature the task of keeping statutes up to date.

c. Greater specificity of legal obligation generates allocative inefficiency as a result of the necessarily imperfect fit between the coverage of a rule and the conduct sought to be regulated. . . . The inherent ambiguity of language and the limitations of human foresight and knowledge limit the practical ability of the rulemaker to catalog accurately and exhaustively the circumstances that should activate the general standard. Hence the reduction of a standard to a set of rules must in practice create both overinclusion and underinclusion. Some conduct is prohibited that would be permitted if the standard that the rules are designed to implement were applied directly to it; other conduct is permitted that would be prohibited under a direct application of the standard. Both effects impose social costs similar to those that an indefinite standard imposes since, as we saw earlier, such a standard, *in application*, will both over- and underinclude. . . .

Our discussion of overinclusion requires two qualifications. First, where the sanction for violation of a legal rule or standard imposes on the violator a cost just equal to the social costs of the violation – simple damages in tort or contract actions approximate such a sanction – socially valuable violations will not be deterred. A rule that makes injurers liable for all of their accidents whether or not they are negligent (strict liability) should not deter them from engaging in behavior that results in nonnegligent (efficient) accidents, since, by definition, their liability will be less than the benefits they obtain from such activity. The rule may have inefficient consequences because the right to be compensated for all accidental injuries may reduce the safety incentives of potential victims below the efficient level. However, this consequence results not from the substitution of a rule for a standard but from the form of the sanction – payment of damages to people injured by the violation. Were the sanction payment of the damages to the state rather than to victims, the inefficient consequences of substituting a rule for a standard would disappear. . . .

Another respect in which our analysis of overinclusion needs to be qualified involves situations where the costs of transactions among the people subject to the rule are low. An example of a rule operating in such a context is the Statute of Frauds, which provides that certain types of contract (*e.g.*, for the sale of land) are unenforceable unless reduced to writing. If the criterion for enforcing contracts for the sale of land were a reasonableness or efficiency standard, many oral land contracts would have to be enforced as expressing the true intentions of the parties. But it does not follow that the Statute of Frauds frustrates many valuable transactions. Since prospective contracting parties can assure enforcement by making a written contract, the major cost associated with the Statute of Frauds, viewed as an over-inclusive rule, is not the prevention of valuable transactions but the legal and negotiating expenses necessary to comply with the rule. These expenses are probably modest. The major benefit is a reduction in the cost of resolving contract disputes. The cost of proving the existence and terms of a contract is reduced; the probability of an erroneous decision is reduced; and the predictability of the outcome of contract litigation is increased. . . .

d. We have thus far emphasized costs incurred in the production of rules and in people's adaptive behavior toward rules. Another (albeit overlapping) type of cost is the cost of hiring experts – lawyers – to advise and counsel on compliance with the law and to operate tribunals and represent the parties before them when a legal dispute arises.

It might appear that rules, by reducing the law's uncertainty, would reduce the demand for experts in its interpretation. It is true that the substitution of rules for standards may reduce the number of legal disputes and hence the demand for trial lawyers. But the conduct of litigation is a relatively minor source of the legal profession's income. So far as the much more important activity of lawyers in counseling and advising is concerned, the substitution of rules for standards may increase the demand for lawyers' services. . . .

The demand for lawyers is affected not only by the choice between rule and standard but also by whether the rule is statutory or judge-made. Precedents, unlike statutory rules, are typically implicit rather than explicit rules. Higher levels of ability and training are required to master implicit rules. Hence we predict that lawyers will be more numerous and better paid in countries where many legal rules take the form of precedents – such as the United States – and also that competition with lawyers from members of other professions will be more intense in areas of the law characterized by explicit rules, as we observe with accountants in the tax area.

e. We have assumed up to now that an increase in the specificity of a legal prohibition always increases the certainty of the prohibition. This is incorrect; it may reduce it, thereby imposing the sorts of cost usually associated with standards. Compare the following alternative methods of defining the crime of statutory rape: sexual intercourse with a female under 16; sexual intercourse with a female who the defendant knows or should know is under 16. The first rule is more precise on its face than the second, but more uncertain in its application to primary behavior because it may be hard for potential defendants to determine age accurately. The first rule may induce the defendant (especially if risk averse) to confine his attentions to females obviously much older than 16. Observe, however, that it imparts greater certainty than the second rule to the litigation process since, in a legal proceeding, the female's actual age can be ascertained more readily than the defendant's knowledge. As we saw earlier, greater certainty at the litigation stage indirectly increases the efficiency of primary behavior. So the costs of the first rule may be lower than the costs of the second rule after all.

This example makes clear that precision can be measured only by reference to whom the rule is addressed to. It may be precise to one audience (adjudicators), imprecise to another (potential violators). The example also suggests an additional point about the costs of overinclusion: they may be low if the lawful conduct deterred (here, intercourse with females who look younger than 16 but are not) is not considered socially very valuable.

B. Implications of the Model

A fundamental implication of the model is that anything that increases the benefits, or reduces the costs, of legal precision, other things remaining the same, will increase the optimum number (precision) of rules. It follows that if economic optimality is important to the actual choices made by society in designing a legal system, we can expect to find (1) more efficient (optimally precise) rules in the criminal area, (2) more overinclusive rules in areas where the sanction is simple damages or where transaction costs are low, and (3) more rules in areas where the relevant primary behavior is homogeneous. . . .

The model also yields a number of implications with respect to the allocation of rulemaking between the legislative and judicial branches of government. . . .

A necessary condition of equilibrium in the formal model is that the marginal cost of statutory rules exceed that of judge-made rules. This is because the marginal benefits of statutory rules tend to be greater. Since part of the social cost of any rule is the cost resulting from imperfect specificity, this condition implies that perfect specificity is less likely to be attained in statutory than in judge-made rules, which corresponds to observation. The greater costs of statutory rules may also explain why such rules are generally more difficult to revise or modify than judge-made rules – assuming, reasonably, that the costs of revising a rule are similar to those of creating a new rule.

The model also implies that an increase in the marginal cost of producing statutory rules will lead to a reduction in the optimal number of statutory rules and an increase in the optimal number of judge-made rules. This has interesting consequences for a class of rules that we have ignored thus far – those promulgated by executive or administrative bodies. Assuming that the cost of such rules is lower than that of statutory rules, we would expect administrative rules to be more detailed, and leave less room for supplementary judge-made rules, than statutory rules, and again this appears to be a true description of the real legal system. In a complete analysis, the substitution effects on private rules would also have to be considered; but we exclude private rules from our analysis. . . .

Lastly, the model demonstrates why the process of deciding a case is, in practice, generally *not* one of searching for the optimal resolution of the conflict giving rise to the dispute. Such an approach would imply that decision was always by general standard (*e.g.*, efficiency) rather than by rule, and would be extremely costly. The use of rules to approximate the results that would be reached by case-by-case cost–benefit analyses is fully consistent with the view that the legal system has as a primary goal the maximization of efficiency. . . .

III. THE DYNAMICS OF LEGAL RULES

Thus far we have largely ignored the costs and benefits associated with the time dimension of legal regulation. Clearly, however, the efficient (or just) solution to a problem may change over time with changes in the economic and technological factors shaping the problem. For example, the development of the air brake, the spark arrester, the electric crossing signal, the steel car, and other railroad safety devices successively altered the relative costs of accident avoidance by railroads and by potential victims of railroad accidents, obsoleting rules of railroad accident law based on the relative costs of avoidance by injurer and by victim as they had existed prior to the development of the safety devices in question. An important cost of legal regulation by means of rules is thus the cost of altering rules to keep pace with economic and technological change.

Obsolescence is not so serious a problem with regulation by standard. Standards are relatively unaffected by changes over time in the circumstances in which they are applied, since a standard does not specify the circumstances relevant to decision or the weight of each circumstance but merely indicates the kinds of circumstance that are relevant. . . .

In general, the more detailed a rule is, the more often it will have to be changed. The greater detailedness of a very precise rule is thus also a source of additional costs, the costs of changing rules. These include the costs, discussed earlier, of producing the new rule plus additional costs arising from the fact that change in the law is a source of uncertainty. A transaction may be subject to a precise and definite rule but if there is a possibility that the rights of the parties to the transaction will in fact be determined by application of a different rule those rights are uncertain. Another name for uncertainty in this context is imperfect precision: if a rule can be changed, one can no longer say definitely that if circumstance X is present, legal consequence Y will follow. Thus the greater the amount of detail in a rule, the lower will be the costs of imperfect precision in one respect and the higher they will be in another.

The rule of stare decisis, which requires that a court adhere to precedent, is founded, in part anyway, on an awareness of the costs in uncertainty of changing rules. Courts in this country do not follow the rule rigidly. It would be highly inefficient for them to do so. As a precedent 'ages', a point is eventually reached at which the social costs generated by its imperfect fit with current reality exceed the benefits of having minimized uncertainty as to which rule would be followed. The principal effect of rigid adherence to stare decisis would therefore be to increase the demand for statutory rulemaking regardless of relative cost. Until very recently, the English courts did follow the rule of stare decisis rigidly, but the costs of such adherence were lower for the English than they would have been for Americans if, as suggested earlier, the costs of statutory rulemaking are lower in England than in America. . . .

The analysis of the dynamics of legal rules may help explain why the number of legal rules has evidently grown over time, at least in the period since the Industrial Revolution. The great increase in the volume of economic activity has increased the costs both of failing to deter socially undesirable activity and of deterring socially desirable activity. This should, by our earlier analysis, have increased the demand for, and hence the quantity supplied of, rules unless the costs of rulemaking have risen equally rapidly.

The dynamic analysis may also explain why the relative importance of legislatures and especially of agencies in the production of rules has grown over time. . . . Judicial processes are ill suited to the rapid alteration of rules. The delays of the judicial process, coupled with its dependence on a sequential sampling process (described earlier) for the formulation of rules, produce significant lags in judicial response to changing conditions. These lags, more serious in a rapidly changing than in a slowly changing society, may not infect legislative (or non-judicialized executive or administrative) processes to the same degree. A factor working in the same direction is that judicial rulemaking activity lays a foundation for inexpensive legislative rulemaking: legislatures often adopt (codify) the rules made by the courts. The costs of statutory production in this form are presumably low; the benefits, which consist of replacing implicit by explicit rules and hence increasing the certainty of legal obligation and reducing the demand for lawyers' services, may be substantial.

We must also consider, however, the increase over time in the cost of statutory rulemaking brought about by the fact, emphasized earlier in this paper, that legislatures cannot be expanded to handle a rising workload without very sharp increases in the costs of enactment. This problem has been met by increased delegation to administrative agencies (as well as by more flexible principles of statutory construction on the part of both courts and agencies). The importance of agencies, relative to courts, as sources of rules has increased dramatically, and this is consistent with the view that society is seeking to adapt to changes over time in the relative costs of different methods of producing rules.

Notes

1. The nature of legal rulemaking, in particular the tension created by the competing demands for certainty and flexibility, has been the subject of a considerable doctrinal literature (see, esp. L. M. Friedman, 'Legal Rules and the Process of Social Change' (1967) 19 Stan. L.R. 786). Though generalizations of judicial behaviour are notoriously difficult, it seems clear that judicial attitudes have altered significantly over time (cf. P. S. Atiyah, *From Principles to Pragmatism* (1978) – the view that English judges are now less concerned to lay down specific rules governing common law rights gains further support from two important recent decisions of the House of Lords on the limits of negligence: *McLoughlin* v. *O'Brian* [1982] 2 All E.R. 298 and *Junior Books Ltd.* v. *Veitchi* [1982] 3 All E.R. 201).

2. In analysing the economic implications of the problem, Ehrlich and Posner concentrate on rules as providing guidelines for behaviour and their model suggests, in particular, that while greater specificity typically reduces transaction costs, this benefit must be weighed against the social costs arising from overinclusion (the deterrence of desirable activities) and underinclusion (the failure to deter undesirable activities). A. I. Ogus, ('Quantitative Rules and Judicial Decision Making' in P. Burrows and C. Veljanovski (eds.), *The Economic Approach to Law* (1981), ch. 9) applies the model to two areas of judicial rulemaking in English law, and seeks to show that judges move

towards an apparently optimal degree of specificity through an iterative process. This contrasts with the prediction expressed in L. M. Friedman, *The Legal System: A Social Science Perspective* (1975), p. 292, that 'living rules of law will move towards objectivity as part of their life cycle . . . they tend towards mechanical, quantitative forms. They have a theoretical resting point at which they are perfectly quantitative or mechanical'.

3. It should, however, also be recognized that the form of legal rules will be influenced by objectives other than behavioural guidance. In some cases, this will be less important than the institutional goal of resolving the conflict between the parties to the litigation, for which purpose notions of procedural or distributional justice may take priority: infra, Notes to Section C. From a broader perspective, Kennedy has argued that while specific rules in private law typically serve economic, individualist, aims, the responsiveness of different sections of the community to such rules will vary (responsiveness being a function, *inter alia*, of information and wealth) and that altruistic concerns may, therefore, explain a greater generality of legal principle: 'Form and Substance in Private Law Adjudication' (1976) 89 Harv. L.R. 1685.

4. The choice between generality and precision has important implications for the enforcement of public law (K. C. Davis, *Discretionary Justice: A Preliminary Inquiry* (1969); J. L. Jowell, *Law and Bureaucracy* (1975), ch. 5). If a regulatory goal (e.g. the socially optimal level of pollution) requires different behavioural limits for different groups of individuals or firms, then, in terms of administrative costs, it is cheaper for enforcement agencies to individualize enforcement strategy under a general standard than for legislatures or bureaucracies to impose precise, differentiated rules. But the benefits derived from this approach must be weighed against the difficulties experienced by those who are regulated in predicting the levels of enforcement and the problem of rendering the agency accountable legally or politically. See G. M. Richardson and A. I. Ogus, 'The Regulatory Approach to Environmental Control' (1979) 2 Urban Law and Policy 337.

C. Civil Procedure

R. A. POSNER

*

Economic Analysis of Law[4]

THE ECONOMIC GOALS OF THE PROCEDURAL SYSTEM

The goal of a procedural system, viewed economically, is to minimize the sum of two types of cost. The first is the cost of erroneous judicial

---

[4] From *Economic Analysis of Law* (2nd edn., 1977), ch. 21, with omissions. Reprinted by permission of Little, Brown and Company.

decisions. Suppose the expected cost of a particular type of accident is 100 and the cost to the potential injurer of avoiding it is 90 (the cost of avoidance by the victim, we will assume, is greater than 100). If the potential injurer is subject to either a negligence or a strict liability standard, he will avoid the accident – assuming the standard is administered accurately. But suppose that in 15 percent of the cases in which an accident occurs, the injurer can expect to avoid liability because of erroneous factual determinations by the procedural system. Then the expected cost of the accident to the injurer will fall to 85, and since this is less than the cost of avoidance, the accident will not be prevented. The result will be a net social loss of 10, will it not? Not necessarily. We must not ignore the cost of operating the procedural system. Suppose that to reduce the error rate in our example from 15 percent to anywhere below 10 percent would require an additional expenditure of 20 on the procedural system. Then efficiency tells us to tolerate the 15 percent probability of error, for the cost of error (10) is less than the cost necessary to eliminate the error cost (20), and the economic objective is to minimize the *sum* of the error and direct costs of the procedural system.

The analysis is incomplete in two important respects, however. First, whatever causes errors in favor of the industry in some cases (lying witnesses, for example) will probably also cause errors in favor of accident victims in others. . . An error that simply inflates the industry's liability in cases where it has been negligent or otherwise culpable (the accident victim convinces the court that his damages are greater than they really are) will tend to make safety equipment more valuable to the industry . . . But if the error results in the imposition of liability in circumstances where additional safety equipment would not have reduced the industry's liability (the accident may not have occurred at all, or may have been caused by someone other than a member of the industry), the industry will have no incentive to purchase additional safety equipment . . .

Second, the social cost of a reduction in the industry's incentive to avoid accidents is likely to be partially offset by the increased incentive of victims to avoid accidents. The effect . . . is to increase the expected uncompensated accident cost to victims and therefore the incentive of victims to prevent accidents. . . .

THE DECISION WHETHER TO SETTLE OR GO TO TRIAL

Since settling a dispute out of court is normally much cheaper than going to trial, the settlement rate is an important determinant of the direct costs of resolving legal disputes. . . .

That cases are ever litigated rather than settled might appear to violate the principle that when transaction costs are low, parties will voluntarily transact if a mutually beneficial transaction is possible; since the parties to a legal dispute are ordinarily just two in number, transaction costs should be low. In fact the vast majority of legal disputes *are* settled without going to trial . . . This is as economic theory would predict but we have still to explain the small fraction that go to trial.

As with any contract, a necessary (and usually . . . sufficient) condition for negotiations to succeed is that there be a price at which both parties would feel that agreement would increase their welfare. Hence settlement negotiations should fail, and litigation ensue, only if the minimum price that the plaintiff is willing to accept in compromise of his claim is greater than the maximum price that the defendant is willing to pay in satisfaction of that claim; for example, if the plaintiff won't settle for less than $10,000 and the defendant won't settle for more than $9,000, settlement negotiations will fail.

The principal determinant of each party's best settlement offer is how he expects to fare in litigation. If the plaintiff's expected gain from litigating is $10,000, he will not settle for less than $10,000 (unless perhaps he is risk averse, a complication we postpone); and if the defendant expects to lose only $9,000 if the case is litigated he will not settle for more than $9,000. Moreover, the best settlement offers will be adjusted upward by the plaintiff and downward by the defendant to reflect the costs of settlement. If those costs are, say, $500 for each party, then the plaintiff's best offer will be $10,500 and the defendant's $8,500 . . .

The expected gain (loss) from litigation depends on three factors: the judgment if the plaintiff wins, the probability of his winning, and the costs of the litigation. The plaintiff's net expected gain, under the American system where the winning party's litigation costs are not reimbursed by the loser, is the judgment if he wins discounted by his estimate of the probability that he will win, minus his litigation costs. The defendant's expected loss is the judgment if he loses discounted by his estimate of the probability of losing (or, stated otherwise, of the plaintiff's winning), plus his litigation costs . . .

The condition for litigation may be expressed symbolically, as in inequality (1), where J is the size of the judgment if the plaintiff wins, P_p is the probability of plaintiff's winning as estimated by the plaintiff and P_d is the defendant's estimate of that probability, and C and S are the costs of litigation and of settlement, respectively, of each party. This is a very simple model because it assumes that both parties are risk neutral and that the stakes in the case, the costs of litigation, and the costs of settlement are the same for both parties; we shall relax some of these assumptions later.

The condition for litigation,

$$P_p J - C + S > P_d J + C - S \tag{1}$$

may be expressed equivalently as

$$(P_p - P_d)J > 2(C - S). \tag{2}$$

If the parties agree on the probability that the plaintiff will win in the event of litigation, the left-hand side of (2) goes to zero and the case will be settled so long as litigation costs exceed settlement costs; a fortiori will it be settled if one party is more pessimistic than the other, so that $P_p - P_d$ is negative. In general, then, litigation will occur only if both parties are optimistic about the outcome of the litigation. This formalizes our earlier point that uncertainty is a major factor in the litigation rate; a numerical example will help nail down the point. Suppose that J is \$10,000, C \$1,000, S \$100, P_p .9 and P_d .6. That is, the plaintiff thinks he has a 90 percent probability of winning but the defendant thinks plaintiff has only a 60 percent probability of winning – a divergence of estimates reflecting uncertainty about the probable outcome. Plugging these values into (2), we find that litigation will occur, because the left-hand side of (2) is \$3,000 and the right-hand side only \$1,800. In terms of (1), plaintiff's minimum settlement offer is \$8,100, and the defendant's maximum offer only \$6,900, so there is no settlement price that will make both parties consider themselves better off than if they litigate.

Inequality (2) brings out the important point that, other things being equal, the higher the stakes in a case the more likely it is to be litigated. The intuitive explanation for this result is that when the stakes are small the potential gains from litigating as perceived by the parties are also small and tend to be dominated by the higher costs of litigation relative to settlement.

Let us relax some of the assumptions underlying our simple model. Suppose the stakes in the case are not the same to both parties, perhaps because the parties have different rates at which they discount a future to a present value ... The critical question is how they diverge: inequality (1) implies that if the plaintiff's J is smaller than the defendant's, litigation is less likely than if they are the same size; it is more likely if the defendant's J is smaller than the plaintiff's.

Or suppose the parties are not risk neutral. If both parties are risk averse, the likelihood of litigation will be less ...; if the parties differ in their risk preferences, the analysis is similar to that of a difference in the stakes.

Now let us consider how particular factors, including procedural rules, might affect the settlement rate. We begin with pretrial discovery. A full exchange of the information in the possession of the parties is likely to facilitate settlement by enabling each party to form a more accurate, and generally therefore a more convergent, estimate of the likely outcome of the case; and pretrial discovery enables each party to compel his opponent to disclose relevant information in his possession. One may wonder why compulsion is necessary, since the exchange of information is a normal incident of bargaining. But such an exchange is less likely in a settlement negotiation than in an ordinary commercial transaction. If a commercial negotiation fails, the parties go their separate ways; if a settlement negotiation fails, the parties proceed to trial, at which surprise has strategic value. Each party has an incentive to withhold information at the settlement negotiation, knowing that if negotiations fail, the information will be more valuable at trial if the opponent has not had an opportunity to prepare a rebuttal to it.

A well-known study of judicial administration argues that allowing a winning plaintiff interest on the judgment from the date of accident (or other event giving rise to his claim) would not affect the settlement rate, even if the plaintiff had a higher discount rate than the defendant.[5] In fact, the addition of prejudgment interest will reduce the likelihood of a settlement whatever the discount rates. Suppose that, before the addition of interest, and ignoring for a moment litigation and settlement costs, the expected value to the plaintiff from litigating is 120, and the expected loss to the defendant is 100 (this was the example used in the cited study). If interest is added, say at an annual rate of 6 percent, for one year, the expected gain to the plaintiff will increase to 127.2 and the expected loss to the defendant to 106. The difference is larger — 21.2 instead of 20 — and this will increase the likelihood of litigation. In terms of inequality (2), the effect of interest is to make J larger. . . .

As prejudgment interest increases the likelihood of litigation by increasing the stakes, so delay would seem to reduce the likelihood of litigation by reducing the stakes, assuming that the parties have positive discount rates . . . But this conclusion must be qualified in two respects. If the defendant's discount rate is higher than the plaintiff's delay may reduce the likelihood of a settlement by causing the defendant's maximum settlement offer to shrink faster than the gap between the offers. Moreover, delay increases uncertainty as to outcome . . . which as we have seen can be expected to reduce the chances of a settlement. . . .

[5] H. Zeisel, H. Kalven and B. Buchholz, *Delay in the Court* (1959), pp. 133–6.

EXPENDITURES ON LITIGATION

If settlement negotiations fail, there is a trial for which each party purchases legal services and other litigation inputs. The purchase of such inputs increases the expected value of the litigation to the purchaser by increasing the probability that he will prevail, but at the same time increases the cost of the litigation. The party optimizes his litigation expenditures by spending up to the point where a dollar in such expenditures increases the expected value of the litigation to him by just a dollar. The process of arriving at an optimum level of expenditures is complicated, however, by two factors. First, the parties will frequently find it mutually advantageous to agree not to incur a particular expenditure (for example, by stipulating to a fact so as to obviate the need for testimony on it); since only two parties are involved in the normal lawsuit, we would expect such transactions to be frequent. Second, every expenditure decision by one party affects the expenditure decision of the other by altering the probability and hence expected value of an outcome favorable to the other party, much as every price or output change by an oligopolist alters the optimum price and output of his rivals. If we assume that each party, in deciding how much to spend on the lawsuit, takes account of the effect of his expenditures on the other party's, then . . . there is no equilibrium level of expenditures – no level at which neither party has an incentive to alter his expenditures further.

If instead we assume that neither party in deciding how much to spend takes account of the effects of his expenditures on the other party, then we must modify our earlier conclusion that divergent expectations with respect to the outcome of a case are bound to make litigation more likely. In some cases, it could have the opposite effect. If both parties are highly optimistic about the outcome, each may decide to spend very heavily on the case . . . The excess of the parties' litigation costs over their settlement costs will grow by the sum of the additional expenditures projected, but the gap between the plaintiff's mimimum settlement offer and the defendant's maximum offer may well grow more slowly because of the mutually offsetting character of their additional expenditures; if so, the likelihood of the parties' litigating rather than settling the case will decline. . . .

One thing seems reasonably clear, however, parties will tend to spend more on a litigation the greater the stakes. The expected benefit of the expenditure, as mentioned, derives from its effect in increasing the probability of a favorable outcome and is therefore magnified by any increase in the value (or cost) of the outcome. And the greater are the expected benefits of expending resources on litigation, the more, presumably, will be spent. But also the more is spent, the lower will be the probability of an erroneous result . . . Hence we would expect bigger cases, other things being equal, to be decided correctly a higher proportion of the time than smaller cases: an erroneous conviction *or* acquittal is less likely in a capital murder case than in a speeding case.

ACCESS TO LEGAL REMEDIES

The principal litigation input is lawyers' time. The cost of that time is relevant not only to the direct costs of legal dispute resolution but also to its error costs. The higher the cost of litigation to the plaintiff the larger must be his stakes in the case for him to be able to obtain legal redress. The point is not that he will be forced to settle if his litigation costs exceed his stakes (discounted by the probability of a successful outcome) but that he will not be able to obtain more than a nominal settlement because he cannot in such a case make a credible threat to litigate in the event that settlement negotiations break down. Hence, where litigation costs are high, the legal system will frequently fail to correct inefficient practices or reduce transaction costs. The resulting inefficiency may be very large even though the individual case is, by hypothesis, one in which the stakes are relatively small; the aggregate stakes involved in many small cases may be substantial.

The cost of legal services is occasionally an obstacle to vindication of a claim even when the plaintiff's stakes are very large, but here the legal profession has devised an imaginative solution. Suppose a plaintiff has a claim of $100,000 and a 50 percent probability of vindicating it. The discounted value of the claim is $50,000 and would justify him in expending up to that amount in litigation costs to protect the asset. (He is assumed in this example to be risk neutral.) But suppose the claim is his only asset. Ordinarily this would be no problem: one can borrow a substantial sum against an asset as collateral. But it is not always possible to borrow against a legal claim. Banks and other lending institutions may be risk averse (because of government regulation of financial institutions) or may find it difficult (costly) to estimate the likelihood that the claim can be established in court. These factors may make the interest rate prohibitively high. And many legal claims (for example, a personal injury claim arising from an accident) are by law not assignable – in order to prevent the 'fomenting' of litigation – and so are worthless as collateral.

The solution that the legal profession has devised is the contingent fee contract. The lawyer lends his services against a share of the claim. Risk is reduced because the lawyer specializing in contingent fee matters can pool many claims and thereby minimize the variance of the returns. Specialization also enables him to estimate risks more precisely than could a conventional lender.

It has been argued that contingent fees are often exorbitant; but it is easy to be misled here. A contingent fee must be higher than a fee for the same legal services paid as they are performed. The contingent fee compensates the lawyer not only for the legal services he renders but for the loan of those services. The interest rate on such a loan is high because the risk of default (the loss of the case, which cancels the debt of the client to the lawyer) is so much higher than that of conventional loans.

There have always been techniques for aggregating a number of small claims into one large enough to justify the costs of suit – or, stated otherwise, for realizing economies of scale in litigation. A department store performs this function with respect to the claims of its customers against the manufacturers whose products are sold by the store. The customer who purchases defective merchandise may not have enough at stake to sue the manufacturer but he will not hesitate to complain informally to the department store. The store will replace the merchandise or refund the customer's money and, if several customers complain, will pool these complaints and present them to the manufacturer. If the latter is unwilling to reimburse the store for its costs in responding to the customers' complaints, the store will be able to make a credible threat to take legal action against the manufacturer.

The contemporary class action presents an opportunity for generalizing this technique. . . . If all of [the] claims are aggregated in a class action, the stakes in the action will be large enough to defray the costs of suit and the cartel will be brought to bar.

The class-action device may seem, however, of rather limited utility in the very cases where it is most needed – where the individual claim is very small. The defendant can be compelled in such a case to pay a judgment equal to the costs of his violation – but to whom? The costs of identifying the injured purchasers and distributing to them their individual damages may exceed the judgment. To be sure, the most important point, on an economic analysis, is that the violator be confronted with the costs of his violation – this achieves the allocative purpose of the suit – not that he pay them to his victims. And our earlier emphasis on the importance of receipt of damages by the injured party to motivate him to operate the legal machinery is inapplicable here, since the stakes are too small to induce any victim to bear any of the burden of obtaining legal redress. But there are still problems. First, the costs of actually effecting compensation to the members of a numerous class may be extremely high and in some cases may exceed the benefits in deterrence yielded by the action. Second, the absence of a real client impairs the incentive of the lawyer for the class to press the suit to a successful conclusion. His profit from the suit is determined by the legal fee he receives rather than by the size of the judgment. No one has an economic stake in the size of the judgment except the defendant and he has an interest in minimizing it. The lawyer for the class will be tempted to offer to settle with the defendant for a small judgment and a large legal fee, and such an offer will be attractive to the defendant.

A class action such as we have described places the lawyer in the position of an entrepreneur rather than an agent, which is good although contrary to tradition, but it also relieves him of accountability, which is bad, because his private goal diverges from the social goal of obtaining a judgment equal to the social costs of the violation. The problem is not present where the individual members of the class have substantial stakes in the outcome, and this observation provides a practical argument for permitting a state to sue as *parens patriae* in cases where a violation of law has inflicted a small harm on each of a great many of its citizens.

The English and Continental practice of requiring the losing party to a lawsuit to reimburse the winning party's attorney's and witness fees (indemnity) might appear to provide an alternative to the class action as a method of vindicating small claims. No matter how small the claim, the claimant will not be deterred from pursuing his legal remedies by the cost of litigation since his litigation expenses will be reimbursed if he wins. But there are several disadvantages to the practice, compared with the class action. First, the indemnity is not in fact complete, primarily because the plaintiff's time and bother (which may be considerable in relation to the value of the claim, if it is small) are not compensated. Second, unless the plaintiff is certain to prevail, his expected cost of litigation may easily exceed the expected value of the litigation. Suppose his claim is for $1, the probability of his winning is 90 percent, and his litigation expenses are $100. Then the expected gain from litigation is $.90 and the expected cost $20 (assuming his opponent's litigation costs are also $100), so he will not sue. Third, indemnity lacks an important economizing feature of the class action. The class action permits the amalgamation of a multitude of small claims, enabling economies of scale to be realized. Suppose there are 1000 identical claims for $10 each, the cost of litigating each one is $100, and the probability of prevailing for the plaintiff is 100 percent. If all 1000 claimants sue – as they may since each stands to net $10 from suit – then $100,000 will be spent in the aggregate to vindicate those claims. Had the claims been aggregated in a class action, the expenses of the suit might have been only a small fraction of this cost. It would be an error to conclude, however, that, were the class action not a feasible alternative, indemnity would result in a socially excessive amount of litigation because $100,000 would be spent litigating claims 'worth' only $10,000. The claims would be litigated only if, ex ante, the parties derived greater utility from litigation than from settlement. The point is not that indemnity would be inefficient in this situation but that a class action would be more efficient.

The case for indemnity should not be evaluated solely from the standpoint of its effect on the meritorious small claim. An important question is its effect on the likelihood of litigation generally. This question can be illuminated with the help of the model of the decision to litigate introduced earlier. With indemnity, the condition for litigation, inequality (1) in the earlier analysis, becomes

$$P_p (J + C) - C - (1 - P_p) C + S > P_d (J + C) + C - (1 - P_d)C - S. \tag{3}$$

One difference between this formulation and (1) is that, with indemnity, the gain to the plaintiff if he wins (and loss to the defendant if he loses) includes the plaintiff's litigation expense (C) as well as the damages awarded (J). Another difference is that the plaintiff's expected gain from litigation must be reduced by defendant's litigation expense (also C) discounted by the plaintiff's subjected probability of loss, $1 - P_p$ (for example, if plaintiff thinks he has a 60 percent chance of winning, he necessarily also thinks he has a 40 percent chance of losing). A similar adjustment is necessary for the defendant's expected loss from litigation.

Inequality (3) can be rewritten

$$(P_p - P_d)J > 2 [(P_d + 1 - P_p)C - S]. \tag{4}$$

The only difference between this formulation and (2) (the parallel condition for litigation without indemnity) is the right-hand side. It will be larger or smaller in (4) than in (2) depending on whether $P_d + 1 - P_p$ is larger or smaller than 1. (If it is smaller than 1, the right-hand side of (4) will be smaller than the right-hand side of (2), thus making litigation more likely under the indemnity system.) It will be larger than 1 only if P_d is larger than P_p — that is, only if the defendant rates the plaintiff's chances of prevailing higher than the plaintiff himself does. But, as noted earlier, in those circumstances litigation will not occur anyway. Thus for purposes of assessing the effect of indemnity on the likelihood of litigation we can confine our attention to the class of cases in which P_p exceeds P_d. In all such cases indemnity makes litigation more likely than it would be without indemnity. . . .

But this analysis is incomplete. First of all, by increasing the variance of the possible outcomes of litigation, indemnity discourages litigation by the risk averse. Without indemnity, the plaintiff receives $J - C$ if he wins the suit and pays C if he loses; the range of outcomes is thus from

$J - C$ to $-C$. With indemnity the range is broader, from J to $-2C$. The analysis for the defendant is similar.

Second, the cost to a party of exaggerating the probability of his prevailing is greater under an indemnity system. . . Hence indemnity should result in a greater convergence of the parties' estimates of the probable outcome of the litigation, thereby reducing the litigation rate. This suggests, incidentally, a possible reason why the indemnity approach is followed in England but has never caught on in the U.S. The rigid adherence to stare decisis by English judges and the smaller use of the jury in England than in the U.S. mean that litigation outcomes are probably more predictable in England than here. This in turn suggests that a mistaken prediction as to outcome is more culpable, i.e., more avoidable, in the English system and therefore that penalizing such mistakes is more likely to reduce their incidence than under a system where much mistaken prediction is inevitable given the greater uncertainty of litigation. The closer the judicial process approaches to complete randomness, the less economic purpose is served by penalizing mistaken predictions; it is tantamount to making people liable for their unavoidable accidents, a liability that has negligible economizing properties. The detailed statutory codes, professional judiciary, and absence of juries which characterize the Continental legal systems would on this analysis explain why the indemnity rule is followed on the Continent as well as in England.

Third, if we drop the unrealistic assumption that the parties' litigation costs are exogenous, and instead assume that they are a positive function of the stakes in the case, we see that indemnity, by increasing each party's perception of the gain to him from a victorious outcome, may, by our earlier analysis of the effects of an increase in the stakes when litigation cost is endogenous, actually reduce the probability of litigation.

It is consequently unclear that the indemnity system on balance raises the litigation rate. And it has other effects that must be considered in any total evaluation. If as we have assumed the legal error rate is indeed a negative function of the parties' litigation expenditures, then indemnity should reduce the error rate. It should further reduce legal error by encouraging the meritorious small claim and, conversely, by discouraging the 'nuisance' claim – a frivolous claim presented only in the hope that the defendant can be induced to settle for at least a nominal sum.

Notes

1. Economists have analysed civil procedure in the context of their perspective of law as a set of behavioural incentives. This is partially captured by

Posner's cost-effectiveness goal of minimizing the sum of direct and error costs. A more general model would also examine the impact of procedural rules on the incentives to avoid litigious matters. K. E. Scott ('Two Models of the Civil Process' (1975) 27 Stan. L.R. 937) draws a useful distinction between two models of the civil process. The first is the conflict resolution model 'that sees civil process primarily as a method of achieving peaceful settlement of private disputes'. This model, which underlies the way most lawyers view the courts, stresses such factors as the degree of harm, compensation, fairness and minimizing the abuse of procedure by such practices as vexatious litigation, champerty and maintenance. In contrast the behaviour modification model' sees the courts' rulings as a way of 'altering behavior by imposing costs on a person'. It focuses primarily on the behaviour of defendants rather than the rights of plaintiffs, on whether the former confront the appropriate set of costs and incentives, and the efficiency, consistency and predictability of legal procedures.

2. Error costs can take many forms. Statisticians frequently distinguish type I errors (failing to convict or penalize the guilty) from type II errors (convicting/penalizing the innocent). The significnce of these errors will depend on the severity of the penalty. In a criminal case, where the accused cannot insure against the penalty and may be liable to imprisonment, a type II error will have serious consequences and is more likely to be avoided. This may explain why the standard of proof is higher in criminal than civil cases. On error costs see R. A. Posner, 'An Economic Approach to Legal Procedure and Judicial Administration' (1973) 2 J. Legal Stud. 391; G. Tullock, *Trials on Trials – the Pure Theory of Legal Procedure* (1980). See, further, on the problem of overinclusion and underinclusion, Ehrlich and Posner, supra, Section B.

3. The majority of civil cases are settled out of court because it is cheaper (H. L. Ross, *Settled Out of Court: the Social Process of Insurance Claims Adjustment* (1970)). The economic model discussed by Posner suggests that litigation occurs because one or both parties are overly optimistic about their chances of winning. (The model was originally developed and formalized by W. M. Landes, 'An Economic Analysis of the Courts' (1971) 14 J. Law and Econ. 61. See, also, J. Gould, 'The Economics of Legal Conflicts' (1973) 2 J. Legal Stud. 279; A. Friedman, 'The Analysis of Settlement' (1969) 22 Stan. L.R. 67). If litigants are rational utility maximizers then alternative methods of allocating legal costs will have predictable influence on their willingness to go to court (S. Shavell, 'Suit, Settlement and Trial: A Theoretical Analysis Under Alternative Methods For the Allocation of Legal Costs' (1982) 11 J. Legal Stud. 55). Litigation may also arise because the parties cannot agree on the sum that will settle the dispute (R. Cooter and S. Marks, 'Bargaining in the Shadow of the Law: A Testable Model of Strategic Behavior' (1982) 11 J. Legal Stud. 225).

4. Some economists have questioned the social efficiency of the adversarial system. G. Tullock (op. cit. ch. 6; 'The Efficient Organization of Trials' (1979) 28 Kyklos 745; 'Public Decisions as Public Goods' (1971) 79 J. Polit.

Econ. 912) has argued that it leads to excessive expenditure on litigation and that judges are undermotivated to seek out efficient solutions. It may also be socially inefficient to rely on the private financing of litigation. Legal rules and precedent have public good qualities – a binding precedent not only decides the case but also influences the behaviour and welfare of all potential litigants. Legal rules may be underproduced since individual litigants will not take into account the total benefits.

5. The model has also been applied to investigate the impact of litigation on the development of precedent. Some (e.g. P. H. Rubin, 'Why is the Common Law Efficient?' (1977) 6 J. Legal Stud. 51; G. L. Priest, 'The Common Law Process and the Selection of Efficient Rules' *ibid.*, 65) have argued that the very existence of litigation encourages an evolution towards efficiency, since there is an incentive on the parties to settle claims based on efficient rules, but to challenge, and thus eventually to secure the correction of, inefficient rules. More recent work has indicated that this is only one of many possible outcomes. The type of cases and their effects on substantive legal rules depend crucially on assumptions regarding the behaviour of the litigants and the judiciary (P. D. Carrington, 'Adjudication as a Private Good: A Comment' (1979) 8 J. Legal Stud. 303, 312–17); the parties may be content with inefficient rules (or motivated to challenge efficient rules) on distributional grounds (L. Kornhauser, 'A Guide to the Perplexed Claims of Efficiency in the Law' (1980) 8 Hofstra. L.R. 591, 627–34).

J. PHILLIPS, K. HAWKINS and J. FLEMMING

*

Compensation for Personal Injuries[6]

The legal process for settling claims arising from deaths and personal injuries is basically one of informal negotiations in which the courts are used as a last resort. Judgments made in those few cases where a settlement cannot be reached conform to a tariff which is also subsequently used by legal advisers when estimating the likely outcome of a court judgment.

There are two major reasons for many settlements out of court being smaller than the expected value of a court judgment. Both arise from the asymmetrical position of the two parties in a typical injury claim, which is derived from the existence of a market in liabilities, but not claims. The claimant is typically an individual who may be making a claim large in relation to his means and having no expectations of making any future claim. The defendant, on the other hand, is typically

[6] (1975) 85 Econ. J. 129–33, with omissions. Reprinted by permission of Cambridge University Press.

an insurance company facing many claims every week, each representing a very small part of the wealth of its ultimate owners.

The relative frequency of claims enables the insurance company to extract virtually all of the 'joint profit' represented by the saving in costs arising from a settlement out of court. The individual claimant stands to gain nothing from teaching the insurer that he meant what he said when he said he would take the claim to court. The relative importance of the claim to the two parties implies that effective risk aversion is asymmetrical, the claimant being very averse, the defendant virtually neutral.

In the simplest case where only the quantity of damages, and not liability, is subject to dispute, negotiations are based on estimates of x, the amount of damages a court would award. If each party (the claimant 1, and the defendant 2) bears his own share of the total costs (which are assumed given) C_1, C_2, then the net expected gain to the claimant of going to court is

$$E_1 = \bar{x}_1 - C_1$$

where $\bar{x}_1$ is the [expected damages].

If he were risk neutral this is the lowest sum for which the claimant would settle and, as we have seen, he is unlikely to get more. If, however, he is risk averse he would settle for $S_1, \ldots$ *i.e.* for a sum giving equal *utility* to that expected from going to court. . . .

. . . D_1, the discount factor for risk, is defined as $D_1 \equiv E_1 - S_1 > 0$. The actual settlement S should therefore be made up of three components:

$$S = \bar{x}_1 - C_1 - D_1$$

the expected court award, less the claimant's costs, less a discount factor for risk.

The preceding simple example ignores three other relevant considerations: it assigns no role to the defendant's expectations; it is based on each party paying his own costs, which is not typical; and it ignores the duration of proceedings. We take up each of these points below.

Since the insurance company gets all the benefit of not going to court its expectations are not relevant in determining the size of out-of-court settlements. If it makes as low an offer as it expects to be accepted, the offer will depend on the company's beliefs about the claimant's expectations as to x. The insurance company's expectations about x affect the decision to settle out of court, not the size of the settlement.

The general principle relating to the costs of court actions is that the loser pays. If liability is agreed, and only the amount of damages is in dispute, it is not clear how the loser is to be identified. The system of payments into court renders this principle applicable, and as it is a common practice it requires analysis. Under this procedure the defendant pays into court a sum which the claimant can take in full settlement of his claim. If, however, he pursues his case in court and is awarded less than this sum, he pays all the costs incurred from the date of the payment. These are likely to be substantial, since costs associated with a court hearing are particularly heavy. To simplify the analysis, however, it is assumed that the losing claimant pays the total costs incurred by both parties.

If the claimant were risk neutral the effect of the practice of 'paying in' would be to raise settlements in most cases. . . .

[P]aying in reduces, but does not eliminate, the cost component in the shortfall of settlements from court awards. Risk consideration may, however, offset this effect. Under the system of paying in, the claimant's net gain . . . has a greater variance. . . . Thus under the paying-in system the risk discount is almost certainly larger than the D derived above.

As to the role of delay in reaching a settlement, a claimant can generally expect no interest and almost certainly faces a much higher effective interest rate than does the defendant, who thus gains whether he actually delays settlement or threatens to go to court, with the delays which this involves.

Evidence that insurance companies are able to exploit claimants' risk aversion to their advantage in negotiations is provided by an article written for American loss adjusters entitled 'Creating Risk in Negotiation and Settlement Techniques':

the attorney will accept the offer, not because he feels that it is adequate, but because he recognises that settling the case at that figure represents the most prudent means of eliminating the uncertainty of the outcome of the case. . .[7]

Since the system of informal negotiated settlements is preferred to court judgments by both rational litigants and the legal profession on grounds of court costs and time, any attempt to arrive at an economically just level of compensation for all widows and injured claimants must encompass the negotiation process. Certainly, a no-fault insurance scheme such as that recently adopted in New Zealand . . . would remove the under-compensating effect of costs, risks and delays. Alternatively, rewarding these costs by higher levels of court judgments above the original economic loss suffered would have the effect of raising the levels of negotiated settlements.

---

[7] P. Clayton [1966] Ins. L.J. 465, 472.

K. E. SCOTT

*

Standing in the Supreme Court —
A Functional Analysis[8]

The Economics of Judicial Services. The usual method in our society of establishing the amount of some good or service to be produced, and the distribution of its consumption, is through the price system and market mechanism. The differing values people attach to a commodity will be reflected in the demand schedule, and (assuming no externalities) the costs of producing it will be reflected in the supply schedule, and the two will be brought into equilibrium through a market price. The services of the judiciary, however, are provided through government, substantially at the expense of taxpayers in general rather than individual litigants. Once we depart from a market solution and the principle that the users of a service shall bear the full costs of rendering it, there is no longer a way to determine precisely what is the appropriate size and capacity of our . . . judicial system. It is necessary to rely on the legislature to form a judgment as to the right amount to invest in the judicial system and to appropriate annually, presumably on the basis that the social benefits created by the last dollar spent are worth at least a dollar.

The subsidization of judicial services creates a problem in determining not only the proper amount to provide, but also its distribution. Borrowing a simple diagram from economics may help to put the matter more clearly. In Figure 1 the *DD* curve represents the amount of judicial capacity that would be demanded by persons in the society at different price levels for court and trial time, and the *SS* curve represents the social costs per court hour (or other 'unit' of judicial services) of supplying a court system of different sizes. On a fully costed basis the public would use and pay for a court system of size Q_1, at a price to litigants of P_1 per court hour. When society socializes most of the costs of the judicial system, leaving to litigants only some filing fees, witness fees, transcript charges and the like, the price of use of the courts drops from P_1 to P_2, with a resulting increase in demand for court services from Q_1 to Q_2. The price decrease will bring into the court system a set of additional cases.

It would be possible for the legislature, seeing this, to increase the size of the judicial system to Q_2, but this would greatly increase the cost

[8] (1973) 86 Harv. L.R. 645, 670–2, with omissions. Copyright © 1973 by the Harvard Law Review Association. Reprinted by permission of the author and the Harvard Law Review.

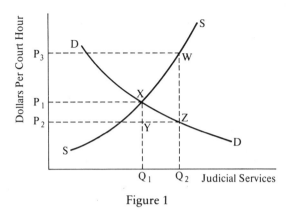

Figure 1

of the judicial system, for it would represent a subsidy not of P_1XYP_2 but of P_3WZP_2. The fact that the problems of court congestion and delay are chronic suggests, not surprisingly, that legislatures are habitually unwilling to supply the amount of judicial services that is in fact demanded at the artificially low prices charged to litigants by the courts. This legislative response seems quite understandable, unless the purposes of subsidizing court costs are equally applicable to all categories of litigation and all types of litigants.

If the legislature does nothing and leaves the judicial system at Q_1, there will be excess demand. One way of handling excess demand is by queues, and this characterizes in part the current practice in our judicial system. People line up and wait for their turn on the court calendar. In effect, the price of court decision is driven above P_2 by delay costs, back toward P_1, at which point the lines would no longer lengthen. Such an outcome is hardly to be desired. It increases the cost of adjudication for those whom society wished to assist and amounts to a transfer of the subsidy, in diminished amount, to those whose waiting costs are relatively low. It adds to the costs of other litigants who join the line. Furthermore, it contributes to a frequent over-estimation of the effect on congestion of adding several judges to a court; as they cut into the backlog, delay costs are reduced, which in turn brings additional cases into the system.

. . . Another possible response, and one that lies within the ability of the judiciary to institute by itself, is to screen cases – to weed out those actions, some of the ones brought into the court system because the price was lowered from P_1 to P_2, which society does not intend to subsidize and which are therefore, in a quite literal sense, not worth deciding. This is a function which, in the context of judicial review of government action, a doctrine like standing can serve and, in an imperfect and not wholly conscious way, has served, in that aspect of the doctrine that is primarily concerned with the plaintiff and the injury or adverse effect that has been visited upon him. . . .

Notes

1. The rules and costs of civil procedure also affect the net compensation received by plaintiffs. In personal injury cases insurance companies will be better bargainers and able to settle claims for substantially less than the damages the plaintiff would have received in court. (D. Harris, et al., *Compensation and Support for Illness and Injury* (1984) ch. 3). One way to increase net settlement sums is to change the procedural rules in favour of the plaintiff. Elsewhere Phillips and Hawkins ('Some Economic Aspects of the Settlement Process: A Study of Personal Injury Claims' (1976) 39 M.L.R. 497, 512–13) have proposed that a 'bonus' be paid to successful plaintiffs as a 'financial reward for the costs, risks and delays of receiving compensation'. Such a bonus would raise the net compensation received by the plaintiff and increase the deterrence effects of the law.

2. Scott addresses, *inter alia*, the problem of delay as a substantial cost of litigation. It affects both the number of cases coming to court and the sums for which plaintiffs are willing to settle. Recently, steps have been taken to reduce the delay and costs involved in appeals to the Court of Appeal (see *Practice Note* (Court of Appeal: New Procedure) [1982] 1 W.L.R. 1312). Supply-and-demand analysis indicates the possible futility of such reforms. If they are effective in decreasing delay costs, litigation will become cheaper and more cases will be forthcoming. The effects will be less per case delay and a greater individual subsidy to each litigant, but the social costs and government subsidy to the courts will increase. The effects and welfare losses are identical to that of price control (supra, Chapter 7, Section C).

3. Rationing court time by non-market means not only causes delays but is inefficient. Those cases which involve the largest stakes have to wait in line with less important ones. This cost can be reduced by allowing litigants with more serious cases to jump the queue (cf. the 'leap-frogging' procedure for appeals to the House of Lords introduced by Administration of Justice Act 1969, s. 12), levying a charge for judicial services or increasing the number of judges and courts. The last solution is only justified if litigation produces significant beneficial externalities (such as better and clearer laws).

4. It is important to recognize that the courts represent only one method of resolving disputes. If they become too costly, disputants will turn to other forms – small claims tribunals, arbitration, out-of-court settlement, penalty clauses and performance bonds. The court is in competition with these other techniques of dispute resolution and the business will flow to the one that offers the best service at the lowest price. See, generally, R. B. Ferguson, 'The Adjudication of Commercial Disputes and the Legal System, in Modern England' (1980) 7 Brit. J. Law and Soc. 141 and, on the current importance of arbitration, D. D. Hacking, 'A New Competition: Rivals for Centres of Arbitration' (1979) 4 Lloyd's Maritime Comm. L.Q. 435.

CASES CITED

INDEX